The History of Scottish Education   VOLUME TWO

The History of
Scottish Education

VOLUME TWO   From 1872 to the present day

James Scotland
Principal of Aberdeen College of Education

University of London Press Ltd

SBN 340 09548 2

University of London Press Ltd
St Paul's House, Warwick Lane, London EC4

Printed in Great Britain by
T. & A. Constable Ltd, Edinburgh

Preface

IT is more than forty years since Alexander Morgan published his *Rise and Progress of Scottish Education*. John Kerr's *Scottish Education, School and University* came out before the First World War. And these are the only two histories of education in this country which may reasonably claim to be complete. Grant's magnificent work, now almost a century old, confined itself to the *Burgh Schools in Scotland*, Strong's dealt with the secondary field only and Professor Knox covered a period of only two hundred and fifty years from 1696 to 1946. The studies by Stewart (*The Story of Scottish Education*) and Mrs Mackintosh (*Scottish Education Yesterday and Today*), valuable as they are, are mere sketches. There seems therefore to be a place for a new comprehensive history, and this book attempts to fill it.

The subject is by no means an artificial creation. That there is such a thing as "Scottish" education is shown by a long series of independent statutes and the fact that, even today, the Department of Education and Science has no authority north of the border. It seems likely therefore that many centuries of independent development, whether their results are good or bad, have produced certain principles, certain ways of tackling problems, which may be called "Scottish traditions". The book's first title indeed was "The Scottish Tradition in Education". As it was being written however it became increasingly clear that it was a general history of Scottish education, and so I have called it just that.

One more point. History is not a catalogue of facts covering the acts parliaments passed, the departments they set up, the way things were paid for. It is a record of what people said and thought and felt, as well as what they did, especially in this case what children and their teachers felt and thought. Much of this book therefore reports what went on in the classrooms of other centuries, and for this preoccupation with detail, *ce superflu, si nécessaire*, no apology is made.

J. S.

Contents

ACKNOWLEDGEMENTS

Photographs are reproduced by courtesy of the following: Aberdeen Journals (facing page 193); Education Department, University of Aberdeen (facing pages 112, 128, 176 and 192); Scottish Field and Dunfermline College of Physical Education (facing page 177); Fox Photos Ltd (facing pages 113 and 129).

LIST OF ABBREVIATIONS

A.C.1
Argyll Commission. *First Report by Her Majesty's Commissioners, appointed to inquire into the Schools in Scotland.* H.M.S.O. 1865

A.C.2
Argyll Commission. *Second Report: Elementary Schools.* H.M.S.O. 1867

A.C. Burgh Schools
Argyll Commission. *Report on Burgh and Middle Class Schools.* H.M.S.O. 1867

A.C.E.S.
Advisory Council on Education in Scotland

Albemarle
Albemarle Committee. *The Youth Service in England and Wales.* H.M.S.O. 1960 (Cmnd 929)

A.U.R.
Aberdeen University Review

Aurora Borealis Academica
Aurora Borealis Academica: Aberdeen University Appreciations, 1860-89. Aberdeen University 1899

Ayr Academy
Air Academie and Burgh Schule 1233-1895. Compiled for the Academy Bazaar by David Patrick and Others. Ayr 1895

BAIN, *Stirlingshire*
BAIN, ANDREW. *Education in Stirlingshire from the Reformation to the Act of 1872.* (Scottish Council for Research in Education. U.L.P. 1965)

BARCLAY, *Banffshire*
BARCLAY, WILLIAM. *The Schools and Schoolmasters of Banffshire.* Educational Institute of Scotland (Banffshire Branch) 1925

BELFORD, *Centenary Handbook*
BELFORD, A. J. *The Centenary Handbook of the Educational Institute of Scotland.* E.I.S., Edinburgh 1946

BLACK, *Paisley*
BLACK, C. STEWART. *The Story of Paisley.* Cook, Paisley 1948

BONE, *Inspection*
BONE, THOMAS R. *School Inspection in Scotland 1840-1966.* Glasgow University Ph.D. Thesis 1966

Book of the Jubilee
The Book of the Jubilee, in commemoration of the Ninth Jubilee of the University of Glasgow, 1451-1901. Students Jubilee Celebrations Committee, Glasgow 1901

BOYD, *Ayrshire*
BOYD, WILLIAM. *Education in Ayrshire through Seven Centuries.* S.C.R.E., U.L.P. 1961

B.J.E.S.	*British Journal of Educational Studies*
BUCHAN, *Parish School*	BUCHAN, JIM. *From Parish School to Academy: the Story of Education in the Parish of Peterculter*. Aberdeen County Council 1967
CAMPBELL, *Curriculum*	CAMPBELL, C. A. B. *The Scottish School Curriculum 1885-1923*. Glasgow University Ed.B. Thesis, n.d.
CANT, *St Andrews*	CANT, R. G. *The University of St Andrews: a Short History*. Oliver and Boyd, 1946.
C.C.M.	Committee of the Privy Council on Education in Scotland, *Minutes and Reports 1839-1939*. H.M.S.O. annually
CHAMBERS, *Peebles*	*Charters and Documents relating to the Burgh of Peebles with Extracts from the Records of the Burgh, A.D. 1165-1710*. Ed. W. Chambers. Scottish Burgh Record Society, Edinburgh 1872
CLARKE, *Short Studies*	CLARKE, JOHN. *Short Studies in Education in Scotland*. Longmans 1904
College Courant	*The College Courant:* Journal of the Glasgow University Graduates' Association
CORMACK, *Peterculter*	CORMACK, ALEXANDER A. *Education in the Eighteenth Century: the Parish of Peterculter, Aberdeenshire*. Published by the author 1965
CORMACK, *Cramond*	CORMACK, ALEXANDER A. *William Cramond 1844-1907*. Published by the author 1964
COUTTS, *Glasgow*	COUTTS, JAMES. *History of the University of Glasgow from its Foundation in 1451 to 1909*. Maclehose, Glasgow 1909
COWIE, *Arbroath*	COWIE, IAN M. *Education in Arbroath*. St Andrews University Ed.B. Thesis 1960
CRAMOND, *Elgin*	*Records of the Burgh of Elgin, 1234-1800*. Ed. Cramond, Edinburgh 1903
C.S. Minutes	Glasgow Church of Scotland Normal College Committee. *Minutes*. MS
DEAN, *Spinning Schools*	DEAN, IRENE F. M. *Scottish Spinning Schools*. S.C.R.E., U.L.P. 1930
DEMOGEOT and MONTUCCI	DEMOGEOT, J. C., and MONTUCCI, HENRI. *De L'Enseignement Secondaire en Angleterre et en Ecosse*. Paris 1870
DOBIE, *S.L.C.*	DOBIE, THOMAS B. *The Scottish Leaving Certificate 1888-1908*. Glasgow University Ed.B. Thesis 1964
EDGAR, *Early Education*	EDGAR, JOHN. *History of Early Scottish Education*. Thin, Edinburgh 1893
Education in the North	*Education in the North.* Journal of the Aberdeen College of Education. Aberdeen 1965 on

EYRE-TODD, *Glasgow* EYRE-TODD, GEORGE. *History of Glasgow from the Reformation to the Reform Acts.* Jackson Wylie, Glasgow 1931, 1934

FAIRLEY, *Compulsory Education* FAIRLEY, JOHN A., *The Beginnings of Compulsory Education in Scotland.* Glasgow University Ed.B. Thesis 1965

FASTI *Fasti Academiae Mariscallanae Aberdonensis: Selections from the Records of the Marischal College and University, 1593-1860.* New Spalding Club 1889

F.C. Minutes Glasgow Free Church Normal School Committee. *Minutes.* MS

FEARON, *Burgh Schools* Schools Inquiry Commission (FEARON). *Burgh Schools in Scotland.* H.M.S.O. 1869

Five Centuries *University of Glasgow through Five Centuries.* Glasgow 1951

500 Year Book *The Five Hundred Year Book to Commemorate the Fifth Centenary of the University of Glasgow, 1451-1951.* Ed. Hamilton. Students' Fifth Centenary Committee, Glasgow 1951

Fortuna Domus *Fortuna Domus: a Series of Lectures delivered in the University of Glasgow in Commemoration of the Fifth Centenary of its Foundation.* Glasgow 1952

General Assembly E.C.R. General Assembly of the Church of Scotland, *Education Committee Reports*

General Assembly P.P.R. General Assembly of the Church of Scotland, *Presbyterial and Parochial Reports*

Glasgow Past and Present *Glasgow Past and Present by Senex, Aliquis, J. B. et al.* Robertson, Glasgow 1884

GORDON, *Keith* GORDON, J. F. S. *The Book of the Chronicles of Keith, Frange, Ruthven, Cairney and Botriphnie: Events, Places and Persons.* Forrester, Glasgow 1880

GRAHAM, *Social Life* GRAHAM, HENRY GREY. *The Social Life of Scotland in the Eighteenth Century.* Black 1909

GRANT, *Edinburgh* GRANT, ALEXANDER. *The Story of the University of Edinburgh during its First Three Hundred Years.* Longmans Green 1884

GRANT, *Burgh Schools* GRANT, JAMES. *History of the Burgh Schools of Scotland.* Collins 1876

HARRISON, *Merchant Company* HARRISON, JOHN. *The Company of Merchants of the City of Edinburgh and Its Schools, 1694-1920.* Merchants' Hall, Edinburgh 1920

HORN, *Edinburgh* HORN, D. B. *A Short History of the University of Edinburgh, 1556-1889.* Edinburgh University Press 1967

HUTCHISON, *Stirling*   HUTCHISON, A. F. *History of the High School of Stirling.* Mackay, Stirling 1904

INSH, *School Life*   INSH, GEORGE PRATT. *School Life in Old Scotland.* E.I.S., Edinburgh 1925

JESSOP, *Angus*   JESSOP, J. C. *Education in Angus.* S.C.R.E., U.L.P. 1931

KERR, *Memories*   KERR, JOHN. *Memories Grave and Gay.* Nelson n.d.

KERR, *Code of 1905*   *Nelson's Annotated Scotch Code, 1905.* Ed. John Kerr. Nelson n.d.

KERR, *Other Memories*   KERR, JOHN. *Other Memories Old and New* (also entitled "Leaves from An Inspector's Logbook"). Blackwood 1904

KERR, *Scottish Education*   KERR, JOHN. *Scottish Education, School and University, from Early Times to 1908.* Cambridge University Press 1913

KNOX, *250 Years*   KNOX, H. M. *250 Years of Scottish Education, 1696-1946.* Oliver and Boyd 1953

LAURIE, *Dick Bequest 1865*   LAURIE, S. S. *Report on Education in the Parochial Schools of the Counties of Aberdeen, Banff and Moray, addressed to the Trustees of the Dick Bequest.* Constable, Edinburgh 1865

LAURIE, *Dick Bequest 1890*   LAURIE, S. S. *Report to the Trustees of the Dick Bequest on the rural public (formerly parochial) schools of Aberdeen, Banff and Moray.* Constable, Edinburgh 1890

LAURIE, *Dick Bequest 1904*   LAURIE, S. S. *General Report to the Governors of the Dick Bequest, 1890-1904.* Constable, Edinburgh 1904

LAW, *Edinburgh*   LAW, ALEXANDER. *Education in Edinburgh in the Eighteenth Century.* S.C.R.E., U.L.P. 1965

LEASK, *Interamna Borealis*   LEASK, W. KEITH. *Interamna Borealis, being Memories and Portraits from an Old University Town between the Don and the Dee.* Rosemount Press, Aberdeen 1917

LOCHHEAD, *Scots Household*   LOCHHEAD, MARION. *The Scots Household in the Eighteenth Century.* Moray Press 1948

MACGEORGE, *Old Glasgow*   MACGEORGE, ANDREW. *Old Glasgow: The Place and the People from the Roman Occupation to the Eighteenth Century.* Blackie 1888

MACKAY, *Highlanders*   MACKAY, DAVID N., ed. *Home Life of the Highlanders, 1400-1746.* Glasgow 1911

MACKIE, *Glasgow*   MACKIE, J. D. *The University of Glasgow 1451-1951.* Glasgow 1954

M'LEAN, *Fordyce Academy*   M'LEAN, DOUGLAS G. *The History of Fordyce Academy: Life at a Banffshire School, 1592-1935.* Banffshire Journal 1936

MACLEAN, *Northern University*   MACLEAN, NEIL N. ed. Leask. *Life at a Northern University.* Rosemount Press, Aberdeen 1906

M'NAUGHT, *Kilmaurs*   M'NAUGHT, D. *Kilmaurs Parish and Burgh.* Gardner, Paisley 1912

M'URE, *Glasghu Facies*   M'URE, JOHN. *Glasghu Facies: A View of the City of Glasgow.* Tweed, Glasgow n.d.

MARWICK, *Edinburgh*   *Burgh Records of Edinburgh 1403-1583.* Ed. J. D. Marwick. Edinburgh 1869

MARWICK, *Edinburgh Charters*   *Charters and Other Documents relating to the City of Edinburgh, A.D. 1143-1540.* Ed. J. D. Marwick. Edinburgh 1870

MARWICK, *Glasgow*   *Charters of the City of Glasgow, 1175-1649.* Ed. J. D. Marwick. Edinburgh 1894

MASON, *Rural Education*   MASON, JOHN. *A History of Scottish Experiments in Rural Education.* S.C.R.E., U.L.P. 1936

MASSON, *Melvin*   MASSON, DAVID. *James Melvin, Rector of the Grammar School of Aberdeen.* Aberdeen 1895

MORGAN, *Makers*   MORGAN, ALEXANDER. *Makers of Scottish Education.* Longmans 1929

MORGAN, *Rise and Progress*   MORGAN, ALEXANDER. *Rise and Progress of Scottish Education.* Oliver and Boyd, Edinburgh 1927

MORRISON, *Compulsory Education*   MORRISON, JAMES L. *The Implementation of Compulsory Education in Scotland from 1883 to 1914.* Glasgow University Ed.B. Thesis 1966

MUIR, *Anderson*   MUIR, JAMES. *John Anderson, Pioneer of Technical Education, and the College He Founded.* Smith, Glasgow 1950

MURRAY, *Old College*   MURRAY, DAVID. *Memories of the Old College of Glasgow: Some Chapters in the History of the University.* Wylie, Glasgow 1927

NEILL, *Bonhill*   NEILL, JOHN. *Records and Reminiscences of Bonhill Parish.* Bennett and Thomson, Dumbarton 1912

N.S.A.   *The New Statistical Account of Scotland, by the Ministers of the Respective Parishes.* 15 volumes. Blackwood, Edinburgh 1845

NORRIE, *Old High School*   NORRIE, JESSIE A. *Memories of the Old High School.* Kidd, Dundee 1924

Northern Iris   *The Northern Iris: a Periodical.* Stevenson Aberdeen 1826

OGILVIE, *Cruickshank* OGILVIE, JOSEPH. *John Cruickshank, Professor in the Marischal College and University of Aberdeen*. Adelphi Press, Aberdeen 1806

O.S.A. *The Statistical Account of Scotland, drawn on by Sir John Sinclair from the Communications of the Ministers of the Various Parishes.* Creech, Edinburgh 1793-6

OSBORNE, *Scottish and English Schools* OSBORNE, GERALD S. *Scottish and English Schools: a Comparative Survey of the Past Fifty Years.* Longmans 1966

PAGAN, *Sketches* PAGAN, JAMES. *Sketches of the History of Glasgow.* Stuart, Glasgow 1847

Parker Committee 1, 2, 3 Parker Committee on Schools and Training Colleges, *Three Reports.* H.M.S.O. 1888

PATON, *Rutherglen* PATON, GEORGE. *The Development of Education in Rutherglen, with particular reference to the period of the School Boards, 1872-1918.* Glasgow University Ed.B. Thesis 1960

PORTEOUS, *Crieff* PORTEOUS, ALEXANDER. *The History of Crieff from the Earliest Times to the Dawn of the Twentieth Century.* Edinburgh 1912

Primary Education in Scotland Scottish Education Department. *Primary Education in Scotland.* H.M.S.O. 1965

Primary School in Scotland Scottish Education Department. *The Primary School in Scotland.* H.M.S.O. 1950

Quatercentenary Book *Studies in the History and Development of the University of Aberdeen.* Ed. P. J. Anderson. Aberdeen University Press 1906

RAIT, *Aberdeen* RAIT, ROBERT S. *The Universities of Aberdeen: a History.* Bisset, Aberdeen 1895

RENWICK, *Glasgow* *Records of the Burgh of Glasgow.* Ed. R. Renwick. Edinburgh 1911

RENWICK, *Lanark* *Extracts from the Records of the Royal Burgh of Lanark, 1150-1722.* Ed. R. Renwick. Glasgow 1893

RENWICK, *Stirling* *Extracts from the Records of the Royal Burgh of Stirling, 1519-1666.* Ed. R. Renwick. Glasgow Stirlingshire Society 1877

RITCHIE, *Forres* RITCHIE, JAMES B. *Forres: Its Schools and Schoolmasters; a Record of 300 Years.* Forres 1926

Robbins Report Robbins Committee. *Report on Higher Education.* (Cmnd 2154) H.M.S.O. 1963

ROBERTS, *Dunbartonshire* ROBERTS, ALASDAIR F. B. *The Operation of the Ad Hoc Education Authority in Dunbartonshire between 1919 and 1930.* Glasgow University, Ed.B. Thesis 1964

Roberts Report	Scottish Education Department. *Measures to Secure a More Equitable Distribution of Teachers in Scotland.* H.M.S.O. 1966
ROBERTSON, *Leith*	*South Leith Records, compiled from the Parish Registers for the Years 1588-1700.* Ed. D. Robertson. Elliot, Edinburgh 1911
ROSS, *Royal High School*	ROSS, WILLIAM C. A. *The Royal High School.* Oliver and Boyd 1949
RUSK, *Infant Education*	RUSK, ROBERT R. *A History of Infant Education.* U.L.P. 1933
RUSK, *Training of Teachers*	RUSK, ROBERT R. *The Training of Teachers in Scotland.* E.I.S., Edinburgh 1928
SAUNDERS, *Scottish Democracy*	SAUNDERS, LAURANCE J. *Scottish Democracy, 1815-1840: the Social and Intellectual Background.* Oliver and Boyd, Edinburgh 1950
Scots Magazine	*The Scots Magazine, a Monthly Miscellany of Scottish Life and Letters.* Glasgow 1924-31
S.E.D.R.	*Education in Scotland: Annual Report by the Secretary of State for Scotland.* H.M.S.O.
S.E.J.	*The Scottish Educational Journal*
SHARPE, *Selkirk*	SHARPE, J. *Selkirk: Its Church, Its School and Its Presbytery.* Lewis, Selkirk n.d.
SHEWAN, *Meminisse Juvat*	SHEWAN, ALEXANDER. *Meminisse Juvat, being the Autobiography of a Class at King's College in the Sixties.* Aberdeen U.P. 1905
SHEWAN, *Gymnasium*	SHEWAN, ALEXANDER. *Spirat Adhuc Amor: the Record of the Gym (Chanonry House School) Old Aberdeen.* Rosemount Press, Aberdeen 1923
SIMPSON, *Bon Record*	SIMPSON, H. F. MORLAND. Ed. *Bon Record: Records and Reminiscences of Aberdeen Grammar School from the Earliest Times by Many Writers.* Ballantyne Press, Edinburgh 1906
SIMPSON, *Aberdeenshire*	SIMPSON, IAN J. *Education in Aberdeenshire before 1872.* S.C.R.E., U.L.P. 1947
SKINNIDER, *Catholic Education*	SKINNIDER, MARTHA M. *Catholic Elementary Education in Glasgow, 1818-1918.* Glasgow University Ed.B. Thesis 1964
SMITH, *Broken Links*	SMITH, JOHN. *Broken Links in Scottish Education.* Nisbet 1913
S.S.P.C.K., *Account*	Society in Scotland for Propagating Christian Knowledge. *Account of the Society from Its Commencement in 1709.* Edinburgh 1774
S.S.P.C.K., *State*	Society in Scotland for Propagating Christian Knowledge, *State of the Society 1729.* Edinburgh 1729

STOW, *Training System* — STOW, DAVID. *The Training System of Education, Religious, Intellectual and Moral, as Established in the Glasgow Normal Training Seminary.* Blackie 1845

STRONG, *Secondary Education* — STRONG, JOHN. *A History of Secondary Education in Scotland.* O.U.P. 1909

STUART, *Aberdeen* — *Extracts from the Council Register of the Burgh of Aberdeen, 1643-1747.* Ed. John Stuart. Scottish Burgh Records Society 1830

T.E.S. — *The Times Educational Supplement*

T.E.S.S. — *The Times Educational Supplement (Scotland)*

TOWILL, *Merchant Maidens* — TOWILL, EDWIN S. "The Minutes of the Merchant Maiden Hospital", in *Book of the Old Edinburgh Club*, vol. xxix. Constable, Edinburgh 1956

T.S.A. *Aberdeen*, etc. — *The Third Statistical Account of Scotland.* Collins:
Aberdeen City. Ed. Hugh C. Mackenzie, 1953
Aberdeenshire. Ed. Henry Hamilton, 1965
Argyll. Ed. Colin M. MacDonald, 1961
Ayrshire. Ed. John Strawhorn and William Boyd, 1951
Banff. Ed. Henry Hamilton, 1961
Bute. Ed. A. Cameron Somerville and William Stevenson, 1962
Dumfries. Ed. George F. B. Houston, 1962
Dunbarton. Ed. Margaret Dilke and A. A. Templeton, 1959
East Lothian. Ed. Catherine P. Snodgrass, 1953
Edinburgh. Ed. David E. Keir, 1966
Fife. Ed. Alexander Smith, 1952
Glasgow. Ed. James Cunnison and John B. S. Gilfillan, 1958
Kirkcudbright. Ed. John Laird and David G. Ramsay *and Wigtown.* Ed. M. C. Arnott, 1965
Lanark. Ed. George Thomson, 1960
Moray and Nairn. Ed. Henry Hamilton, 1965
Peebles and Selkirk. Ed. J. P. B. Bulloch, 1964
Renfrew. Ed. H. A. Moisley, and A. G. Thain, 1962
Stirling. Ed. Robin C. Rennie and *Clackmannan.* Ed. T. Crouther Gordon, 1966

TURNER, *Edinburgh* — *History of the University of Edinburgh 1883-1933.* Ed. A. Logan Turner, Edinburgh 1933

Veterum Laudes	*Veterum Laudes, being a Tribute to the Achievements of the Members of St Salvator's College during Five Hundred Years.* Ed. James B. Salmond. St Andrews 1950
Votiva Tabella	*Votiva Tabella: a Memorial Volume of Saint Andrews University in connection with its Quincentenary Festival.* St Andrews 1911
WADE, *Post-Primary Education*	WADE, NEWMAN T. *Post-Primary Education in the Primary Schools of Scotland, 1872-1936.* U.L.P. 1939
WARRICK, *Old Cumnock*	WARRICK, JOHN. *The History of Old Cumnock.* Gardner, Paisley 1899
WATT, *Aberdeen and Banff*	WATT, WILLIAM. *The History of Aberdeen and Banff.* Blackwood 1900
WILLIAMSON, *Old Greenock 2*	WILLIAMSON, GEORGE. *Old Greenock, embracing Sketches of its Ecclesiastical, Educational and Literary History, Second Series.* Gardner, Paisley 1888
WILSON, *Tales and Travels*	WILSON, JOHN. *Tales and Travels of a School Inspector.* Jackson, Glasgow 1928
WILSON, *Mathematical Teaching*	WILSON, DUNCAN K. *The History of Mathematical Teaching in Scotland to the End of the Eighteenth Century.* S.C.R.E., U.L.P. 1935
WILSON, *Junior Student System*	WILSON, JOHN D. *The Junior Student System and Preliminary Training between 1906 and 1950.* Glasgow University Ed.B. Thesis 1964
WOOD, *Edinburgh*	*Extracts from the Records of the Burgh of Edinburgh, 1589-1655.* Ed. R. K. Hannay and Marguerite Wood. Edinburgh 1927
WOOD, *Sessional School*	WOOD, JOHN. *Account of the Edinburgh Sessional School and the other Parochial Institutions for Education Established in that City in the Year 1812.* Edinburgh 1830

PART I

Education by the State
1872-1945

CHAPTER I

Educational Expansion

IN 1872 the state openly acknowledged its direct responsibility for educating the people of Scotland. Three-quarters of a century later this undertaking had expanded out of all prophecy. Every Scottish child had the absolute right to be educated for at least ten years according to his age, ability and aptitude. No fees need be paid. If he possessed any talent and his parents were willing to let him continue his education, higher secondary schooling was free and there were usually bursaries to take him to a degree or a diploma. If he suffered from mental or physical handicap the state would provide special educational treatment as long as he required it. He was entitled to free milk and cheap meals, free medical inspection and treatment, bursaries, travel grants and lodging, cheap clothing if his parents were poor, cheap holidays and assistance in finding a job. The most striking feature of Scottish educational development after 1872 was this extension of the meaning of the word "education".

It is a generalisation but not perhaps too inaccurate to discern two main periods between 1872 and 1945. In the first, extending roughly to the end of the nineteenth century, the principal educational effort was expended in making the Act work – in eliminating inefficient schools for example and coming to terms with the idea of a state system, with the concept of education as a public service. Thereafter the deficiencies of the Act became too important to be kept in the background. Secondary schooling, the administrative unit, social welfare – the terms of the problems were stated, and the years between 1890 and 1945 were occupied in finding solutions. Throughout the whole period however, as in all periods, there were emergencies and crises, political, social and economic, and a large proportion of time in education was spent not in planning for the future but in coping with the present. And of course, understandably but fruitlessly, in yearning for the past.

The immediate effect of the 1872 Act was to reduce substantially the number of schools in Scotland. In 1867 the Argyll Commission had found 4,443 in the districts surveyed; there were probably over 5,000 altogether. In 1879 the total had shrunk to 3,893, made up as follows[1]

Type of School	Number
Public elementary	2,503
Aided non-public	605
Other elementary (recognised as efficient)	508
Higher class public	17
Higher class non-public	260

The few elementary schools not recognised as efficient which neverthe-less contrived to remain in existence can hardly have raised the total much over four thousand. This reduction was partly at the expense of the church schools but mainly due to the disappearance of the worst type of adventure schools. When the public institutions could offer better instruction as cheaply, the private dominie could hardly make a living, except perhaps by relying on snobbery.

Between 1875 and 1914 the figures published in the reports of the Committee of Council show a steady but slow increase in the number of schools receiving financial aid from the government. Just over 3,000 out of the 3,893 enumerated above were state-aided in 1879. This followed a rapid rise between 1872 (with 1,902) and 1875 (with 2,720). As late as 1909 however the total had increased no further than 3,312 The percentage of public schools in this total did rise, however[2].

Year	Percentage
1872	—
1875	71·1
1879	83·4
1885	81·4
1890	85·0
1895	87·1
1900	88·4
1905	88·9
1909	89·1

The reason was that, although Roman Catholic and Episcopal schools increased their numbers, those of the Established and Free Churches almost vanished.

Among these public schools a small but interesting group was made up of the 'side' or 'sub' schools which were permitted in thinly peopled districts where the inspector approved the accomodation. They had to meet on not less than a hundred and fifty days a year. In the early 1920's there were sixty-four in Inverness and twenty-four in Shetland, while in Harris there were thirteen besides the eleven ordinary public schools. The total in 1931 was a hundred and sixty-one. Thereafter their numbers dwindled: in 1936 they had fallen in the Highland Division to a hundred and one – forty in Sutherland, thirty-three in Ross, nineteen in Inverness, seven in Orkney and two in Caithness.[3] Their value in isolated farming communities must have been considerable, but, since they were often held not in specially built accommodation but in farmhouses at the head of remote glens, the loneliness of the teachers was a constant affliction, and was often mentioned by inspectors in their reports.

UNRESOLVED PROBLEMS AFTER 1872

The Act of 1872, while it advanced Scottish Education greatly by giving it system, left several problems unresolved. For one thing few people in Scotland were satisfied with the administration of their schools from London. The Duke of Richmond's description of the Scotch Education Department as "simply a room in Whitehall with the word 'Scotland' painted on the door" was generally applauded. In many fields besides education there was steady pressure for more Scottish control of Scottish affairs, and the movement culminated in 1885 in the establishment of a Secretary for Scotland. The Department however remained almost exclusively in London until the twenties of the next century, and its headquarters did not come to Edinburgh until 1939.

The system of local administration set up by the 1872 Act worked well for almost half a century, but there was an increasing conviction that the area controlled by each school board was too small. No change was made until 1918, when an act substituted the county for the parish as the local unit, reducing numbers from almost a thousand to less than forty. These new authorities were elected expressly for the administration of education. This fact was from the beginning an invitation to opposition, and little more than a decade passed before the Local Government (Scotland) Act of 1929 transferred power in local educational affairs to the county councils, where it remains.

A second problem unresolved and even complicated by the Act of 1872 was the provision of secondary education. Elementary instruction was now well within the reach of all, but since the school boards were not permitted to use the education rate for maintaining higher class public schools, it is possible that the percentage of children going forward to some form of secondary instruction actually decreased. At the same time the increasing technical needs of industry made higher education essential. The last decade of the nineteenth century was the period in which a number of statutes provided money for secondary and technical schools, but with no adequate instruments for the allocation of these funds. There were soon indeed too many sources of income; the confusion visible in the sixties in elementary education was now transferred to secondary. As before, this confusion resulted from too many attempts to solve the same problem. The systematic organisation of secondary schools was not achieved until 1945, and then with no finality.

THE EXTENSION OF EDUCATION

Apart from these problems the history of Scottish education after 1872 shows continual extension in many directions. School life for instance was steadily lengthened. The Act had made education compulsory from five to thirteen, with exemption for children obtaining a certificate of proficiency in the three Rs. An Act of 1883 raised the leaving age to fourteen but allowed "half-time" after ten. In 1901 all exemptions by examination were abolished,[4] and seven years later the 1908 Act made the system more efficient by introducing entering and leaving dates. The 1918 Act provided for the raising of the leaving age to fifteen on a date to be fixed; education authorities were instructed to make preliminary surveys of requirements, but the difficult conditions of the twenties and thirties delayed the move. A bill was introduced without success in England in 1930; Scotland required only a statutory regulation, but when the English measure was defeated in the Lords no action was taken north of the border.[5] At last the 1936 Act fixed a date – September 1939 – a notable example of unfortunate timing. For almost six weeks the regulation was presumably in effect, for an Appointed Day Order was issued on 3 August 1939 and the Education (Emergency) (Scotland) Act, which cancelled the change, was not passed until 12 October. Thereafter the war prevented educational advance. The 1945 Act took up the struggle again, with more success.

The education provided by the 1872 Act, despite the new rate, was not free; there is a traditional Scottish conviction that people set greater value on anything for which they have to pay. For another fifteen or twenty years therefore all but necessitous children paid perhaps 2d or 3d a week for their schooling. Acts of 1889 and 1890 made funds available and the boards then abolished fees in their elementary schools, but secondary education was not free until the Act of 1945, though in most areas practice was in advance of legal permission. Higher education had still to be paid for and even with bursaries and grants this might still require heavy sacrifice by parents and young people.

Towards the end of the nineteenth century interest in the general welfare of children became increasingly positive all over Britain. In the nineties there were pioneers like Margaret Macmillan and progressive authorities like the school boards of Bolton and Govan which believed that the schools were the best place to attack the poverty and disease which seemed endemic in British towns. The average person was aware of slum conditions but either ignored them or pacified his conscience with charitable donations. But when 800 out of 1,200 volunteers for the Boer War were rejected in Manchester there was national concern:[6] a Committee on Physical Deterioration was appointed, and its report in 1904 caused general disquiet. Various school boards introduced schemes for medical inspection. The 1908

Act made medical supervision compulsory and allowed boards to serve meals where they thought fit. Thereafter more and more was done for the child at school. The fundamental principle was stated in the 1945 Act – no child must be allowed to suffer from any removable handicap to deriving full benefit from his education.

BETWEEN THE WARS

The effect of the First World War on Scottish education was considerable, though not as shattering as that of the Second, perhaps because there were fewer welfare services in 1914-18 to be removed from the children. The provisions of the 1908 Act had barely had time to make their effect: the army which died at Loos and the Somme was described as the finest Britain ever had, but the comparison was with the "regular" forces of the past, and there was still a high rate of rejection for physical defects in the early years of the conflict. As the war dragged on however it brought insoluble problems. Over 800 teachers had gone on service in the first few weeks and the shortage of young men in the schools was to have an effect lasting for a decade or more and duplicated in the later war. There was a general decline in attendance and senior pupils particularly became discontented. The best were eager to go to fight; many saw chances of well-paid employment in munition factories; all were bored with long hours in dark, crowded rooms under tired, ageing teachers.

There were two good effects of the war however. One was a general determination to repay those who had fought, not merely with money but by bringing higher education within their reach. The scheme for the Higher Education of Ex-Service Students trained almost 6,000 in the first five years of its existence at a cost of £1,303,310.[7] It is interesting that the largest proportion of individual awards was for the study of medicine.

The second and earlier effect of the war was as always to stir people out of their daily round and make them ready for experiment and change. It is more than a coincidence that, in England at least, the four great Education Acts of the last century have been passed in time of war. Although Britain did not fight in the campaigns of 1864, 1866 and 1870, she was vastly interested in the emergence of the German Empire. The 1902 Act was not unaffected by the lessons of the struggle with the Boers and those of 1918 and 1944 were clearly hastened by the interest in fresh beginnings which wars seem to engender. In many ways the Scottish Act of 1918 was a statesmanlike and far-sighted measure, involving "complete re-organisation of the whole fabric of the Scottish educational system outside of the Universities".[8] Its comparative lack of success was due to the hard times which followed the war and which were all the more depressing by contrast with (somewhat gilded by memory) conditions before 1914 for the middle and upper classes. Almost at once expenditure had to be cut, and education, essentially a long-term asset, suffered. Circular 34, issued by the Scottish Education Department on 18 January 1921, began the demand for reductions. On a direct order from the Cabinet the watchword was not "what can we do?" but "what can we do without?".[9] Cuts in building and maintenance followed and many of the praisworthy schemes of 1918, like compulsory further education, never came into effect at all.

There was some improvement during the twenties in the economic condition of Britain, although a tendency to look for remedies in terms of the pre-War world did not help. The early thirties however brought the effects of the collapse of credit in America, and the Great Depression spread over practically the whole western world. Teachers were forced to accept cuts in salary as an alternative to unemployment. As it was, only those with training records above average could count on a post at once. New building was again reduced. There was no question of extending school life. Yet the streets were full of unemployed youths, rusting at corners in the shadow of empty factories and docks. Classes for unemployed juveniles, founded in Glasgow as early as 1924, were soon extended to Aberdeen, Motherwell and Greenock, and renamed "Junior Instruction Centres". They had dwindled in numbers by 1930, but were soon unfortunately filling up again. The Unemployment Insurance Act of 1935 put the onus on the education committees of supplying courses for young people under eighteen. Their aims were to keep bodies and minds fit and alert, to give useful training, and significantly to give them an interest in life. In 1935 attendance in the centres rose to thirty thousand. They were scattered all over the central valley of Scotland.

The general recovery of economic balance and orders in heavy industry brought by preparation for war gradually dissipated the Depression. With it went the junior instruction centres. The last closed on 17 December 1941. Their premises however continued to be used in the building shortage following the Second World War.[10]

THE EFFECT OF THE SECOND WORLD WAR

By 1941 the War was already over two years old. Its impact on Scottish education was undoubtedly severe. As we have seen, the raising of the leaving age was suspended. The most obvious immediate effect was the evacuation of children to "safe areas", for air raids were expected to destroy parts of the cities. Circular 121, issued on 19 June, had made all arrangements, and in the first three days of September, just as the war began, 101,774 children left the built-up areas. Conditions in the "receiving areas" were strange and crowded. Even though many of their own teachers accompanied them, the children were unsettled, and for many the first winter of the war was one of loss or at best marking time. As the "phoney war" stretched out, many returned without permission to their parents in the cities, where no schooling was available.

Within a year of the outbreak, moreover, 94 schools were wholly and 199 partly occupied for military purposes. The resultant shortage of school places made it impossible to maintain the pre-war standard of education. In addition many young teachers went off at once to the Services or "war work". In time the age of reservation for male teachers was fixed at thirty-five. As in the First World War, there was a serious shortage of qualified teachers.

In December 1939 the government claimed to be providing education for ninety-six per cent of the children in the receiving areas, sixty-eight per cent in "neutral areas" and eighteen per cent in the sending districts. A year later they had managed to stabilise the position: the figures were 95·3, 93·2 and 70·8 per cent.[11] Even these showed a serious deficiency in the towns. And in any case the standard of education provided was not high. Some schools had to operate a "shift" system, by which pupils attended for only half a day, and this continued until 1942. The general decline may be seen from the fact that the Senior Leaving Certificate, which was awarded under emergency arrangements during the War, was unquestionably easier to obtain. Five per cent more candidates were awarded certificates in 1945 than immediately before or after the conflict.[12] This is hardly a grave, but it is a significant variation.

The fall in educational standards, and the impact of the War on home life, with fathers in the forces and mothers at work, had their effect in encouraging delinquency. One excellent result was the birth of the Youth Service, implementing the voluntary work of organisations like the Scouts, Guides and Boys' Brigade. It was established on 3 September 1942 by Circular 244.

If anything, the War served to expand welfare arrangements in schools. The meals service was widened, and there was a stirring of public interest in planning for the future, as shown in the pamphlet on "The Scottish School" prepared in 1943 by the Educational Institute of Scotland and that on "Education in Scotland" drawn up in the same year by the Association of Directors of Education.[13] The culmination was the Act of 1945.

EDUCATIONAL AIMS

The general aims of education in the period from 1872 to 1945 suggest that Disraeli's two worlds were still in existence. George Watson's Ladies College in 1920 was intended

> to prepare girls for a cultured home life, or for the University and those many professions now open to women, and to enable them to bear themselves worthily in any sphere of life they may choose and in every land to which fate may lead them.

The corresponding Boys' School sought

> to train strong men, capable of filling a place in the world and of leading an honourable life in any sphere which they are called on to occupy.[14]

Modestly as they were expressed, these aims assumed for their pupils a more important place in society than awaited the children of the elementary schools. One of A. S. Neill's main grievances in the system as it existed in 1915 was the stress it laid on practical success; the main "supplementary courses" were in domestic science, commerce and agriculture.

A high proportion of parents would have supported such a practical bias; indeed they did not believe the authorities went far enough. "Bairns are gettin ower muckle eddication noo-a-days", said one to Neill.[15] "What eddication does a laddie need to herd kye?" And the master at Cullen had a complaint in 1877 from a Free Church elder against his children being taught "profane songs" like "Ye Banks and Braes".[16] But there were exceptions, if we are to believe Lewis Grassic Gibbon:[17]

> Most said it was a coarse thing, learning, just teaching your children a lot of damned nonsense that put them above themselves, they'd turn round and give you their lip as soon as look at you. But Chae was sitting down himself by then and he wouldn't have that. "Damn't man you're clean wrong to think that. Education's the thing the working man wants to put him up level with the Rich."

This was the attitude which had built the Workers' Educational Association; right up to the end of the period there were many men of thirty and over who had left school too early, and were keen to repair the ruins of missed opportunities.

For most people concerned, parents, teachers and children themselves, education remained an earnest matter, especially before 1914. "Be not deceived" was one headmaster's favourite text, "God is not mocked; for whatsoever a man soweth, that shall he also reap". Another in 1889

> spoke to the children about the necessity of working hard during the time before them,

as he noted in his log-book. A third was more concise: "Busy, boys, busy!"[18] The attitude is hardly surprising: it is sometimes difficult to remember or imagine how near the serious things were in the world

of 1914. In the space of three years in one Aberdeen school one young
teacher died and two others had time off to nurse dying sisters; a year
or two later a pupil-teacher also died.[19] Absences of staff and pupils
were both more frequent and more prolonged. One of the happier
features of the period in fact was the gradual lightening of the educational atmosphere, though, remembering the resilience of children,
it would be a mistake to overestimate the gloom before 1914.

The changes which did come had to battle against well-rooted
conservatism. Neill, the apostle of freedom for children, was dismissed
when he tried his ideas in an elementary school in Angus. His views
were admittedly extreme – a fact of which he was not unaware: "'I
expect that I *was* a sort of bombshell', I laughed"[20] – but it is notable
that when he founded a freedom school of his own, it was outside
Scotland. The attitude which infuriated him, the Old Guard view, is
perhaps nowhere better stated than in a letter written by Professor
Ramsay in October 1908 when he resigned the presidency of the
Classical Association of Scotland. What he deplored were the "emolli-
ents" working to soften the Scottish character – the removal of fees;
free books; taboos on hard tasks and home lessons; the forbidding of the
tawse; the devising of new modes of learning; the showering of bursaries
on just and unjust without an examination; "No young person will
read a book which is not illustrated." A whole complicated educational
machine, he complained, was "now operated by one lever in a distant
signal box".[21] The rights and wrongs of the Professor's attitude are
open to argument, but he represented a strong, sincere body of opinion
which appears in every generation.

REFERENCES

1. *C.C.M. 1879*, xxvii
2. *C.C.M. 1872-1909*, my figures
3. S.E.D., *Report by the Secretary of State for Scotland 1919-1920*
   Robertson, 13; *1922-3* Thomson, 57; *1931-3*, 9; *1936-7* Lang
   C/128
4. KNOX, *250 Years*, 108, 118
5. *S.E.D.R. 1929-30*, A/4
6. LOWNDES, G. A. N., *The Silent Social Revolution: an Account of the
   Expansion of Public Education in England and Wales 1895-1935*
   (London 1937), 227-8.
7. *S.E.D.R. 1923-4*, A/24
8. *Circular No. 1*, 5 April 1919
9. *S.E.D.R. Circular No. 34*, 18 January 1921
10. *S.E.D.R. 1925-6* Wattie, 53; *1929-30* Clark, 83; *1935-6*, A/52
11. *ibid*
12. *S.E.D.R. 1951*, 19

13. KNOX, *250 Years*, 226-7
14. HARRISON, *Merchant Company*, 45-7
15. NEILL, A. S., *A Dominie's Log* (Jenkins 1915), 58
16. CORMACK, *William Cramond*, 37
17. GIBBON, LEWIS GRASSIC, *Sunset Song* (Jarrolds 1937), 115
18. BULLOCH, " 'Billy' Dey", *A.U.R.* iii 8, Feb 1916, 112; *Demonstration School Logbook*, 10 June 1889, 23; M'LEAN, *Fordyce Academy*, 117
19. *Demonstration School Logbook*, 88, 146
20. NEILL, A. S., *A Dominie Dismissed* (Jenkins 1917), 166
21. *Proceedings of the Classical Association of Scotland* (Pillans and Wilson, Edinburgh 1908-9), 5

CHAPTER 2

The System of
Educational Administration

IN local administration, the period from 1872 to 1945 saw a movement towards larger and more powerful authorities, and in central administration a movement towards freedom from English control. The first was achieved by 1930, the second substantially by 1940.

THE SCHOOL BOARDS – BUILDING AND ATTENDANCE

The Act of 1872 called into existence almost a thousand school boards, charged with the duty of providing places for all the children in all the parishes of Scotland. There were 987 parishes in 1872, but a few were content to unite for educational purposes; in 1913 there were 972 boards, and five years later, when they were abolished, the number had shrunk to 947.[1] The size of the area administered varied widely. In the south-west the urban parishes expanded rapidly into sizeable towns: in 1891 Maryhill, part of Glasgow, had a population of 29,296, and only ten years later the census return was 48,130. Govan was so large in the last decade of the nineteenth century that it was provided with its own Secondary Education Committee, on a par with the four main cities. The other extreme was seen in the Highland and rural areas: in 1905, when Lanarkshire (including Glasgow) had only fifty boards for 1,314,810 people, Perth had seventy-nine for 123,991 and Berwick thirty-two for 31,128. Lyne and Megget had a school board in 1913 for a total population of 98, Cranshaws for 159 and Dumbarton (Landward) for 220. It was estimated in that year that the education of half the country was being locally administered by no more than 56 boards.[2]

Under the 1872 Act the boards were constituted at a special election by four-pound owners and occupiers, and there might be anything from five to fifteen members. To begin with these came mainly from the professional and well-to-do classes. The first board of Urquhart and Glenmoriston comprised the parish and two Free Church ministers, the factors of local land and two other gentlemen. At Crieff the seven members included two bankers, two solicitors, a doctor and the minister. Rutherglen had two bankers, a surgeon, an architect, a manufacturer, a colliery manager and a pawn broker. Ministers especially had the

interest and the time: there were four among the six members at
Cardross.[3] Within a couple of decades however places were being
taken by successful tradesmen and farmers and the boards attracted
growing criticism: one inspector found instances of a teacher being
grudged a salary exceeding the income of one member, and it was
suggested that where members were elected by the "operative classes"
they were not prepared to spend money on higher education. The
parsimony of the boards was indeed proverbial, but it merely reflected
public sentiment: a certain Mrs Anderson was defeated at the 1911
election in Rutherglen because she had spent £132.5.10½ on a new
homecraft department for Gallowflat school.[4]

Friction with teachers was by no means uncommon, especially
where board members inspected the work, as they were entitled to do.[5]
A. S. Neill in 1915 saw them as bodies whose only aim was to keep
down the rates. At Alloway in 1878 an influential local lady found fault
with the quality of the sewing, and said so in presence of the pupils.
The teacher spoke back, refused to apologise and received a month's
notice. Some teachers, for instance in Kelso and Ardrossan, denied
the right of boards to inspect, but legal proceedings, while they left
the position vague, made it virtually impossible to exclude them from
the school. In Lerwick at the end of the century a series of disagree-
ments culminated in the board's dismissing the rector, Mr Young.
The Scotch Education Department disapproved of the board's action,
and the Educational Institute of Scotland blacklisted the school.
Shetlanders however were stubborn: they appointed a new headmaster
who was not a member of the Institute, and he appears to have enjoyed
adequate success.[6] Clearly the boards had much power, and their
arbitrary use of it in many cases was a powerful influence in shaping
teachers' attitudes. Yet the strength of local feeling could still make
itself felt, at least in the early part of the period. An attempt by the
local board to transfer Fordyce Academy to Portsoy in 1914 failed,
and so did an effort in 1918 by the education authority to reduce it to
a primary school.[7] After 1945 there were to be few such victories over
the central or regional authorities.

The boards varied widely in efficiency. Some of the earliest circulars
issued by the Scotch Education Department cast an unflattering light
on them: one dated 1873 set out[8]

> the proper mode of conducting correspondence with the Department:
> Paragraph 1. Letters addressed to this Department should be
> written on foolscap paper and on consecutive sheets, beginning with
> the first.

Nevertheless the work done by many boards was impressive. The
main difficulty was that their problems were never static: by the time
all the children of 1872 had been provided for the steady rise in urban
and fall in rural population had altered the picture. Between 1872 and

1904 the population of Scotland increased by a quarter, and the average attendance at public schools rose by from fifty to seventy-five per cent.[9]

The main problem in 1872 was accommodation. In Hamilton for instance the board's census showed that of the burgh's 2,211 children between five and thirteen years old 824 would now be attending school for the first time and rather less than half the required number of places was available. In 1873, 466 of Bonhill's 1,678 children went to no school and no fewer than 925 ran wild in Rutherglen.[10] In many parishes therefore the boards took over the schools of the Established and Free Churches and occasionally some of the better private institutions, though many were hardly attractive, as the reports showed:

> Miss Child's school – this is a girl's school. It is situated in Millgate. There are no offices and no playground, but the schoolroom affords accommodation for the regulation number of 62.

New building was also required: in Rutherglen for example, where the board had at its disposal the burgh school, Macdonald's and the Free Church building, three new schools were erected in 13 years, the new burgh, Farie Street and Stonelaw, to be followed soon by Gallowflat. The towns on the whole coped better than the Highlands and islands, where overcrowding was the rule for years:[11]

> 1874 Dec, 14. Admitted 5 pupils this week. Writing deficient, some of the pupils having to write on the harmonium, and on the coalbunker.

Several boards became famous for the work they did and the spirit of adventure they showed. On more than one occasion Her Majesty's Inspectors took the chance to mention the "marvellous work" of Glasgow and Govan, and a walk through the western streets of the city today confirms this. In 1874 Glasgow had 27 schools – including the ancient grammar school, handed over by the town council – with accommodation for 9,645 pupils. By 1883 there were 62, exactly half of them newly built, and the total accommodation was 43,939. Together with six other school buildings in that year the programme had cost the board half a million pounds, and the annual expenditure was now £120,000. Govan School Board by 1877 had built ten schools and in 1885 it acquired the private Bellahouston Academy for £15,000, making it a public higher class school. Edinburgh was fortunate in taking over the Heriot schools, but in effect only three out of twelve were purchased for permanent use. In any case by 1878 the school board of the capital had nine new schools built and three building. A black spot was Leith, where as late as 1884 there was still no provision for a third of the children of school age; the board was officially characterised as "willing but dilatory".[12]

The first rush of board school building lasted from 1873 until about

1879. It was not always prudently undertaken: Her Majesty's Inspectors complained that they were never consulted.[13] Nor was it unqualified philanthropy: in Angus the inspector commented that though they were liberal in erecting schools, they were not in providing houses for the teachers, an important matter in rural districts.[14] Between 1873 and 1907 however the Scottish boards spent ten and a half million pounds on building.[15] The effect of this ambitious effort was to be felt in the mid-twentieth century, when many of the buildings available were nearly 80 years old, solid and durable but antiquated in design; an extensive programme of renewal was required. Classrooms were cubes, too high to be economical, draby painted in green or brown, with rows of desks clamped to the floor, preventing experiment in anything but "class" teaching. Many in the country schools still had open fires. The old "gallery" rooms were slow to disappear – 1929 in the Aberdeen Demonstration School – and the common pattern of seventies building was a ring of classrooms in a solid rectangle of red or grey stone, arranged around a central hall with a vast glass roof to give light. The main feature of the hall came to be its Dux Board and its War Memorial. As classes became legally smaller partitions were constructed inside rooms, and there were schools in Glasgow where it was hardly possible to conduct a lesson in defiance of the noise from all sides, for the hall often did duty also as gymnasium and dining-room. The playground was half an acre of concrete, with a "shed" for protection against the rain and two sets of lavatories. Set in a cavern of tenements, such a school needed all the light it could attract; nevertheless there was much more stone than glass in its walls. Rural schools had the advantage only of smaller size and airier surroundings; some of them were even older than 1872. At Auchtertool in Fife the schoolhouse in 1948 was a modernised building 400 years old; Jane Welsh had lived in it before her marriage to Carlyle and it was said to have witnessed their secret meetings. A score of buildings in Ayrshire at the same time dated from before the Act, but it is doubtful whether any was quite as primitive as that at Newburn in Fife, which was served by coal fires, oil lamps and dry sanitation. In Aberdeenshire, Overton parish school, taken over in 1872 by the School Board, was still in use in 1955. Small wonder that the comments of inspectors in school log-books increasingly commended devoted work in conditions varying from inadequate to "touching the low point of seemly and sanitary accommodation". One in 1893 complained of country schools that "at present the decencies of modern civilisation are unrepresented in school offices" (lavatories).[16] Yet the achievement of the boards remains: whereas in 1872 there were places for only 281,688 pupils in Scotland, the figure in 1903 was 948,308.

Besides building new schools the boards found themselves occupied enforcing attendance. For almost all normal Scottish children, since few could afford a tutor, attendance at school was rendered compulsory by the 1872 Act, "cramming information down people's throats with a policeman's staff".[17] The boards had to appoint officers, and in cases of severe or recurrent default to prosecute parents. From 1878 onward a child might leave school at the age of ten if he satisfied the inspector that he could read, write and show reasonable proficiency in arithmetic, but even this was abolished in 1901; meanwhile the leaving age was raised to fourteen.

Some of the boards, especially in the north-east, did their duty with zeal. Elsewhere however the compulsory clauses were not enforced. Attendance officers, poorly paid, had to take other jobs to make ends meet and could not afford to alienate local parents. In 1874, 6,342 summonses were issued, but the boards were unwilling to proceed to extremes, or perhaps a summons was enough to bring conformity, for there were only 156 prosecutions in that year, with 110 convictions. Parents made over 3,000 applications for their children's exemption, and of these 2,000 were granted. One Sheriff produced the remarkable judgment that the requirement of a man under the 1872 Act to send his child to school between the ages of five and thirteen could be met by attendance for one day! In some towns, one inspector complained, attendance was more irregular *after* the Act; in Nairn in 1883 it was slightly over sixty per cent, in Skye from thirty-five to sixty.[18] Seasonal absence was high, as the school log-books show, with boys used as herds, caddies and beaters:[19]

> The attendance is yet small as is generally the case till after the Martinmas term, when the children engaged herding cattle, etc., come home for the winter.

> The scholars have been greatly thinned owing to several leaving for the summer work in the fields and especially for herding cattle, for which a great many under thirteen have also left.

An inspector listed occasions for absence as lambing and potato-planting (April-May), turnip-thinning (June-July), sheep-shearing (July), harvest (August-September) and potato-lifting (October). Coastal towns had similar problems.[20]

> 1873. August 15. Classes imperfectly formed owing chiefly to the absence of the fishermen's children, who will not return from Fraserburgh, etc., for some weeks.

Whenever there was a wreck local children would be absent collecting useful salvage. The 1878 Act recognised the problem by permitting a maximum of six weeks employment a year for husbandry and fisheries. But no act could cope with the climate:

> The weather during a great part of the year is of the wildest and roughest character. Terrific gales swept over the islands ... and the rain comes down in cold, solid slices, at a cutting angle, so as to wet

B

through the thickest clothes in a few moments. There is no shelter anywhere and there must be therefore very many days in the year in which it is impossible for the younger children to attend at all.

The larger towns had their own problems:

28 May 1889. Flitting Day. Attendance considerably affected by it and by the wet day.

There was also in many parts a fluctuating and recalcitrant population, "too intoxicated to answer our enquiries" or, as in Glasgow in 1879, excessively discreet:

William came to window and said his mother was out and had key with her – saw mother sitting up in bed.

People in Glasgow who were comfortably off showed no more enthusiasm for schooling: they often removed their children with them to houses down the Clyde in May and June. But the main destroyer of attendance was poverty: in Rutherglen as late as 1917[21]

the lack of boots and the prolonged time taken for boot-mending cause a number of children to be kept at home.

Edinburgh in 1882 found 101 cases of children selling newspapers outside the permitted hours and many more offered matches long after dark. The answer of parents who were prosecuted was simple – "are we to starve?" – and some sheriffs were very lenient.[22]

Improvement was slow over the years. The figures are difficult to interpret because of the children who attended schools outside the public system, but there is no doubt that many parents contrived to evade their obligations, often with the connivance or at least the knowledge of the boards. Even the freeing of elementary education in 1890 had little immediate effect, and although half a dozen years later the closing of many adventure schools brought more pupils into the state system, especially in the infant classes, only forty-eight per cent of children between five and six were then on the public registers and only 79.5 per cent of those between six and seven. There was still a discrepancy in 1914 between the estimated number of children in the population and the actual number on school rolls. In Ayrshire in the nineties eighty-three per cent of children of appropriate ages were at school, in Scotland as a whole in 1903 eighty-five per cent. By 1950 the figure for five-year-olds was eighty-one per cent, for all other ages up to fifteen ninety-four per cent.[23]

We may conclude therefore that the work of the school boards in improving attendance, while often quite efficient, was not their most successful. On the other hand, some boards showed commendable zeal. When continuation classes were given some statutory recognition in 1908, the Act of that year gave local authorities power to make them compulsory up to seventeen. The first authority to make use of this was the school board of Hoddam in Dumfries, and its young men and women were the first in Britain to be compelled to receive education up to the age of seventeen. East Kilbride shortly followed the example.

THE SCHOOL BOARDS – VOLUNTARY DUTIES

Building and attendance were the main duties of the school boards. The measure of their efficiency perhaps was the extent to which they were willing to undertake additional duties. A few experimented in the early years of the twentieth century with schemes for improving the physical welfare of their pupils. In 1904 the school boards of Edinburgh, Dunfermline, Kirkcaldy and Govan had medical inspection arrangements, and in Glasgow, though no examinations were held, teachers recorded their children's measurements and tested their eyesight. There were also arrangements in Glasgow for feeding and clothing necessitous children through Day Industrial Schools, Day Refuges, the Poor Children's Dinner Table Society and the Buchanan Institution.[24]

By that time however most of the local boards were, as one inspector noted, marking time "in the expectation that they were to be superseded by a wider authority".[25] The largest part of their effective work had been done in the previous thirty years, and on their achievement then they should be judged. They had encountered much severe criticism, mostly before they were set up. Teachers on the whole had not wanted them, being fairly sure of their employment under the old system and fearing that trouble-makers would contrive to be elected. In 1865 the convener of the Free Church Education Committee had stated his opinion that unscrupulous politicians would soon rule the roost in the boards and cheap education and low rates would be election slogans.[26] Certainly these gloomy forecasts were not always proved wrong. But on the whole the boards worked well. Several were not only efficient but farseeing: they were unwilling to confine their work to elementary education, and ready to set up higher-class schools when funds could be found.

THE 1918 AUTHORITIES AND THE 1929 COMMITTEES

The Munro Act of 1918 ended the existence of the school boards. Clearly there were too many, and the areas they administered were too small for efficiency. Since 1892 secondary education committees had been controlling finance, each in one county or large town, and they suggested an administrative unit of a handier size. The government's intention was to put power into the hands of the county councils, as it had done in England by the Act of 1902, but there was much Scottish opposition, partly on the ground that education should be the care of men specially elected for the purpose and partly out of pure conservatism. A Bill of 1905 proposed the substitution of District for Parish school boards, based on county council districts. The effect would have been to reduce the number of authorities to 111, but the bill failed to secure passage. The debates on the Liberal Education Act of 1908, which proposed no change in educational areas, opened the affair again. Mr Munro Ferguson, for the Opposition, moved an amendment which would allow the creation of wider areas, calling the school boards "as obsolete as the Poor Law districts" and claiming that their smallness opened the way for "the heavy hand of the Department". Unfortunately he also got lost in some recondite Old Testament allusions, and Sir Henry Craik, seconding, confessed that he was not always sure what Mr Ferguson was talking about. Craik asked the very pertinent question whether 980 boards, however well intentioned, could all aspire to be pioneer educators; in his view the Government was in a hurry to get its act passed, and that was why no change was proposed. The Lord Advocate, replying, made much of the "time-honoured parish system" and the need to maintain local interest. He pointed out how difficult it would be for people in Sutherland to travel to any central town, only to have an English member remark that English counties were already committed to such arrangements, apparently without hardship. But all the arguments were in the air: the Government had a solid majority of 158 to 29.[27]

In the end the 1918 Act went further than the original proposals: it provided for the election every three years by proportional representation of education authorities with an existence separate from that of the county councils. There were thirty-three counties in Scotland, and five large burghs – Glasgow, Edinburgh, Aberdeen, Dundee and Leith. Thus thirty-eight authorities – reduced to thirty-seven in 1920 by the amalgamation of Leith with Edinburgh – took the place of 947 school boards; 987 members replaced over 5,000.

Their powers and duties rapidly expanded. Besides maintaining the public schools of their district they were permitted to contribute to other educational institutions, including the universities and higher colleges. They were expected to supply nursery schools for children under five where the demand was sufficient. They had to attend to the mental health, nourishment and physical welfare of children. To make attendance at secondary schools easier they were to pay fees, maintenance grants and the cost of travel or lodging.

These multiplying commitments greatly increased the cost of educational administration and the new authorities were unpopular from the start: the rise in Dunbarton within a year or two was 111 per cent. Nevertheless the government was disinclined to extend their rating powers; its original bill had committed authority to the county councils and the teachers' organisations had been annoyed when the Department gave way on the *ad hoc* principle:[28]

> Education is so important that it cannot be left out of the great stream and tendency of social service.

As it was, the central powers clearly regarded it as no more than a stage, and within little more than a decade the *ad hoc* authorities were superseded by the county and city councils, working through education committees. There were thirty-five of these committees: Kinross was amalgamated with Perth and Nairn with Moray. The majority of the committee was drawn from the councillors, but at least two members were nominated by local churches or denominational bodies interested in education. It discharged all the educational functions of the council with three exceptions – raising money by rate or loan, approving and authorising expenditure and incurring any not authorised by the council. In short the education committee might propose many interesting plans, but the last word was always with the county treasurer.

The main criticism of the education committees stressed the obvious fact that the majority of their members had no special knowledge of educational problems, might indeed be abysmally ignorant of them. The situation was not improved by the express exclusion of teachers. Since the only contact of councillors with schools was in their own childhood or in specially organised visits, their experience tended to be a generation out of date. Such a comment however applies to any branch of democratic government, central or local, and it was at least partly met by the appointment of a permanent servant of the council, the director of education. The first circular issued by the Department after the 1918 Act advised each authority to appoint an executive officer; not all however, complied, and after the transfer to county councils, there was a tendency to double the post with that of county clerk. The 1945 Act put an end to that by making the appointment of a separate director obligatory and specific.[29]

SCHOOL MANAGEMENT COMMITTEES

The framers of the 1918 Act clearly felt that the establishment of larger authorities carried the danger of losing touch with individual schools; their answer was to order the setting up of "School Management Committees" for schools or groups of schools.[30] Members were to be drawn from parents and teachers as well as the authorities, but their powers were narrowly confined, excluding all important functions like appointment and dismissal of staff, building of schools and general finance. In the first year or two after the Act 489 of these committees were set up in Scotland, with members distributed as follows:

1,350 members of education authorities
1,299 parents
 890 town and parish councillors
 887 ex-members of school boards
 851 teachers
 182 representatives of transferred schools
  13 others.

In the event, like so many good ideas on paper, school management committees were not widely accepted in Scotland. They fought a running battle with the education authorities, which were jealous of their powers; the one in Dunbarton for instance required that its permission be sought for any expenditure over £10 and refused to allow attendance officers one record book each.[31] In return one of the management committees took the authority to task for using its school without permission. In such an uneven contest the authorities were bound to win, with the inevitable consequence that the management committees, left in their own view to do nothing but menial duties and "dirty work" like enforcing attendance and prosecuting parents, wasted away. At some meetings not enough people appeared to elect themselves as the required body. The liaison they were intended to promote was later undertaken by parent-teacher associations.

THE COMMITTEE OF COUNCIL AND
THE SCOTCH EDUCATION DEPARTMENT

Central administration after 1872 was the responsibility of the Scotch Education Department. From the outset however this body aroused disappointment among people interested in Scottish education. As early as 1847 the Synod of the United Presbyterian Church, in a document containing six recommendations on education, had suggested that

> stated returns should be made to the Privy Council or to a National Board of Education.

Three years later the "National Educational Association of Scotland" declared:

> There should be a general superintending authority to see that duties are not neglected, to prevent abuses, to check expenditure, to collect statutes and to spread knowledge and enlightened views.

In the next two decades opinion hardened into a desire for a National Board, preferably located in Edinburgh, with powers to direct policy as well as disseminate information. The "Scotch Education Department" set up by the 1872 Act certainly failed to satisfy this desire. It gave the new Scottish Committee of the Privy Council the administrative assistance of a separate civil service department and thus achieved independence of the English system. But when its composition was announced it was found to have the same President and Vice-President as the English, and to share also its Permanent Secretary. Since the last two posts were the most effective, it could be expected only to bring Scottish education into line with English, a step which, having regard to the educational history of the two countries, could hardly meet with approval north of the border. A protest submitted by a meeting of the Church of Scotland in Glasgow pointed out that there was

> no reasonable security that the Department will have adequate knowledge of Scottish circumstances.

The duty of forming policy nominally fell to the Committee of Council. It is not clear how it discharged this duty. Lord Sandon admitted in the Commons that it never met and that all its work was done by an office staff brought up in the English tradition. The practice of issuing all edicts in the name of "My Lords", which continued until the appointment of John Struthers as permanent secretary in 1904, was said to be no more than a matter of courtesy. On the other hand the first Scottish secretary, Sir Henry Craik, claimed that[32]

> for many years the influence of the Lord President in Scottish education was real and not nominal only. The Committee, I can answer for it, did frequently meet, and to good purpose, when I had the honour of being its secretary.

This may have been an expression of Craik's modesty: certainly the major reforms during his tenure of office were his own work.

Wherever the power lay it was not in Scotland. Government of course was neither blind nor arbitrary: the Scotch Code of 1873 for instance was an attempt to meet peculiarly Scottish requirements and its provisions showed real differences from those in the English document. But this was not enough. Between 1872 and 1885 numerous pamphleteers and interested bodies conducted a campaign against the two objectionable features of the administration – that it was run by Englishmen, and that it had its headquarters in London. The most open path of reform was to confer permanency on the Board of Education set up in Edinburgh to co-ordinate the work of the school-boards; in 1877 a petition to Lord Beaconsfield ensured its continuance for another year.[33] Attempts were made to extend its duties to control endowments, grants, inspection and the training of teachers. In 1879 however it was allowed to lapse, and for six years more the unpopular regime continued.

Sir Francis Sandford, the Permanent Secretary who acted for both English and Scottish departments, was a man of great power and energy, but he was clearly overworked in attempting to enforce the

two Acts. Moreover there was a legacy of English ignorance of Scottish
affairs. His predecessor, Mr Lingen, finding that Kirkwall Burgh
School taught Latin, Greek, French and mathematics, withheld a grant
on the ground that it could not possibly be intended for the working
classes. He later handsomely acknowledged his mistake, but the inference of his English background is clear. The Revised Code itself had
been imposed on Scotland as the result of an enquiry into English
conditions. Under Sandford this tendency continued: one Scottish
inspector reports a conversation between two members of the Department staff.[34]

"Where is Skye?"
"I'm not quite sure, but I think it's not far from the Orkney Islands".

After the disappearance of the Edinburgh Board, educational rebels
joined in the agitation for a Secretary for Scottish affairs. The discontent
culminated in a public demonstration in the capital in January 1884.
A parliamentary bill introduced in the same year failed because of the
Franchise Bill difficulties. In the following year Lord Rosebery
introduced a new bill, and although Gladstone's government fell,
Salisbury allowed it to go through. The importance of education in
the duties of the new Minister is shown by the title of the measure:

An Act for appointing a Secretary for Scotland and Vice-President
of the Scotch Education Department.

Although the new Secretary held inferior rank and was not a Secretary
of State until 1926,[38] he was given a separate Permanent Secretary,
Henry Craik, and undoubtedly an attempt was being made to meet
some of the Scottish demands. Nevertheless the reform was not
enough to satisfy all those who expostulated. For one thing a vague
Scottish Committee of Council was still in nominal control. For another
the new Secretary would be a very busy man: his duties under the 1885
Act formed an imposing list, ranging from police duties and public
health to prevention of river pollution, wild bird protection and the
keeping of the Great Seal in Scotland. Finally, although a new home
was found for the Scotch Department, it was at Dover House in
Whitehall,[36] there was still no prospect of a transfer to Edinburgh.

The reason given was not agreeable to Scottish *amour propre*. During
a Lords debate in 1884 Lord Balfour of Burleigh expressed the official
attitude:

I very much doubt whether it is possible for the government to
allow such a large spending department as the Education Department
has become to have an office away from London.

For many years therefore, during the secretaryships of Craik and
Struthers, headquarters remained in London. In Edinburgh there
were only such minor establishments as the offices of the Accountant

at 33 York Place, and those of the Endowment Commissioners at 46 George Street. Early in the twentieth century, after a good deal of pamphlet agitation, the Department relented so far as to open a branch office at 14 Queen Street, under the care of an assistant secretary, George Macdonald. On 1 January 1921, when Macdonald succeeded Struthers as Secretary, he did not transfer his headquarters to London, and so, without official warrant, the concentration of administrative power in Edinburgh was achieved. Until the opening of St Andrews House in 1940 however the address of the Department appeared in the Civil Service List as Dover House. It may be added that a somewhat obscure tribute was paid to Scottish sentiment in the Act of 1918, when the title of the Department was altered from "Scotch" to "Scottish".

Just before the outbreak of the Second World War the antique tradition of ascribing ultimate power to the "Lords of the Committee of Council" was at last broken.* From 1939 education became one of the responsibilities of the Secretary of State for Scotland, and all subsequent acts laid duties on him. By an order of 4th August 1939 he delegated all his educational functions, including some not previously subject to the Committee of Council, to the Scottish Education Department. In 1940 the first Report of the Secretary of State appeared, after a century of Reports by the Committee of Council.

CRAIK AND STRUTHERS

The legal arrangement that decision of policy have been left to the Committee of Council and later to the Secretary of State, while the Department carried them out, has not been by any means a fiction. Nevertheless men in public affairs are seldom experts in education, and they rarely have enough time to devote to administrative matters. In consequence it is safe to state that many of the changes in Scottish education during the last three-quarters of a century have been introduced at the instigation of the Department, and the importance of its permanent secretaries can hardly be overstressed. These changes are not of course easy to trace, since the central authority has seldom made any statement of its principles. An exception to this rule occurred in 1904, when the general principles governing the conduct of the Committee of Council were described as: first, to maintain three distinct grades of day schools – elementary, intermediate and secondary – each giving a general, humanistic, unspecialised training; second, to adhere to the "characteristic national principle" of dual control in subsidies; third, to test efficiency not written by examinations on a set syllabus but by general inspection, thus conferring considerable freedom on the schools.[37] The second and third of these principles

* This body last met in 1913.

were rooted in tradition, but the first was largely evolved by the reforms introduced during the nineties by Henry Craik.

As might be expected, the earlier secretaries, working in a formative period, made their influence more readily felt. Sir Francis Sandford held office from 1870 to 1884, while the new school boards were finding their feet and the flaws in the Acts were appearing. The most effective contribution to Scottish education in this period was the first independent Schools Code, which was largely the work of Dr Kerr, one of Her Majesty's Inspectors, and appeared in 1873. It covered such matters as building grants, teacher training and certification, and evening schools; and, as we shall see, it introduced at last to Scottish schools the pernicious doctrine of "payment by results". Sandford retired in 1884 and was succeeded by Patrick Cumin, but within a year Cumin's connexion with Scottish education was broken when a separate Secretary was appointed.

This was Henry Craik, later created a baronet for his services. He held his position for almost two decades, and during that time the entire aspect of Scottish education changed. Almost at once he set about freeing the schools from "payment by results"; the last traces vanished in 1889. Elementary education rapidly became free for all children between three and fifteen. Turning his attention to higher instruction, he carried through numerous administrative measures which resulted in the establishment of a "higher grade" as well as a secondary system, and so opened advanced classes to poorer children, since the new schools were eligible for government grants. He encouraged instruction in art and science as well as in the older academic subjects, and in 1897 the administration of science and art grants was taken over by the Department. His interest in the standard of secondary education was shown by the introduction of regular inspection of higher class schools and in the first leaving certificate examination. The Secondary Education Committees established in 1892 were based on the county as an administrative unit, and helped to point the way to future reorganisation of local control. Finally it was largely during Craik's tenure that the problem of the training and certification of teachers was tackled, though Provincial Committees were not set up until 1905; he had an important part in permitting the colleges from 1901 onward to set their own curricula. He has also been described as a pioneer of physical education. It is unlikely that he himself gave birth to so many new ideas, but he was a constant driving force. The statement of principles quoted above dates from May 1904 and may perhaps be taken as his testament.

Craik was certainly one of the two most influential men in Scottish education during the second half of the nineteenth century. (The other was Simon Laurie, first professor of Education in the University of Edinburgh, superintendent of Church of Scotland schools and Visitor and Examiner for fifty years to the Dick Bequest.) On Sir Henry's resignation in December 1905 to commence a career in Parliament, he was succeeded by John Struthers. The latter had a wide knowledge of the schools: he had been an inspector for almost the entire period of Scottish educational independence, having been appointed in 1886 and taken into the central system in 1897 at Dover House. He held office until 1921 and his strong will may be traced in many contemporary developments. The remodelling of the teacher training system under Provincial Committees came at the beginning of his period, the institution of a National Committee at the end. Where Craik had emphasised the value of physical education, Struthers gave considerable importance to manual training as an element in ordinary schooling. By a series of generous grants he strengthened Craik's higher grade system and later extended it logically by dividing post-primary pupils into secondary and non-secondary groups. Such a move, justified by the economic conditions of the time, was to cause much trouble however to his successors as the climate of educational opinion changed. Finally, it was during his secretaryship that the Acts of 1908 and 1918 were passed. His Department had a great deal to do with their framing and it was their job to carry them into effect.

These were fundamental changes, yet they were often brought about quietly by civil servants, without the thunder of parliamentary debate.* Despite its efficiency – or perhaps because of it: "the more efficient the Department", wrote Professor Laurie, "the worse for the country" – the S.E.D. was not popular. Most of its innovations had to be introduced against stern opposition. The Leaving Certificate examination "might deny children in small schools the right to a higher education". The Classical Association of Scotland thought that the Department "appeared to be trying to Germanise Scottish education".[38] Struthers, a forceful man, was personally unpopular, the inevitable fate of any reformer, made worse by the unpalatable fact that the reformer represented the state.

HER MAJESTY'S INSPECTORS

Throughout the period Her Majesty's Inspectors continued to maintain contact between the Department and the schools. In the early days of the school boards they were kept busy interpreting the wishes of Dover House, and the part they played directly in local administration was not small. As local efficiency increased, however, their duties tended towards supervision rather than polite control. Their first task was to ensure that the Acts were being carried out and that public money was being wisely spent, and the legacy of payment by results was a long series of personal conflicts and tensions. At first examination of

---

* A popular method of legislation was by Minute of the Committee of Council, which avoided the long delays of parliamentary procedure.

all classes took place at the end of the school year, but, as Circular 223 pointed out,

> it is alleged, and their Lordships believe with much truth, that in many schools the work of the year is practically accomplished a month or two before inspection.

The rest of the time was spent by the teacher preparing by dill for pupils to make a good impression. No fixed month of inspection therefore became the rule, but for a number of nervous teachers and headmasters these occasions were severe emotional trials. As the twentieth century progressed there was a general movement to stress the advisory rather than the monitory aspect of inspectors' work "His Majesty's Educational Advisers", the Norwood Report of 1941 wished to call them. They were not only to advise the Department on local conditions and act as educational experts in their fields but also to advise and encourage young teachers. Not until after the Second World War however, despite improving relations, was there general agreement that the advisory function was sufficiently stressed. Visits, especially on short notice, were often emotional occasions, and there was a good deal of banter about "back-room boys"[39]

> Nae doot fin God made Rectors gweed
> He'd Higher Leavin's in his heid.
> And fin He gart Directors growe
> He'd gweed intentions in His pow.
> But fin He sent Inspectors doon
> Dyod! fa kens *fut* wis in His Croon?

Not all of it was so good-natured, though on the whole it was less outspoken than in the 1870s and 1880s, when the *Educational News* often attacked inspectors by name: "personal fads, of which Mr Dunn seems to have his fair share", "the unhappy manner and method of inspection pursued by Mr Waddell", "as a teacher in (North Forfarshire) I would be most happy to hear of (Mr Muir's) removal". The fact that many inspectors championed teachers threatened with dismissal by the school boards probably helped to improve relations.[40]

Additional duties were delegated to the Inspectors as the educational structure was developed. From the beginning of the twentieth century the training of teachers was left in the hands of the colleges, but the inspectors approved teaching marks and decided as before whether a probationer was entitled after two years to his "parchment" certificate. As one educational body after another was constituted inspectors were used as assessors, maintaining contact with the Department, giving advice when asked but never directly formulating policy. They appeared on teacher training committees, the National Joint Council, the Advisory Councils. Meanwhile from 1888 they were mainly responsible for the administration of the Leaving Certificate examinations.

One duty they were never called on to perform was the inspection of religious teaching, which by the 1872 Act was expressly removed from their province. Whether this was valuable was debatable: in too many schools the Bible period dwindled into useful time for daily administrative tasks or at best a perfunctory gabble through the Gospels. Since the state was of the opinion that religious teaching was worth giving, it would appear that some inspection of it was not unreasonable. In England it caused little disturbance.

In 1874 there were twenty-three inspectors, with thirteen assistants. Ten years later there were twenty-five with four sub-inspectors and twenty-one assistants, and the number increased steadily to over ninety after the Second World War.[41] From 1884 their reports – a fruitful source of educational information – were organised according to the new "divisions", Northern, Western or Southern. In 1908 the Highland made its appearance, though for a long time its report was bracketed with the Northern.[42] Each was under the supervision of a Chief Inspector. There were many men of great ability and influence. Sir John Struthers, we have seen, began his career in the inspectorate. Dr John Kerr, appointed before 1872, rose to become Senior Chief Inspector in 1887 and held that post for ten years.[43] The first Scottish Code, issued in 1873, was largely his work, and he was a pioneer of the plan whereby some training college students were encouraged to attend classes at universities. William McKechnie, who became Secretary in the 1920's, and William Arbuckle, Secretary in the 1950s, were men of considerable distinction who rose through the ranks of the inspectorate. Both were knighted. The first woman inspector of general subjects was not appointed until 1930, the second four years later. Promotion of a woman to charge of a district dates from 1936, to the post of Chief Inspector from the 1950s. Particularly in its senior branches, however, the inspectorate remained and remains predominantly male.

As a body, Her Majesty's Inspectors discharged their somewhat circumscribed duties with tact and efficiency. That their time was increasingly spent in uninspiring administration was probably a tribute to the growing efficiency of the system. It may be guessed however that many of them would still be willing to face with pleasure some of the problems which exercised their predecessors in the late nineteenth century, when Dr Kerr had to visit outlying Highland schools on horseback, and Dr Wilson could inspect a class in the Orkney Islands with all its parents watching, and one proud father, as his child reached the top, exclaiming in rapture :"Weel done Johnny! Weel done my laddie!"[44]

THE ADVISORY AND RESEARCH COUNCILS

Section 20 of the Munro Act made it lawful for an Advisory Council to be set up by Order in Council.[45] From the early years of the century the English Board of Education had profited from the advice of a consultative committee, and it was felt that the Secretary of State ought to have the assistance of the country's best educational brains. The Act provided that two-thirds of the members should represent the views of various interested bodies and that the Secretary should "take into consideration" any advice or suggestion the Council made. Rather over a year later, in January 1920, an Order in Council constituted the first Advisory Council on Education in Scotland.

Its main work was not accomplished in this period; that was to come in the late forties. Between 1920 and 1940 a number of useful reports were issued, including one on the education and training of primary women teachers (1933) and another on technical education in the day school system (1936). On the whole however it hardly lived up to expectations, and in 1942 it was reconstituted to consist of twenty-five members, of whom seventeen would represent the education committees, the Educational Institute and the Association of Directors of Education. The Secretary of State appointed chairman, vice-chairman and secretary, and special committees might be established for specific matters. Every three years it was to be reconstituted, but this provision was not always observed.

The Act of 1918 also instructed education authorities to set up local advisory councils within three months. Little was heard of these; however, one member of parliament described them as "the fifth wheel on the coach."[46] A much more promising development occurred in research, for which the Act made no provision. Educational experiments on a more ambitious scale were being conducted in the United States and Russia in the early twentieth century; in Scotland the lead was taken by the Educational Institute, which set up a committee on educational research in 1919. Eight years later this body collaborated with the Association of Directors of Education to found the Scottish Council for Research in Education. The aims were to organise and aid research and to publish reports, with the co-operation of all education authorities. In 1928 the Scottish Education Department gave its approval in principle to the foundation, but insisted on a progressive widening of the bodies represented; in time these included, besides the founders, the Association of County Councils, the Association of Counties of Cities, the National Committee for the Training of Teachers, the training colleges, the universities, the Scottish branch of the British Psychological Society and the Association of School Medical Officers.

For some years money to finance the Council's projects was not easy to find. In 1932 it took the wise step of becoming a limited company; meanwhile grants from the E.I.S. and the authorities were fortunately supplemented by the Carnegie Trust. The Act of 1945 permitted the Secretary of State to make grants in aid of educational research, and the Regulations issued in the following year brought the Council within the scope of the scheme.[47]

A series of valuable reports was published. In some cases, after the

SYSTEM OF EDUCATIONAL ADMINISTRATION 31

original work had appeared at a fairly moderate price, the author was
further encouraged to prepare a short statement and summary for
publication at a shilling or two in a special "teachers edition". There
were studies in various curriculum subjects like Professor Vernon's
reading test and Dr Neill Wright's work on arabic numerals; works
on Scottish educational history – in Aberdeenshire, for example, in
Angus, Stirlingshire, Ayrshire, Edinburgh and the spinning schools of
the Highlands; and monographs on such special topics as selection for
secondary education and the prognostic value of university entrance
examinations. Certainly the most ambitious project – unique indeed
in present-day education – was the Mental Survey intended to shed
light on the trend of Scottish intelligence. In 1932 and again in 1947
all the children aged from $10\frac{1}{2}$ to $11\frac{1}{2}$ on a selected day were given a
group test of intelligence. Certain smaller sub-groups were also indivi-
dually tested. The results were published over a number of years; there
was no agreement on the construction to be placed on the evidence, but
the evidence itself was a major contribution to educational information.

REFERENCES

1. CURTIS, S. J., *History of Education in Great Britain* (Universities
   Tutorial Press 1961), 248; SMITH, *Broken Links*, 144
2. *C.C.M. 1902-3*, 62; SMITH, *Broken Links*, 144; *Nelson's Annotated
   Scotch Code, 1905*, 294
3. MACKAY, *Urquhart and Glenmoriston*, 400; PORTEOUS, *Crieff*, 195;
   SHEARER, *Rutherglen Lore*, 174; MURRAY, *Cardross*, 59
4. STRONG, *Secondary Education*, 217; WILSON, *Tales and Travels*,
   76; PATON, *Rutherglen*, 21
5. Kelso School Board *v.* Hunter
6. NEILL, *Dominie's Log*, 133; BOYD, *Ayrshire*, 196-7; *Anderson
   Educational Institute*, 26
7. M'LEAN, *Fordyce Academy*, 61-5
8. *S.E.D. Circular*, 24 Oct 1873
9. CLARKE, *Short Studies*, 42
10. *Hamilton Past and Present*, 66-7; SHEARER, *Rutherglen Lore*, 174;
    NEILL, *Bonhill*, 86
11. SHEARER, *Rutherglen Lore*, 175; COWIE, *Arbroath*, 220; *Logbook of
    Drumgeith School*, 83, qu. FAIRLEY, JOHN A., *The Beginnings of
    Compulsory Education in Scotland*, Glasgow University Ed.B.
    Thesis 1965, 44
12. *C.C.M. 1875-6* Ross, 151-2; *1883-4* Kerr 126; *1877-8* Middleton
    187; *1885-6* Kerr 199; *1886-7* Wilson 162; *1878-9* Wilson 226-7;
    1884-5 Wilson 203
13. *C.C.M. 1881-2* Ogilvie, 140
14. *C.C.M. 1875-6* Dey, 129

15. KERR, *Scottish Education*, 392
16. Circular from T. A. Stewart, H.M.I., July 1893; *T.S.A. Fife*, 633; *T.S.A. Aberdeenshire*, 171
17. Mr Lowther, M.P. for York, in 1870 Debates, qu. FAIRLEY, *Compulsory Education*, 19
18. GRANT, *Burgh Schools*, 316; *C.C.M. 1877-8*, 199-200; *1883-4* MCLEOD 140; MORRISON, JAMES L., *The Implementation of Compulsory Education in Scotland from 1883 to 1914* (Glasgow University Ed.B. Thesis 1966), 28-9; LAMONT, qu. MORRISON, *Compulsory Education*, 68
19. *C.C.M. 1886-7* Struthers 229; *1905-6* Boyd 327; *Logbook of Tomintoul Parish School*, Oct 1873
20. CORMACK, *William Cramond*, 24; *C.C.M.* 1876-7 Scougal 143
21. *Demonstration School Logbook*, 28 May 1889; *Education (Scotland) Act 1878*, section 7 (3); *Board of Education Report 1873*, Appendix xiv, 94; *Policy and Operations of the Glasgow School Board 1873-79*, qu. FAIRLEY, *Compulsory Education*, 147; *C.C.M. 1897-98*, 374; PATON, *Rutherglen*, 75
22. FAIRLEY, *Compulsory Education*, 156-9
23. BOYD, *Ayrshire*; *S.E.D.R. 1950*, 86; *C.C.M. 1913-14*, 9
24. *C.C.M. 1904-5*, 399
25. *C.C.M. 1905-6*, Boyd 321
26. *C.C.M. 1867-8* Woodford; *A.C.I*, NIXON
27. *Parliamentary Debates, Fourth Series*, vol 196, 130-150
28. *Report of the Education Reform Committee 1917*, set up by the teachers' organisations
29. *Education (Scotland) Act 1945*, section 48
30. *Education (Scotland) Act 1918*, section 3
31. *S.E.D.R. 1919-20*, 43; ROBERTS, ALASDAIR F. B., *The Operation of the Ad Hoc Authority in Dunbartonshire between 1919 and 1930* (Glasgow University Ed.B. Thesis 1964), 54-76
32. SCOTT, "The Government of Scotland", *Scots Magazine*, iv 15-16
33. *General Assembly E.C.R. 1877*
34. KERR, *Memories Grave and Gay*, 74-5; WILSON, *Tales and Travels*, 5
35. *Secretaries of State Act, 1926*
36. *S.E.D. Circular No. 69*, 31 Aug 1885
37. *C.C.M. 1904-5*, 263
38. *Proceedings of the Classical Association of Scotland, 1908-1909*, 77
39. MILNE, J. C., *Poems* (Aberdeen 1963), 97
40. BONE, *Inspection*, 158, 200
41. *C.C.M. 1874-5*, xlix; *1893*, 126; *Public Education in Scotland*, H.M.S.O. 1963, 13
42. *C.C.M. 1884-5*, 160, 180, 202; *1908-9*, section D
43. *C.C.M. 1887-8*, xxxiii

44. *S.E.D.R. 1930-31*, C/37; *1934-5*, G/25; WILSON, *Tales and Travels*, 153-4
45. *Education (Scotland) Act 1918*, section 20
46. Galland in debate on the second reading, qu. ROBERTS, *Dunbartonshire*, 41
47. *Education (Scotland) Act 1945*, section 78

CHAPTER 3 | # The Finance of Education

RATES, FEES, GRANTS, THE EDUCATION (SCOTLAND) FUND

THE pattern in which Scottish education was to be financed for a century was fixed by the Act of 1872. Before then schools had always depended on fees and endowments, with, since 1834, an annual grant made by Parliament "to aid local exertion in maintaining schools";[1] the Act ratified these sources and went further. Instead of forcing heritors – often against their will – to sustain a parish school, it authorised the new boards to levy a rate on local owners and occupiers. The Argyll Commission, which had recommended the move, had estimated that a rate of twopence in the pound would be sufficient in rural areas, though in towns it might have to be twopence-halfpenny. Almost from the beginning these figures were found to be inadequate. In 1880 for example the rate in parishes of Elgin, Skye and Southern Ross varied from threepence to 2s 2d. Even so, they were not always punctually paid: five years later the vexing backwardness of children in Skye was blamed by the Department on local unwillingness to pay, and Circular 76 drew this to the notice of districts concerned.[2] Thereafter local rates, though they formed a diminishing portion of educational expenditure, rose steadily. At Bonhill in Dunbartonshire for instance the rate in 1873 was sixpence; in 1888 it had dropped to 5½d, but 1900 saw a rise to 8¼d and 1911 to 1s 2¾d. In 1903 the average rate for the whole country was 11½d. It was higher in the burghs (1s 1d) than the rural parishes (10¼d), and very high in all the cities except Edinburgh. Thinly populated areas also suffered: in parts of Argyll, Inverness and Ross it was over 2s. On the other hand the average in Berwick and East Lothian was only 8d, and Kinross escaped with 5½d.[3] A general increase after 1907 was due to the use of certificated teachers by requirement wherever possible; one critic remarked darkly "It has yet to be proved that the new system will produce better teachers than the old method did".[4] In 1952 the ratepayers of Glasgow paid something over five shillings on every pound of rent; rather over a quarter of all the revenue raised by local rates went on education.

The reluctance of crofters in Skye and other remote areas to pay the rate was not unreasonable. Where there were few ratepayers the charge was bound to be high, and school building suffered. From 1884 onward the Department recognised this in a Minute inaugurating the system, continued even in the 1945 Act, whereby specially liberal grants were made to Highland schools. The problem was one facet of the perennial difficulty of local government finance, that the poorest areas have to bear the highest rates.

Since education was compulsory and they were also compelled to pay rates, parents were reluctant to meet the school fees which continued to be charged for two decades after the 1872 Act. They might claim inability to pay, but that meant a means test imposed by the parochial board. If they simply refused to disburse, they might be summoned before the Small Debt Court. The result was virtually constant tension between them and the unfortunate schoolmaster, who had to collect the money. School log books leave no doubt of the importance attached to this matter: William Cramond's at Cullen for instance noted:[5]

1874. Nov. 12. Lost ten minutes discussing a question of fees with a parent.

The dominie of Irvine in 1888 was more eloquently concise:[6]

Fees, fees, fees!

The problem was finally solved by Acts of 1889 and 1890, which freed elementary education. The money was found mainly by the government, and it did not push up the rates; it was therefore a popular move and inevitably spelt the end of the small adventure school.

The step was part of a process by which the state very slowly accepted general financial responsibility: it was in 1890 also that schools were released from the need to justify their grants by results. Since 1873, eleven years after England, the principle had been in operation: the grant depended on the results of an individual examination of each pupil by a visiting inspector, and the amount payable for each success was laid down. The school managers received 4s a year for each pupil in attendance; there were also payments of 1s 6d for discipline and 1s for singing, both fairly nominal. Three shillings was paid for an individual pass in reading and the same each for writing and arithmetic; 2s was the figure for grammar, history and geography. No grant at all was made unless needlework and "cutting out" formed part of the course for girls. Inspection was highly mechanical: a passage and a few sums were dictated, then children were lined up and the inspector heard them read while at the same time marking their writing and arithmetic. The worst features of the 1862 Code had probably been discovered and removed: in testing reading for example the inspectors made allowance for intelligent knowledge of the material, and higher study was encouraged by grants for performance in "specific subjects" beyond the sixth standard. But the fundamental fault had not been eliminated: the principle based on the belief that children were of equal capacity and developed at the same rate in an environment evenly favourable. School boards and managers demanded a high percentage of passes, to the exclusion of all non-essential subjects. The teacher was often paid part of the grant personally and felt direct pressure. The form of the examination induced rigid methods of cramming: a child was failed for three mistakes in dictation or for having two sums incorrectly set out. He might have to divide 54 by ·00009 or rhyme off the capes of Western Europe. It was hardly surprising that the appointment of a separate Scottish Secretary led to the end of the system: Craik abolished individual inspection in the lower classes in 1886 and in 1890 throughout the elementary school. (Even with general inspection however there was still a system of special rewards and punishments. Evidence of "exceptionally meritorious work" might attract an increase of 6d [for each pupil, but the opposite would lose 6d or even 1s a head, and "observable neglect to teach manners, etc." might also cost 1s.[7])

The problem of financing secondary education was still being nibbled at. The Education and Local Taxation Account (Scotland) Act of 1882 provided £60,000 a year for this purpose; in 1897 control of Science and Art grants was transferred to the Department; and in the following year another Local Taxation Account Act allowed £35,000 more. The first higher grade schools, which appeared in 1900, were able to draw for maintenance on the rates. The general effect of so many statutes, each providing a specific annual sum for a specified purpose, was to make educational finance extraordinarily complicated. The Department in particular was responsible for managing a number of comparatively small funds. One of the main aims of the 1908 Act therefore was to simplify the administration: this it did by establishing the Education (Scotland) Fund, which became the central bank account of the Department. Into it in each financial year were paid the sums allotted under the Acts of 1890, 1892 and 1898 out of the Local Taxation Account, together with the General Aid Grant voted annually by Parliament.[8] From 1918 on the procedure for estimating the General Aid Grant was laid down by formula: the financial year 1913-14 was adopted as the "standard year", and a sum equal to the amount granted in that year was paid; the excess of the grant paid in any year in England and Wales over their 1913-14 grant was then calculated, and a sum equal to eleven-eightieths of that figure was allotted to Scotland.[9] This was the "Goschen formula", calculated on a basis largely of population. After 1929, when the work of education authorities was transferred to the county councils, an annual grant equal to the sums previously paid out of the Local Taxation Account was also guaranteed. Finally certain sums payable to maintain the Teachers' Superannuation Account were added.[10] These became the main sources of income for the Education (Scotland) Fund.

The Fund grew rapidly: in 1914 it amounted to £663,355, in 1926 to £6,841,000, in 1938 to £9,333,108.[11] After each World War the fall in the value of money inflated the figures, and after 1945 they were further swollen by the development of social assistance. Most of the Fund (about three-quarters) was expended in grants to local authorities. An increasing proportion – 3·6 per cent in 1921, 12·7 in 1931, 19·3 in 1938 – went in superannuation contributions and benefits and about 1·5 per cent in grants to central institutions. Voluntary schools claimed a decreasing share – 3·6 per cent in 1921, but only 1·2 per cent in the thirties. Other outlay, with no single item amounting to much over one per cent, was devoted to teacher training, university aid and the cost of running the Scottish Leaving Certificate.[12]

INCOME AND EXPENDITURE, 1918-45

The responsibility for providing places in the public schools was left throughout the period with local bodies – school boards until 1918, education authorities from 1918 to 1929, county councils thereafter. The cost increased annually: it was £9,372,000 in 1919-20, but over fourteen millions in 1938-9 and over twenty-two in 1945-6. The expenditure on each pupil rose from £14 in 1932-3 to nearly £18 in 1937-8.[13] The Secretary of State's annual reports give a useful analysis of where the money came from and where it went. By 1945 over two-thirds was being provided by Departmental grants, rather over a quarter by the rates, a tiny fraction (less than one per cent) by fees, which lingered at a non-economic level in secondary and a few elementary schools almost throughout the period, and in some cases beyond. The Code allowed Boards to maintain "a certain number" of schools with fees in the infant department and elsewhere, and there were still forty-seven of these in 1905.[14] In Glasgow most secondary places became free at the end of the nineteen-twenties, but half a dozen "non-regional" schools like Allan Glen's, Hillhead and the Boys' and Girls' High Schools were still charging fees in the sixties. The main reason generally given for their continuance was that they helped to exercise a certain control of entry into schools with a tradition worth guarding, but it is difficult to believe that no more equitable method could be found. Local bursary competitions were not the answer: in the thirties the main Glasgow examinations were in the second and fourth years, by which time pupils were unlikely to change schools, and the Corporation's fee-paying institutions were often regarded as the preserve of the professional classes.

By far the largest item of local expenditure (two-thirds of the total) was on the salaries and superannuation of teachers. Repairs and maintenance accounted for 16 per cent and the remainder went mainly on administration charges.

ENDOWMENTS

The history of endowments in Scotland after 1872 was one of rationalisation and simplification. The process had begun four years before, when Professor Laurie reported on the schools of the Edinburgh Merchant Company, recommending their conversion into private fee-paying institutions. An Act of 1869 made it possible for such a change to occur, and the Merchant Company took advantage of it in 1870 to convert the Merchant Maidens' Hospital into the Edinburgh Institution for Young Ladies. The Governors of George Watson's Trust opened a Ladies' College a year later; the only other school to take advantage of the Act was Bathgate Academy.[15] Hutchesons' Girls School was begun in 1876 under a private act.

The Colebrooke Commission was established in 1872 to deliberate on the state of all educational endowments. It divided them for convenience under five heads – hospitals, drawing £80,000 a year; schools, with £60,000; university, with £21,500; general endowments like the Dick Bequest, which totalled £10,000; and a number of mixed benefactions, producing £18,500. The Commission recommended that a general register should be established, that the proportions of mixed endowments should be made clear, that all restrictions to scholars of a certain name be removed and that the twenty-six endowed hospitals should be thrown open as fee-paying day schools, with bursaries as a reward of merit.[16] The Endowed Institutions (Scotland) Act of 1878 brought some of these recommendations into effect and set up a Commission under Lord Moncrieff to attend to their administration. This existed until 1881, but the Act was not a conspicuous success, and it was followed by a more efficient one in 1882, which made inspection compulsory in higher-class schools and had therefore considerable effect in secondary education.[17] Its executive, the Balfour Commission, sanctioned many useful reforms, including the conversion of several hospitals into selective day schools. It also simplified and reorganised many local schemes: in Glasgow, for instance, bequests were grouped after 1882 under four heads – Hutchesons' Educational Trust, the Glasgow City Educational Endowments Board governing seven single benefactions including Anderson's, Bell's, Murdoch's and Maxwell's, the Glasgow General Endowments Board with five including Wilson's, Gardiner's and Graham's, and the Glasgow and West of Scotland Technical College, governing Anderson's College, the College of Science and Arts, Allan Glen's School and the Atkinson Institution.[18] The arrangement undoubtedly simplified the finance of education in the city.

The most famous of the general endowments in Scotland continued for some years to be the Milne and Dick Bequests. The Milne Trust, which had concentrated before 1872 on paying the elementary fees of the poor, found that the Act placed responsibility for this on the school boards, and therefore transferred its attention, with the permission of the Court of Session, to higher branches. The Dick Bequest continued without revision until 1890. In the seventies and eighties 122 schools in the three eligible counties of Aberdeen, Banff and Moray – about four-fifths of the total schools in the area – were deriving advantage from the scheme. Between 1878 and 1888 an average of thirty-six pupils went every year from these institutions to the Universities, while another fifty took courses in teaching, pharmacy, law, or, if girls, studied for the L.L.A. In 1888 9·3 per cent of all pupils in Dick Bequest schools were beyond Standard VI. Over 9 per cent were studying Latin, 5·2 per cent mathematics, 4·5 per cent French, 1·5 per cent Greek and 0·1 per cent German. These proportions were much higher than in ordinary elementary schools.

In 1890 the trustees decided to revise the conditions of the Bequest, in order to encourage attendance beyond Standard VI, teach higher subjects in the rural schools, and particularly avoid the misuse of the fund by allowing it to be squandered in relieving the rates. The new proposals were expensive, and as a result the operation of the Bequest was limited to 130 schools. At the same time, however, the examination for teachers wishing to participate was made a little easier: graduation, which had previously been less difficult than the test, was now accepted in place of an examination.

The effects of the revision were described by the Inspector, Professor Laurie, reporting in 1904, as highly satisfactory. A very large proportion of masters in the ordinary elementary schools of the north-east were graduates; whatever their professional competency, their intellectual adequacy was not in doubt. In 1903, out of over 21,000 children in the benefiting schools, rather over 12 per cent were in advanced classes. Almost exactly 10 per cent were taking Latin, the same number French, 9 per cent mathematics, 1·5 per cent German and 0·7 per cent Greek. In that year 935 children gained the junior leaving certificate and 417 the higher, four of them with honours. On an average 146 children passed directly every year into secondary or central schools, thirty-eight into training colleges, thirty to the universities, while nine took the pharmacy examination and five that of the Law Agents. The general suspicion that the lower subjects were being neglected for the benefit of brighter children was stoutly repudiated by Professor Laurie, and he produced many witnesses to prove his case. Undoubtedly, though somewhat academically biased, the Dick Bequest assisted materially in raising the standard of education in the north-east. As the state took over complete responsibility for secondary as well as primary education, however, the Bequest changed the use of its funds: by the nineteen-fifties it was producing a nominal payment in some schools of about twenty pounds a year.[19]

The Balfour Commission was a very efficient body: its Report in 1889 resulted in making available for higher education a large sum of money, and several hospitals, including Heriot's and Morgan's, were converted into fee-paying day schools. The Acts of 1908 and 1918 however transformed the picture of secondary education and educational finance. In consequence a Committee on Endowments was appointed in 1927 under the chairmanship of Lord Mackenzie. After an enquiry, it recommended the establishment of an executive commission to review endowments; this body would hold office for a limited period, and endowments would then pass under the control of the Scottish Education Department.[20]

These recommendations were given force in the Educational Endowments (Scotland) Act of 1928, which appointed an executive commission with powers for three years to alter schemes in the public interest. The commissioners were directed to pay attention to the desires of the founder and to local interests, however, as well as to general economy. Certain endowments were expressly excluded from the reorganisation unless their governors requested that they participate; they included university and theological funds, the Carnegie Trust, and any bequests made after the 1928 Act. In the event the work of the executive commission was not complete until 1936. It reviewed the terms of 1,540 endowments, and organised 1,296 of them in 129 schemes, producing an annual revenue of over three hundred and fifty thousand pounds.[21]

The Education Act of 1946 devoted the whole of Part VI – sections 115 to 134 – to the reorganisation of endowments. Its provisions were not new: as a consolidating statute it brought together the main features of four previous acts. The same four categories as under the 1928 Act, for example, were exempted from reorganisation, though the date for "new endowments" moved to 1946. Powers for reorganisation were given, not to an executive commission, but to the Secretary of State; he was instructed to appoint one of his officers Registrar of Educational Endowments, and so to maintain an up-to-date register of all such benefactions.[22]

A number of independent bodies remained in Scotland, charged with the administration of groups of endowments. In most cases their work became concerned more and more with peripheral services. After 1946, for example, there was not only free schooling at all stages under the age of fifteen but a fairly generous supply of public bursaries; the East Lothian Trust directed its efforts to providing additional equipment and assisting in running holiday camps.[23] Endowments, in short, had completed what service they could contribute in extending education: the Hyndford Mortification, which still yielded twenty-two shillings a year to the headmaster of Pettinain (the "dominie's whisky money") was a fair example of a quaint anachronism.[24] They were now relics of a less enlightened era, and as the state's contribution spread, greater ingenuity was required to find a profitable way of expending ancient bequests.

REFERENCES

1. *Scotch Code of 1905*, article 3
2. *C.C.M. 1880-81* McLeod, 144; *1885-6*, 117
3. *Nelson's Annotated Code of 1905*, 287-9
4. NEILL, *Bonhill*, 89
5. CORMACK, *William Cramond*, 28
6. BOYD, *Ayrshire*, 173
7. *S.E.D.R. 1960*, 102-3, 105; *1951*, 68-9; *Scotch Code of 1905*, article 19B; BONE, *Inspection*, 84
8. *Education (Scotland) Act 1908*, section 15
9. *Education (Scotland) Act 1918*, section 21
10. *Education (Scotland) Act 1946*, section 69
11. *S.E.D.R. 1939*, 77
12. *S.E.D.R. 1920-21*, 46; *1931-2*, 44; *1939*, 77
13. *S.E.D.R. 1939*, 66-7
14. *Scotch Code of 1905*, article 133, 134
15. TOWILL, *Merchant Maidens*, 1; MORGAN, *Makers*, 103-5; HARRISON, *Merchant Company*, 34-5
16. MORGAN, *Rise and Progress*, 106; KNOX, *250 Years*, 80-85
17. *C.C.M. 1885-6*, xxx
18. AIRD, *Old Glasgow*, 186-7
19. *T.S.A. Aberdeenshire*, 670; LAURIE, *Dick Bequest 1904*, 16-17
20. KNOX, *250 Years*, 214; MORGAN, *Rise and Progress*, 110
21. KNOX, *250 Years*, 214-17
22. *Education (Scotland) Act 1946*, sections 115, 116, schedule 8
23. *T.S.A. East Lothian*, 155
24. *T.S.A. Lanarkshire*, 590

CHAPTER 4 | # The Elementary Schools

CHURCH SCHOOLS

THE effect of the 1872 Act within a few years was to confine elementary education almost entirely within the public schools. Church institutions, except those of the Roman Catholics, rapidly dwindled in number. There can be only one justification for any church schools, the conviction that they have benefits to confer which can be had nowhere else. Before and immediately after the Reformation in Scotland the main benefit was education itself; there were virtually no alternative schools at all. The eighteenth and nineteenth centuries brought many types into existence, run by individuals and corporations representing many shades of opinion; the church schools came more and more to represent the religious doctrines of their own sects. As the state slowly accepted educational control the danger in many minds was the establishment of schools which would be not only non-sectarian but even secular, giving no religious instruction whatever. Until the last quarter of the nineteenth century therefore there was good justification for running schools under the aegis of a church. The Act of 1872 however guaranteed the teaching of religion in schools according to the tenets of the presbyterian faith and to the satisfaction of most adherents of both the Established and the Free Churches. Since within the schools there was often considerable liberality – one (admittedly private) teacher, asked what catechism he taught, answered "ony ane they like to bring"[1] – it might be expected that there would be a steady disappearance of presbyterian schools, including those of such predominantly religious bodies as the S.S.P.C.K. and the Gaelic Societies. On the other hand Episcopal and Roman Catholic authorities might be expected to make every effort to expand their own provision.

The Gaelic schools vanished almost at once. Those of the S.S.P.C.K., already dwindling in numbers, also closed down within a comparatively short time. The Argyll Commission had found 202 in 1867; a list drawn up in 1897 showed one survivor only, and that vanished shortly afterwards.[2] The table overleaf shows the trend in church schools run by the main denominations with government aid.[3]

Within a few years of the Act therefore something like eighty per cent of the schools run by the presbyterian churches were closed (the

Year	Church of Scotland	Free Church	R.C.	Episcopal	Others	Public	Total
1872	519	523	22	46	792	—	1902
1875	476	151	92	66	—	1935	2720
1880	145	39	126	73	235	2438	3056
1890	62	18	166	74	146	2651	3117
1900	27	6	188	68	71	2744	3104
1905	20	6	201	66	69	2882	3244

figure of 476 for Church of Scotland in 1875 includes those normally appearing as "others" – Gaelic Societies, S.S.P.C.K., etc.) Thereafter these institutions dwindled steadily until, just before the First World War, they were a handful kept in existence by special local conditions; some were the practising schools of the training colleges until 1906.

The Church of Scotland assembly schools were closed quite early: the last two, at Crathie and at Whalsay in Shetland, vanished in 1879. The situation of the Church of Scotland schools which remained is of interest. In 1896, when the total was still thirty-seven, Aberdeenshire accounted for seven, Perthshire six, Moray three, Ayrshire three, Nairn and Shetland two each, with the rest scattered all over the country. Fourteen years later, in 1910, there were two each in Aberdeen and Perth, and one each in Inverness, Kirkcudbright, Midlothian and Shetland. The last Free Church schools, apart from those connected as practising classes to the Training Colleges, were in Caithness and Aberdeenshire. In some cases, particularly among Free Church institutions, the school was attached to the kirk building and used for ecclesiastical as well as scholastic purposes; these were slower to close than others.[4]

Few of these schools of course were taken over by the school boards. They were often small, badly ventilated and poorly appointed, and the public authorities, with the backing of public money, usually found it more economical to build new schools. By 1915, when the last transfers of schools under the 1872 Act took place, only 118 out of the original 519 Church of Scotland buildings had been taken over. Something like 400 were defunct. Out of about 600 Free Church schools (of which 100 had not been in receipt of government aid) 162 were transferred and about 450 died; their accommodation had clearly been a little, but not a great deal better. Out of forty-five schools run by the United Presbyterian Church only two were taken over.[5]

The Episcopal Church on the other hand made an effort to provide schools for children of its faith. Within a few years after the 1872 Act the number had increased from forty-six to about seventy and there it remained for twenty years. By 1918, when new conditions of transfer were offered, there were between fifty-five and sixty Episcopal schools receiving government aid. Apart from the use of their own catechism, they showed no variation from board schools and their rolls usually

held more presbyterian than Episcopal pupils, while many children of
their faith attended the ordinary schools. The main Episcopal areas
were along the east and north-east coasts: in 1910 Aberdeenshire had
eleven schools, Banff four, Kincardine three, Edinburgh seven and
Midlothian three. [6]

The Roman Catholic Church adopted a less compromising attitude.
Within three years of the Act its twenty-two schools had become
ninety-two, and by 1880 126. Thereafter a dozen or so were added
every five years, the total in 1910 reaching 224. The main Catholic
areas were in the south-west, to which Irish immigrants continued to
flock during the years before the First World War. The size of their
families made more schools essential: Glasgow (including Govan) had
thirty-two in 1910, the rest of Lanarkshire forty-three, Ayrshire
twenty-one, Renfrew twenty and Dunbarton ten. Nine schools in
Inverness, seven in Aberdeen and six in Banff showed the provision
for children of the Old Faith. [7]

It was not fair however, as one inspector pointed out in 1876, to
compare these institutions with ordinary Scottish schools: the material
they had to work with was too poor. The fault lay also with the teachers:
indeed they were described as the weakest part of the schools, whose
general management was "beyond praise for its energy and educational
fervour". [8] Teachers were almost all uncertificated, and those who had
qualifications had seldom been to any college. Where economy was of the
utmost importance uncertificated men and women were welcome, and
the Catholic schools came to rely fairly heavily on ex-pupil-teachers.
Few of their staff were prepared to attend a course in any Episcopal or
Presbyterian institution, and the nearest Roman seminaries, at Liverpool
and Wandsworth, were too far and too expensive for all but a handful
of young men and women. In 1894 a college for Roman Catholic
women was opened in Glasgow, but its effect was slow to register.
In any case, few of its first students were natives of Scotland. [9] Even
with the aid of a government grant, the Roman schools were rarely
rich enough to offer an attractive salary to a teacher, and their standards
of staffing remained until 1918 distinctly lower than in Protestant
schools.

In 1918 there were 327 voluntary schools in the country receiving
a grant of money from the government. Of these 228 belonged to the
Roman Catholic church, forty-nine to the Episcopal communion, two
to the Church of Scotland, one to the Free Church and forty-seven
were "unclassified" under denominational heads. The act of that year
opened the door to public support for these schools: under section 18
their managers might offer them for transfer to the local education
authority, which, according to the decision of Lord Murray in the
Bonnybridge case in 1928, must accept them at a fair price. Moreover
the authority was bound to take over the staff as it stood. In future
these institutions became ordinary public schools in all but one or two

important matters. Teachers were to satisfy their employers, the education authority, of their professional competence, but their Church had the right to scrutinise their religious position. Most important of all, the time spent in religious instruction and observance and the methods used were to conform to "use and wont".

Such a handsome offer was accepted by most voluntary schools. For a time some Roman bishops, including the Archbishop of Glasgow, stood out, but the teachers were in no doubt of the proper course of action:

> The Bill offers you Catholic schools for Catholic children taught by Catholic teachers under Catholic control as far as religion is concerned. . . If you refuse to accept this offer you are faced with educational starvation. . . At present the burden is more than you can carry, and it is only by the exercise of the most rigid economy and the payment of starvation wages to your teachers that your schools are able to maintain a bare existence.

The matter was settled by a letter from Rome.[10]

Within two years only thirty-five schools remained outside the public system, including three Catholic, two Episcopal, two Church of Scotland and one Free Church. Within the system the Roman Church continued to open new schools: there were 231 in 1923, 244 in 1931 and 254 in 1938, and the expansion continued after the Second World War. A large part of this development occurred in the Glasgow area, where thirty-seven schools in 1923 became forty-eight in 1931 and fifty-four in 1938.[11] The Papal Encyclical on the Christian Education of Youth (*Divini Illius Magistri*) stated the attitude of the Mother Church when it condemned schools of mixed religion, and except in comparatively remote areas the Catholic authorities in Scotland adhered strictly to that principle. At Skermorlie in Ayrshire in 1947 about a score of Catholic children attended the ordinary public school and a few came over from Wemyss Bay; on the other hand at Carnock and High Valleyfield in Fife three years later most of the Protestant children attended Catholic schools; but these cases were rare. Even where there was a rapid growth of the Catholic population, almost all the children travelled long distances after passing the primary stage. In Ayrshire for example, before St Joseph's Kilmarnock offered a full secondary course, the brightest Catholic pupils journeyed daily to Glasgow.[12]

In contrast the story of the Episcopal schools after 1918, both in size and numbers, was one of steady shrinkage. On the eve of the Second World War only thirty-five remained, and the decline continued afterwards. So few students presented themselves at the Episcopal Training College that it closed at the end of session 1933-34, though the church retained representation on Provincial Committees.[13] By 1958 there were only twenty-five schools left, with 2,697 pupils, 0·3 per cent of the

Scottish figure. Nine of these institutions were in Edinburgh and six in Aberdeen, with a handful in Argyll, Moray, Glasgow and St Andrews.[14]

The success of the arrangement made by the 1918 Act was clear; indeed it was a matter of envy in countries where the religious problem remained difficult. A situation had been reached in which all the religious safeguards required by the Christian churches in Scotland had been granted by the state, and there was no need on these grounds for any denominational school to stand outside the public system. Where they did, the reasons had to be sought elsewhere.

ADVENTURE, INDEPENDENT AND NURSERY SCHOOLS

The old Scots "adventure school", run for a meagre livelihood by a man or woman of small means and smaller scholarship, did not long survive the 1872 Act. Not unnaturally people preferred on the whole to send their children to the public schools where inspection guaranteed a certain standard of efficiency; only in fairly remote areas, where it was inconvenient for pupils to travel far in winter, was there still a field for the teacher "on chance". An example was to be found in Crossbost on the island of Lewis in 1881, where a pupil teacher who failed to secure a place in a training college opened an establishment in opposition to two local board schools. His venture, which seems to have had some success, was actually managed by a member of the local school board. Already however the adventure schools were being described as "relics of an almost defunct system". The appearance in 1889 of free elementary schooling virtually killed the few which still existed.[15]

"Voluntary" schools, run by private bodies outside the state system, did not die out altogether. In Ayrshire in 1877 there were still 8,800 pupils on the rolls of schools which received no government aid, and these represented 4·4 per cent of the total attendance in that county.[16] The reason for the existence of these independent schools, as they came to be described, was mainly private profit, but they acquired – or aspired to – a dignity never associated with the adventure schools. Their owners, as might be expected, attempted to provide facilities and services not yet found in the state system. For thirty years at least after the 1872 Act there was clearly a want of secondary instruction, and the majority of the independent schools concentrated on this part of the course. At the elementary stage the stress was usually on "preparatory" schools, coaching children for admission to selective secondary institutions, and there was also, unexpressed but obvious, a "snob" appeal. "X Ladies College" and "Y Preparatory School for Boys" continued throughout the period to attract the children of ambitious parents, especially in the cities, where haphazard building often placed working-class and even slum-clearance areas beside "good residential" districts, with one public school serving all.

One field in which the state was slow to compete was nursery education. A hundred years ago it was not uncommon, especially in urban areas, to find children under five in school: at Robert Owen's infant school in New Lanark there were youngsters of three and even two. There was a tendency however to absorb them early into the ordinary teaching; the nursery school as we know it did not exist. The effect of the 1872 Act, which set the starting age at five, was to force younger children out, since there was barely room for all the pupils of school age.

The early years – and particularly the second decade – of the twentieth century saw the beginning of "nursery" schools. The greatest single pioneer was Margaret McMillan, born in the United States of Scottish parents and brought up in Inverness. With her sister Rachel she undertook social service work in England, and a series of unhappy experiences with adolescents in the shabbier parts of London convinced her that she must concentrate on reclaiming slum children while they were still in their most impressionable years. In 1908, with the aid of an American philanthropist, Jacob Fels, she opened a school clinic at Bow. It was not a success but an enlarged version at Deptford did much better. Finally in 1914 she opened a nursery school at Evelyn House, Deptford, consisting of a shelter in a garden and beginning with six children under five. What she tried to give them was "nurture", without which they could never really have education[17]

> for education must grow out of nurture as the flower from its root, since nurture is organic; it is the right building of nerve structure and brain cell . . . Much of the money we spend on education is wasted because we have not made any real foundation for our educational system.

She took the pattern of a nursery in a comfortable home and adapted it to care for over three hundred children. They came in at 8 a.m., had their baths and breakfasted on porridge, milk and brown bread. Thereafter all through the morning they gathered experience, in the garden if possible, as they ran about strengthening their bodies and sharpening their senses. At 11.45 they had dinner, then went to asleep, again if possible in the open air. The afternoon was spent in music, dancing and speech. A tea of milk pudding and brown bread and butter followed at four and mothers came to collect their children soon after five.

Something of this nature became the pattern for the nursery schools of the twentieth century, which had great potential for transforming education. "For me", wrote Dr Kerr, the inspector,

> the greatest single contribution to practical education in our time has been the demonstration of the Nursery School as the requirement of every child of civilisation.

Nevertheless the movement made slow progress. St Saviour's Child-Garden, opened in the Canongate of Edinburgh with three children in 1906, was one of three in Great Britain, and by 1912 there were no more than ten. St Saviour's, which expanded to take fifty children, followed the Macmillan pattern (though anticipating her work) with the stress on practical activity with plastic materials, free play, songs and tableaux; the garden, though no more than a piece of reclaimed waste, was for long the centre of their work. A few of the oldest pupils, aged 6 or 7, had formal lessons in the three Rs, but the most rewarding work was with the youngest: when the parish minister received the Military Cross, they cut out their own crosses in cardboard and awarded them to such gallant youngsters as the little girl of four who "got a bomb on her heid and never said nothin".[18]

In 1918 the Glasgow School Board set up about a dozen nursery classes each for thirty-five children, providing three meals a day in a hostel; this was a wartime measure to accommodate working mothers and ended with peace. In that year, when there were 110 nursery schools in Paris alone, England had eighty and Scotland only twelve.[19] The 1918 Act empowered the new authorities to provide such schools where necessary, but the permission was seldom used, and the cuts of 1921 virtually wiped it out. In 1928 there were only four schools in Glasgow with trained nursery teachers and a few without, almost all run by voluntary managers. The nursery class in the Aberdeen Demon-stration School remained for twenty years the only one in the north. A few authorities, notably Edinburgh, Dundee and Elgin, made some contributions to independent schools.[20] There were nineteen in the country in 1932 and five schools had nursery classes; just over 700 children were on the rolls. Only three schools were supported by public bodies. Private schools existed in Edinburgh (9), Glasgow (3), Aberdeen, Dundee, Elgin and Paisley, and there were nursery classes in Glasgow, Greenock and Paisley.[21] The main expansion was confined to a few years at the end of the Second World War. The Act of 1945 made it the duty of education authorities to establish nursery schools wherever there was sufficient demand among parents,[22] but in the next two decades Scottish education was busy with other matters, and nursery provision, public and private, rested at about 5,000 places, with no prospect of further expansion.

HOURS AND HOLIDAYS

Rules governing the daily conduct of elementary schools were laid down by the Scotch Education Department in Codes. The first, promulgated in 1873, extended to Scotland the principle of "payment by results", and it was not a success. One of Craik's early steps as Secretary of the Department was to abolish individual inspection.

Until 1939 there were separate Codes for Elementary and Secondary Education, printed annually with any necessary alterations, and giving fairly specific instructions on grants, fees, curricula and the size of classes. Early in the period the pattern of the school year – and the school day – became fixed. The session ran from late August or early September to late June or early July; the main holiday periods were ten days at Christmas:

> 21 Dec 1888. Gave out the Christmas Holidays. The teachers seem to need a rest very much;[23]

a week at Easter – called in some areas "the Communion holidays" – and two months in summer, arranged to suit local conditions. Roman Catholic institutions, with many church holidays during the session, had only six weeks, and the practising schools of the training colleges normally remained open into July, so that demonstration classes were available for teachers' courses. The latter arrangement was not popular: many parents withdrew their children to suit their own holidays. There were also some local days off – Lanimer Day in Lanark, for example, and the annual "Timmer Market" in Aberdeen; the other breaks were occasional favours by royal command. When George V was crowned the vacation lasted a week, but his son allowed only three days and his grand-daughter two. Important visitors to the town might bring a half-holiday, and so might great occasions like the capture of Pretoria in 1900 and Armistice Day in 1918. There were also quainter but no less exciting occasions: Aberdeen had a half day on 28 January 1918 to "see a tank in motion" and Deskford Parish School a whole holiday on 3 May 1899 "for washing out the Kirk".[24]

Soon after 1872 the hours of opening became fixed: by what is now an old tradition the school day lasted from nine till four and there was no work on Saturdays. A few institutions had a little latitude at either end of the day, but in public schools the six-hour day was established, with 200 days of opening each session. Only in the English-type independent schools like Loretto was the pattern different; there, part of the afternoons was devoted to games and there might be lessons between four and five-thirty and "prep" from eight to nine in the evenings.[25]

CURRICULUM

As its name suggests the "elementary" school's function was to teach the elements, the three Rs; the later change of name to "primary" was to be evidence of a totally new concept. Article 19A of the Code pre-scribed the teaching of reading, writing and arithmetic from the ages of five to twelve, and with them physical exercises (military drill for seniors), drawing, poetry, "singing by note", and needlework for girls. Nature knowledge and "object lessons" on such topics as water, sun,

D

porosity, the cat and silver[26] came in for juniors, as did geography and oral English; seniors had history as well. In fact most of these were regarded as "frills"; in many schools even after the Second World War the whole morning and part of the afternoon were devoted to the three Rs, with the lion's share for arithmetic. Attempts at varying the pattern were dismissed by the majority of teachers as "fads" (defined by A. S. Neill as "half-formed ideas that a sub-inspector has borrowed from a bad translation of a distinguished foreigner's treatise on education, and handed on to a deferential dominie"[27]), and, half-formed or well-grounded, shared the fate of desuetude. Dewey's ideas, propounded at the end of the nineteenth century, were being tried by pioneers within ten years, but they were not endorsed by the Department or the training colleges until the thirties, and it was another twenty years before they were accepted practice in many schools. The Dalton Plan, experimented with in the twenties, left little trace in secondary classes and none at all in primary. Even those who made variations were a little self-conscious about it. The Aberdeen Practising School had musical drill in its infant department in 1891, action songs and kindergarten work and object lessons, but explained them in the log-book as necessary "to relieve the strain of ordinary routine".[28]

Ordinary routine was formal and factual. The Third Schedule of the Code laid down the scheme of needlework for girls under seven, for example, as needle drill, position drill, the hemming of strips with coloured cotton, knitting pin drill and the knitting of small squares on a strip with two needles. The objective in history was some knowledge of the British story, "advancing from an outline knowledge of the main periods to a more detailed study year by year". The teacher at Eastfield school in Rutherglen in 1876[29]

instead of an object lesson gave a special lesson to Standard IV on history, showing them how to make out a summary of the principal events in Scottish history with dates from Robert the Bruce to the Union of the Crowns.

English sought to develop a taste for good literature by composition, systematic home reading and committing lines to memory. The Code was also economical:[30]

One of the reading books in the Senior Division must be a manual of history, suitable for use as a reading book.

Next to the three Rs the most universally taught subject in Scottish elementary schools before 1872 was religious education. The Act laid down that such instruction should continue according to use and wont[31] and this provision was repeated in later statutes. Its nature however changed greatly. As a subject it was expressly excluded in 1872 from inspection nationally; the Department ruled in 1883 that there was nothing to prevent a local board using money from the

School Fund to inspect the efficiency of religious teaching themselves,[32] but the practice did not become common. For a few years the General Assembly Committee offered grants for religious teaching based on inspection by their own officer. A detailed syllabus was drawn up, of which the following are examples:[33]

Infants: The Creation and Fall, the Deluge, the life of Joseph, the birth and early life of Jesus; memorise Psalm 23 or Paraphrase 2 and the Lord's Prayer.

Standard VI: Ahab, Jehoram, the history of Judah from Hezekiah to the Captivity, the Acts; memorise Psalm 104 or 107, Paraphrase 48 or Hymn 1, the Doctrine of the Resurrection and parts of the Shorter Catechism.

In Session 1876-7 Mr McQuarrie inspected 260 schools; of these 85 were put forward for examination by 38 boards. Two years later however the demand became too great – 105 boards wished to submit 267 schools – and the strain on the Committee's finances was inordinate.[34]

It is probable that for many years Scripture and catechism lessons were taught with diligence and care by most teachers, especially since the training colleges were run by the churches until 1906. The drift away from religion in the community did not become critical until after 1945. Moral lessons on the importance of such daily virtues as honesty and fellow-feeling were also popular. The way in which these were taught was not, it is true, always approved: one inspector wrote of an entry examination in 1878 to the colleges:[35]

I was greatly disappointed with the character of the answers given to the questions on moral discipline. The motives appealed to were often inadequate and even ignoble, and the chief "argument" by which a large number of the candidates propose to deter children from wrong doing is an exaggerated description of future punishment, both in this world and the next. It is noticeable that with regard to wantonly injuring telegraph wires, it has only occurred to five or six of the writers to suggest the very simple expedient of giving a lesson on the telegraph, and explaining its beauty and manifold uses, before proceeding to moralise on the sinfulness of throwing stones at it.

Throwing stones at telegraph wires hardly comes under the category of deadly sins – though postage stamps of the Soviet Union in the nineteen-twenties preached a similar lesson to "young pioneers" – but the reliance of Scottish teachers on the threat of punishment, human or divine, as a deterrent to evil-doing is highly typical. The Fifth Schedule of the Code also enjoined instruction in the laws of health, thrift, investment and insurance, trade and employment, the institutions of government and the British Empire. There was one notable omission throughout the period: "if I mentioned sex in School", wrote A. S. Neill in 1915,[36] "I should be dismissed at once."

METHODS AND DISCIPLINE

The methods by which these subjects were taught were determined largely by the size of classes and the shape of rooms. In 1872 it was still possible to find a hundred children or more in the care of one teacher. In 1905 the maximum number for a certificated teacher was reduced from seventy to sixty; there were lower maxima for assistants and pupil teachers. The Code of 1928 reduced the top figure to 50, still too large and in areas of teacher shortage no more than a pious hope. The "staffing ratio" (number of pupils to each certificated teacher) showed a better position:

Session	Ratio (all schools)
1913-14	40·8
1924-25	31·6
1935-36	28·2
1946-47	25·9

But this is always artificial, since all the pupils are being taught but not all the teachers – headmasters, infant mistresses, etc. – are teaching; small rural schools also force down the national average. In many urban schools classes of well over fifty were common in the twenties and thirties, making experiment impossible.

On the whole the traditional Scottish principle of co-education prevailed. There were few elementary schools in the public system with classes of one sex only, and in secondary departments common classes were generally accepted: in the city of Aberdeen in 1950 for example only three public and three private schools were not mixed.[37] The meaning of co-education however should be clear: in the elementary departments it was the practice for boys and girls to sit in the same classrooms but not usually, except at the infant stage, to mix freely. There were usually separate playgrounds, cloakrooms, even staircases in city schools, and mixing was not encouraged. Where there were enough girls of the same level of ability in secondary schools, they formed a class, otherwise there was a mixture. This meant usually that boys and girls, save perhaps in music lessons, followed a separate career in the lower forms of large urban secondary schools, though not in country districts. In the upper forms numbers were generally too small to allow segregation.

Methods of teaching, like the curriculum, remained formal throughout the period, fixed in a pattern of "chalk and talk". At Buckie in the

1880's, apart from the daily marking of the register and two periods a week of copy-writing, all the work was done standing. It was purely mechanical, with great stress on accuracy and no real contact with the world outside. Apart from the prohibition of sitting down few schools before 1914 would have differed much. There were weekly tests and monthly examinations[38] and a general atmosphere of earnest endeavour ironically caught by the Buchan poet, John C. Milne:[39]

> Fae Monday morn till Friday nicht I'd yark the learnin in
> Though I widna touch the fancy frills, for that wid be a sin!
> Nae drawin, singin, dancin – they're the cantrips o the Deil!
> Na, I widna hae sic ongauns in my couthy country skweel.
>
> But O the reams o writin a' my littlins aye wid dae!
> And siccan lists o spellin's ilka nicht they'd learn for me!
> And dyod the aul' Director wid dance a highland reel
> Gin he cam, but that's nae likely, te my couthy country skweel.

The more progressive schools might depart from this rigidity – by dramatisation of history and poetry for instance, by "nature rambles" and visits to places of local interest. There were also school concerts or cantatas in June and perhaps a half-day to see *Peter Pan* or the arrival of Barnum and Bailey's Circus. Such excursions were generally infrequent and invariably regarded as breaks in the normal pattern of hard, serious work.

Such a pattern demanded unquestioning, preferably silent obedience. The Inspector's report of 1882 on the school at Cullen stated:[40]

> In the junior department there should be sustained quietness and instantaneous obedience.

The inevitable result with healthy children was to raise problems of discipline. The tawse was still in daily use; on the walls of the same school's shed might be read the local version of an ancient rhyme:[41]

> Dr Cramond is a godly man
> He goes to the Kirk on Sunday
> He prays to God to give him strength
> To strap the loons on Monday.

Yet it was in this period that the conscience of teachers and board members troubled them over excessive "belting". The same Dr Cramond, forced to inflict corporal punishment in 1886 for "rioting and disobedience", reflected that this was the tawse's first airing for two years, and he ruled that all his teachers wishing to punish must do so in his room and his presence.[42] The author of *Old Greenock* believed in 1888 that[43]

the use of the taws is now generally more honoured in the breach than in the observance, and when employed was, upon the whole, a safer instrument of punishment than the cane, the use of which ought to be strictly prohibited.

On the other hand Dr Kerr, H.M.I., reported in 1887 that, though corporal punishment was rare on the day of inspection, visits without notice showed it to be common.[44] As the twentieth century advanced opposition strengthened, but in the sixties it was still in use.

Prizes were also slow to disappear; indeed they showed little sign of doing so, especially in large secondary schools, where Speech Day might include well over an hour devoted to a shuffling procession, punctuated with dwindling bursts of applause. Books and dux medals were also common in elementary classes; Langholm School Board tried offering money rewards amounting to £9.3s in one session, but the S.E.D. expressed strong disapproval. A few critics attacked the practice of rewarding intelligence and application repeatedly, but only one or two were able to make as practical a gesture as the headmistress of Laurel Bank School in Glasgow, who from the end of her first session gave a book to every pupil with a note inside of the subjects in which she had done well: "we valued all our pupils".[45]

TEACHING AIDS

There was a steady improvement in material aids. The common writing surface as late as 1900 was the "slate", a rectangle framed in wood on which calculations could be made and washed out easily. Slates were prohibited as insanitary in many public schools before the end of the First World War, but private infant classes were still using them in the twenties.

Textbooks as time went on were better produced and more widely used. Under the board system, when penny-pinching was the rule, they were often closely printed on inferior paper with smudgy illustrations. The 1930's, especially after the economic crisis, showed a marked improvement in ideas and quality. A few history books for the elementary school give plentiful evidence of this. Madalen Edgar's *Stories from Scottish History*, published by Harrap in 1906, was essentially a patriotic collection of stories culled from Scott's *Tales of a Grandfather* and illustrated by romantic paintings – "Mary's Farewell to France", "The End – Fotheringay", "The Last March of Edward I". It had one photograph, of Stirling Castle. The tales were more graphic than convincing – Wallace and the trout, "The Black Douglas shall not get you" – and the language was high-flown for children: "his hatred of the Scots was so inveterate", "Edward was dreadfully incensed". Only a dozen years later Lewis Spence's *Story of Robert the Bruce*, produced in 1918 by the Oxford University Press, showed much more attention to the social background, with a description of life in the turf-and-sod houses of Annandale. There were also attempts at recreating the feelings of men: atrocities were not simply recited, they were "the actions of desperate men". Legends like the spider were identified as legends. The illustrations, line drawings, included sketches of the Brooch of Lorn, ring mail, castle ruins and a map of Bannockburn. Despite fairly intricate language on occasion and an explicit pointing of moral lessons in the last chapter – hardly to be evaded in 1918 – the book had much more of the feeling of history than its predecessor. B. I. Magraw's *Stories of Early Modern Times*, published in 1932 by the Oxford University Press – an English book much used in Scottish schools – clearly showed the trend in history teaching. Its illustrations, nearly fifty in less than a hundred pages, were from contemporary sources in the main, with attributions, and there were questions at the end of each chapter to be answered by the pupils' own investigations.

The most striking change in teaching methods was in the use of instructional aids mechanically operated. The Advisory Council in its report on the subject in 1950 kept its feet on the ground by stating roundly that[46]

> the most important visual aid at the command of a teacher in the classroom is the blackboard, and every classroom should therefore have ample blackboard space.

Nevertheless schools were built after 1930 to take advantage of two valuable educational aids, school broadcasts and the throwing of pictures on a screen. Experiments in school broadcasting began in the twenties: in March 1928 for example the qualifying class at an Aberdeen school was taught a lesson in the studio at Belmont Street while a man from the B.B.C. acted as link in the school classroom.[47] Within a year or two the Schools Broadcasting Service was well established: at the end of 1933, 260 schools were taking the courses. In 1935 however, although quite a large number of sets were in use, no less than 56 per cent were the personal property of teachers and 32 per cent had been provided by voluntary effort; only 12 per cent came from the education authorities. In Ayrshire, a large and not unprogressive county, the first set was not provided until that year.[48] In 1938 about 1,000 schools, a third of the Scottish total, had listening facilities.

As we saw in Volume One, the teacher in Niddry Street School, Edinburgh, was using a magic lantern in 1862. Its successor was the filmstrip projector, which did not come into general use however until after the Second World War; even then Scottish schools were noticeably slower than English to adopt it. Moving pictures were first used north of the border in schools about 1924.[49] A Scottish Educational Film Association was set up by interested teachers and educationists, with panels for research and production, but despite its work instructional films were not quickly incorporated in the curriculum. In 1947 there were 590 projectors in Scottish schools, a number which compared favourably with England's 2,400, but only 16 were fitted with sound, against 1,000 south of the border.[50] What was more significant was the use made of films and broadcasts. Except in a few experimentally minded schools, they were regarded as interruptions – pleasant, but occasionally irritating – to the main current of work, and in too many classrooms their lesson was neither prepared for nor reinforced by the teacher. For the children too the cinema and the radio still trailed clouds of glory as entertainment, and therefore were "not really education".

HIGHER ELEMENTARY EDUCATION

The average child might be expected to have mastered the elements by the time he was eleven or twelve years old. If he could satisfy the authorities, he might then be permitted to leave school; the Scotch Education Department recognised this in its "Labour Certificate". The Act of 1878 stated that no child might be employed under the age of ten, but between ten and thirteen he might leave if his standard of performance in the three Rs was approved by one of Her Majesty's Inspectors. The performance required was in reading plain narrative, in writing to take five lines of dictation "in a fair, small hand", and in arithmetic notation up to a million, with the four simple rules, money and time.[51] Labour Certificates, intended as a concession to impecunious parents, were issued until all attendance exemptions by examination were abolished in the Act of 1901. On the whole they were widely used; not many children left school as soon as they were ten, but few remained to thirteen. They must have had a tendency, like payment by results (which in a way they were), to discourage the teaching of subjects other than the rudiments.

But if a pupil did not leave school at once there remained the problem of what to teach him after he mastered the three Rs. Secondary education was not for him: in the nineteenth century that was still a different kind from elementary. The solution from 1891 to 1898 was a system of "specific subjects" – languages, mathematics, agriculture, commerce, navigation and domestic science – whose rudiments pupils might study for a year or two. A goal was provided by the Merit Certificate which, like the Higher Leaving Certificate, was a creation of Sir Henry Craik. Circular 119 of January 1891 announced its institution, and the first examinations were held in the following year. Open to all pupils aged thirteen or over, it certified the satisfactory completion of an elementary course in the three Rs, two "class subjects" (English, history, geography, needlework or elementary science) and one specific subject. In an effort to maintain freedom and a good standard of achievement no grant was to depend on performance in the examination.[52]

In the opinion of inspectors the Merit Certificate was slow to achieve popularity but its worth was considerable. In the first year 2,346 were awarded, 6,177 in the first three years of its existence. Mr Andrew, reporting in 1900, declared that it was having "a most stimulating effect", since it gave elementary education a definite aim and goal. From 1898 to 1903 a section of the elementary school working towards the certificate was named the "'advanced department".

The first years of the twentieth century however saw a change in the official if not the general attitude to the organisation of education. Children were staying longer at school – the Education Act of 1901 raised the age for compulsory attendance to fourteen – and it was becoming increasingly clear that a system teaching nothing but the elements was out of date. The term "primary" began to take the place of "elementary", showing that all children were entitled to at least two stages of education. What was not yet accepted, as we shall see in the next chapter, was that the second stage need be in "secondary" schools. Post-primary education continued to be given in primary institutions, and the names given to it are significant: from 1903 to 1923 there were "supplementary courses", thereafter until 1936 the term was "advanced divisions".

Supplementary courses were intended to last two years and to have a vocational bias, although they also included general subjects like literature. In country districts they were conducted mainly in the ordinary elementary schools, but in towns a number of "central schools" were established, devoted entirely to the conduct of these courses.[53] The Inspectors' reports of 1904-1905 contain a description of a typical supplementary course undertaken for seven months by a clever girl in a good school. Bookwork occupied the mornings, fifteen hours in a week, while ten hours in the afternoons were devoted to practical instruction. The English course included *The Talisman, Enoch Arden, Evangeline, The Merchant of Venice, A Christmas Carol, Rab and His Friends* and *The Abbot*, with précis of all to be composed. The pupil also had to get by heart *Yarrow Revisited, God's Acre*, parts of *Evangeline, The Day is Done, The Legend Beautiful, A Psalm of Life, The Brook* and the *Ode on the Death of Wellington*. Ten library books were read. An essay was written once a fortnight. There was a course on citizenship and one on the history of India and the Colonies. Mathematical studies included the higher rules of arithmetic, with decimals and the metric system. There were talks on hygiene, with twelve lectures by a doctor on sick nursing. Meanwhile the practical studies of the afternoons comprised music and physical exercises, practical housewifery, cookery, laundrywork, needlework and dressmaking. Good teachers found plenty of scope. Brother Guerin of St Andrew's Boys in Glasgow took his supplementary class in 1904 to the Fishmarket and the Cathedral, to a pottery, a newspaper office and the People's Palace. He found lesson material in the *Glasgow Herald* and had them recording weather trends:[54]

Part of the day was good and was varied with a snowstorm and hailstorm – the very ideal of what we might hope for.

Supplementary courses lasted until 1923, when they were replaced by "advanced divisions". They came in for much criticism almost throughout their existence. The standard of work done was generally held to be poor, inferior to secondary schooling in content, premises and equipment, and certainly not regarded as equivalent by industrial and business concerns.* One great weakness of the courses was the lack of trained staff; many moreover who were willing to work there found themselves inadequately prepared by the Scottish academic tradition. The tendency towards early specialisation which the vocational part of the course encouraged was deplored. Nevertheless much of the criticism was uninformed and the supplementary courses were firmly defended by inspectors as introducing youngsters to the treasures of literature, if for no other reason.[55] Perhaps their chief value lay in the contribution they made towards a broader official conception of "post-primary" education.

The new attitudes at the turn of the century also put an end to the Merit Certificate; its function was changed in 1903 to that of a "qualifying examination", ascertaining which pupils were fit to undertake a two-years course after mastering the elements. There was at first no general written examination; instead there were at least three tests in each school every session.[56] A general standard was maintained by making the award of a pass conditional on the approval of inspectors: that is to say, the examination was the responsibility of the Department, not the school boards or managers. It was never highly regarded. In its favour was the fact that it marked an approximate break between primary and higher studies, but the notion of "qualifying" (implying that there were children who did not qualify) tended to erect a barrier like the "free place" examination in England and at the same time to encourage conscientious teachers to cram pupils for the test. Like all external examinations, it was regarded as a hurdle to be cleared by as many candidates as possible, not as an instrument to distinguish those of greater and less ability so that the poorer ones might not be overstrained. Incidentally, whether because of the standard demanded or excessive caution among teachers who presented children only when they were well prepared, the average age at which a pupil passed the examination was, in the north-east at least, distinctly higher than intended: in 1909 in Aberdeen city it was twelve years and ten months, in the county 12·9, in Kincardine 12·7, in Orkney 12·10 and in Shetland 13·2.[57] The average child would not have enough time left for a full two-years course as the Department intended.

Opposition to the opprobrious term "qualifying" continued after the First World War. Circular 44 of 1921 finally abolished the old type

* There were exceptions in a few urban central schools.

of national qualifying examination: the Department's inspectors ceased to run it in 1924, and thereafter education authorities were left to organise "promotion" (the more fashionable term) in their own way. For the next twenty years this meant a written examination, mainly in English and arithmetic, with in some areas tests in other subjects too. One feature was to remain common to all areas and unchanged for generations – the constricting influence the examination exercised on all work in the senior division of the elementary school. If performance in the test determined, as it did, whether a pupil went to a secondary, an intermediate or an "advanced division" (virtually non-secondary) course, there was a demand by parents which conscientious teachers found hard to resist for meticulous preparation directly aimed at the examination, and most pupils in schools "worth their salt" spent their years from ten to twelve learning handy rules, working countless examples, mastering the pattern of arithmetical problems, analysing, parsing and writing shapely essays on "The Adventures of a Penny". It was occasionally possible to buy books of qualifying-type questions, and where these were not available, there were always copies of old papers.

By 1945 in short the elementary school was in a strange condition. Just when there was general agreement that a syllabus confined to the rudiments was impossibly constricting, just when the school was ready to spread its wings, the qualifying examination kept its pupils in their last two years rigidly applying themselves to the three Rs. A radical change after the Second World War was essential.

REFERENCES

1. KERR, *Memories*, 112
2. *C.C.M. 1877-8* Walker, 197; *1896-7*, 34-49; *A.C.2*, xxxiv-xxxv.
3. *C.C.M. passim*
4. *General Assembly E.C.R., 1879*; *C.C.M. 1896-7*, 34-49; *1910-11*, G/46-57; opinion of counsel on Free Church schools, Oct 1873, qu. J. EDWARD GRAHAM, *Manual of the Education Acts* (Blackwood 1911), 318-321
5. *S.E.D. Memorandum on Religious Instruction in Scotland*, Table 2 (Cmnd. 6426)
6. *C.C.M. 1910-11*, G/46-57
7. *ibid*
8. *C.C.M. 1875-6* Ross, 155; *1881-2* Ross, 150
9. *C.C.M. 1888-9*, 241; *1895-6* Kerr, 424
10. Glasgow and West of Scotland Catholic Teachers' Association, 'Letter to Catholic Parents', qu. PATON, *Rutherglen*, 105-6; SKINNIDER, *Catholic Education*, 125
11. *S.E.D.R. 1919-20*, 18

12. *T.S.A. Ayrshire*, 209, 383; *T.S.A. Fife*, 395, 450
13. *S.E.D.R. 1934-5*, A/41
14. *Episcopal Church Education Report, 1958*
15. *C.C.M. 1881-2*, Sime, 180; *1878-9* Dey, 147; *1890-91* Ogilvie, 258; JESSOP, *Angus*, 214
16. *C.C.M. 1877-8* Hall, 148
17. Margaret Macmillan, in a broadcast address, November 1927
18. HARDY, LILEEN, *The Diary of a Free Kindergarten* (Gay and Hancock 1917), *passim*
19. *S.E.D.R. 1919-20* Fraser, 32-3; STRONG, JOHN, *The Education (Scotland) Act, 1918, with Annotations* (Oliver and Boyd, 1919), 17
20. *Demonstration School Logbook*, 1938, 115; *S.E.D.R. 1929-30*, A/3
21. *S.E.D.R. 1932-3*, A/32
22. *Education (Scotland) Act 1945*, section 1
23. *Demonstration School Logbook*, 11
24. *Deskford Parish School Logbook*, qu. BARCLAY, *Banffshire*, 237; *Demonstration School Logbook*, 264
25. *Loretto's Hundred Years*, 145-6
26. *Stonelaw Infant School Logbook*, qu. PATON, *Rutherglen*, 56-7
27. *Demonstration School Logbook*, 126
28. *Demonstration School Logbook*, 73
29. *Eastfield Landward Board School Logbook*, 9 June 1876, qu. PATON
30. *Scotch Code of 1905*, article 3 (8)
31. *Education (Scotland) Act 1872*, Preamble
32. *S.E.D. Letter*, 7 Feb 1883, qu. *Nelson's Code*, 303
33. *General Assembly E.C.R., 1877*
34. *General Assembly E.C.R., 1879*
35. *C.C.M. 1877-8*, 256
36. NEILL, *A Dominie's Log*, 77
37. *T.S.A. City of Aberdeen*, 409
38. JOHN TAYLOR of Rathven, paper to E.I.S., 1923, qu. BARCLAY, *Banffshire*, 118; *Demonstration School Logbook*, 13
39. MILNE, *Poems*, 64
40. *Cullen School Logbook*, 28 June 1882, qu. CORMACK, *Cramond*, 40
41. *ibid.*, 58
42. *ibid.*, 43
43. WILLIAMSON, *Old Greenock 2*, 159-60
44. *C.C.M. 1887-8*, Kerr, 254
45. KERR, *Nelson's Annotated Code*, 220; *Laurel Bank School 1903-53* (Smith, Glasgow, 1953), 9
46. Advisory Council on Education in Scotland, *Report on Visual and Aural Aids* (H.M.S.O.), 9
47. *Demonstration School Logbook*, 16 March 1928, 23
48. *S.E.D.R. 1933-4*, A/31; *1935*, 13; *T.S.A. Ayrshire*, 212
49. *S.E.D.R. 1938*, A/21

50. A.C.E.S., *Aids*, Appendix II, 42
51. *Code of 1892*, article 29
52. *C.C.M. 1890-91*, 126
53. WADE, NEWMAN T., *Post-Primary Education in the Primary Schools of Scotland, 1872-1936* (U.L.P. 1939), 86
54. *C.C.M. 1904-5* SCOUGAL, 388; *St Andrews Boys School Logbook*, 1904, qu. SKINNIDER, *Catholic Education*, 84
55. *S.E.D.R. 1922-3*, Wattie, 44
56. *C.C.M. 1903-4*, 14
57. *C.C.M. 1908-9*, Dunn

| The Secondary Schools

SECONDARY EDUCATION AFTER 1872

"THE Act of 1872", wrote Dr Dey, one of Her Majesty's Inspectors, three years after its passage, "is excellent, but it does not encourage higher education".[1] By the end of the century educational writers were prepared to go much further in criticism: one described the act as "disastrous to secondary schools".[2] Its aim was undoubtedly to establish a national system of elementary education and all forms of higher schooling had in consequence to take a minor place. Secondary education was not altogether forgotten: section 62 permitted the new school boards to accept the transfer of burgh schools with an advanced curriculum under the name of "higher class public schools", and in the following year eleven town councils, including Glasgow's, transferred their schools to the boards. But the financial provision for the new institutions was not enough to make others follow. The boards were allowed to borrow on the security of the rates to build new higher class schools, but not to maintain them in repair, which had to be done out of endowments, fees or grants from well-wishers. The schools got no share of government grant, and nothing from the rates except for the payment of examiners. By 1888 the number had risen no higher than twenty. The Parker Committee on Training Colleges and Secondary Schools, reporting in that year, remarked that Glasgow was taking good care of its high school but Aberdeen was not, and in many smaller burghs the charge of starving higher education was well founded. At Strathblane, Latin, Greek and mathematics were "little taught after the Act". In Ayrshire the work of Ayr and Irvine was "badly reduced" and Kilmarnock saved some only by having science classes under the Science and Art grant at 9 a.m. and "ordinary classes" beginning at 10. Lord Balfour, in evidence before the 1888 Committee, alleged decline in several famous schools, including Madras College, Perth, Aberdeen and Edinburgh.[3]

The higher class public schools also suffered from the competition of private and endowed foundations and from the system of teaching "specific subjects" begun in 1873 in the elementary institutions and providing all the higher education that most pupils desired. The latter encouraged promising scholars to dissipate their talent in the study for a short time of unrelated topics, and more generally retarded the development of a complete secondary system. In 1879 when there were only seventeen higher class public schools there were no less than two hundred and sixty which could qualify for the title of "higher class non-public."[4] Attendance at the public schools fell away: the roll of Edinburgh High School, which amounted to four hundred and forty in 1878-9, averaged only two hundred and fifty-eight from 1886 to 1888, due partly to the attraction of the Merchant Company's schools. (It is significant however that Edinburgh Academy showed the same decline – from four hundred and sixty-one in 1862 to about two hundred and fifty in the middle eighties.)[5] It is fair to say with Dr Kerr that[6]

> the state-aided school was child, the burgh school the step-child of the board.

Secondary education therefore was left increasingly to schools outside the public system, and these were in two main groups, private and endowed. The former included those modelled on the English Public Schools whose foundation we noted in Part III of Volume One – Loretto, Glenalmond, Merchiston Castle – as well as such exclusive day schools as the Edinburgh and Glasgow Academies. Loretto for example achieved recognition as a Public School in the mid-eighties.[7] Private ventures like the Aberdeen Gymnasium and Kelvinside Academy in Glasgow were able to flourish for a time, still barely troubled by state competition.

The last quarter of the nineteenth century moreover saw the rapid provision of secondary education for girls. Professor Laurie recognised the need: in the course of a report to the Merchant Company in 1868 he wrote:[8]

> The truth is that the intellect of women is a very difficult growth, and that it is interwoven with her imagination, her affection and her moral emotions much more intimately than in man. What the world wants is not two men, a big one in trousers and a little one in petticoats, but a man and a woman.

The effect is seen in the foundation of private schools like St Leonard's, opened in 1877 by the St Andrews School for Girls Company, with as its first headmistress Miss Louisa Lumsden, one of the first three women to pass the Cambridge Tripos. It was the earliest Scottish boarding institution for girls on the lines of a Public School, offering full secondary courses in all the main academic subjects except science. (Music and advanced drawing were available outside school hours.) As few of its pupils would ever earn their own living it was able to ignore "vocational studies."[9] Girls' day schools also appeared: in Glasgow for instance there was Westbourne, founded in 1877. The encouragement and support given by University professors is worth noting.

The other group of secondary ("higher class") schools which expanded rapidly at this time was the endowed institutions. Many were formed by converting the funds of Hospitals, which were under severe criticism because of[10]

> the prevalent tyranny and deceit incident to youths constantly confined together alone in such monastic establishments.

Under Endowed Institutions Acts of 1878 and 1882* many hospitals, intended to provide the rudiments for indigent children, became secondary schools for middle-class pupils: they included George Heriot's, Hutchesons' Grammar, the Morgan Academy, George Watson's and Robert Gordon's Colleges, Allan Glen's, and for girls George Watson's Ladies College, Hutchesons' Grammar School for Girls and the Edinburgh Institution for Young Ladies. The change met a strong demand. In 1869 there had been 428 pupils on the registers of the Merchant Company's schools; a year later there were 3,400, in 1871, 4,100 and by the end of the century 6,000. George Heriot's held 180 boys in 1885, a thousand a year later.[11] (The needs of poor but talented children were met to some extent by providing scholarships and free places.) The Acts of 1878 and 1882 dealt in all with 158 schools, of which 77 were closed at once, 47 transferred to school boards and 34 left under their governing bodies. New endowed schools at this time included Waid Academy, Anstruther, founded in 1884 under the will of Lieutenant Andrew Waid, R.N., "for the sons of east coast fishermen", and Spier's School Beith, begun in 1888, which so flourished that in 1905 it had seven in the first hundred bursars at Glasgow University.[12]

The success of the board schools as a whole served to underline deficiencies in secondary education, and a few minor efforts were made to improve the situation. An Act of 1878 extended the right to maintain and repair buildings from government grant to higher class public schools, but since assistance in paying salaries, always the largest single item of current expenditure, was expressly forbidden, the Act was largely ineffective. A letter to the Scottish Education Department in 1880 suggested the establishment of a centre for higher education in each board's area, but was not accepted.[13] The Balfour Commission, reporting in 1890, deplored the conditions in general:[14]

> School boards and teachers have no real inducement to provide education beyond the stage which the law declares to be compulsory, and poor scholars have little opportunity of pursuing their work beyond that stage.

After 1872 in short there were two separate, virtually isolated educational systems. The elementary ladder rose through infants, juniors and seniors to the advanced department; the secondary stages were infant, lower, middle and upper; and once a child was fairly committed to the former he had little prospect of transfer.[15]

* See Chapter 3.

SECONDARY EDUCATION COMMITTEES AND
THE LEAVING CERTIFICATE

There was no sudden alteration in the situation. A series of small, almost timid steps in the eighties and nineties contributed however to a piecemeal change. The Educational Endowments Act of 1882 made inspection compulsory in higher class schools, previously visited only at the pleasure of the school boards. Six years later the report of the Parker Committee on training colleges and secondary schools showed the way to reorganisation. It recommended new committees administering areas of approximately county size, with a public secondary school in every area, capable of sending pupils to the universities. Higher education should not be tacked on to the elementary course but given in specifically secondary schools. To give a definite aim a leaving certificate ought to be introduced, conducted for the time being by the Scotch Education Department, later perhaps by an examination board. The funds for the scheme might come partly from fees, which should be as high as possible, with exemption for poor boys of talent, but mainly by parliamentary grants for this specific purpose.

Much of this came into effect in the next decade. The Acts of 1889 and 1890 which established county councils and freed elementary education had subsidiary effects almost immediately on secondary work. In 1892 a parliamentary grant was made to English councils to abolish elementary fees, and as it would have been unfair to deny Scotland her equivalent because she had already taken the step, the Education and Local Taxation (Scotland) Act of the same year granted a sum of £265,000. Sixty thousand pounds of this was disbursed through the Scotch Education Department for the extension of secondary schooling.[16]

Since this was to be an annual grant and the school boards were not suitable bodies for conducting the finance of secondary schools, it became necessary to constitute appropriate committees. A departmental minute of 11 August 1892 established thirty-five Secondary Education Committees of the pattern recommended by the 1888 Report, one for each county, five for the burghs of Aberdeen, Dundee, Edinburgh, Glasgow and Leith, and one for the very large urban parish of Govan. Each committee consisted of members from the county council, and from the burgh and parish boards, with an Inspector in attendance. Where there were local trusts financing secondary education they were represented: the Edinburgh committee for example had three representatives of the town council, three of the school board, one inspector, one representative of the Merchant Company and one of Heriot's Trust.[17]

They were instructed without delay to submit schemes to the Department for approval, and the resultant plans showed diverse interpretations of their duties: some, like Aberdeen and Edinburgh, included provision of scholarships and free places, while others, like

E

Selkirk and Berwick, virtually left administration to the school boards.[18] The importance of these bodies however was to spread beyond secondary education: they demonstrated the tendency towards wider administrative regions, and their success undoubtedly influenced the framers of the 1918 Act. The equivalent was generally well used, though there were a few cases of waste in state-aided schools whose "secondary work" was simply a facade intended to attract grants.[19]

Additional sources of revenue appeared at the end of the century. In 1892 Science and Art grants, which had been dispended by the Science and Art Department in Kensington for forty years, were being drawn by five Scottish schools including Allan Glen's and Robert Gordon's College; the total money received in Scotland was about £4,000. Allan Glen's, first in this field, had earned a grant of £58 as early as 1879, and by 1896 the figure had grown to £2,332, despite a technical department with only one chemistry laboratory holding twenty-four pupils in a school of four hundred. Robert Gordon's earned its first Science and Art grant in 1882.[20] A certain amount of literary as well as scientific instruction was permitted to qualify a school for grant after 1897 and at the same time the administration of the system north of the border was transferred to the Scotch Education Department. The sum drawn in that year was £67,000,[21] and in the following year another £35,000 was made available to secondary and technical education annually by the Local Government (Scotland) Act.

But the crucial development in the period was the institution of a goal for secondary education in the form of a Leaving Certificate. The Universities had taken a few steps in this direction with their Local Examinations, introduced by Edinburgh in 1865, St Andrews in 1867, Glasgow in 1877 and Aberdeen in 1880.[22] Glasgow organised the examination at a number of centres – Dumbarton, Greenock, Kilmarnock, Hamilton and Rothesay besides the city – and in 1879 instituted a "higher "grade on the model of the Cambridge examination. Edinburgh in 1883 was conducting tests in forty-seven centres for 891 candidates, 746 of whom were girls. The examiners probably had two aims – to give the secondary schools some idea of the standard required for entry to college, and to provide some objective for clever girls whose sex barred them from a university course. In fact, no preliminary examination yet existed and few boys bothered to work for a test which had no legal backing. Girls made good use of it, but when, with the advent of the Preliminary Examination in 1892, women were admitted to degree courses, the Local Examinations were discontinued.[23]

All the witnesses before the Parker Committee in 1888 agreed that a national examination would avoid the multiplying of external tests by different managers and authorities, and a committee of secondary teachers including the headmasters of Edinburgh Academy and High School, Glasgow Academy and High School, Kelvinside Academy, Allan Glen's, Dundee High School, Aberdeen Grammar School and

Dumbarton Academy, suggested the setting up of an examination board for Scotland on the pattern of the Oxford and Cambridge Board. By 1885 various inspectors were recommending in their reports the award of a certificate. In 1887 a kind of pilot examination in mathematics was tried out in twelve schools; the examiner, Professor Chrystal, reported favourably on the results.[24] Circular 91 of November 1887 asked for the comments of interested bodies, including the universities, on suitable subjects and a desirable standard. The universities, which held a monopoly of certificates of general education, were expected to offer resistance, and they did in fact request a right of control. The Department agreed to consult professors on subject content, but rejected the general principle; the universities rejected such a compromise. A conference held in February 1888 however, with Craik as chairman, decided that a leaving certificate should be awarded from that year onward. Craik took considerable interest in the certificate, supervising it throughout his remaining period of office. It was his decision for example which restricted it at the outset to higher class schools. Glasgow and Edinburgh universities refused at first to accept the certificate for arts entrance, but gave way in 1889.[25]

The basis of award, set forth in Circulars 93 and 94, was to be a written examination, and in drawing up the papers the framers accepted suggestions from the Oxford and Cambridge Board.[26] The examiners were to be professors of the universities. To meet expenses candidates were to pay a fee of half a crown. There were to be two grades – the first, or "higher", that of the senior local examination of the universities, declaring fitness to enter on a three-year arts course; the second, or "lower", guaranteeing his ability to undertake a medical course. Almost at once, perhaps to cater for Oxford and Cambridge, a third, or honours grade was added, of the standard of examination for the Indian Civil Service. Circular 95 announced the subjects in which papers would be set – English (including history and geography), mathematics, Latin, Greek, French, German, conics, analytical geometry and dynamics; examples of papers were also provided. One guiding principle was that no special curriculum should be set, so that there might be no effort to prepare candidates specially for the examinations: in English and Latin, for example, there were no prescribed books. A candidate might present himself in one or more subjects.

The questions in the first papers were notably straightforward, even on the higher level: compare the following examples from the papers of 1888 and those of the mid twentieth century:

Give some account of the Danish Invasions of England, and of the settlement reached by King Alfred in the Peace of Wedmore. (History, Higher Grade, 1888.)

Estimate the importance of the Norse invasions of England and Scotland up to the time of Cnut. (History Higher Grade, 1958.)

Give a short account of the relations between England and Scotland between 1542 and the execution of Queen Mary. (History Higher Grade 1888.)

Estimate the importance of John Knox in Scottish history. (History Higher Grade 1958.)

Name and give the chief works of any two leading writers of
   (a) Drama (excluding Shakespeare)
   (b) Epic poetry
   (c) Satiric Poetry. (English, Higher Grade, 1888.)

"Though Chaucer scarcely ever refers to contemporary events, yet he is the social historian of his age". What references or allusions does Chaucer make to contemporary events, and what kind of historical information can we derive from his works? (English, Higher Grade, 1959.)

Classify Shakespeare's plays, either in order of time or according to subjects. (English, *Honours* Grade, 1888.)

From your reading of any of the tragedies or histories discuss the qualities which Shakespeare considers a sovereign ruler ought to have. (English, Higher Grade, 1958.)

Trace with an outline map the course of one of the leading rivers in England, in Scotland, *and* in Ireland, naming in each case the towns upon its banks, (Geography, Higher Grade, 1888.)

Write explanatory notes on the following:
   (a) Emigration from the Scottish Highlands to the Lowlands of Scotland and abroad:
   (b) Immigration into Malaya:
   (c) Nomadism in the Sahara: and
   (d) Shifting cultivation in Central Africa. (Geography, Higher Grade, 1958.)

The same tendency towards wider and more exacting questions may be seen in the mathematical and scientific subjects.

Twenty-nine schools presented 972 candidates for the first examinations in 1888, including six in Edinburgh, two in Perth, three in Glasgow (the High School, Academy and Kelvinside) and one in Aberdeen (Gordon's College). Four thousand three hundred certificates – one for each subject passed – were awarded in the first year. In 1889 there were 2,066 candidates, taking 9,200 papers in 42 schools. Many authorities at once accepted the certificate as a guarantee of fitness for entrance to further training – the War Office, the universities of Edinburgh, Glasgow, St Andrews and Cambridge, the General Medical Council and the Societies of Solicitors and Accountants.[27]

A further important step was taken in 1892, when the Department extended entrance to pupils in all schools which had efficient higher

departments but were not classified as "higher class". Their exclusion
until then had been attacked by the universities and the Educational
Institute as blatant class distinction, but Craik's aim was to safeguard
the future of secondary education in Scotland. As soon as state aid was
provided for this in 1892 he opened the certificate to the "semi-
secondaries". Sixty-three state-aided schools with higher departments
took advantage at once: in Glasgow for instance these included City
Public, Whitehill, Albert Road, Bellahouston and Hamilton Crescent.
By 1898 there were over 16,000 candidates for the certificate, presented
by 76 higher class and 322 public schools. When a year later the
higher grade schools came into being many began presenting at once.
Unfortunately some presentations were clearly frivolous or at best
sanguine: in 1905 thirty-three pupils presented on the lower grade in
one school in the west produced only five passes; in another only one
out of twenty was successful; in a third only three out of forty-three.
All three were higher grade schools. The percentage of passes disclosed
annually until 1905 averaged sixty-seven, varying from fifty in mathematics to seventy-six in German; the standard varied from year to
year.[28]

Almost from the outset the Department found it necessary to guard
pupils against overtaxing; to this end it refused to disclose results, but
certain schools took delight in publishing them and an unworthy
competition developed. At the end of the nineteenth century some
candidates were being presented at the age of eleven or twelve.[29] As an
experiment in preventing this the practice began in 1900 of offering
passes in groups of subjects. Craik had resisted this for a long time,
claiming that very few pupils could secure one, but after a period of
experiment the Department gave warning in 1902 that this was to
become the only method of gaining an award. The "highers" became
a curriculum certificate, for which not only satisfactory performance
in the examinations but also the completion of a four-year higher
course were essential. The candidate had to show passes in four
subjects on the higher standard, or in three highers and two lowers.
Moreover he must have reached the age of seventeen.[30] The award was
no longer open to those schools – and there were several – which had
made a practice of presenting candidates in lower English or arithmetic
only, but to give them time for improvement the 'group' system did
not become the rule until 1908. In 1911 the course was extended to
five years and because this in itself was something of a safeguard against
early presentation, the minimum age clause was revoked.[31] The problem
of overtaxing was undoubtedly reduced but not eliminated.

There were other changes in the administration of the certificate
before 1914. One effect of the group provision was to make the "honours"
grade unnecessary, indeed a temptation to overpressure. It was abolished
in 1908 and never reappeared, despite occasional agitation for an
approximation to the English "credit" system. In the following year

the Education (Scotland) Fund was set up, and one of the first charges on it was the expense of the Leaving Certificate.[32] Meanwhile new subjects were added. Science appeared, mainly on a basis of oral and practical testing, in 1899, and specialised certificates were introduced in technical and commercial subjects (not yet as part of the "Highers") in 1906. Candidates on the whole continued to be presented almost exclusively for the older and more academic disciplines.

Not all the effects of the Certificate were salutary: more than once the Department had to complain about its misuse:[33]

> My Lords strongly deprecate the practice of presenting a candidate again for a subject he already got the previous year,

and

> It is impossible to deprecate too strongly any tendency to gauge the quality of teaching in a school simply by the number of honours certificates gained by its pupils.

There was also a constricting influence on the secondary syllabus. But by providing a goal at which to strive and a link with the universities and especially by making itself available to board as well as private schools the certificate played a central part in the development of Scottish secondary education. The rector of George Watson's Boys stated in 1908, that, thanks to the stimulus of the leaving certificate, work was being done in secondary schools which a quarter of a century before had taken place in the arts classes of the universities.[34]

DEVELOPMENTS IN THE TWENTIETH CENTURY

The main public schools which undertook work for the certificate were those set up in 1899 to give education on a "higher grade" than elementary to the cleverer pupils from poorer families. The new schools represented one of the reforms attributed to Craik's influence; they were quite distinct from elementary institutions and offered a course lasting for at least three years, with a bias either scientific or commercial and a general curriculum embracing English, history, geography, higher arithmetic and drawing. They were intended to prepare pupils for a career in industry, but soon outgrew this idea. The first opened in 1900 and within a year there were thirty-one in the country with 3,271 scholars. In 1903, when the supplementary courses were introduced in elementary schools, offering similar vocational opportunities, the higher grades became more liberal and in many places extended their courses to five years. Some became secondary schools in the true sense, though they were not so recognised until 1923: they included Oban High School, Dumbarton Academy, Vale of Leven, Airdrie and Rothesay Academies, Campbeltown and Lanark

Grammar Schools. Under article 134 of the Code fees were charged in many, including seven in Glasgow.[35]

The commercial course for girls remained short: there was only one full three-year programme of this type in Glasgow in 1902 and it was poorly attended. The percentage of boys and girls completing their courses in 1908 was only about thirty – as high as forty-four in Strathaven, as low as ten in Johnstone. But by the end of the First World War Mr Jamieson, Inspector in the Southern Division, was justified in writing that the term "higher grade" had for many years had no more than a financial distinction from "secondary".[36] The work of the best schools was impressive: the walls of Whitehill held photographs of five Snell Exhibitioners. Moreover the higher grade school was generally much more popular than the higher class; by 1908 there were few districts without one. In 1910 there were two hundred, with only fifty-five higher class public, and in 1920, when all those offering a secondary course were recognised as secondary institutions, the total of higher grade was one hundred and ninety-six, with a roll of 31,050.[37] They may claim to have played the largest part in re-establishing a connexion, in circumstances vastly altered by the Industrial Revolution, between the Scottish elementary schools and the universities.

By 1905 the public schools were providing as much secondary education as the non-public – 8,999 pupils against 8,922.[38] The provision was not to be free or compulsory until the 1918 Act, though several authorities – Banffshire was one – anticipated the statutory requirement.[39] The independent schools steadily lost ground. Of thirty-four left under their own governing bodies by the Act of 1882, only thirteen remained in the middle nineteen-twenties, and no more than a handful could struggle along without aid from the state. The recommendations of the Mackenzie Departmental Commission, set up in 1927 to consider the position of endowed schools since the 1908 and 1918 Acts, led to one new measure, the Educational Endowments (Scotland) Act of 1928. It added one new school to the roll of independents, Dollar Academy, which was withdrawn from the Clackmannan authority and given its own managers;[40] there were thus fourteen endowed schools in the traditional sense of the term at the end of the Second World War.

But these had to be helped. With the steep rise in costs during the twentieth century only the most financially favoured schools could hope to continue an independent existence. Glasgow Academy and Merchiston Castle School became companies, and in 1920 the War Memorial Trust took over the management of the former. The history of Kelvinside Academy throws light on similar difficulties. Founded in 1877 by the Kelvinside Academy Company as a private school for boys of the upper classes on the west of the river Kelvin, it had a subscribed capital of £13,000 and an initial loan of £10,000. That the venture was launched at all is evidence of the opportunities for private schools at the time, but it was unfortunate from the beginning. While the building was rising in Kirklee the Glasgow Academy sold its old quarters to the School Board and a new structure was established in Hillhead; meanwhile not far away the Govan School Board founded a new high school. Since the initial cost of the Kirklee building was £35,000 Kelvinside was in debt from its earliest days. In 1915 its old boys had to open a subscription list to avert bankruptcy, and the solution was not found until 1922, when the War Memorial Trust took over management. Thereafter the Academy was more flourishing, its numbers, which had fallen from 267 in 1882 to 137 in 1913, rising sharply to 314 in 1922-3.[41]

Other private schools depended on liberal endowment. The John Neilson Institution in Paisley had a windfall in 1889 when six small charity schools were closed by the Balfour Commissioners and the money released was used to increase scholarships at Neilson to 120. At the same time it confined its course to the secondary stage.[42] The only major foundation between the two World Wars was made in Troon by Mr Charles Marr, who died in London in 1919 leaving £330,795 to be spent on furthering education in his birthplace. Almost £240,000 was spent on building Marr College, incorporating such amenities as a stage, cinema, radio equipment, a pipe organ in the hall, a museum and art gallery, classrooms panelled in cedar and mahogany and floored in polished oak, and windows of Vitaglass; the College was surrounded by fifty acres of playing fields. Building and staffing were complete in 1930, but legal difficulties delayed opening until 1935. The rest of Mr Marr's legacy was used for bursaries, including free education at the secondary level for every child in Troon. On this last £90,000 was spent in the thirty years following his death.[43]

Many schools however had to surrender their independent existence. Bellahouston Academy was bought in 1885 for £15,000 by Govan School Board. Allan Glen's, where the standard of scientific instruction at the end of the century was high – it was one of two Scottish schools presenting candidates successfully for the advanced and honours science examinations of the Board of Education, and had been directed since 1886 by the Royal Technical College – was transferred in 1912 by statute to the Glasgow School Board. Waid Academy passed in 1921 from a board of governors to the education authority of Fife and James Gillespie's in 1908 to the Edinburgh School Board.[44]

But although the boards and their successors were establishing themselves in the post-elementary field, a new administrative division was appearing which was to endure throughout the period and far beyond. This was the distinction between "secondary" and "intermediate" education. In 1902, not long before his retirement, Craik had introduced a third certificate, the Intermediate, which marked the completion of a three years course in mathematics, language, English and science, with the passing of an examination. As the title suggested the Department was trying to distinguish a form of education intermediate between elementary and secondary: the 1908 Act[45] defined the terms. Within five or six years of its institution however the new examination came to be regarded as a half-way stage in the course for the Leaving Certificate, and although many children left after their third year this attitude persisted until after the First World War.[46]

The Act of 1918 assisted the unification of the educational system by placing all types of public schools under the new local authorities, and sought to facilitate attendance at higher institutions.[47] It was followed in December 1921 by Circular 44, which abolished the central qualifying examination and left decisions on transfer at twelve to the new authorities; undoubtedly the attempt was to get rid of the concept of "qualifying". But Circular 44, which also abolished the "intermediate" certificate as a halfway stage to the "highers", substituted two new documents, each intended to mark the end of a course. The first, established in 1923, was the Day School Certificate (Higher), awarded by the Department on the results of a national examination, and testifying to the completion of a three years course in a higher grade school, with passes in at least four subjects including arithmetic and English. The Day School Certificate (Lower), instituted a month later, could be gained at the end of a two years course, and was awarded at the discretion of local authorities, with the approval of His Majesty's Inspectors. In 1923 also two distinct codes were issued for running schools – the Day Schools Code and the Secondary Schools (Scotland) Regulations. The former organised elementary institutions, with "advanced divisions" offering quasi-secondary courses in central schools, which numbered forty-three between 1934 and 1945, or most commonly in primary "tops".[48] In the 1920s more than half the urban elementaries had such "tops". Many children unfortunately left school without completing either Day School Certificate, and less than twenty per cent of primary schools with advanced divisions offered three-year courses.[49] Higher grades on the other hand were run under the Secondary Regulations.

The Day School Higher on the whole possessed some standing. In 1931 when 3,055 leaving certificates were awarded there were 3,351 Day School Highers. The Act of 1936 recognised however that, at least in name, all children over the age of twelve should receive "secondary" education. It also provided for the raising of the leaving age in 1939 to fifteen, thereby envisaging three secondary years for all. A distinction was retained nevertheless between "junior secondary" courses of three and "senior" of five years and this was a crucial point, since it fostered jealousy, frustration, pressure, disappointment and strain, if not among all pupils, at least among many parents. The Act proposed to abandon Day School Certificates in 1940 and to substitute a Junior Leaving Certificate. In form it would resemble the Day School Higher, since passes would be required in four subjects, including English and arithmetic. The third however would be the "characteristic subject" of the course taken – a language, commerce, technical subjects – and the fourth would be either science or another characteristic subject. A further valuable reform would be the issue of the certificate every six months, thus reducing the penalty for being born in an inconvenient month of the year.

In fact the new certificate was never awarded. The Day School Certificates lapsed in 1940 as proposed, but the circumstances of war made it unwise to embark on a new scheme, though local authorities were allowed to issue their own documents. When in 1947 the leaving age was raised the Department thought it advisable to refrain from imposing a pattern on timetables by introducing a new certificate: the junior secondary school was to be left alone to work out its own salvation, which might legitimately vary from one authority to another. What did remain until the sixties was a division into five-year sheep and three-year goats. Even professional training was separate – a special certificate for secondary, a primary certificate with endorsement for work in the advanced division.

CURRICULUM

If change and experiment were frequent in this period in the organisation of secondary education they were much less evident in content and methods. In the last quarter of the nineteenth century the classics were still firmly enthroned; indeed in the north-east, where the Bursary Competition counted for so much, their "Arctic grip" held until the outbreak of the First World War. In Fordyce Academy in the eighties and nineties the top class spent all their forenoons on the Version, which commanded 500 out of the total of 850 marks; there was a page a day of Latin and the same of Greek vocabulary to memorise, and an extra class on Horace at 7 a.m. on Saturdays, with Friday evening sessions just before the Bursary Examination.[50] When the advent of the higher grade schools and the growth of science as a school subject sapped the position of classics, their supporters fought a long rearguard action. Thus we find Dr Stewart, His Majesty's Chief Inspector of Schools, remarking in 1902 as he opened a new school at Mortlach:[51]

> I am strongly of opinion that, as a training in accuracy, research, discrimination, taste and the feeling of style, this exercise (Latin versions) is unequalled and unsurpassed,

and in 1914 at a meeting of the Classical Association of Scotland[52]

> Miss Patton, Boroughmuir, thought the average girl could learn classics with great profit and pleasure if she had not to spend so much time on Science at school.

The Association did not favour experiment. In 1906, when Dr Wright Henderson advocated learning a language by reading plenty of it, stigmatising claims of "good grounding" as excuses for teaching minute and irrational grammar, his paper was not welcomed – "What can we throw overboard?" "Our grammar is thoroughly rational and essential". Eight years later Miss Bentinck-Smith, headmistress of St Leonards, was politely frozen out when she preached the heresy that the attempt to teach classics to the average girl should be given up, and in 1911 a report by two members on the new oral approach at the Perse School, Cambridge, was met with general agreement that it was not suitable for Scotland.[53]

This stubborn defence was not unsuccessful: it kept Latin in an important place throughout the period, though Greek slowly declined. Presentations for the Leaving Certificate tell an interesting story (page 76).[54]

Besides Latin the most important subjects in the secondary curriculum were English and mathematics. The former became central in all courses, especially when a pass on the higher grade was made obligatory for the award of a group certificate. Much time was spent on grammar and interpretation; literature was usually studied according to canons of good taste dictatorially laid down. At Dundee in 1882[55]

> Little they recked what we really knew of Shakespeare and Milton, if we could only reel off glibly that "Shakespeare was the greater genius but Milton the sublimer man". Mr Valentine saw to it that we were able to do that,

and at the Royal High School in 1900[56] English was

> buried beneath a shroud of glossary, a pall of critical exposition, a tomb of grammatical and expository notes.

The headmaster of Aberdeen Demonstration School noted in 1910 that Class I was reading *As You Like It*, "which is far too difficult for them".[57]

On the other hand good teachers broke the shackles of examination and tradition. Dr William Dey's top class at the Old Town Grammar School in Aberdeen in the eighties read Spencer's *Education* and his *Study of Sociology*, John Stuart Mill's *Liberty* and *Representative Government*, Bain's *Mind and Body*, Huxley's *Lay Sermons* and Carlyle unlimited, an earnest but potentially stimulating prescription, while at Loretto in the nineteen-twenties

> Our greatest joy had been when Mr Smith read a part. He had the gift of making a character appear before you, no matter what type it might be. His majestic mien when reading such parts as Brutus or Hamlet was supreme; he could reduce us to helpless laughter over the Gravediggers; and I am positive that no-one who was privileged to witness his rendering of the fearful entry of Lady Macbeth round the classroom door will ever forget it.[58]

(1) ALL PRESENTATIONS

Year	Candidates	English	Latin	Greek	French	German	Maths	Science	Art	Music	Tech	Comm	Dom	Spanish	Gaelic
1888	972	724	443	315	486	265	584								
(%)		74·5	45·5	32·4	50·0	27·3	60·1								
1908*	10827	9117	4674	858	8220	1535	8795								
(%)		84·2	43·2	7·9	75·9	14·2	81·2								
1933	7296	4971†	3059	387	5166	927	5478	2600	786	84	4	141	104	121	39
(%)		68·1	41·9	5·3	70·8	12·7	75·1	35·6	10·8	1·2	0·05	1·9	1·4	1·7	0·5
1946†	8245	6458†	2947	220	5939	1150	6456	3951	985	192	302	448	258	76	42
(%)		78·3	35·7	2·7	72·0	14·0	78·3	47·9	12·0	2·3	3·7	5·4	3·1	0·9	0·5

(2) HIGHER PRESENTATIONS

Year	Candidates	English	Latin	Greek	French	German	Maths	Science	Art	Music	Tech	Comm	Dom	Spanish	Gaelic
1888	972	200	131	92	150	82	140								
(%)		20·6	13·5	9·5	15·4	8·4	14·4								
1908*	10827	2758	1551	349	2630	513	2396								
(%)		25·5	14·3	3·2	24·3	4·7	22·1								
1933	7296	4971†	1148	180	2828	320	3125	1672	434	53	1	66	67	24	35
(%)		68·1	15·7	2·5	38·7	4·4	42·8	22·9	5·9	0·7	0·01	0·9	0·9	0·3	0·5
1946†	8245	6458†	1244	129	2946	410	3946	2909	671	144	260	366	207	23	40
(%)		78·3	15·1	1·6	35·7	5·0	47·9	35·3	8·1	1·7	3·2	4·4	2·5	0·3	0·5

* includes the Intermediate Certificate presentations.   † Higher standard only available.

In general however by the thirties English literature in many secondary schools meant a partly understood and poorly appreciated study of Shakespeare (*A Midsummer Night's Dream, Twelfth Night, The Merchant of Venice, Julius Caesar, Macbeth* and *Hamlet*), Chaucer's *Prologue*, Milton (*Lycidas, L'Allegro* and *Il Penseroso*, Book I of *Paradise Lost*), a few Romantics (notably *The Ancient Mariner*), Gray's *Elegy*, Sir Roger de Coverley, *Old Christmas* and *Roast Pig, Ivanhoe, Pride and Prejudice* and *The Cloister and the Hearth*. A few teachers opened magic casements; too many dictated character sketches of Brutus and Cassius or the rhyme scheme of the sonnet.

Mathematics showed the same pattern of rigid prescription in most schools with occasional glimpses of more adventurous methods like the models and cut-outs adopted by Mr McArthur in the seventies in Aberdeen Gymnasium.[59] The entrance examinations for teacher training colleges at that time show the content of the subject. It was clearly more a male than a female preserve: the paper in "Euclid, algebra and mensuration" was for boys only, and there was a special, easier arithmetic paper for girls. Instead of being asked to face a succession of problems – "an estate is divided between two claimants", "the wheels of a locomotive are $2\frac{1}{2}$ metres asunder" – female candidates were requested to multiply 456,978 by 789 and to subtract 90·41 from 300.[60] This distinction operated for many years and was accepted by the pupils: one woman remembered that girls in Dundee in the eighties learnt Euclid by rote and were lost if ABC were substituted for XYZ.[61]

Science, which had been examined orally and practically since the nineties, became a subject in the Leaving Certificate examination at the start of the twentieth century, and in this field also a sex differentiation developed. It became the accepted rule that physics and chemistry – "real science" – were for boys, biology rather more for girls, although the latter – "all about your insides" – was regarded as rather daring for young ladies.[62] Chemistry was a series of experiments, dictated by the teacher and not noticeably inter-related; much importance was attached by masters and inspectors to the careful writing-up of laboratory notebooks. Discovery methods were rare throughout the period, though botanical excursions were not uncommon and at least one teacher in the seventies offered to dissect any animal brought in after the vacation; he received a dead cat.[63]

History and geography were regarded as subsidiary subjects, given a minor time allocation and generally taught as a "second string". Laurel Bank in 1904 claimed to be one of the first schools in Scotland to employ a history specialist.[64] In the Leaving Certificate examinations before the 1920s both subjects were part of the English paper; thereafter history remained with English, but geography became part of the Science group. On the whole, perhaps because there were fewer experts to teach it in the formal way to which they were accustomed, geographical instruction was more lively, with mapping excursions, clay models and

rural visits to study the lie of the countryside, all in the first years of
the twentieth century.[65] History was mainly a recital of political events,
with no mention of social or economic patterns. Leaving Certificate
questions certainly became more testing – fewer began with
"Describe . . ." and more with "Explain . . ." – but this merely reflected
changes in the form of notes dictated by the teachers. Moreover the
history of Scotland was neglected: it was generally restricted to the
primary school and came to an end in 1746 on the field of Culloden.
As a political record it is generally so confused and unedifying that this
is hardly surprising: as one inspector reported in 1879,[66]

> one year of school life is quite enough to devote to such an uninter-
> esting subject as Scottish history, which consists merely of three
> grand events: the reign of Bruce, culminating in the battle of
> Bannockburn, the Reformation of which Knox is the central figure,
> and the Union. All else is a mere chronicle of murders, personal
> squabbles among the nobles, occasional battles in the country and
> frequent battles on the border – all barren events in which we trace
> little development or progress among the people.

But there is no mention here of the daily life of people in the towns or
on the land, nothing of the evidence to be found in place-names,
street-names, museums and libraries, photographs – nothing in short
of the very stuff out of which historical study can be made.

In the thirties there was some attempt at change. An excellent
instance was the campaign of the Departmental Secretary, McKechnie,
against "lumber in the curriculum". Textbooks appeared as in the
primary schools, which printed extracts from contemporary authorities
and set the pupils to work on their own. One for instance, dealing with
the affairs of Scotland in the eighteenth century, reproduced passages
from Burnet on Glencoe, Chamberlayne on presbyterianism, some
clauses of the Act of Union and extracts from the memoirs of Sir
John Clerk of Penicuik; it gave suggestions for further reading, notes
on the Darien Scheme and Scots Law, and various exercises – "Find
out what a presbyterian believes", "write an argument between two
people concerning the Act of 1707".[67] But that was an English history
book. The full impact of these efforts was muffled by the strong tendency
to teach towards certain questions "spotted" as "likely to come up"
in the Leaving Certificate. It was still possible – indeed it was in the
fifties – to walk into a fourth- or fifth-year classroom and hear the
teacher droning out notes at dictation speed on the fiscal policy of
Walpole or the causes of the French Revolution.

Modern languages steadily took a more important place, especially
after their recognition at the end of the century as university subjects
in their own right. For most of the period French was almost exclusively
the first study, with some German, a little Spanish or Gaelic and a
handful of students of any other tongue. In 1888 two-thirds of modern

language presentations for the Leaving Certificate were in French, one-third in German. Thereafter percentages were as follows:[68]

Year	French	German	Spanish	Gaelic
1908	84·3	15·7	—	—
1933	82·6	14·8	1·9	0·6
1946	82·3	15·9	1·1	0·6

Much of the work was a grim hunt for mechanical accuracy, with grammar-books the important texts. As one headmaster put the matter[69]

> There's no need for that; it's not Boarding-School French that is wanted here. These pupils will never be in France; they are only taking French as a subject for the Leavings and the Bursary Competition.

"These pupils will never be in France"; he was speaking in 1912! He concluded by remarking that "only twenty per cent of the marks are given for oral work", leaving the inference obvious, and he would have been applauded by many Scottish language teachers throughout the period, who sought to turn out pupils who could write correct French but need neither speak it nor understand it when spoken. When an Inspector found poor pronunciation, as one did in Aberdeen in 1907, his remedy was to recommend that "the phonetic chart should be constantly in use".[70]

All other subjects, with one exception, were regarded as peripheral, at least for academically minded pupils. Art, generally called "drawing", was a subject for relaxation. The Department's recommendation in 1907 was "representation of objects, natural and fashioned, singly and in harmoniously arranged groups", though some lively teachers, especially in girls' private schools, became more ambitious: in St Leonard's in 1927 there was outdoor sketching, life drawing, mural decoration, lino printing and book illustration, and the Aberdeen Demonstration School eight years later was commended for integrating the subject with English lessons.[71] It did not achieve a place in the Leaving Certificate until 1924, at the same time as Music.

Physical education was also essentially a spare-time occupation, though the advent of the Keep-Fit movement in the nineties gave it some importance. Physical drill first appeared in the Day School Code of 1895.[72] In some schools it had been introduced before, but in general the exercise taken naturally by exuberant children during two daily intervals was held to be enough. The end of the century brought the nation up sharply with the shocking evidence of the Boer War medical examinations, showing a very low standard of physical efficiency among the poor. In the sunless caverns of the towns rickets were the rule. Circular 279 of the S.E.D., issued in 1900, urged the need for controlled physical exercise, and a Royal Commission appointed in 1901 investigated the possibilities of physical training. Reporting in 1903, its evidence added to the national alarm, and a Committee on Physical Deterioration was appointed in the following year, while a school syllabus was produced and the first Inspector of physical education nominated.[73] The usual practice in most schools, even those for girls, was to employ a retired soldier as a drill sergeant, but the opening of colleges training teachers of physical education ensured a supply of qualified instructors. Thereafter the subject widened its province until in 1946 the Primary Report of the Advisory Council placed physical welfare as one of the three fundamentals of education.

Clever pupils were expected to undertake academic courses; other boys might be trained more specifically to earn their living with their hands, while girls learnt how to make a home. The Technical Schools (Scotland) Act of 1887 gave permissive powers to the school boards which had complied with the 1872 provisions to establish schools for technical instruction, but it had two weaknesses – it was merely permissive, and it left the meaning of the term in doubt; it became a dead letter. Nevertheless attempts were still made to promote handwork teaching: in 1902 for example the Duchess of Sutherland was the moving spirit in proposing the building of a technical school at Golspie at the expense of the Duke and of Andrew Carnegie.[74]

For the next thirty years technical training was held to be the business of continuation classes and technical colleges, and there was considerable expansion of these institutions. The Act of 1918 made it possible for authorities to open centres in which young people who had just left school might be trained on "day release" from their firms. But all these measures accepted the principle that vocational education in the technical sense should not begin until the child had left school. There was some warrant for such a view: unless he obtained his "general" (or to use the more fashionable term, "liberal") education before he was fourteen, he was unlikely to get any at all. It was not commonly agreed – though philosophers like Whitehead and Dewey were hammering the point home – that technical training was an indispensable part of the liberal curriculum. In Scottish schools the result was a tiny handwork department, consisting often of a single room, in which a few elementary processes in working with wood were taught to a handful of boys, generally those too poorly endowed to tackle the stiffer "academic" subjects. There were exceptional schools, of course, in which handwork was well taught.

The proposed raising of the leaving age to fifteen reopened the problem, especially since the effects of the Depression were still felt when the Act of 1936 was passed. In 1937 the Advisory Council suggested the institution of preapprenticeship classes to fill the year between fourteen and fifteen which would be such a problem from 1939 onwards. A few local authorities accepted the proposal, but it never received more than the encouragement of the Department.

Girls took "domestic subjects" or "homecraft", by which terms were meant needlework, cookery, laundrywork and home management. Of these needlework had been the commonest feature of a girl's education for centuries: in the dames' schools of the 1600s and 1700s sewing was oftener taught than reading. When specific subjects were introduced in 1875 no girl was permitted to take even one unless she also undertook a course in domestic economy. Unfortunately the besetting bookishness of Scottish studies operated here too, with no practical application whatever. It rapidly became popular however: the Inspector in Renfrew, Bute and Argyll examined two girls in 1875 but 3,468 in 1881. In 1882 there were 24,204 presented in Scotland; about two-thirds passed.[75]

By 1882 forty-one schools were teaching practical cookery, which became popular both with girls and their parents, though some resolute feminists opposed it as a retrograde step when they were campaigning to win women freedom from the kitchen. Moreover the Code of 1882 offered a special grant for cookery and stressed the importance of needlework. The next twenty years saw the development of laundrywork and the appearance of Colleges of Domestic Science – some dated from the seventies – throughout Britain. In the Code of 1900 cookery, laundrywork and housewifery were officially organised into a course known as "household management".

Two years later the first temporary inspectresses were appointed. Both dealt with cookery, one in the southern, the other in the western region. Thereafter domestic subjects made and kept their place in the curriculum: like technical subjects they were included in the Scottish Leaving Certificate. They suffered however from a similar handicap, being regarded primarily as the province of pupils "not good enough for anything else". It is certainly less intellectually taxing to bake a sponge than to solve a quadratic equation, but complete success is no easier. And the value of both is not open to doubt.

Agriculture, as we have seen, was the subject of a series of scholastic experiments by the Society for Propagating Christian Knowledge. It seemed clear that rural schools should help boys to become farmers, and the Committee of Council made grants for this purpose in the 1840s. In 1876 it also recognised agriculture as eligible for science and art grants, and in 1883 it became a specific subject. It had to be examined however and was therefore, like domestic economy, taught mainly from a textbook. Towards the end of the century it was felt to be unsuitable for elementary schools and faded from their curricula. In secondaries, even in country areas, it was never very popular; indeed between the wars it was discontinued in many. In practice it included horticulture: there were fifty school gardens in 1909. But nineteen years later there were only eight schools in Scotland with any form of rural course, two doing dairying and six poultry-keeping.[76]

The one study not primarily academic which was regarded as essential for all pupils was religious instruction. At the Gymnasium

F

in the seventies three verses of Proverbs were assigned for repetition daily, and on Sundays there was something from the metrical psalms. Not surprisingly the subject was remembered by the pupils as "a burden we had to bear".[77] The situation for a number of reasons did not improve. Religious teaching was not inspected by the Department. It had no place in the Leaving Certificate. Moreover the climate of opinion was changing, especially in the appalled disillusionment brought by the massacres of the First World War. By the thirties R.I. was allowed two periods a week in every Protestant school, but much of the teaching was superficial and unenthusiastic. The situation in Roman Catholic schools was different; spiritual matters were the reason for their existence.

EXTRA-CURRICULAR ACTIVITIES

The conviction that life was earnest, that school was a place for work, if necessary by compulsion, died hard. Nevertheless the period, in secondary as well as elementary schools, saw a growing recognition of the need to provide for relaxation, and if time for this could not be found between nine and four o'clock or in weekday evenings consecrated to homework, there were always Saturday mornings and the useful hour between four o'clock and teatime. This was the era in which extra-mural activities established themselves, especially in urban schools, whose pupils did not have miles to travel. Sport was at first permitted rather than encouraged, with the boys clubbing together to buy a ball and arranging their own fixture lists, but later it was organised. For boys there were football, rugby and cricket, for girls netball and hockey, though the independent schools might also attempt more select sports like lacrosse and fencing. The gymnastic specialists produced by the Colleges of Physical Education had much to do with the rapid expansion in the twentieth century. Most pupils welcomed it, but not all, since not all were attracted to team games. For this minority the result might be unhappy, with the authoritarian tradition applied to making them conform.

Many less energetic societies also sprang up. The most popular were choirs, debating societies and dramatic clubs, all of which appeared in many schools at the beginning of the century. The annual stage presentation, generally at the end of the session, but rehearsed for months before, became part of the pattern of school life, though not in many minds of education, except insofar as it refreshed young minds for serious effort. A few adventurous schools presented Sheridan, Goldsmith or even Shaw, but for the majority the alternatives were a Shakespearian comedy, not too outspoken, and Gilbert and Sullivan.

Another enterprise was the School Magazine, serving partly as an opportunity for creative writing and occasionally illustration, but also as a forum for opinion and a chance to poke fun at authority. These productions, like the societies, tended to appear first mainly in the nineties or the Edwardian decade. They were in the main sober publications, edited and administered by the English department; even when pupils were nominally in control, the need for censorship was generally accepted. An average Magazine might be expected to contain a message from the Headmaster, School News (who's out, who's in), a list of duxes and prizewinners, reports on athletic and society activities and on the higher educational prowess of former pupils, some crude verse from the junior forms and *vers libre* from the upper, a good deal of parody, semi-affectionate references to the foibles of well-known pupils ("who carries whose books home at four?") and teachers ("have you got that, boy? well fix it!"), and photographs of the recent school visit to Stratford or Paris or the Mediterranean.

Even in leisure pursuits the authoritarian bias remained strong. Discipline in class was still founded on corporal punishment or the threat of it: "they are most affa strick and hiv terrible hard Tags" wrote one wag in the Fordyce Academy magazine of 1913.[78] Various devices were borrowed from English practice, prefects and school captains for instance, but pupils were not often trusted to make a free election, and the nominees were seldom given real power. The "house" system was not generally adopted until after 1945. Nevertheless there was much talk of "the school tradition" and even in young institutions like the higher grade schools this was not unjustified. From the nineties onward Former Pupils' Clubs appeared in large numbers, with organised sport for younger members and annual dinners for all, at which there was a great deal of sentimental jollity and a general agreement that the school concerned had been, at least in their day, one of the best in Scotland.* Moreover the two World Wars in their own tragic way fostered the school spirit. From 1919 the central feature of most secondary school halls was the War Memorial Board with its list of fallen Old Boys. The attitude in many schools may be exemplified by one country headmaster who, when the bells and whistles of Armistice Day were heard, remarked levelly, "Quiet there! go on with your translation, John", but who when it came to Prize Day that year broke down and could not finish his address: "However the public may see them, they will always be for me *my* boys".[79]

REFERENCES

1. *C.C.M. 1875-6* Dey, 132
2. CLARKE, *Short Studies*, 50-51

* One of the interesting questions in the years after the Second World War, when the team spirit was less generally applauded, was to be the possible effect on F.P. clubs.

3. GUTHRIE SMITH, J., qu. BAIN, *Stirlingshire*, 240; Committee on Training Colleges and Secondary Schools (Parker Committee), *Third Report* (H.M.S.O. 1888), BALFOUR; BOYD, *Ayrshire*, 186; MORGAN, *Rise and Progress*, 170

4. *C.C.M. 1879-80*, xxvii

5. *Parker Committee 3*, Duff and Carmichael

6. KERR, *Scottish Education*, 301

7. *Loretto's Hundred Years*, 10

8. TOWILL, *Merchant Maidens*, 74

9. *St Leonard's School 1877-1927* (O.U.P., Milford n.d.), 3-10, 36-8

10. OGILVIE, *Cruickshank*, 83

11. KERR, *Memories*, 312-13

12. *T.S.A. Fife*, 595; BOYD, *Ayrshire*, 187

13. MORGAN, *Rise and Progress*, 178; *C.C.M. 1881-2* OGILVIE

14. Balfour Commission, *Seventh Report*, H.M.S.O. 1890, viii

15. See KERR, *Annotated Code of 1905*, 82

16. *C.C.M. 1891-2*, 105-7

17. *C.C.M. 1892-3*, 137-8; *1895-6*, 138

18. *C.C.M. 1893-4*, xli-lviii

19. MORGAN, *Rise and Progress*, 181

20. RAE, *Allan Glen's School*, 37, 125, 128

21. STRONG, *Secondary Education*, 244; MORGAN, *Rise and Progress*, 181-2; *C.C.M. 1896-7*, 144

22. KNOX, *250 Years*, 127; CANT, *St Andrews*, 120

23. COUTTS, *Glasgow*, 451; GRANT, *Edinburgh*, 157-8

24. *Parker Committee 3*, xvi; *Circular 74*, 15 Jan 1886; *C.C.M. 1886-7*, 110-122

25. BONE, *Inspection*, 142; THOMAS B. DOBIE, *The Scottish Leaving Certificate, 1888-1908* (Glasgow University Ed.B. Thesis, 1964), 44-8, 92

26. *C.C.M. 1893-4*, 141

27. *C.C.M. 1887-8*, xlvii; *1888-89*, xxviii

28. *C.C.M. 1892-3*, 222; *1891-2*, 169-176; *1897-8*, 181; *1905-6*, 313; DOBIE, *S.L.C.*, 92-3

29. *S.E.D.R. 1951*, 9

30. *Circular 340 (1902)*

31. *S.E.D.R. 1951*, 10

32. *Education (Scotland) Act 1908*, section 15

33. *Circular 366 (1904)* para 5; letter from Craik, qu. KERR, *Annotated Code of 1905*, 224

34. ALISON, *Secondary School Journal*, Nov 1908, 66

35. *Day Schools (Scotland) Code 1899*, ch. ix; *C.C.M. 1899-1900*, 15; *1900-1*, 2; *1905-6*, 15; *1908-9*, Section E

36. *S.E.D.R. 1920-21*, Jamieson, 46; *C.C.M. 1902-3*, 717; *1908-9*, Andrew, C/66

37. KERR, *Scottish Education*, 323-5; WADE, *Post-Primary Education*, 110; KNOX, *250 Years*, 120
38. KERR, *Annotated Code of 1905*, 295
39. STRONG, *1918 Act*, 12
40. KNOX, *250 Years*, 218
41. BRODIE, WILLIAM, *Kelvinside Academy 1878-1923* (Glasgow 1924), *passim*
42. BLACK, *Story of Paisley*, 201
43. *T.S.A. Ayrshire*, 614
44. *Royal Technical College Calendar, 1914-15*; *C.C.M. 1901-2*, 740; *T.S.A. Fife*, 595; HARRISON, *Merchant Company*, 38
45. *Education (Scotland) Act 1918*, section 34
46. *S.E.D.R. 1925-6*, 12-14
47. *Education (Scotland) Act 1918*, section 4
48. WADE, *Post-Primary Education*, 164-5, Table 24
49. WADE, *Post-Primary Education*, 207, Table 28
50. M'LEAN, *Fordyce Academy*, 108, 130-4
51. BARCLAY, *Banffshire*, 139
52. *Proceedings of Classical Association, 1913-14*, 87
53. *Proceedings of Classical Association, 1906-7*, 16-22; *1910-11*, 97; *1913-14*, 88
54. *S.E.D.R. 1951*, 15-17, my percentages
55. NORRIE, JESSIE A., *Memories of the Old High School* (Kidd, Dundee 1924), 34
56. qu. ROSS, *Royal High School*, 68
57. *Demonstration School Logbook*, 230
58. BUCHANAN-DUNLOP in *Loretto's Hundred Years*, 155
59. SHEWAN, *Gymnasium*, 124
60. Education Department Examinations, Christmas 1875, 15-18
61. NORRIE, *Old High School*, 94
62. NORRIE, *Old High School*, 113
63. SHEWAN, *Gymnasium*, 133
64. WATSON in *Laurel Bank*, 11
65. *A.E.I. Centenary*, 40; JIM BUCHAN, *From Parish School to Academy: the Story of Education in the Parish of Peterculter* (Aberdeen County Council 1967), 26; *Demonstration School Logbook* 1912, 243; 1931, 56
66. *C.C.M. 1878-9* Dey, 154
67. FIRTH, *Ginn Series for Grammar Schools*, 1936-1949
68. *S.E.D.R. 1951*, 15-17, my percentages
69. M'LEAN, *Fordyce Academy*, 177
70. *Demonstration School Logbook*, 210
71. *St Leonard's School*, 53; *Demonstration School Logbook*, II, 89
72. *C.C.M. 1910-11*, Jamieson, B/25
73. *C.C.M. 1910-11*, Jamieson, B/26
74. *C.C.M. 1901-2*, Walker, 762

75. *C.C.M. 1881-2*
76. MASON, *Rural Education*, 165
77. SHEWAN, *Gymnasium*, 177
78. M'LEAN, *Fordyce Academy*, 76
79. *A.E.I. Centenary*, 51

CHAPTER 6

Social Assistance

FREE EDUCATION

> The school has become a central institution for the last quarter-
> century's development of many new services under the County
> Council; children's welfare foods are distributed, a savings group
> is run and a lunch-hour canteen-dining-hall caters for mid-day
> hungry mouths – a great contrast to the work of the ancient classical
> dominie.[1]

IN some ways the most striking development in modern Scottish
education has been a sweeping extension in the meaning of the word.
Four or five clauses in the Act of 1908 show early evidence of this
tendency: they compelled school boards and managers to provide
medical inspection and supervision for pupils, and permitted them to
provide cheap meals, assistance with travel, lodgings, books and equipment, and employment information; moreover sections 3, 5, and 6
made special arrangements for handicapped and neglected children.[2]
These provisions represented the first systematic intervention in such
matters by the state; the principle however had been enunciated in
the closing years of the nineteenth century, particularly by such
reformers as Margaret Macmillan, whose interest in education arose
through social welfare work. It seems obvious today – and is stated
explicitly in the 1946 Act – that every child should have such physical
assistance as will ensure his taking full benefit from his instruction.
But the early years of the twentieth century found Britain still busy
with legislation to provide reasonable living and working conditions
for most of her adult population; and the children's turn came later.

The first step in public social assistance for education was to make
the process free. There was reason in the suggestion that where a man
was forced to send his child to school, he should not have to pay money
as well. As we have seen, therefore, the Local Government Act of
1889 abolished fees in all compulsory classes under the Scottish Code,
and in the following year the Local Taxation (Customs and Excise)
Act provided forty thousand pounds, which were used to do away
with fees in Standards IV and V. Thereafter elementary education in
Scotland was to be had free by any child whose father would accept

it. It is interesting to note, however, that though this relief brought in many younger children, the percentage of these on public registers as late as session 1896-1897 was still by our standards low: 48·27 per cent of five-year-olds and 79·49 per cent of six-year-olds.[3] Some attended private schools, but many were still at no school at all.

The abolition of fees for secondary education was much slower in coming. Under article 134 of the Code of 1909, for example, almost all higher grade schools charged fees, admittedly fairly small, and they continued to do so until the twenties and thirties. The first statute to provide that education should be freely available for as long as a child's abilities entitled him to instruction was the Act of 1945.[4]

It was also in the 1930s that "free education" was interpreted to include the provision of books, writing materials and equipment. There had been provision in various areas before. The parish school at Kennoway in Fife for example had free books in 1882 and Banffshire children in 1890 were receiving needles, thread, pens and ink.[5] The Act of 1908 had allowed boards to award books where these were thought to be required[6] but in most cases this was interpreted as referring to poorer children. In 1939 however free books and stationery were given to all in the state schools, and the Act of 1945 made the practice compulsory. From 1918 onwards it was also lawful for authorities to provide books for general reading, usually by arrangement with local libraries.[7]

PHYSICAL AND MENTAL WELFARE

A more obvious form of assistance attempted to improve the physical condition of scholars. As we have seen a good deal of alarm was caused by the results of medical examinations for the Boer War and the Territorial Army, and by the Report of the Committee on Physical Deterioration, but the problem was of long standing. In the nineties the death roll among children under a year was 127·9 per 1,000, and we have already noted the high absence rate among pupils and teachers: of seven hundred students who qualified at Aberdeen Church of Scotland Training College between 1874 and 1895, fifty-five died in the same period. People near the poverty line accepted death as an ever-present fact, indeed in a perverse way they enjoyed it, with "demonstrations of exaggerated grief", but they did little to avoid it: St Saviour's Free Kindergarten for example had much trouble at first in cultivating their garden because their neighbours, disdaining refuse buckets, threw what they were finished with out of the nearest window.[8]

The earliest attempts at conquering the problem were free or cheap mid-day meals for needy or far-travelled children: in 1888 Mr Stewart of the inspectorate reported that warm dinners were being provided

in many country schools in the north and at the same period the school
board of Dundee found such meals a useful incentive to attract children
to school. In 1887 it gave 8,466 free, 23,993 at a halfpenny each, and a
few at a penny.[9] Peterculter children in 1884 could buy a bowl of soup
for a halfpenny, broth on Monday and Tuesday, potato on Wednesday
and Thursday, pea on Friday, prepared in a local cottage. A penny
dinner scheme was organised in 1888 by the headmaster of a Roman
Catholic school in Bridgeton, who helped to found a football club to
finance it, Glasgow Celtic. In Pitsligo in Aberdeenshire in 1905 hot
soup or potatoes or turnips were supplied by local farmers and cooked
by the school cleaner, while six years later Aberlour parish school
served 150 warm dinners daily by public subscription and mission
halls in Edinburgh gave free breakfasts on Sunday mornings.[10] But
these practices, though widespread, were not universal, and since no
public money was available for feeding and clothing necessitous
children, a number of voluntary institutions – day industrial schools
and refuges, the Buchanan Institution and the Poor Children's Dinner
Table Society – tried to fill the gap. The last-named served 850,000
dinners in 1909.[11]

At the same time, just before the First World War, some boards,
notably in Edinburgh, Dunfermline, Kirkcaldy, Govan and Glasgow,
were experimenting with medical inspection. The Carnegie Trust
founded a College of Hygiene and Physical Education at Dunfermline
in 1905 and financed medical inspection of all school children in the
same town from 1906; Dunfermline was also the first Scottish burgh
to benefit from the offer of free treatment.[12] In Glasgow in 1905
teachers were recording as part of their duties children's physical
measurements and standards of eyesight. By 1908 only a very small
number of the largest boards however paid doctors to conduct medical
examinations. The Act of that year laid down that "a school board may,
and where required by the Department, shall" provide for medical
examination and supervision. To begin with only large boards were
compelled, and since their authority was in towns, where the problem
was worst, this was not unsuitable. Five years later however the Act of
1913 compelled all boards and managers to provide medical treatment
for all necessitous children.[13]

The War broke out before the full effect of these provisions could
be felt. The 1918 Act made no mention of medical supervision, but the
Scottish Board of Health Act of the following year placed the scheme
under the supervision of the new board it was creating.[14] Compulsory
inspection of children was now becoming the rule, though in many
areas it was not effective until the thirties. The Act of 1945 stated the
law clearly: it became the duty of an authority to provide for medical
inspection and offer treatment for all the children in its schools. A
parent must submit his child for inspection, but need not accept
treatment.[15]

In the twenties an independent, largely voluntary movement began, concerned with the mental health of children. At Glasgow University in 1925 the Departments of Education and Psychology opened the first Scottish "child guidance clinic", whose aim was to study and advise on "problem children", boys and girls who because of physical, mental or social handicap found themselves maladjusted to their environment, or mentally unable to take full advantage of their schooling. At the outbreak of the Second World War there were eleven of these clinics – three each in Edinburgh and Glasgow, and one each in Aberdeen, Dundee, Paisley, Greenock and Kilmarnock. All but one were voluntary, the exception being run by the Glasgow authority.[16] The Act of 1945 encouraged authorities to open clinics and "county psychologists" were appointed in many districts for the first time.[17]

It was the Depression which brought to attention once more the need for free meals and clothing. The Education (Scotland) Act of 1930 had given authorities power to issue milk during the morning interval; now between 1931 and 1933 there was a rise of twenty per cent in free meals and sixty-six per cent in free issues of clothing; in the latter year 35,000 Scottish children received dinners free and 110,000 clothing. There were 15,000 pairs of free boots in Lanarkshire alone.[18] Thereafter there was a fall in the figures as trade recovered. With the outbreak of war again however and the breaking up of normal homes the need revived: Aberdeen Demonstration School for instance served meals daily at 3d each from September 1940, together with cod liver oil in the nursery and an issue of sweets from Canada and the United States, "at which children, staff and headmaster rejoiced exceedingly"[19]. In 1943 twenty-two per cent of Scottish children were being fed in school. The Act of 1945 made it the duty of authorities to provide milk and a mid-day meal for all children, though they might levy a small charge on parents who could afford to pay.[20] In effect this meant that all children except for a small number of resolute individualists received a third of a pint of milk during the morning interval; where cooking and dining facilities existed they also received a warm two-course dinner every day at a small weekly charge. Necessitous children not only had their dinners free, but might have all their meals, even on holidays and at week-ends.

BURSARIES, TRAVEL, LODGING, EMPLOYMENT

After education had been freed and the worst poverty removed, there still remained a number of obstacles. There were the "clever poor" who had more right to secondary and higher education than their parents' means could command. The traditional Scottish solution was the "bursary" provided for centuries by beneficent lairds and merchants. In the first half of the twentieth century an attempt was made to extend this throughout the country. The Act of 1908 gave secondary education committees the duty of administering endowments schemes in their areas; the 1918 measure went a step further in empowering the new authorities to pay fees, defray expenses and grant bursaries for bright children, even as far as the universities. All authorities submitted bursary schemes under the Act during the next eight years.[21] Nevertheless education authority bursaries, especially at school, were not plentiful before 1939. The Act of 1945 repeated in more precise terms the powers of its predecessors.[22] In the sixties however there were still many men and women of manifest ability who had left school long before their ability was extended, and who had spent the rest of their lives regretting the fact. Their influence was felt in various educational debates, particularly when a Socialist government was in power. By contrast, if their plans succeeded, one of the problems for the nineteen-eighties and nineties would be to find a balance in a community with few able but undereducated citizens.

Education was (and is) always difficult also for the child whose home was remote from the nearest school. An Inspector's report of 1877 pointed out:[23]

> There is another small school for 12 or 15 children kept in a room in a farmhouse by the side of Loch Katrine. Several of the scholars have to row themselves, or be rowed by their mothers, to and from the school, across the loch, which is there nearly a mile wide; the passage is not infrequently impossible, and is often attended with considerable risk.

For children under twelve the answer was often the one-teacher unit, with a roll of perhaps twenty boys and girls and an age range of seven years. In the lonelier districts of Argyll, Inverness, Ross and certain other counties however this was not a sufficient answer: children were no longer expected, as their fathers and grandfathers had been, to walk miles over moorland to and from school. The Acts of 1908 and 1918 permitted the authorities to make travel grants or arrangements, while that of 1945 laid down the duty of providing transport for children living outside walking distance, defined in the Code as two miles for those under eight, three for those over eight.[24]

The commonest provision was a school bus, calling at various farms and road-ends; where public services were reasonably handy pupils might be given free tickets or a grant to buy them. In remoter areas more ingenious solutions were required, taxis for example, as in East Lothian and some parts of Ayrshire and Lanarkshire in the late forties, a bicycle or even a pony in the north.[25] If all else failed the teacher might travel to the child: there were a few travelling teachers at work in the remotest areas, especially among the western islands.

Sometimes the solution was to provide board and lodging for the child near the school. The reason might not be simply remoteness:

one particular school might be best for the child, or his home might not be good. The Acts of 1908 and 1918 gave authorities permission to offer such lodging where they thought good, and that of 1945 confirmed this, though the consent of the parents had to be secured. Lodging might be in private houses: from Stenton in East Lothian for instance the best older pupils in 1948 went to Knox Academy and lodged in the village of Gifford at the expense of the education authority. In such cases the authority had to choose a landlord whose religious views were acceptable to the child's parents. Even so, however, not all fathers and mothers were satisfied: at Stenton there were claims that the boarded pupils were less amenable to discipline when they came home, and in any case took less interest in the life of their own community.

The commonest practice was to build hostels beside the main secondary school of the district. The first was opened at Dumfries in 1908 when Dr Thomas McKie bequeathed his mansion for that purpose. Andrew Carnegie provided one at Stornoway, and others appeared between the wars in Lerwick, Breadalbane, Hawick and Portree. In 1934 there were three in the county of Ross and six in Inverness. The average cost about 1930 ranged from £35 to £55 a session, and was often at least partly recovered from parents; after the Second World War however these charges rose steeply. By 1948 there were ten Scottish hostels for girls and nine for boys.[26]

No travel or boarding arrangements, however smooth and efficient, were universally popular. The Third Statistical Account had many complaints:[27]

The Education Act of 1918 has not been favourable to local community life in Cardross any more than in other villages. It has entailed the transfer of all children of twelve years and over from the village school to secondary schools in Dumbarton and Helensburgh. This has proved detrimental to village life, as well as to the local school.

And there was an unfortunate effect on the pupils themselves, who, as the schoolmaster of Clatt wrote,[28]

leaving early in the morning and coming home in the evenings, they are learning to become strangers to home and restless wanderers.

There was also the problem of the child who represented a source of family income while still at school, and who might be exploited when he was too young to protect himself. The Education (Scotland) Act of 1878 prohibited altogether the employment of children under ten; those from ten to fourteen might be employed only if they gained an inspector's certificate of competency in the three Rs. During holidays these provisions did not apply. Thereafter the principle was established: children might leave school before the prescribed age only if they had achieved a reasonable academic standard. There remained the case, very common in both town and country, of the child who took a paper round, or a milk delivery, or helped his parents in their shop, and might be at work from five a.m. until school time and as late as eight or nine o'clock in the evening. The Act of 1918 attacked this evil, by forbidding the employment of children under thirteen during school hours, before 8 a.m. and after 6 p.m. on a school day; if a child over thirteen had not been granted exemption, the same rules applied to him.[29] The Education (Scotland) Act of 1946 gave authorities, which had to enforce this law, the sanction of fines on parents and employers.[30]

ABNORMAL CHILDREN

With such assistance and protection normal children might be expected to derive as much benefit from their schooling as they were prepared to accept. A few however were not normal, and they also had to be catered for. Humanity made it difficult to find a general term for subnormal children: "handicapped", intended to show that their weakness was not their fault, acquired an undesirable ring, and the Act of 1945 called them "pupils requiring special educational treatment".[31] In any case this was a more precise name, since a pupil not at all handicapped might require special treatment.

As we have seen provision for these children was made in Scotland as early as the eighteenth century; from 1872 however the state took over the main responsibility. The Act of 1890 made grants to institutions for training blind children and deaf mutes, and that of 1906 obliged the school boards to provide education for such children where parents were unable to do so. In the years between the world wars the trend was to reduce special classes in ordinary schools and open more schools specially designed for this work:

Year	Classes	Schools
1930	60	52
1932	55	55
1934	52	57
1936	47	62
1939	46	62

Of the special schools listed in 1938 only a dozen were run by boards of management with direct aid from the Scottish Education Department; the remainder were established and maintained by the education authorities. Of the sixty-three in existence there were forty-six in the four cities, including twenty-four in Glasgow and fifteen in Edinburgh. Some counties had no special school, and some, including all the smallest, offered no provision of their own, sending handicapped children to neighbouring counties. During the Second World War the centralising trend continued, so that by 1947 there were eighty-five schools but only twenty-six special classes.

Most of these institutions were intended for children less spectacularly handicapped – the mentally deficient, physically crippled, and
those with impaired sight and hearing. Pupils just below the borderline
at which they might receive benefit from normal teaching were longest
in achieving special provision: as long ago as 1897 there were four
institutions for blind children and four for the deaf and dumb in
receipt of state aid;[32] in 1938 there were five of the former, three of the
latter. The majority of totally blind pupils went to the Royal Blind
School in Edinburgh; Donaldson's in the same city was probably the
most celebrated school for the deaf. It had reserved ninety-six places
for them since 1848 but from the outset expressly excluded mentally
defective children.[33]

Not all children in need of special treatment were mentally or physically handicapped. There was also the social misfit, the "young delin-
quent", often the product of his environment. It was to prevent these
developing that women like Margaret Macmillan and Lileen Hardy
opened their nursery schools:[34]

> Surely these dear children can never degenerate in later life to the
> class of unemployed and unemployable to which so many of their
> relatives belong?

and reduction of juvenile crime was the measure of success of Mission
and Ragged Schools. Once delinquents had developed however they
had to be dealt with – cured if possible, but in any case dealt with. In
1872 the institutions catering appropriately were the industrial and
reformatory schools. The former, regulated by the Industrial Schools
Act of 1854 and controlled after 1860 by the Home Department, were
intended for vagrant and homeless waifs, to prevent them sliding into
crime. For some time they remained residential, but an Act of 1893
extended the English system of day industrial schools north of the
border. Reformatories, begun by the Youthful Offenders Act of 1854,
dealt with ascertained delinquents; before the Reformatory Schools
Act of 1893 only children who had served a term of imprisonment
were committed to them.[35]

The Children and Young Persons (Scotland) Act of 1932 brought
together industrial and reformatory institutions in one category. Each
school of the new type was to cater for both delinquents and unfortunates, and it had to be "approved" by the Scottish Education Department; it was seldom used however until other methods had failed –
probation, detention in a remand home, committal to the care of a
local authority. All but one or two were under voluntary management,
with direct aid from the Department. As might be expected there were
no co-educational establishments. The staff, although they had no
special course of training, were subject to inspection, and rather more
highly paid than those in ordinary schools. The work however was
clearly a vocation, albeit a rewarding one.

Training in the schools was forced by the general intelligence of most pupils to concentrate on practical work like gardening, shoe-making and brick-laying. The important influence in any case was physical and moral rather than intellectual: the health of the pupils almost invariably improved, and the personal influence of individual members of the teaching and domestic staff might be crucial. Discipline was strict, though slowly relaxing over the period; in the last resort however it had to depend on the sympathy, discernment and unsentimental devotion of the teachers, together with, in Roman Catholic institutions especially, considerable reliance on religious training. There seemed for a time at least to be some evidence of success: the number of pupils decreased after the Second World War. But a reversal of this trend thereafter only served to demonstrate the perpetual complexity of the work. If delinquents are made by society, even partly, no improvement can be looked for without radically improving society; if the problem is one of human nature, the solution is even harder to find.

REFERENCES

1. *T.S.A. Aberdeenshire*, Clatt, 643
2. *Education (Scotland) Act 1908*, sections 3, 4, 5, 6, 20
3. *C.C.M. 1889-90*, 110-11; *1890-1*, xvi; *1896-7*, xv-xvi
4. *Education (Scotland) Act 1945*, section 11
5. *T.S.A. Fife*, 582; CORMACK, *Cramond*, Logbook 7 Oct 1890
6. *Education (Scotland) Act 1908*, section 3
7. *Education (Scotland) Act 1945*, section 11; *Education (Scotland) Act 1918*, section 5; *Demonstration School Logbook*, 135
8. STRONG, *1918 Act*, 18; *Joseph Ogilvie and His First 21 Classes* (Aberdeen 1896) 17; HARDY, *Free Kindergarten*, 13, 107
9. *C.C.M. 1888-9* Stewart, 282-3; *Parker Committee 3*, Moncur
10. BUCHAN, *Parish School to Academy*, 22-3; BARCLAY, *Banffshire*, 158; HARDY, *Free Kindergarten*, 36; *T.S.A. Aberdeenshire*, Pitsligo 341; SKINNIDER, *Catholic Education*, 67
11. *C.C.M. 1904-5*, 399; MORRISON, *Compulsory Education*, 99
12. *T.S.A. Fife*, Dunfermline, 349
13. *Education (Scotland) Act 1908*, section 4; *C.C.M. 1914-15*, 14; *Circular 321*, 31 March 1909
14. *S.E.D.R. 1919-20*, 24-5
15. *Education (Scotland) Act 1945*, section 38
16. *S.E.D.R. 1939*, A/42
17. *Education (Scotland) Act 1945*, Section 6
18. *S.E.D.R. 1933-34* A/25
19. *Demonstration School Logbook*, ii, 156-68
20. *Education (Scotland) Act 1945*, section 36

21. *Education (Scotland) Act 1908*, section 30; *Education (Scotland) Act 1918*, section 4; *S.E.D.R. 1926-7*, A/18
22. *Education (Scotland) Act 1945*, section 32
23. "Notes from the Past", *S.E.J.* 13 Dec 1963
24. *Education (Scotland) Act, 1908*, section 3; *Education (Scotland) Act 1918*, section 4; *Education (Scotland) Act 1945*, section 34; *Schools (Scotland) Code 1950*
25. *T.S.A. East Lothian*, Saltoun, 272; *T.S.A. Ayrshire*, 208
26. *S.E.D.R. 1928-9*, A/24; *1929-30*, A/26; *1933-4*, A/20; *1948*, 34
27. *T.S.A. Dunbartonshire*, 206
28. *T.S.A. Aberdeenshire*, 643
29. *Education (Scotland) Act 1918*, section 16, 17
30. *Education (Scotland) Act 1946*, section 136
31. *Education (Scotland) Act 1945*, section 7
32. *C.C.M. 1896-7*, 34-49
33. *Documents relating to Donaldson's Hospital*, Edinburgh 1902, xi, 59
34. HARDY, *Free Kindergarten*, 116
35. KNOX, *250 Years*, 181-2

CHAPTER 7 | # The Training of Teachers

THE POSITION AFTER 1872

THE Act of 1872 made no provision for the training of teachers. It demanded that all new teachers after that date should be certificated, but left the work of professional preparation in the care of the churches. Since training was the safest path to certification most entrants in the following two decades, except graduates, for whom there was other provision, went through one of the colleges. As early as 1877 a letter from the Scotch Education Department stated the official opinion that the number of students at church colleges was too great for the demand, and proposed to reduce it from 971 to 700 with effect from 1880. In 1883 the proportion of teachers with some training in Scottish schools was as follows:

	Masters	Mistresses
Period of Training	*(per cent)*	
Two years	61·5	68·6
One year	9·9	4·6
Less than one	2·5	0·3
None at all	26·1	26·4

In short, only one teacher in four was completely untrained. The Departmental Committee on Training Colleges, reporting in 1888, counted 3,601 male certificated teachers, of whom three-quarters were "fully trained", and the corresponding figures for women were 3,425 and two-thirds. Some school boards – Glasgow for example where in 1895 the proportion of trained to untrained teachers was twenty-six to one – would employ nothing but trained teachers for new posts. Others, more remote, could not afford to be so strict: in the other parishes of the Western Division the ratio was about five to two. Roman Catholic schools, with no Scottish seminary until 1895, were in the worst position, yet they could boast five trained to four untrained teachers on their staffs. Untrained teachers, both Protestant and Catholic, included a large number of university graduates, but inspectors were universally convinced that a training college man was to be preferred to an untrained graduate.[1]

G

THE CHURCHES AND PUPIL TEACHERS

Scotland's training institutions remained until the end of the century under the management of various churches, but the training they gave was not rigidly denominational. For one thing all of them after 1872 came under the inspection of the same man, Dr Wilson.[2] In 1888 the Parker Committee reported that about sixty or seventy per cent of students in the Presbyterian colleges belonged to the parent denomination, training centres often being chosen according to practical convenience rather than conscience. Even the staffs of the Church of Scotland and Free Church institutions, other than the Rectors, were not religiously tested. In 1890 for example the Established Church college in Edinburgh had two United Presbyterian lecturers, one Free Churchman and an Episcopalian.[3] By the turn of the century collaboration between the Presbyterian colleges was common: they had periodic conferences and, from 1902, a common prospectus. The process had gone so far, indeed, that Dr Stewart, Her Majesty's Inspector, suggested in 1900 that it was time for them to be combined.[4]

The position of Episcopalians and Catholics was less simple. Some of the former elected to attend the Presbyterian colleges, though there was an Episcopalian institution for women in Edinburgh. Its Principal, the Reverend Dr Smith, complained in evidence before the Departmental Committee of 1888 that his students, having completed their course, were frozen out of the Scottish schools, and as many as three-quarters had to go to London or other parts of England for a post. The Committee pointed out that the College output was thirty a year, that only eight were required by Scottish Episcopal schools, and that half the students in any case came from northern England. There appears to be a legitimate deduction that a number of school boards preferred Presbyterian to Episcopalian applicants for posts, and that several Episcopalian students preferred to take their training in Presbyterian colleges. Catholics were less inclined to mix, though one witness before the same Committee stated that a few were attending the Church of Scotland institution in Glasgow at the time. On the other hand this was stated by another witness to be uncommon, and the convener of the Free Church Education Committee deposed that there were none in his colleges. In 1872 a Roman Catholic girl had done well in the Free Church entrance examination and had been granted a bursary, but her case seems to have been very rare.[5]

In general then there was little to choose on denominational grounds between the Church of Scotland and Free Church Colleges. Yet the latter institution in Glasgow, particularly in the seventies, for which period the minutes of both colleges are available, enjoyed an atmosphere of superior tranquillity and efficiency. The first case to warrant mention in the Free Church minutes after 1872 occurred in September 1885, when three students, who had absented themselves from classes for two hours and had been found by the Rector in a public house, were severely censured, deprived of part of their bursary and compelled to read a public apology.[6] All other difficulties in Cowcaddens were financial. On the other hand, the five years after 1872 at the Established Church College were not at all placid. In 1875 there are references to five different students who were admonished for neglect of studies and disrespect. A few months later a pupil teacher had to be warned about poor conduct and inadequate preparation. The standard of work produced was not always satisfactory: Dr Wilson had to request several explanations, a thing he never had to do at the Free Church College. Moreover the staff was not happy with its Rector. The master of the Training Department, in particular, was cautioned once or twice, and the Rector stipulated that he must not leave the College during working hours without permission. The rules for discipline laid down by the Rector, Mr Leitch, became increasingly positive and severe, without apparent success. Finally, in the spring of 1877, unrest reached a climax. In the "riot of 7th June", which broke out when a holiday was postponed and several bursaries were withheld on grounds of discipline, seventeen students absented themselves without leave, several crackers were exploded in class, and a meeting of protest was held in the lobby outside the Rector's room. Three of the lecturers, who did not see eye to eye with Mr Leitch, appealed to their students in their own way, thereby widening the breach. The Rector sought to rusticate eleven students and asked several of his staff to resign, but he failed to carry the Committee with him. The upshot was that Leitch himself and the three malcontent masters were requested to resign, and a number of male students were "signally punished" by the Education Department. Nevertheless it was some years before the institution recovered from a situation in which "the general discipline and moral tone of the male students was very bad, and relations between staff and students were very strained". As late as 1894 a comparison of the results of certificate examinations showed only 149 of the first class in Dundas Vale against 210 in the Free Church institution of the same size.[7]

From 1874 to 1906 the Established Church ran three colleges; the third, for women only, was opened in the earlier year in Aberdeen, and extended in 1887 to male students. Teacher training, indeed, during the last thirty years of the nineteenth century, was "the principal permanent function of the General Assembly's Education Committee."[8] In 1877, just before the reduction in numbers enforced by the Scotch Education Department, almost five hundred students were taking a two-year course in Glasgow, Edinburgh and Aberdeen. All, except for a handful of women, had been pupil teachers; the most brilliant were awarded Queen's Scholarships, one or two secured Gaelic scholarships offered by the Church, and the rest were self-supporting.[9] The session, after changes enforced by the 1875 Code to bring it into line with the universities, ran from August to June instead of January to November, and the entrance examination was held in July of each year. It was conducted by the Education Department, with papers in reading, writing and dictation, English grammar, composition, arithmetic (with algebra and three books of Euclid), the geography of the earth (including maps), outlines of British history, musical notation, transposition and singing, school management, Latin or another language, and scripture (including the parables and Shorter Catechism). The papers, revised by Her Majesty's Inspectors, were ranked and passed on to the Assembly committee, which chose the best candidates for admission. There was room for no more than a third of those who passed, and the Committee gave special consideration to those who did well in the religious test. The prescription for this examination included the Old Testament up to the Book of Judges, and some examples of the problems set are:[10]

> Give an outline of the life of Abraham, and point out those events in which his "faith" was strikingly exemplified.
> Define a Parable. State the subject of which the Parables of Our Lord mainly treat.
> "What is Justification?" Give the words of the answer, with Scripture proofs.

Despite the imposing nature of the examination, the College staffs had occasion to complain of the poor standard of work done by applicants. In 1879 only twelve out of three hundred passed in Latin,[11] and complaints continued to be made for many years as part of the general attack on the low standard reached by pupil teachers.

The Committee of 1888 stated its opinion that the course of study in training colleges tended to be unduly narrow, since it was restricted to elementary subjects and methods of instruction, and crushed into two years; for any higher studies a university training was essential.[12] The subjects taught in 1877 may be seen from the timetables on the following pages of the Established Church Seminary in Glasgow.[13]

A striking feature of these timetables is the amount of time spent on general subjects at no very high standard; it was still necessary, despite Stow's strictures, to educate as well as train the student.* The curriculum of professional training included lectures on school organisation and discipline, a course on "Practical Educationists" and one on the "art of teaching", with daily practice in the attached day school, whose pupils ranged in age from three to fifteen, and half-day visits to various Glasgow elementary schools like Oatlands, Dobbie's Loan and Kennedy Street. Five years later the curriculum for women was changed by the Department's advice to include psychological principles, and in 1883 the Inspector gave his approval to a much more ambitious professional course at the Dundas Vale College, including forty lectures on the

* The Free Church colleges were in no better condition in this matter.

MEN – FIRST YEAR

	9-10	10-11	11-12	12-1	1-2	2-3	3-4
Monday	Grammar Sch. Man. Dictation	Arith. Maths.	History Geog.	Latin	Rel. Ed. Reading Compos.	Magnet- ism Electr.	Drawing
Tuesday	do.	Physi- ology	do.	Latin Hist.	Geology	Music	do.
Wednesday	do.	Arith. Maths.	do.	Latin	Rel. Ed. Reading Compos.	Magnet- ism Electr.	do.
Thursday	do.	Physi- ology	Greek	Latin Geog.	Geology	Music	do.
Friday	do.	Arith. Maths.	do.	Latin	Rel. Ed. Reading Compos.	Magnet- ism Electr.	do.

MEN – SECOND YEAR

	9-10	10-11	11-12	12-1	1-2	2-3	3-4
Monday	Arith. Maths.	History Geog.	Grammar Latin Reading	Rel. Ed. Sch. Man. Greek	Teaching	Music	Drawing
Tuesday	Physi- ology	Geology	do.	do.	Latin	Magnet- ism Electr.	do.
Wednesday	Arith. Maths.	History Geog.	do.	do.	Teaching	Music	do.
Thursday	Physi- ology	Geology	do.	do.	Latin	Magnet. Electr.	do.
Friday	Arith. Maths.	History Geog.	do.	do.	Teaching	Music	do.

Male students also had drill on two mornings each week from 8.30 to 9 a.m.

WOMEN – FIRST YEAR

	9-10	10-11	11-12	12-1	1-2	2-3	3-4
Monday	History Geog.	Grammar Compos. Sch. Man.	Arith.	Dom. Econ. Needlework	Rel. Ed. Dictat. Reading	French	Drawing
Tuesday	do.	do.	do.	do.	French	Music	do.
Wednesday	do.	do.	do.	do.	Rel. Ed. Dictat.	French	do.
Thursday	do.	do.	do.	do.	French	Music	do.
Friday	do.	do.	do.	do.	Rel. Ed. Dictat.	Botany	do.

WOMEN – SECOND YEAR

	9-10	10-11	11-12	12-1	1-2	2-3	3-4
Monday	Dom. Econ. Needlework	Rel. Ed. Sch. Man.	Teaching	History Geog.	Arith.	Music	Drawing
Tuesday	do.	do.	do.	Grammar Dictat. Reading	do.	French	do.
Wednesday	do.	do.	do.	History Geog.	do.	Music	do.
Thursday	do.	do.	do.	Grammar Reading Botany	do.	French	do.
Friday	do.	do.	do.	History Geog.	do.	Music	do.

science of education, with special reference to Spencer and Locke, and twenty on educational history. The "great educators" treated were Luther, Ascham, the Jesuits, Comenius, Milton, Locke (three lectures), Rousseau, Pestalozzi (three), Jacotot, Bell, Lancaster, Froebel (three), Arnold and Stow (two).[14]

One interesting feature of the timetables reproduced above is that there is no period set aside for lunch. The visiting inspector in 1883 remarked that some provision for a hot meal was badly needed in most colleges, and probably no more than a few minutes were allowed for the consumption of sandwiches. It is hardly surprising that the medical history of the students was more eventful than at the present day; Dr J. R. Dickson reported in 1877 that[15]

> of the health of the students attending the College this year I have to report: of the females one died, another was invalided; of the males two were invalided, another was off for a few weeks having ruptured a blood-vessel; the others have all enjoyed as good health as in any previous year. No cause of illness could be attributed to connection with the College.

The course culminated in a government examination for a certificate of competency. Students leaving college were graded "Excellent", "Good', "Fair and "Under Fair", the percentages in each category in 1877 being 15·1, 37·6, 32·2 and 15·1[16]. Thereafter their performance in the Inspectors' examination was marked, if successful, by a certificate of Class I, II, III or IV.

Apart from the general atmosphere of efficiency already mentioned in Glasgow, the features of the Free Church colleges showed few variations from those described in the Established Church institutions. One for women was opened in Aberdeen in 1875, a year after that of the Church of Scotland, and was extended to men in 1887. So similar were the colleges of the two churches that in evidence before the Departmental Committee of 1888 Dr Dickson, convener of the Church of Scotland committee, proposed their amalgamation under joint management.[17] Entrance examinations, curriculum, timetables and certificate examinations were identical or similar. In both types pupil-teachers formed over ninety per cent of the intake, and since many Free Churchmen attended an Established college and *vice versa*, it is not easy to find reasons for their choice. One possible answer refers to conditions of residence. The Church of Scotland college possessed a large boarding-house in Glasgow, and it was laid down by the Committee in 1876 that all girls not at home in the city or its immediate neighbourhood must reside in this hostel. The Rector of the local Free Church college, on the other hand, stated in 1888 that residence was unnecessary, since students could be at home in Airdrie, Hamilton, Greenock, Coatbridge or Renfrew by 4·30 p.m.[18]

The administration of the two types of college shows great similarity.

There are the same formal but sometimes grim medical reports. Students appear to take their work equally seriously: in 1873 Dr Adams of the Free Church reported that[19]

> with one exception there has been no serious ailment. Nothing beyond petty disorders of digestion as will occur among young individuals, who are occasionally careless in the times of taking food, or of going to rest, when eagerly absorbed in their studies.

No more than a handful failed to fulfil the conditions of their training by refusing to adopt a teaching career: the first in the history of the Free Church College in Glasgow did not occur until 1883, when one man broke off his course to enlist in the army.[20] The career of one girl at the end of the century may stand as typical of many others. In January 1895, at the age of eighteen, having already had a secondary education, she became a pupil teacher in the Dovehill centre in Glasgow. A contract was signed between the Glasgow School Board and her father as surety, by which she undertook to teach from three to six hours a day and for twenty-five hours a week. In return she was paid £16 in her first year and £20 in her second, and given five hours a week of instruction in teaching after school hours. She was liable to dismissal without notice for idleness, disobedience or "immorality of a gross kind". After two years she gained her Pupil Teacher's Certificate, an imposing document setting out her entire course and signed by the Chairman of the School Board, the Convener of the Pupil Teachers' Committee, the Clerk to the Board, the Headmaster of the Day School and the Headmaster of the Pupil Teachers' Institute. In October 1897 she entered the Free Church College in Cowcaddens, though her own denomination was Church of Scotland; she gained a Queen's Scholarship on the result of her entrance examination, being placed 37th in the College list and 109th in Scotland. After a two year course she was awarded her certificate in June 1899, signed by the Rector and his entire staff. Finally, after two years as a probationer, she was eligible for her "parchment certificate" and became a qualified teacher.

For twenty years after 1872 the only church college other than those already mentioned was run in Edinburgh by the Episcopal Church. It remained independent until 1920 and in the half-century after 1867 (when it was reserved for women) it trained 1,744 students, turning out about 30 each year. Many of these came from, and even more returned, south of the border. One other college, small as it was, is of interest – St George's Edinburgh, founded in 1886 to meet the need for training women teachers, especially for secondary schools. Its students were presented for the diploma of the Teachers' Training Syndicate of Cambridge. Two years later a high school for girls was founded in connexion with it.[21]

The young men and women who took up a teaching career in the last quarter of the nineteenth century came mainly from the industrial classes, though some women were daughters of clergymen and doctors. Well over ninety per cent had been pupil teachers and this would seem to justify the scheme as a whole.[22] Nevertheless throughout the period it came under sustained criticism. The system, wrote Dr Stewart, H.M.I., in 1894[23]

> has never flourished in the soil of this country nor adapted itself to the needs of our schools. It is a compromise at best; and like all other compromises, while it does not provoke active hostility, it affords satisfaction to nobody.

The work was hard: in Edinburgh many had to teach from 8.30 to 3.30, then attend instructional classes and conclude with five hours of homework.[24] Small wonder that, as one Aberdeenshire pupil teacher remembered,[25]

> it was not a joyous thing to go into the school at half past seven of a winter's morning, and teach the livelong day, in the prospect of lessons again at night.

Conditions of service were restricted: candidates had to be of the same sex as the teacher they served, though in a mixed school girls were allowed to work with a master so long as[26]

> some respectable woman, approved by the managers, be invariably present during the whole time that such instruction is being given.

Many regarded the course simply as a convenient method of getting a higher education, and this they were entitled to do, since their teaching fulfilled their contract. Homework in Cullen in 1875 included Xenophon, Livy and Melvin's Latin prose.[27] Nevertheless the number who fell by the way or refused to go on into training colleges aroused criticism.[28] Moreover the standards achieved were not high: in the view of the Director of Studies of the Edinburgh Training Centre, "what was generally the fact is that he could manage a class and maintain discipline."[29] In Dumfries, Kirkcudbright and Wigtown, out of 146 examined by the inspector in 1877 only nine were classified as "good", with ninety-two "fair" and forty-five "below fair". By the end of the century it was clear that the days of the system were numbered; in 1904 it had virtually died out in rural areas.[30]

CONCURRENT UNIVERSITY COURSES

The girl whose training we traced had one interesting entry on her college record. It stated that she had attended a class in mathematics at Glasgow University concurrently with her training. This arrangement had been in operation since 1873. Its origin was dissatisfaction with the quality of the average teacher's personal education at the end of his course: the colleges, one of their principals later wrote, "tended to produce mechanical, mill-horse teachers".[31] The content of the syllabus, as shown in the 1905 examinations, seems to bear this out. English in the First Year included parsing, analysis, grammar, a study of *Comus* (Book Two) and Carlyle's *Essay on Burns* and to "write plain prose on a given subject"; the Second Year prescription was *The Tempest, The Advancement of Learning* (Book One), eighteenth-century English literature and an essay. History involved "a general knowledge of the most important events of English and Scottish history, with dates" and especially eighteenth-century British history, with marked reference to the constitution, military operations and literature. Mathematics dwelt much on Euclid and ventured no higher than the binomial theorem.[32]

The credit for publicly suggesting concurrent attendance at university classes was claimed by an inspector, Dr John Kerr, who recommended it in a report of 1865. Permission was given in the Code of 1873 and two years later thirty-two students were taking advantage of the arrangement.[33] Between 1874 and 1878, as numbers increased steadily, one hundred and ten men enrolled from the Church of Scotland colleges in Glasgow and Edinburgh and 263 from those of the Free Church. In 1881, 53 out of 171 men in the Established Church institutions attended. Thereafter however, though there was no readily assignable reason for fluctuation, the total tended to decline – 191 from all colleges in 1886, 182 in 1887, only 159 in 1888.[34] Ten years later, when John Adams became rector of the Free Church Training College in Glasgow, he insisted, with only two exceptions, on all male students with the necessary qualifications attending university classes, and the opening of the universities to women caused the figures to rise again: in 1902 one hundred and thirty of the two hundred and fifty students in Adams' college were involved.[35]

The subjects studied were usually Latin, Greek or mathematics. It was possible however for the more gifted student to win a bursary offered by the training college and so return for a third year to the university. He had to provide some of his own books and was expected to study for the qualification of Literate in Arts which, lacking the status of a degree, was yet a warrant of satisfactory higher education. Two bursaries are mentioned in the Edinburgh Church of Scotland College in 1877, but the first in the Free Church intended for third year study dates from 1890.[36]

The work of these concurrent students did not always meet with university approval. Professor Ramsay deposed in 1888 that most of them lost a great deal of time over examination periods in each institution, and added that few were able to attend for more than an hour a day. On the other hand many were distinguished students. At the Glasgow Established Church College in 1880 nine students took seven-

teen university prizes, and Free Church candidates won twenty-two
out of sixty given in 1892 in the classes of mathematics, Latin, Greek,
English and logic. Some determined scholars continued their studies
after they began work and took a degree of the University of London;
others were able to graduate after a shortened course at Glasgow,
Edinburgh or Aberdeen.[37] The most celebrated student in the history
of the Free Church colleges was the above mentioned John Adams,
who qualified at Cowcaddens, Glasgow, in 1876, graduated at the
university in arts and science, and became headmaster of a school in
Port Glasgow. From there he went as rector to the Free Church
Training College in Aberdeen, returning in 1898 to take over the
Glasgow institution. His tenure of that post lasted only four years,
during which time, with the permission of the Committee, he was
appointed lecturer in education at Glasgow University, and at the
invitation of McGill University spent the summer of 1902 investigating
the condition of Protestant schools in the province of Quebec. In
August of the same year he was appointed Professor of Education in
the University of London, and left Glasgow to continue a brilliant
career which culminated in a knighthood.[38]

There was a sharp decline before the First World War in the number
and proportion of training college students in such courses – 46 per
cent in 1906-7, 22 per cent in 1911-12.[39] The principle of concurrency
none the less was upheld in various sets of training regulations during
the first half of the twentieth century. Until 1912 the duration of a
concurrent course was three years; thereafter it was extended to four,
with modification of professional classes to suit individual requirements.
In Aberdeen Training College twenty or thirty students entered on
the concurrent course each session, not always at the first year, though
many never completed a degree. With a hiatus between 1925 and 1931
the course continued to thrive moderately until after the Second World
War. From 1945 however the entries dwindled, and there were many
cases of students discontinuing the course in favour of consecutive
rather than concurrent study. The last four-year students completed
their course in 1955.[40]

UNIVERSITY LOCAL COMMITTEES

One problem which this arrangement was designed to tackle was that
of providing more trained teachers for the higher class and higher
grade schools; the scheme took students in training and raised their
educational standard. An alternative was to take university men (and
later women) and give them training as teachers. We have already seen
that St George's College in Edinburgh attempted to provide the equivalent for women; for men provision had existed since 1873, when article
47(c) of the Scotch Code laid down that any graduate, after three

months training in a state-aided school approved by a Senior Inspector, might qualify for a certificate. He was examined by an Inspector, and had to teach lessons in arithmetic and reading.[41] There was general agreement among critics, however, that this requirement, demanding only eight hours of training a week for twelve weeks, was too lenient. Professor Laurie stated before the Departmental Committee of 1888 that a minimum period of six months continuous training was essential, and the Committee backed this in its general recommendations. Meanwhile in 1884 more than one of the universities had indicated a desire to take a hand in training teachers, and entered into correspondence with the Scotch Education Department. As early as 1872 one of Her Majesty's Inspectors, Mr Jolly, had advocated the establishment of university Departments of Education, including training classes; now the Senates of Aberdeen and St Andrews proposed schemes whereby a Professor of Education would deliver lectures on philosophy and instruction in teaching methods, while practice would be conducted in local schools. The difficulties of such an arrangement were recognised to be the lack of suitable practising schools, especially in St Andrews, and the existence of two perfectly good training colleges in Aberdeen.[42] The gallantry of the universities in offering to conduct classes on how to teach day by day in the schools might also have warranted mention.

In the event nothing was done to alter the law for another decade. In 1887 however one of the universities decided not to await a change: Edinburgh instituted a professional diploma for teachers, while Glasgow had a similar step under consideration. It consisted mainly of theoretical instruction; restricted to arts graduates of Edinburgh, it was conferred on the results of an examination in the theory, art and history of education, with reference to Locke, Milton, Comenius and the lectures given during the course. It was intended as a qualification for secondary teachers, but was not granted official recognition by the Education Department until 1895.[43] The recommendation of the Departmental Committee of 1888 was that training institutions should continue to occupy the centre of the system, though some combination with the universities was desirable. This encountered the difficulty that the universities, conscious of their high educational standing, were unwilling to admit inferiority in any undertaking to such vocational institutions. There was no general practice yet of graduates attending training colleges for instruction.

In 1895 the Department recognised the desires of the universities. The Code of that year stated that it would recognise Local Committees set up by any of the universities to give professional as well as academic training to students. Bursaries were also provided for: on the analogy of the "Queen's Scholars" at training colleges, a number of candidates might receive awards as "Queen's Students". At the same time all university Diplomas of Education were recognised; they were in time to become the first stage of a higher degree in education.[44]

Aberdeen and St Andrews at once took advantage of the new provisions, and opened Local Committees in the session beginning in 1896, each with three students. Another centre appeared in 1901 at Dundee, where there were eleven students, under the aegis of the University of St Andrews. The number of Queen's Students increased rapidly from 6 in 1896-7 to 69 in 1898-9, 110 in 1900-1 and 333 in 1905-6.[45] Glasgow was slow to set up a Local Committee. The decision was not taken until May 1903, when the first meeting to constitute the body was held. It made use of the arrangements already operating elsewhere, modelling its "student's obligation" on that of Aberdeen and its form of application on that of St Andrews. The Committee contained representatives of the school boards, the Educational Institute of Scotland, the Royal Technical College and the local churches besides the University. John Clark, university lecturer in education, was appointed Director, and the headmaster of Shields Road School Master of Method. A music master, a medical officer and a Lady Warden (who would also teach needlework and methods) were also engaged at once. There were thirty students in the first session, receiving a professional course consisting of needlework, gymnastics, science, singing, drawing, English, religious knowledge, phonetics and methods. A number of local schools – five at first, their names disclosed by the giving of honoraria to the janitors – were used for criticism lessons. Soon the attendance had risen to 150 and planning for 1906 was on a basis of 350.[46]

PROVINCIAL COMMITTEES AND JUNIOR STUDENTS

The needs of Roman Catholics were met in 1894, when a house was acquired in Dowanhill, Glasgow, and a training college opened for women by Sister Mary of St Wilfrid and four other sisters of Notre Dame, a teaching order which had been responsible since 1854 for a similar college at Liverpool. Its first two classes each contained twenty-three students and the course extended over the customary two years. The first visit by an inspector, which occurred in May 1895, showed some interesting facts. There was an entrance fee of £5, and books and stationery had to be paid for. There were no bursaries for this, but all tuition was free. The practising schools were inconveniently situated, at least ten minutes away. One was built beside the college in 1897, but visits continued to five nearby Catholic schools. Comparatively few of the early students were natives of Scotland, and it is legitimate to wonder whether the problem was quite as urgent as the inspectors' reports had suggested, or alternatively whether Catholic men and women were sufficiently alive to it.[47]

There was now provision for the training of both primary and secondary teachers; the danger was that this might contribute still further to the widening gap between the two types of schools. School boards began to encourage students to aim as high as possible: in 1902 seven girls left the Glasgow Free Church college because Govan School Board allowed them to attend Queen Margaret College and teach at the same time. The status of the training institutions was raised, however, when in 1901 the Scotch Education Department put an end to the external examination which had come at the end of the course. Minute 329 of that year gave the colleges complete liberty to draw up their own courses of education and conduct all their own examinations. This gave the work a powerful stimulus, and the Department found no cause to repeal its decision.[48]

By the end of the century a girl intending to be a teacher might, according to her talent, ambition and religious persuasion, receive training in any of a dozen institutions. The Established and the Free Church had three colleges each, in Glasgow, Edinburgh and Aberdeen. The Roman Catholic and the Scottish Episcopal Church had one each. There were three and there would soon be four university departments operating under Local Committees. Finally there was St George's College in Edinburgh, supplying women secondary teachers. The Departmental Committee of 1888 had considered the abandonment of denominational colleges, which seemed to many critics wasteful of money and effort, but it decided that substitution would be difficult, and so recommended their continuance, with liberal government grants. By 1905 however the annual output of all these colleges was only seven hundred, leaving four hundred places a year to be filled by the untrained.[49] It was generally felt that the central authority must combine all facilities in a system.

In November 1904, just as Struthers was taking over as Secretary of the Department, a letter was sent to all colleges inviting representatives to a meeting in Edinburgh. A Minute followed on 30 January 1905 establishing new bodies called "Provincial Committees for the Training of Teachers". There were to be four provinces, based on the universities, with provision for a fifth, when it became expedient, at Inverness. Each committee would provide courses of training for both primary and secondary teachers. School boards, if they wished to qualify for grant, must provide facilities for teaching practice, a stipulation of great value for the training courses. Committees were to erect training centres as soon as possible and appoint directors of studies.

The position of existing training bodies was described. Local Committees would terminate their work on 31 July 1905 and become subcommittees to train King's Students until the new bodies could take full charge. The churches might if they desired sell or rent their premises and turn over their work to the new authorities, who would guarantee that staff would be employed and religious dogma respected; church representatives would be co-opted to the new Committees.[50] These guarantees satisfied the Education Committees of the Established and Free Churches, whose colleges were duly transferred; the Episcopal College came under the Edinburgh Committee; but the Roman Catholic institution maintained an independent existence.

The effect of the new legislation may be studied in detail in Glasgow, whose first Provincial Committee had five members elected by the University Court, four representing the Central Institutions, twenty-three from school boards as far afield as Inverness and Ross (with two, three and four members for the larger boards), three managers of important secondary schools, three co-opted members who were actively engaged in schools or colleges in the province, Church representatives and the Chief Inspector as an assessor. The Church of Scotland and the Free Church could each nominate five representatives; they also added the proviso, which was accepted, that religious instruction must be an integral part of the curriculum of study.[51]

The next problem was accommodation. The six Presbyterian colleges were handed over in May 1907, and the new system came into force in October of the same year. In Edinburgh the Free Church Rector retired, and Dr Morgan of the Established College became Director of Studies. In Glasgow the Free Church Rector retired, and a similar arrangement was made possible. All members of the two staffs who wished to continue were employed. There was however a sharp rise in the number of students, and accommodation was stretched to the limit. Edinburgh used three buildings, in Chambers Street, Moray House and Johnstone Terrace Practising School. Glasgow had Dundas Vale, Cowcaddens and some class-rooms in the University and Queen Margaret College. Aberdeen used the two church colleges and some rooms in the Marischal buildings. St Andrews was worst off, for there had been no church college in the province: the King's student centres at Dundee and St Andrews were coordinated, but more room was urgently required. A Joint Committee was set up in 1906 to standardise procedure throughout the country, and building plans were prepared,[52] but only Edinburgh managed to complete its scheme before the outbreak of the Great War. Moray House was ready in 1913, but hostilities called a halt in the other provinces. Aberdeen and Dundee centres were completed in 1919. The most ambitious building, at Jordanhill in Glasgow, was not ready until 1921, and for a time the Glasgow Committee had to have the use of some lecture rooms and offices in the Royal Technical College.[53] When the new building was opened the organisation of training in Scotland had again been altered.

The establishment of Provincial Committees in 1906 marked the time for revising the regulations governing admission to training and courses available. The pupil-teacher system had now endured a running fire of criticism for sixty years; there was also a general feeling, concentrated by the Educational Institute, that the days of the untrained teacher should be numbered. New Regulations proposed in 1905 revised the law and tackled both problems: two types of students were to be recognised, Senior and Junior, and pupil-teachers were to vanish. There was strenuous opposition to this proposal however, mainly by authorities which had found pupil-teachers a cheap contribution to staffing. Their place was to be taken by Junior Students, who must have reached the age of fifteen and gained an intermediate certificate and would then undertake three years of education and training in a secondary institution recognised as a "Junior Student Centre." The scheme, it was felt, was bound to produce better-educated teachers. But the Kilsyth School Board Chairman's "own candid unbiased opinion" was that "no great breadth of culture is needed to teach a, b – ab and s, o – so,"[54] and there were many of his mind. The substantive regulations of 1906 allowed pupil-teachers to continue along with students of the new category. In effect however they died out, existing ones having their indentures cancelled and becoming junior students. In 1907 there were three hundred and forty-nine pupil-teachers and no junior students, in 1910 twenty-four and two hundred and eighty-one, in 1913 two and two hundred and fifty-three.[55] Few mourned their passing.

The Draft Regulations also proposed to demand training for all Scottish teachers, with an entrance standard at least equivalent to the Leaving Certificate. The Certificate Examination for Practising Teachers (normally untrained) was to be discontinued after July 1907. There was wide opposition to this also on the ground that the schools would be left badly understaffed, and the Department gave way here too, allowing the Practising Teachers' Examination to continue.

The new junior students were to be paid maintenance allowances instead of salaries (thus reinforcing a principle for the financing of training which was to be strongly assailed in the second half of the century, when well-qualified teachers became increasingly scarce). Managers were invited to nominate their schools as Junior Student Centres, appointing one teacher as Master of Method. There was a flood of application and the Chief Inspectors, whose duty it was to adjudicate, found themselves dealing with some strange ones. When Carluke School Board's offer was refused for example it was pointed out that their school had only twelve pupils capable of attempting a post-intermediate course, and only three had completed such a course in the past three years; the laboratories also were bad.[56] Nevertheless all counties except Bute and Kinross had applications granted immediately and in the first three or four years of the scheme thirty-seven higher class schools (out of fifty-five) and seventy-three higher grades were recognised.[57] Within two years there was talk of limiting entry to prevent a glut of teachers.

The course of junior students was not much lighter than the old pupil-teacher "cram": they had to study, as well as the normal Leaving Certificate programme, drill, music, phonetics, woodwork or needle-

Infants at play, Wolseley Street School, Glasgow, around 1890

work, drawing and science;[58] they were also lectured once a week by their Master of Method, usually on Wednesday from four till five, and had to face the ordeal of periodical "criticism lessons". There was strain and over-pressure for many who hoped to go on to teaching through the universities, and especially between 1907 and 1911, when it was permissible for brilliant students to complete the course in two years. In their teaching practice, young though they were, they were often used as relief teachers: one boy remembered that "on one occasion I taught the highest class of an infant school for a solid month".[59] For one reason or another, novelty perhaps or the different climate of pre-war classrooms, there seem to have been few disciplinary troubles, but wastage was always high: 1,223 qualified in 1911 but only 980 went on to full training at the colleges. Most of the rest entered a university, but a number withdrew after their first junior year, and the Department regarded this as reasonable.

At eighteen they were ready to join other entrants as Senior Students in the training colleges for a course lasting two years. This was a professional training comprising school and personal hygiene, psychology, ethics, logic and the history and principles of education; there were also background studies intended to develop general education, but as the Chief Inspector in charge of training wrote in 1920,[60]

> the Scottish system proceeds on the assumption that the general education of the students is in the main complete on entry so that the college course can be devoted in the main to professional training.

While accepting this general principle, the Educational Institute constantly complained of the low educational requirements for entry. Junior Students had their own examination as an easier alternative to the Leaving Certificate tests and in the war years two-fifths of them failed to pass the latter. In 1916, 34 per cent of entrants to the Glasgow Training Centre had no leaving certificate, 45 per cent of those to Edinburgh, and in 1919 the corresponding figure at Notre Dame was 57 per cent.[61] Moreover the failure rate in the colleges, barely two per cent, was far too low.

The college course led to a "general certificate", and there were two others, the "specialist", intended for technical teachers, and one for secondary masters and mistresses. The principle now for the first time enunciated was that all truly secondary teachers must be honours graduates with professional training; for teachers of supplementary courses however a special qualification under "Article 39", to be taken by ordinary graduates, was provided.[62] Most significantly, all teachers at work in 1906 without a certificate were warned that they must undergo training before the end of 1914. Unfortunately the War and its shortages deferred indefinitely the full working of this provision.

Modern infants at work, Gorbals, Glasgow

On the whole the 1906 Regulations met with considerable initial success. In 1905 for example there had been only 9,367 trained certificated teachers in Scotland, but eight years later the number was 15,423. The least popular feature of the scheme was the Junior Student system, especially after 1918, when many careers outside teaching opened for women. In 1918 there were 700 fewer junior students in training than in 1914, and the rate of wastage had risen to 30 per cent.[63] Teaching practice arrangements were recognised, even by the Department, to be unsatisfactory. Only in Edinburgh was there real co-ordination of effort by the training college and the junior student centres of periodical conferences.[64] There was general agreement that the work in the secondary school was too hard for the students and that the line was drawn far too early between the ordinary young person and the teaching aspirant. By 1920 an inspector could state flatly that "the junior student system is not in favour".[65]

NEW COLLEGES

Between 1905 and 1920 two new colleges appeared. The first, opened in 1905, was the Scottish School of Physical Education and Hygiene, founded at Dunfermline by the Carnegie Trust to provide qualified gymnastic teachers as part of the Trust's contribution to the improvements of physical standards in the country.[66] Before that date the most interesting enterprise in this field was the Aberdeen College of Physical Training, opened by Mr George Cruden, who was at various times lecturer in physical education in Aberdeen University and the Free and Established Church Training Centres in Aberdeen and Glasgow, as well as Colonel of the First Volunteer Battalion, Gordon Highlanders. His manual of the subject first appeared in 1889 and went through several editions. For the "Teacher's Certificate" of his college "a knowledge of Cruden's Manual from page 11 to page 189" was necessary. It contained sixty pages on physiology and rules for conducting lessons, two hundred on musical drill, including marching, hoop work, bells and clubs, rifle and bayonet to tunes like "The British Grenadiers", "Hielan Laddie", "Bonnie Dundee" and "Love's Dreamland", and a final forty pages on apparatus training. All his students had to undergo a strict medical examination before entry. His certificate was approved by H.M. Inspectors.[67]

The second new college in this period was the result of an attempt by the Roman Catholic Church to meet the needs of its schools in eastern Scotland. In 1919 the Society of the Sacred Heart began training a few women in a house in Moray Place, Edinburgh; a year later the college was transferred to better accommodation at Craiglockhart Hydro.[68]

THE NATIONAL COMMITTEE

Up to 1918 the cost of training teachers was defrayed by students' fees and capitation grants from the central department, the school boards meeting no part of the expense. The new education authorities set up then were liable for some of the cost and also for the maintenance of students from their own areas. It was therefore advisable to establish a national body, on which the authorities could be represented, to supervise the process of training. A Departmental Minute of 10th February 1920 provided one, the National Committee for the Training of Teachers, with responsibility both financial and general for training policy, its members representative of local authorities.[69] The Committee was reconstituted every three years and met annually, its work being done for the rest of the year by a Central Executive Committee, on which the churches were represented. The duties of the central body were to approve courses, to build and staff colleges, and to provide hostels where these were required. Except for a few minor alterations in a Minute of 1934 these duties remained unchanged until 1958.

Drawing up courses and keeping them going continued as the task of the Provincial Committees, which also retained the management of colleges. In the appointment and approval of staff however the National Committee claimed a say. Most of the daily work of the National Committee was entrusted to an executive officer, first appointed in the mid-twenties; the post was filled throughout its existence by William McClelland, formerly Professor of Education at St Andrews.

Almost at once the denominational colleges and the School of Physical Education at Dunfermline came voluntarily under the control of the National Committee, though they retained their own Committees of Management, with representation on the Central Executive Committee. At the same time St George's College came within the system.[70] The provincial centre at Jordanhill, in the west of Glasgow, opened in September 1921, was described by the Scottish Education Department as "one of the most spacious and commodious buildings of its kind in the world".[71] It used the mansion house of the Jordanhill estate as a students' hostel. The old church colleges at Dundas Vale and in Cowcaddens were bought by the Glasgow Education Authority, and about fifty years later were still in educational use. At the beginning of session 1931-2 the School of Physical Education for men was transferred from Dunfermline to Jordanhill, where it remained, qualifying about thirty students a year after a course lasting three sessions.[72]

In 1925 the centres in Edinburgh and St Andrews collaborated with their universities in an interesting experiment. Professor Godfrey Thomson, Professor of Education in Edinburgh University, became Principal of Moray House Training College also; at St Andrews Professor McClelland undertook the same double employment.[73] The latter centre, by far the smallest of the four main Scottish institutions, continued the experiment under McClelland's successor, Professor Skinner, but on his resignation in 1953, the two posts he had occupied were given to different men. A similar redivision had been made in Edinburgh in 1951, on the retirement of Sir Godfrey Thomson; there was a general feeling in influential quarters that the duties of the posts too often conflicted.

The Episcopal College in Edinburgh continued, under the Provincial Committee, to turn out about thirty women teachers every year. From 1928 all its secular instruction was transferred to Moray House, though it remained in being as a hostel and centre of religious training. The College was finally closed altogether at the end of session 1933-4, though the Episcopal Church retained representation on the Edinburgh Provincial Committee;[74] because of the number of Episcopal schools in the north-east a member was also allotted a place on the Aberdeen Committee. All Episcopal students in future attended their own provincial training centre, and an Episcopal minister gave denominational instruction in each.

To have made St Andrews itself a centre of teacher training would have been absurd, for school facilities were clearly inadequate. The solution found was the building of a college in Park Place, Dundee, begun in 1912, opened in 1920. The college at Aberdeen, also begun before the Great War, opened in 1919.

THE 1924 AND 1931 REGULATIONS

The early twenties saw growing discontent with the system. The junior student principle was no more popular than it had been before the war. The content of the college course came under powerful attack, and there was a movement by teacher organisations to have it extended to three years. The Department declared in 1919 that it saw no benefit in such extension and in any case opposed it because of the need for more teachers from a limited pool of ability.

The recession of 1922 however brought widespread unemployment and a sharp change in the attitude of authority. Two years later new training regulations took a long step towards abolishing the "non-graduate" male teacher. All men desiring a certificate for general teaching in primary or secondary schools must take a university degree, followed by professional training in college. Teachers of art, music, handwork and similar "technical" subjects had to acquire a diploma of a central institution or its equivalent, though handwork students might take their whole course in the provincial centres. Women with degrees would proceed in the same way as men to a college year, but it was open to other women to qualify as "non-graduates", while if they took practical training before leaving school for one, two or three years they could have a shortened college course. Secondary teachers of either sex must be university graduates, with an endorsement for teaching the first three years if they held an ordinary degree, including two years studying the appropriate subject. The junior student system was abolished, though preliminary training was retained.

Reviewing progress between 1911 and 1931, the inspector in charge of teacher training commented on several striking changes. The first was the appearance of a unified administration in the National Committee, the second the ambitious but successful building programme which set up four new centres, three demonstration schools and no less than ten hostels. Third came the virtual elimination, at least in general education, of the male non-graduate, a notable experiment hardly to be found elsewhere in the world, and certainly not in England. Fourth, the general educational level of non-graduate women was slowly but certainly rising, though it could still find room for improvement. Finally, the proportion of university graduates in the profession was rising.[75] Indeed in 1928 the Central Executive Committee announced that preference in admission to training would be given to graduates, and four-fifths of entrants in that session belonged to this group. In short anyone subscribing to the belief that wide general education improved a teacher's professional competence would be satisfied with the trend in Scotland in the late twenties and early thirties. But there was never any real prospect of a totally graduate profession: non-graduate labour was too cheap, especially in years of financial crisis.

In 1931 the Training Regulations were again amended. The instrument issued in that year laid down the Higher Leaving Certificate as the entrance requirement for all women. The course for the primary diploma was fixed at three years, but students might have it reduced to two by taking preliminary training, now restricted to the sixth year at school. This was the last form of preliminary training and it was never a success: from 768 studying by this method in 1930-1 the number fell to 86 in the following session, and did not rise again above 159.[76] The certificates to be gained in colleges were renamed "general", "special" (for honours graduates) and "technical". These regulations remained in force for over thirty years, with occasional minor amendments which slowly eroded the entrance requirements. During that time however the experiment in preliminary training at school fell into increasing disfavour, and in 1950 it was abolished.[77]

THE POSITION IN 1945

Between 1872 and 1945 therefore long strides had been taken in the professional education of teachers. Training had been made compulsory, a rule which repeatedly caused surprise and some resentment among immigrants from south of the border. The educational requirement for entry to training had reached a high point in 1931 with the demand of a group leaving certificate for women candidates in general subjects and a university degree for men. The course of training had been steadily lengthened until by the end of the period no teachers, except a few small groups of technical specialists, could qualify in less than three years, and those intending to teach at the highest secondary level required five years and a term.

In the administration of the system the *ad hoc* principle had triumphed. None of the three main training authorities in England – universities, local education committees and established church – had been left with corresponding rights in Scotland, though the Roman Catholic Church had retained certain privileges. Nor had the Scottish Education Department openly concentrated power in its own hands. The colleges had been given a good deal of freedom to formulate their own curricula and liberated from external examinations, and Departmental inspection had become neither close nor oppressive. At the same time it might have been reasonably claimed that true power still lay with the Department, which provided two-thirds of the money spent on training and could exercise quiet but effective control through the Provincial Committees' estimates. The local authorities, as preliminary training dwindled, lost influence, but they provided the rest of the money and ensured through their representatives that spending by the colleges was less than reckless. The reign of the Central Executive Committee and the Provincial Committees was marked by much close scrutiny of college policies and considerable parsimony.

There remained at the end of the period continual criticism of the training courses. Graduates claimed that they were treated like children, and although some of their criticism was formulated before rather than during their training, it was by no means totally unfounded. The three year primary course for women was charged with deplorably low educational standards, but since the teaching community also required the colleges to restrict their work to professional matters, it was difficult to see how standards could be raised. In any case it was hard for anyone to believe that institutions with a failure rate of two per cent had high standards. Whatever the solution, it was unlikely to be found until the colleges were granted much more freedom and finance to experiment in a responsible way. An improvement in this direction was the main requirement of the next period.

REFERENCES

1. *C.C.M. 1883-4*, xxiii; *1894-5*, 366; *General Assembly E.C.R., 1878 Parker Committee 2*, v
2. *C.C.M. 1874-5*, Wilson, 100
3. *C.C.M. 1890-91*, Kerr, 323

4. *General Assembly E.C.R. 1902*; *C.C.M. 1899-1900, 593*
5. *Parker Committee 2*, Kennedy, Dickson, Mackenzie; *F.C. Minutes*, 5 Feb 1872
6. *F.C. Minutes*, 14 Sep 1885
7. Glasgow Church of Scotland Normal College Committee, *Minutes*, (MS), 11 Sep 1875, 5 Oct 1875, 15 May 1876, 14 Nov 1876, 10 Jan 1877, 6 Mar 1877, 7 May 1877, 19 June 1877, 21 June 1877, 25 June 1877; *F.C. Minutes* 21 Feb 1894; *C.C.M. 1877-8, 278*
8. *General Assembly E.C.R. 1878*
9. *ibid*
10. *General Assembly E.C.R. 1880, 1882*
11. *General Assembly E.C.R. 1879*
12. *Parker Committee 2*, vi
13. *General Assembly E.C.R. 1877*
14. *C.C.M. 1883-4* Wilson, 243; *General Assembly E.C.R. 1877, 1882*
15. *General Assembly E.C.R. 1877*
16. *ibid*
17. *Parker Committee 2*, Dickson
18. *Parker Committee 2*, Morrison; *C.S. Minutes* 14 Nov 1876
19. *C.C.M. 1872-3, 358*
20. *F.C. Minutes*, 5 Feb 1883
21. KNOX, *250 Years*, 148
22. *C.C.M. 1883-4*, 194; *Parker Committee 2*, Morrison; WILSON, *Tales and Travels*, 92
23. STEWART, *Report on Northern Schools, C.C.M. 1894*
24. *C.C.M. 1902-3*, Stewart, 685
25. ABERCROMBY, DONALD, remembering conditions in 1895, qu. BUCHAN, *Parish School to Academy*, 19
26. *Code of 1905*, article 70 (c)
27. CORMACK, *Cramond*, 33
28. e.g. *C.C.M. 1872-3*, Jolly
29. *C.C.M. 1913-14* King
30. WILSON, JOHN D., *The Junior Student System and Preliminary Training between 1906 and 1950* (Glasgow University Ed.B. Thesis 1964), 25; *C.C.M. 1877-8* Barrie, 145
31. OGILVIE, *Cruickshank*, 89
32. *Regulations of 1905*
33. KERR, *Memories*, 301; *C.C.M. 1875-6*, xii
34. *C.C.M. 1878-9*, 271; *1888-9*, 351; *General Assembly E.C.R. 1881*
35. "History of Graduate Training", *S.E.J.* 12 May 1961; *F.C. Minutes* 14 Nov 1902
36. *Parker Committee 2*, 6; *General Assembly E.C.R. 1887*; *F.C. Minutes* 1 Sep 1890
37. *F.C. Minutes* 9 May 1892; *Parker Committee 2*, Kennedy; *General Assembly E.C.R. 1880*

38. *F.C. Minutes* 15 June 1898, 1 May 1899, 9 Apr 1902, 5 Aug 1902
39. WILSON, *Junior Student System*, 152
40. Records of Aberdeen College of Education
41. *C.C.M. 1877-8*, 79
42. *Parker Committee 2*, Laurie; *C.C.M. 1884-5*, 90-103; *1872-3* Jolly, 278
43. *C.C.M. 1894-5*, xxiv; *Circular 179*, 14 June 1895; *Parker Committee 2*, ix
44. *C.C.M. 1894-5*, xxiv
45. *C.C.M. 1896-7*, xxxiii; *1898-9*, xii; *1900-1*, 4; *1905-6*, 22
46. Glasgow University Local Committee for Teacher Training, *MS Minutes*
47. *C.C.M. 1895-6*, 455-6; *1898-9*, 602-3; SKINNIDER, *Catholic Education*, 7
48. *F.C. Minutes*, 25 Sep 1902; *C.C.M. 1902-3*, 760-63
49. KERR, *Scottish Education*, 396
50. *C.C.M. 1904-5*, 223-4
51. *General Assembly E.C.R. 1906*
52. *C.C.M. 1908-9*, Scougal, K/6-7
53. *S.E.D.R. 1919-20*, Smith, 18-19
54. *Educational News*, 17 Feb 1906
55. WILSON, *Junior Student System*, 93
56. WILSON, *Junior Student System*, 81
57. KERR, *Scottish Education*, 402
58. SMITH, *Broken Links*, 130
59. MCINTYRE, R. qu. WILSON, *Junior Student System*, 210
60. *S.E.D.R. 1920-21*, Smith
61. WILSON, *Junior Student System*, 231-2, 246
62. *Teacher Training (Scotland) Regulations, 1906*
63. WILSON, *Junior Student System*, 225
64. WILSON, *Junior Student System*, 112
65. *S.E.D.R. 1920-21*, Smith, 5-6
66. *T.S.A. Fife*, 348
67. CRUDEN, GEORGE, *Manual of Physical Culture and System of Musical Drill for the Use of Teachers in Schools* (Simpkin Marshall 1902)
68. *S.E.D.R. 1920-21*, Smith, 16
69. *S.E.D.R. 1919-20*, 29; *1930-31*, D/3
70. *S.E.D.R. 1921-2*, A/24
71. *S.E.D.R. 1921-2*, Smith, C/11
72. *S.E.D.R. 1932-3*, A/37
73. *S.E.D.R. 1925-6*, 28; *1926-7*, Smith, D/10
74. *S.E.D.R. 1930-31*, D/3-4; *1934-5*, A/41
75. *S.E.D.R. 1930-31*, D/5
76. WILSON, *Junior Student System*, 283
77. *Training of Teachers (Scotland) Regulations, 1949*

The Teacher's Life

CHAPTER 8

THE STATUS OF THE PROFESSION

O a' ye loons and laddies wha hae ta'en a gweed degree,
O dinna be a dominie what iver else ye dae!
For a dominie, like the deevil, never wants for wark and steer!
  O!
  A Dominie's day I widna hae
  For a thousand pounds a year![1]

SECONDARY teachers were better off than elementary, and some in the most famous schools enjoyed real public status, but on the whole the schoolmaster was not highly regarded by his fellow-men. The aristocracy and gentry, who would never have dreamt of patronising a doctor or a lawyer, had no qualms in so treating a dominie, even when he could boast an honours degree. The working community's attitude was often more positively hostile to teachers because[2]

> the most of them were sons and daughters of poor bit crofters and fishers themselves, up with the gentry they felt safe and unfrightened, far from that woeful pit of brose and bree and sheetless beds in which they had been reared. So right condescending they were with Chris, daughter of a farmer of no account, not that she cared, she was douce and sensible she told herself. And hadn't father said that in the sight of God an honest man was as good as any school-teacher and generally a damn sight better?

The source of such resentment was complex. Partly it was based on the conviction expressed above that teachers were ordinary folk who wanted to forget they were ordinary. As Scott wrote,[3] "there's always something grotesque about a schoolmaster," but if this were so, it was at least partly due to the artificial position in which teachers were placed: A. S. Neill pointed out in 1917 that though any respectable farmer might enter a bar without comment, a teacher must not.[4]

There was also undoubtedly an element of jealousy in the general attitude, nowhere better expressed than by Walter Wingate in a "reading" of immense popularity at parties and socials:

He dauners out at nine o'clock
    He dauners hame at four –
Frae twal to ane to eat and smoke –
    And sae his day is owre.

Oh Leezie Leezie fine and easy
    Is a job like yon –
A' Saturday at gowf to play
    And aye the pey gaun on!

When winter days are cauld and dark
    And dykes are deep wi snaw,
And bairns are shiverin owre their wark,
    He shuts the shop at twa.

And when it comes to Hogmanay
    And fun comes roarin ben
And ilka dog maun tak a day
    The Dominie taks ten!

And sae the Board comes smirkin roon
    Wi prizes in their haun
And syne it's frae the end of June
    Until the Lord kens whan.

Oh Leezie Leezie fine and easy
    Is a job like yon –
Sax weeks to jaunt and gallivaunt
    And aye the pey gaun on!

Not all the banter was good-humoured, and even the most popular dominie felt himself obliged on occasion to counter unexpressed criticisms of his "ample leisure". But probably the strongest force in the situation was simply rebellion against someone who had once wielded authority strictly and now no longer could.

SUPPLY BETWEEN THE WARS

Up to the time of the First World War the supply of teachers for all types of schools increased steadily, and classes became smaller. After 1918 however it fluctuated. The Report of the Committee of Council for 1920-21 mentioned that the situation was "giving cause of anxiety, though not alarm", but in a short time the problem had been solved: by 1923 there was a deficiency only in a few Roman Catholic schools, and indeed there was some unemployment. The end of the twenties and the early thirties were lean years for teachers: many of the students completing their training had still not been placed a year later.[5] Some authorities refused to employ any teacher whose training certificate was marked as no more than "promising". Unemployment might have become worse had not teachers accepted a cut in salary between 1931 and 1935, if "accept" is the right word. As it was many qualified men and women had to take posts for several years in private schools, as tutors or outside the profession. The unrest in the fifties and sixties was not unconnected with the fact that many of the most prominent teacher-politicians of these latter days had left college during the thin years of the early thirties.

The 1872 Act had made a certificate of competency, gained by examination, compulsory for all future principal teachers, and the Regulations of 1906 recognised the value of a fully qualified profession by allowing uncertificated teachers only eight years in which to acquire training, with special courses available in the training colleges. In 1903, when there were 20,000 teachers in the schools, three-fifths (12,200) were certificated and another 5,400 classed as "juveniles", mainly pupil-teachers; only 2,550 (about an eighth) were completely uncertificated.[6] Thirty-six years later, at the outbreak of the Second World War, vacancies for untrained masters and mistresses occurred only in remote schools, in some particular posts and in special emergencies. By 1950 the total teaching force had risen to 32,850, but only 880 were without a certificate, including 90 untrained university graduates, 136 men and women who had acquired some training in another country and about 300 "skilled in a practical subject" like needlework or music. From 300 to 350 were stated by the Department to be "seriously sub-standard".[7]

The effect, as might be expected, was a high degree of professional or at least mechanical competence. The aim of the teachers themselves, as enunciated on many occasions by the Educational Institute, was to eliminate uncertificated teachers altogether. Another, more ambitious, was a "graduate profession", and in the years between the Wars it seemed to be coming into attainable distance: the percentage of graduate teachers at work rose from twenty-seven in 1928 to forty-one in 1939,[8] and in the last year sixty-five per cent of newly trained teachers were graduates. Moreover under the Training Regulations of 1924 no male candidate for a certificate to teach general subjects (as distinct from technical studies like art and music) could be admitted without a general degree. It was an experiment of remarkable courage, and it went on for over forty years, but it was made possible only by certain economic and social circumstances, notably the recession in the twenties and thirties and the consequent attractiveness of a "safe job" like teaching. The schools in those days were a very stable community, especially since the mass slaughter of the First World War committed many young women who would otherwise have married to a lifetime in the classroom.* Most

* When they did marry in fact they were obliged to resign.

schools had a Miss Smith or a Mr Jones, frequently more than one, who had been on the staff for a score of years or more, and there were many where a new teacher was an event.

One further consequence of the peculiar economic situation between the Wars was a rise in the academic quality of teachers. In general a woman with a degree was more highly regarded than one without and might expect a wider choice of posts – unpromoted, of course, except as an Infants Mistress – in primary schools. In the secondaries there were few headmistresses, virtually none in posts open to men* and this was largely true also of headships of departments. As a rule men with honours degrees taught in secondary schools and monopolised the promoted posts there, but many were also required to serve an apprenticeship of several years as headmasters of primary schools. There was also, in every graduate class in training, a considerable proportion of people with first class honours: the figures in Aberdeen in various quinquennia were[10]:

Year of College Intake	I Class Hons.	Total with Honours	Percentage with I Hons.
1907-11	13	49	26·5
1912-16	19	78	24·4
1917-21	20	117	17·1
1922-26	42	166	25·3
1927-31	46	185	24·9
1932-36	31	148	20·9
1937-41	18	62	29·0
1942-46	22	71	31·0

These academic aristocrats were often to be found in the more selective schools like Hutchesons', George Watson's and Aberdeen Grammar, but in the thirties at least there were many also in the higher grades. A Third, on the other hand, was regarded as something very inferior, recognised on a lower salary scale, hardly counting as honours at all and certainly barring its holder from all the more lucrative posts.

These views of course were further evidence of the Scottish reverence for academic achievement. There was a well-recognised hierarchy in the profession, scrupulously observed by teachers themselves, with secondary masters more highly regarded than primary, men more highly than women, university graduates more than non-graduates, honours men more than ordinary. A first class degree was worth much more than "excellent" in practical teaching. And in the secondary world the lowest place was reserved for teachers of domestic and technical subjects, so that, writing of a fictitious but thinly disguised grammar school in the thirties, a Scottish novelist could speak (probably without conscious design) of "the whole staff from old Gilmour the Headmaster down to Patterson, who taught woodwork".[11]

* The first woman head of George Watson's Ladies College, Miss Charlotte Ainslie, was not appointed until 1902.[9]

APPOINTMENT AND DISMISSAL

In the independent and often in the direct grant schools headmasters
had an important part in the appointment of their staff. In the public
schools however the duty was entrusted from 1872 onwards to the
boards and their successors, and even between 1918 and 1947, when
School Management Committees existed, the authorities kept it in their
own hands, granting an influential but not decisive voice to the Director
of Education. It became the practice in many areas to employ teachers
in the general service of the authority, with no guarantee that they would
work in any particular school; in its own interest however each authority
gave as much attention as it could to the teacher's wishes. From 1872
also all new appointments were made "during the pleasure of the authority". This implied a certain risk, for some school boards proved to be
capricious. There were two common grounds of dismissal, immoral or
cruel conduct, of which the board had to send notice to the Sheriff,
and incompetence or inefficiency, on which the opinion had to be sought
of one of Her Majesty's Inspectors. There was no appeal in either case.[12]
After a number of arbitrary dismissals however the Mundella Act of
1882 was passed to ensure that no dismissals could occur without proper
deliberation. The Act of 1908 added a right of appeal, by which the
teacher might apply to the Department for an inquiry within six weeks
of his dismissal. If the Department saw fit to hold one, and found the
school board at fault, it could not force the teacher's reinstatement, but
it might compel the board to pay him up to a year's salary in compensation,[13] and this principle remained active under future types of
educational authority. Meanwhile the Act of 1918, in view of the larger
size of the new educational authorities, hedged about dismissals with
added conditions. The authority had to give written notice of a motion
for dismissal not less than three weeks before a meeting to adopt it,
and a copy had to be sent to the teacher; at least half the members of
the authority had to be present at the meeting; two-thirds of those
present had to agree to the resolution.[14] The Act of 1936 added a right
of the teacher to appeal to the Secretary of State. The first duty of the
authority on dismissing a teacher, in any case, was to send a full report
on its action to the Secretary. In short, the Scottish teacher now enjoyed
such security of tenure that dismissals were rarer than they should have
been in the interest of general efficiency.

It is interesting to find that the crimes warranting dismissal included
some new ones brought by changing circumstances. As in the days of
the Jacobites, politics might be important, though they were more
likely to prevent an appointment than to cause dismissal. After the
Second World War there was a strong suspicion that at least one
authority, giving no reason, refused to accept an application for employment from a qualified candidate who was known to be a Communist.
Cruelty to pupils, persistent lateness and inefficiency continued to be

grounds for dismissal, and a new crime which appeared in the inspectors' reports after 1872 was falsification of registers: out of twenty-two certificates revoked or suspended in 1877 nineteen were for this misdemeanour. For ten years thereafter cases were reported regularly, though the numbers dwindled. The influence of payment by results was widespread: the mistress of the infant department at St Patrick's, Coatbridge, for example, showed one hundred and three children on her roll, but an inspector, paying a visit without warning, found only sixty-five.[15] The majority of dismissals however, and almost all cases in which the Secretary of State withdrew certificates to teach, rose from moral misconduct, particularly where it involved pupils.

One unfortunate effect of the over-supply of teachers in the thirties was the rule that a woman had to leave her employment on being married. This was widely enforced until the Act of 1945 included a section stating specifically that marriage must no longer be a disqualification from appointment nor a reason for dismissal.[16] Since a married woman with a young family might be expected to add practical to her theoretical knowledge of child psychology, the provision put an end to an obvious anomaly. It did not however remove the administrative difficulty of twin loyalties, and some authorities continued to employ married women only where spinsters, men or childless widows were not available.

SALARIES AND PENSIONS

We have seen in chapters 4 and 5 something of the conditions in which teachers served during this period. For many reasons, in the public schools at least, their work was essentially *class* teaching. For one thing the ratio of teachers to pupils ensured this: up to 1905 the Code allowed seventy children in the class of a certificated teacher, thereafter sixty until 1939 when the figure was reduced to fifty. Much of the instruction was also carried out by apprentices – pupil-teachers (over a quarter of the force) until 1905 and junior students thereafter – and these could reach reasonable efficiency only in the class situation. Experiments in group and individual work were restricted before 1939 to a few independent masters, generally outside the public system, or to teachers in small rural schools whose circumstances positively enforced such methods.

The record of salaries is one of some improvement, but never to a point at which teachers were generally satisfied; the problem became linked with that of "professional status", and there was always a fundamental disagreement between teachers and their employers on what constituted a suitable minimum and maximum salary for a schoolmaster. Two principles early became accepted. The first stated that the teacher with better academic qualifications should command a better pay: in consequence there were separate scales for graduates and non-

graduates teaching in primary schools. The second, presumably arguing
that men were likely to have more family responsibilities than women,
paid them higher salaries in comparable posts.

In 1870 the average salary of a master in a state-aided Scottish school
was about £111 a year, of a mistress £55.[17] The Act of 1872 left school
boards to determine the amount they would pay, and the old minimum
which had existed since 1696 disappeared. A few boards undoubtedly
exploited their employees, but in general salaries remained fairly steady
during the last three decades of the nineteenth century:

Year	Men			Women		
	£	s	d	£	s	d
1882	136	3	7	67	10	10
1889	133	16	6	62	16	1
1898	142	6	10	69	8	1
1904	149	12	7	75	17	5

The relationship between the sexes was also maintained. Many teachers
enjoyed in addition a free house, which under the Building Rules of
1900[18] must have a parlour, kitchen, scullery and three bedrooms. Men
on leaving college averaged £85 a year in 1877, women £66[19]; the fact
that the latter arrived almost at once near their maximum mirrors the
differential prospects for promotion.

Outside the public system there was more variation. The secondary
schools could afford to go considerably higher, but in 1904, when the
average for public school masters was about £150 a year, Roman
Catholic men had only £107.[20] Moreover all salaries fluctuated with
the economic condition of the country: in 1879 for example, when there
was general commercial depression, they sank by about fifty shillings a
year. The aim of the teachers was to secure some financial guarantee by
demanding a minimum figure, and in 1917 a committee was set up
under Sir Henry Craik as chairman to review the position. The result
was a Departmental Minute of August 1919 which guaranteed a
minimum salary for all men of £150 a year, rising by ten-pound
increments to £250. Women were kept in a lower position, but brought
nearer: their scale began at £130 and rose by five-pound steps to £150,
then by ten-pound steps to £200. There were additional allowances in
recognition of longer training, of graduation and for posts of responsibility.[21] Thus the main principles of payment for Scottish teachers were
established, with two exceptions, the possibility of standard payment for
work anywhere in the country, and equal pay for women.

Between the Wars there was no serious fluctuation, though from 1931
to 1935 industrial depression forced cuts in salary. The economies
enacted in 1931 included reductions in the Education (Scotland) Fund,
in grants to education authorities and by one-twelfth in the minimum
of each teacher's salary.[22] Half the cut was restored in 1934, the remainder in 1935, but teachers had been gravely perturbed by the experience:

it was clear that any large economy in educational expenditure must strike at their remuneration, actual or promised. Meanwhile, in an attempt to attract better teachers, the richer authorities offered bonuses wherever they could justify them. Such competition was naturally resented by less favoured authorities, and a review of the position was due at the outbreak of the Second World War.

It was not until the end of the nineteenth century that statutory provision had been made for contributory pensions to retiring teachers; anything previously available had been a matter of grace and favour. The Elementary School Teachers (Superannuation) Act of 1898 at last dispersed the shadow which must have darkened the lives of many Scottish dominies. It called for annual contributions of £3 by each man and £2 by each woman in the elementary branch of the service. The pensions payable after forty-five years were respectively £39 and £20 a year.[23] But even this modest beginning was restricted; secondary masters remained dependent on voluntary schemes or their own savings. The Act of 1908 extended the government provision to all Scottish schools: the teacher contributed four per cent of his salary, his employers a further two per cent. In return he was guaranteed a modest retiring allowance, at least a pound a week, and a lump sum to assist him in finding accommodation when he left the schoolhouse. There was also provision for a disablement allowance or gratuity and at the worst – if a woman, for instance, forfeited her claim by marriage – contributions were returned. After the Geddes Committee's enquiry of 1922 the teacher's contribution was raised to five per cent and in 1925 that of his employers to the same figure.[24] There the proportions remained until 1954 when they rose to six per cent in each case.

Such a scheme was fair, calculated on the basis of salary earned. Where it failed was in making no provision to revise pensions as the cost of living rose: a teacher who retired in 1938 and was still alive in 1953 at the age of eighty was very badly off, for salaries and prices had soared in the interval. Attempts to cope with this problem took the form of Pensions Increase Acts. Provision also existed from 1937 for teachers over sixty to allocate part of their pension to be set aside for their dependents.

PROFESSIONAL ASSOCIATIONS

Throughout the period under review professional associations continued to thrive in some measure. By far the strongest was the Educational Institute of Scotland, which celebrated its centenary in 1946. In 1874, with the admission of the first women members, it might fairly claim to represent the views of all branches of the profession. Regarded as a body for the furtherance of education in Scotland and the interchange of educational information, it had a fine record. From 1876 to 1918, for

Class at work in Hollybrook School, Glasgow, around 1890

swallowed easily enough

example, it was responsible for the publication of the *Scottish Educational News*; thereafter the title was changed to the *Scottish Educational Journal*, and weekly issues printed some valuable articles on specific topics, though their general concern was somewhat parochially confined to the affairs of the Institute and the party line on educational measures. The Institute's Committee on Educational Research, founded in 1919, was the forerunner and pioneer of the Scottish Council for Research on Education. From time to time Commissions appointed by the Institute produced reports on contemporary topics: there was one in 1898 on secondary education, another in 1910 on education in Lewis, and one the following year on education in Shetland. A panel on Scottish Educational Reform recommended in 1917 the formation of a National Council; another which met during the Second World War was subdivided into eight committees, and produced a scheme for the complete reconstruction of Scottish educational administration. The Institute's programmes of aims generally advocated changes years before they found favour with the government: in 1903 it was recommending that local authorities should supplant the school boards (enacted in 1918), that there should be an Advisory Council (1920), that the central authority should have its headquarters in Edinburgh, not London (1921), that teachers should be trained by provincial boards in university areas (1906) and that there should be superannuation for all teachers (1908). Its aims in 1946 included a further extension of the concept of education, a "united profession", as an attack on distinctions drawn between graduates and others, the institution of a professional degree, and the establishment of educational institutes attached to the Scottish universities.[25]

Regarded as a trade union, however, the E.I.S. showed few of the victories of other unions – a success hardly to be expected perhaps, since teaching is a profession, not a trade. The first organised teachers' strike did not occur until 1961, and its success was a matter of debate. In providing amenities however – life insurance at preferential rates, building loans, car insurance and so on – the Institute was very active.

The weakness of the E.I.S. was in some degree increased by the appearance of smaller associations. The Scottish Schoolmasters' Association, with a fairly long history, produced its own journal and policy, the latter mainly concerned with salaries. There was also a Primary Teachers' Association, Associations of Headmasters and Headmistresses and various groups with special interests. A Secondary Teachers' Association was founded as early as 1885, but amalgamated with the Institute in 1917. In 1944 a similar body, the Secondary Schoolmasters' Association, was set up within the Institute; a year later, feeling that the interests of its members diverged at several points from those of the E.I.S. as a whole, it broke away and took up an independent existence, with the aims

Science at Hyvot's Bank Primary School, Edinburgh

I

to advance secondary education in Scotland, and to safeguard and promote the professional interests of Scottish secondary teachers in all matters, particularly in such as affect remuneration and other conditions of service.

It issued its own journal three times a year. The comparative membership of the main associations just after this period may be gauged by the figures for Ayrshire, where in 1947 all but two hundred of the two thousand teachers employed were members of the E.I.S., only a hundred of the S.S.T.A. Two hundred of the E.I.S. members were also in the S.S.A., which had not yet broken away.[26]

AUTHORITARIANISM

There was no such thing in this period as a "typical teacher", thanks to the wide scatter of qualifications which entitled a candidate to certification, and it was this diversity which prevented the community as a whole from regarding teaching as a profession. Most would have been prepared to accord such status to university graduates and especially secondary headmasters, but few would make the same concession to girls whose training consisted of no more than three (earlier two) years, with a low level of attainment in higher education. In 1879 the Inspector for Renfrew, Bute and Argyll recorded his impression that[27]

> as a class teachers are not well read; many of them leave the training colleges without having formed intellectual tastes or acquired intellectual habits; in entering the work of life these do not feel the need for further culture, and consequently they do not follow out any definite line of reading. They cannot be said to take the same interest in the literature of their profession that physicians and clergymen take in that of theirs.

The last point might have been made, virtually throughout the period, about graduate as well as non-graduate teachers; far too many regarded their training as complete when they took their degree, and "in-service" courses were not popular before 1939.

Nevertheless there were vague stereotypes of "the teacher". To begin with the picture conjured up was increasingly that of a woman: between 1870 and 1900 the percentage of men in the profession dropped from sixty-nine to thirty-six.[28] When people searched their minds for a vignette of the traditional schoolmistress, the result was old-fashioned middle-aged or elderly, sensibly dressed,

> angular, grim,
> proper and prim,
> The Pride of the E.I.S.

When they thought of a man, he was a narrow, rather humourless authoritarian. Mr Chips and Miss Dove did not teach in Scottish schools. The pictures were not entirely fanciful: there were ladies like "Granny" Carmichael in Dundee whose care for sex segregation was so strong that she would not let a girl speak to her brother in school, and men like Dr Wilson of the same establishment who was heard to laugh only once in six years, when he recounted how Romulus beat his brother's brains out.[29] There were also martinets like Dr "Billy" Dey of the Old Town Grammar School in Aberdeen, who might be seen on any weekday morning walking up the road from the New Town in his shabby frock coat and tall hat, carrying an umbrella and a pile of corrected exercises. He set stern standards for himself and his boys – "the night cometh when no man can work" – and his credo, expressed when he was presented with his portrait, might stand for many of his colleagues in Scotland at the beginning of the twentieth century[30]

> I never could accept without large reservations the method of governing boys that underlies the common remarks "Boys will be boys" and "You cannot put old heads on young shoulders." At an early age of my English experience I came to the conclusion that these venerable and pithy sayings, when strictly analysed, are found to contain more of claptrap than of truth. . . . I fully satisfied myself that boys are endowed with a very considerable amount of self-control. I therefore definitely settled in my mind once for all what I was to do and to be in my dealings with boys; and gave them very clearly to understand that I assumed the existence of this power of self-control and meant to hold them responsible for the due exercise of it under ordinary circumstances.

The atmosphere in Scottish classrooms undoubtedly fostered authoritarianism. The main emphasis was on the teacher; lessons were accepted as occasions involving children in self-control rather than self-expression. Moreover, although this atmosphere perceptibly lightened during the period, the Scottish Education Department in its Primary Memorandum of 1950 was still addressing itself to teachers "accustomed to being the centre of attention in their own classrooms, who liked to feel that they were fully in control, and who also erred to a fault on the side of caution".[31] To many no doubt the imputation that they were "boys among men" did less than justice, but almost all were obliged by the system to be "men among boys".

REFERENCES

1. MILNE, *Poems*, 60
2. GIBBON, *Sunset Song*, 65
3. qu. CORMACK, *Cramond*, 63

4. NEILL, *A Dominie Dismissed*, 90
5. *S.E.D.R. 1920-21*, Smith, 3; *1922-3*, 19; *1929-30*, A/36
6. KERR, *Annotated Code of 1905*, 291
7. *S.E.D.R. 1950*, 23
8. *S.E.D.R. 1938*, A/12
9. HARRISON, *Merchant Company*, 38
10. Records of Aberdeen College of Education, my percentages
11. LINKLATER, ERIC, *Roll of Honour* (Hart-Davis 1961), 52-3
12. *Education (Scotland) Act 1872*, section 60; *Education (Scotland) Act 1946*, section 78
13. *Education (Scotland) Act 1908*, section 21
14. *Education (Scotland) Act 1918*, section 24
15. *C.C.M. 1877-8*, 99; *1886-7*, 110
16. *Education (Scotland) Act 1945*, section 51
17. *C.C.M. 1882-3*, xxvi-xxvii
18. *Building Rules 1900*, section 19
19. *C.C.M. 1877-8*, Wilson, 243
20. KERR, *Annotated Code of 1905*, 292
21. *C.C.M. 1879-80*, Wilson, 202; 12 August 1919
22. *S.E.D.R. 1931-2*, 4-6
23. *Elementary School Teachers (Superannuation) Act 1898*; *Rules, 1 April 1899*
24. *Education (Scotland) Act 1908*, section 14; KNOX, *250 Years*, 177-8; MORGAN, *Rise and Progress*, 225-6; *C.C.M. 1904-5*, 24
25. BELFORD, *Centenary Handbook*, ch. 16
26. *T.S.A. Ayrshire*, 210-11
27. *C.C.M. 1878-9*, 192
28. OSBORNE, G. S., *Scottish and English Schools, a Comparative Survey of the Past Fifty Years* (Longmans 1966), 275
29. NORRIE, *Old High School*, 121, 143
30. BULLOCH, " 'Billy' Dey", *A.U.R.*, 110-111; MACKENZIE, "My Last Schoolmaster", *A.U.R.*, iii, 8, Feb 1916, 100
31. OSBORNE, *Scottish and English Schools*, 105

CHAPTER 9

Further Education

THE NEED FOR FURTHER EDUCATION

"WASTAGE" in the upper forms of the secondary schools has always been a chronic disease of Scottish education. Nearly 84,000 boys and girls who entered post-primary education in 1933 had dwindled to 8,500 by the time they reached the fourth year and only 2,500 when in 1938 they came to the sixth.[1] Such a record, whatever action it demands in the schools, produces an unanswerable case for the most flexible provision of further education. The Scottish schools moreover throughout their history remained steadily unvocational: training for a job was generally felt to be something best undertaken while in the job. The original plans of the Scottish Education Department in 1887 contemplated not one but four Leaving Certificates, classical, scientific and technical, commercial and female, but only the first was introduced. Separate commercial and technical certificates were at last instituted in 1902, but they were never popular and lasted only until 1912, reappearing as subjects in the Leaving Certificate only in the thirties.[2] The Committee for Scottish Educational Reform, writing in 1917, reported that[3]

> the fact is that the great majority of business men look with profound distrust on all forms of commercial education that have not been acquired in counting house or warehouse.

By the end of the nineteenth century, with the success of the 1872 Act, further education as a necessity for repairing omissions in elementary literacy had ceased to exist. Throughout the twentieth however it became increasingly important as a vocational instrument, while classes continued to be held with the purpose of widening intellectual and cultural horizons.

ADULT EDUCATION – W.E.A. AND E.M.C.

Adult education not directed towards vocational improvement had two aims, to widen the educational background of the mass of the population in the faith that the result would be better individuals and better citizens, and to train the elite of the working classes for posts of responsibility. In Scotland such aims were found operating in many quarters, predominantly as the effect of humanitarianism, religious sentiment or radical politics. Since the state confined itself largely to providing education in school, the field of adult training remained fruitful, for voluntary endeavour and "cultural classes" were offered by many organisations. At the end of the nineteenth century however the state took a hand here too with the issue of an Evening Continuation School Code in 1893, to encourage instruction in more than elementary subjects. There was provision for languages, English, geography, history, mathematics, agriculture, horticulture, navigation and domestic economy; there were also two interesting courses on "the science of common things" and "the life and duties of the citizen". Although some school boards had already experimented in this field – Hawick, for example, advertised "recreative evening classes" in 1886, with concerts, readings and magic lantern shows – the Code was described within a year of its inception as "a great impulse to improvement".[4] The effect was being strongly felt just before the passage of the 1908 Act: whereas in session 1873-4 only 3,209 evening school pupils were presented for inspection in Scotland, over 100,000 were enrolled in 1906. Classes were being offered in such subjects as wood-carving, military drill, physical exercise, vocal music and fancy needlework.[5]

The Act of 1908 obliged school boards to provide continuation classes for all people over 14 years of age who wished to attend. By 1914 Scotland was taking a leading position in developing such classes, but the First World War curtailed activity and the recession of the twenties and thirties changed the function of continuation courses, which became more useful in checking demoralisation during unemployment. Classes for unemployed juveniles operated from 1922 to 1926 and junior instruction centres after 1935, but they were never a success: neither pupils nor teachers were eager to take part. Indeed no courses for leisure activity were ever so popular as vocational classes unless they offered some prospect of material use: there was a rise in enrolment from 1940 to 1945 for cookery, dressmaking and "make-do-and-mend".[6]

For more serious students – the "elite of the working class" who had once founded the Mechanics' Institutes – there were two more ambitious educational ventures. As early as 1873 the universities were running "extension courses", in which professors and lecturers gave instruction at a fairly high level to men and women whose certificate of admission was their diligence. By then the Mechanics' Institutes were breaking up in many parts of the country and an attempt was made in 1881 to amalgamate these with the extension courses. Moreover the Co-operative Movement was entering adult education at the beginning of the seventies.

Progress was slow however until the early part of the twentieth century, when Albert Mansbridge founded the Workers' Educational

Association. W.E.A. classes were opened in Glasgow in 1905, within two years after the first in Britain, but by 1910 they had failed. An attempt to keep them unpolitical meant little support from the big parties: the Labour Conference of 1907 for instance showed no interest in adult education, though that of 1915 was more sympathetic. Classes began again in Glasgow in 1916, but remained for some years small and unorganised.

A Committee on Adult Education, reporting in 1919, recommended the formation of university extra-mural departments to organise adult education within their provinces. The universities adopted the suggestion with varying alacrity: Aberdeen's department was not set up until 1956.[7] Scotland moreover never showed the same interest as England in the W.E.A., though good work was done. Numbers of students were small compared with those in continuation classes, which in 1938-9 amounted to over 160,000. There were 128 W.E.A. and E.M.C. centres in Scotland in that year, and just under 9,000 enrolments. The students were older and on the whole more earnest: the most popular subjects were current affairs, international problems and economics.

One striking experiment was the establishment of a residential college of further education, offering a distinctively liberal course. In England a working man's college, Ruskin, had been founded as early as 1899, and later such institutions as Ashridge were to become well known. The only Scottish college of the type was at Newbattle Abbey, a handsome country house near Edinburgh handed over in 1933 by the Marquis of Lothian as a residential college for adult workers.[8] The gift was a munificent one, including furniture, books and pictures, but for a variety of reasons the first students could not be enrolled until 1937, and the outbreak of war forced closure just as the college was gathering momentum. It was to reopen in 1945 as an Army Formation College.

TECHNICAL EDUCATION

The complacency in British technical achievement which signalised the Great Exhibition of 1851 was sufficiently shaken by some foreign exhibits there to encourage the foundation of the Department of Science and Art in Kensington. Midway through the eighteen-sixties such smugness was destroyed completely. In 1866 Matthew Arnold returned from a continental tour undertaken for the Education Department and his report drew attention to the vigorous technical schools in Europe, especially Prussia. Next year the first great Paris Exhibition was held; Britain made a poor appearance. Nevertheless the first positive steps to improve the higher branches of technology were not taken until 1873, when the Royal Society of Arts began to conduct examinations whose practical nature made them well received. Six years later these examinations were incorporated in the system run by the City and Guilds of London Institute.

The second Paris Exhibition, held in 1878, was another British humiliation, and the government of Gladstone, thoroughly perturbed, appointed the Samuelson Commission on Technical Instruction, which spent four years investigating arrangements in Britain and on the Continent. Abroad it found technical schools for foremen and higher institutions for employers; there were also special trade and professional schools for women. Instruction was systematic, with better equipment, a higher quality of teaching and state aid to reduce fees to a nominal figure. The Commission's recommendations, issued in 1884, set the pattern for British technical education for many years. The best general preparation was stated to be an up-to-date secondary education in a school of the type of Manchester Grammar School or Allan Glen's, Glasgow. Practical instruction should be left to the workshop, but further technological training was required up to the age of at least nineteen. The government's duty was to provide funds for setting up secondary schools with a modern bias and technical institutes for boys and girls just out of school.[9]

In Scotland the first attempt to make such provision was the Technical Schools (Scotland) Act of 1887, which encouraged school boards to set up and administer schools of the required kind. Only one was ever founded under the Act, however: there was no sufficient definition of "technical", and no funds were laid aside other than the existing Science and Art grants. A second act, passed in 1892, was little better drafted. It placed such schools under the control of county councils and police burghs, but there was no direct grant, and the principle was explicitly stated that instruction was "not to include the teaching of trade, but scientific subjects".[10]

This "essential unity" of technical and secondary education was stressed again in 1895 by the Bryce Commission. In consequence the Scottish schools which benefited from the Science and Art grants were those like Allan Glen's and Paisley Grammar School, which presented pupils for the examinations of the English Board of Education. From 1897 onwards these grants came under the control of the Scotch Education Department, administered by a "Directory of the Science and Art Department".[11] Meanwhile the Local Taxation Account (Scotland) Act of 1898 provided another £35,000 a year to assist secondary and technical education.

During the last quarter of the nineteenth century also, continuation classes had steadily increased in numbers. Some, as we have seen, were mainly recreative; others, intended to provide instruction in reading and writing for men and women whose childhood had been too hard to leave time for such acquirements, dwindled rapidly as the 1872 Act gained strength. But not a few gave quite advanced vocational instruction, preparing students for the examinations of the Science and Art Department or of the City and Guilds of London Institute. The latter had existed since the seventies, and a Central Institution was founded

in London in 1883. Its certificates were soon widely accepted throughout
Britain as trade qualifications. Preparation for them was made in the
evening schools of Glasgow during the late eighties, and in Leith a year
or two later.[12] An Evening Continuation School Code was issued by the
Scotch Education Department in 1893, with the aim of encouraging
higher studies, and was very well received. Seven years later a new Code
reorganised the Scottish system. At the same time, in 1901, higher
technical studies in Scotland were given their distinctive pattern by
the recognition of certain "central institutions", with instruction up to
university level.

CENTRAL INSTITUTIONS

The common pattern of higher education in most modern countries
provides technical and artistic studies along with the older intellectual
disciplines in the universities. In Scotland during the first half of the
twentieth century, while there were university faculties of engineering,
a distinctive feature of the educational system was the "central institution", offering higher courses up to degree and diploma level in technology, applied science, art, music, drama, commerce and other studies.
The first came into existence when the Continuation Classes Code of
1901 gave permission to the Scotch Education Department to exempt
certain regional colleges from the Code's provisions, and deal with them
under special Minutes. Ten were recognised between 1901 and 1909
and one more before 1939. Five others were controlled by the Department of Agriculture. These institutions were to become "the keystone
of the structure of technical education in Scotland".[13] For the highest
forms of their work several received grants from the University Grants
Committee. The steady growth in attendance is shown by the following
table[14]:

Year	Day Students	Evening Students
1903-4	1,537	12,375
1913-4	5,348	11,675
1916-7	3,582	6,294
1919-20	8,931	13,649
1929-30	8,039	11,581
1938-9	9,506	11,775
1942-3	6,624	7,135

In 1938, 2,500 of these Scottish students were working at a level comparable with the standard in universities; the corresponding figure for
the whole of England and Wales was only 4,000.[15]

Probably the most celebrated, certainly the largest of the central
institutions was the Royal College of Science and Technology in Glasgow. As a member of the Royal Commission on Technical Education
wrote in 1899[16]

Technical education in Britain had its beginnings in Anderson's College and in the Glasgow Mechanics' Institute, both of which now form part of the same College.

Its form in the first half of the twentieth century was largely the work of the Endowment Commissioners of 1882, who prepared a scheme for the amalgamation of advanced technical institutions in Glasgow. There were three – Anderson's College or "University", the College of Science and Arts which had developed in 1881 out of the Glasgow Mechanics' Institution, and Atkinson's Institution, founded in 1861 under the will of a local bookseller, for the instruction of artisans. In 1886 an Order in Council combined these into a technical college. At the same time the endowments of Allan Glen's School were reorganised: the work was extended to secondary technical instruction and placed under the supervision of the new college. One part of the Andersonian Institution, the medical school, removed itself westward and retained its independence for another sixty years.[17]

New buildings on an ambitious scale were opened in George Street between 1905 and 1910. Meanwhile in 1908 a college of weaving, dyeing and printing which had been founded in 1876 was amalgamated with the "Tech". When the Imperial College in London received its charter in 1908 there was some feeling that the Glasgow institution had been passed over, but George V provided some mollification in 1912 when he granted the title "Royal"; he had just returned from his tour of India, where he had been much impressed by the work of its old students. In the following year the College was affiliated with the university, so that several years of study in the former might lead to a university degree. At the outbreak of the Second World War the "Tech" was recognised as the chief centre of technical research in Scotland.

There were corresponding institutions in other parts of the country. Edinburgh had the Heriot-Watt College, organised at the same period as the Tech. In 1886, by a similar scheme for the readministration of endowments, the Heriot Trust took over supervision of the Schools of Arts and the Watt Institution. By 1939 its courses were mainly scientific and technological, but they also included commerce, art and music.[18] Robert Gordon's Technical College in Aberdeen had its origins when the day school there was permitted in 1881 to run continuation classes. Evening courses began two years later. In 1886 the Aberdeen Mechanics Institution and Gray's School of Art were transferred to the College and it was recognised in 1903 as a central institution. Its full status as a technical college came in 1910 with the incorporation of a school of domestic science founded in 1888.[19] It offered courses of wider scope than most institutions – science, technology, commerce, domestic science and art. Dundee had its Institute of Art and Technology.

Glasgow and Edinburgh had separate institutions for artistic studies, offering courses in painting, sculpture and architecture, and as a final qualification a Diploma of Art. The Glasgow School of Art, its Rennie Mackintosh building squeezed unimposingly into a narrow site above Sauchiehall Street, had over a thousand students, as had the Edinburgh College of Art.

There was a School of Art for a time in the Glasgow Athenaeum, which had been founded in 1847. In the nineties, when a move to larger premises in St George's Place had made wider accommodation available, the classes in drawing were expanded into a School, but it did not flourish. Much more successful was the School of Music, founded in 1890 out of the singing classes which had been running for over forty years. Within four sessions it had 1700 students and fifty professors, mainly part-time. The curriculum for its principal qualification extended over three years. In 1939 the "Scottish National Academy of Music" was recognised as a central institution.

Also in the nineties the enterprising directors of the Athenaeum expanded their elocution classes into a Department of Elocution and Dramatic Art. It was fairly successful in its early days, its external examiners including Edward Compton, Osmond Tearle and Frank Benson, but doubts are cast on the quality of its work when one reads that the early productions of its students were *Paul Pry*, *The Lady of Lyons* and "the dramatic adaptation of Sir Walter Scott's *Lady of the Lake*". As a dramatic school it lapsed for many years, but it was here that in 1950 a College of Drama was opened as part of the Royal Scottish Academy of Music.

The main institution specialising in commercial studies was the Glasgow and West of Scotland Commercial College which also grew out of classes in the Athenaeum, and was recognised in 1915 as a central institution. Twenty years later a new building was erected in Pitt Street. Commercial colleges were maintained in the other cities by the education authorities; the School of Economics run by the Dundee authority from the 1930s was incorporated in 1953 into St Andrews University.[20]

Domestic science was taught at various times in several institutions. In 1905 for example there were six schools of cookery whose certificates were recognised qualifications for teachers, three in Glasgow and one each in Edinburgh, Aberdeen and Elgin.[21] The two main independent colleges of domestic science however were in Glasgow and Edinburgh. The latter, Atholl Crescent, was founded in the eighteen-seventies by the Misses Guthrie Wright and Louisa Stevenson[22] and like the Glasgow "Do School" became a central institution early in the twentieth century.

Other central institutions under the supervision of the Scottish Education Department in 1939 were the Leith Nautical College and the Scottish Woollen Technical College at Galashiels, opened in 1909 and recognised in 1922. Paisley Technical College, opened in 1890, was not to be recognised until 1950. There were also various colleges supervised by the Department of Agriculture. The West of Scotland had a college of agriculture from 1899, the East from 1901, the North (in Aberdeen) from 1904. There were research institutes in animal nutrition (the famous Rowett, founded in 1913 with John Boyd Orr as its first director), animal genetics (opened in 1919 at Corstorphine by the University of Edinburgh), animal diseases (at Gilmerton, Midlothian, from 1920), plant breeding (Corstorphine 1921), dairy farming (Ayr 1928) and soil research (the Macaulay Institute, set up in Aberdeen in 1930).[23] The Veterinary College in Glasgow was founded in 1862, the Royal (Dick) College in Edinburgh, the first of its kind in Scotland, as early as 1823.[24]

CONTINUATION CLASSES

The central institutions alone however could not take over the provision of all the further education required. The Act of 1908 extended widely the system of continuation classes. It became the duty of school boards to provide classes for young people over 14 in the crafts and industries of their home district, as well as English, hygiene and physical training; they might even, if they desired, make attendance compulsory up to the age of 17.[25] In session 1909-10, in the southern division of the country, about a fifth of the children between 14 and 17 attended courses; the figure was probably smaller in the remoter areas of the north. The school board of Hoddam in Dumfriesshire had the distinction of being the first authority in Britain to compel attendance at such classes, and East Kilbride very soon followed.[26]

The responsibility for running continuation classes was now fixed on local authorities and successive Codes laid down the administrative principles to be used. In session 1937-8 over 161,000 students were taking courses, and in no fewer than 43,000 cases these extended over four years and more.[27] Many were seeking certificates, the demand for which increased steadily after the First World War. The Ministry of Education and the Scottish Education Department instituted National Certificates which could be gained at the end of three, four and five year courses of part-time study. They were awarded in mechanical and electrical engineering, in chemistry, building and naval architecture; in 1938 there were three hundred and twelve candidates at the ordinary and ninety-nine at the higher level. In addition there were also full-time courses for Higher National Diplomas, whose standard was comparable with that of a university degree; thirty-one candidates attempted these in 1938.[28] A somewhat larger number studied for the many certificates issued by the City and Guilds of London Institute, but the majority of students in continuation classes left with no certificate at all.

DAY RELEASE AND PRE-APPRENTICESHIP

It was difficult to blame them: attendance from 7.30 to 9.30 on three evenings a week throughout the winter for several years, sometimes in a centre several miles from home, was not an attractive prospect. Not all apprentices however were forced to work in this way. During the last quarter of the nineteenth century the "half-timer" system was still alive – in some mining areas for example, where alternate days were spent at school and pit, but most notably in Dundee, whose jute industry provided many more jobs for women and children than for men. The system was never satisfactory; probably its most famous alumnus was Harry Lauder, who had a spell at "Stumpie Bell's" school in Gordon's Mill, Arbroath.[29]

Some industries ran apprenticeship classes by day in their own factories or elsewhere: in printing for instance a young man had to attend classes for one day a week during the third and fourth year of his training. He studied English, arithmetic, drawing and his own branch of printing, and at the end of his course might go on to further studies in the nearest art school. An attempt by the plumbing trade to set up a similar system during the nineteen thirties was not successful.

It was reasonable that firms should apply for assistance in such schemes to the Scottish Education Department, and co-operation began as early as 1901 with the establishment of the West of Scotland Joint Committee for the Organisation of Classes in Science and Technology. This body, which devised schemes of work and set examination standards so that the more elementary classes could lead naturally to higher work, was still in existence half a century later.[30] The 1918 Act attempted to put industrial co-operation on a systematic basis by introducing compulsory day release. Each authority was instructed to draw up a scheme for part-time education for all children between leaving school and reaching their sixteenth birthday; later this was to be extended to 18. Their course was to include English and general subjects, vocational instruction and physical training.[31] Each employer was to release some of his young workmen for one day each week, while continuing to pay full salary. On the whole larger firms were prepared to co-operate: as early as 1911 textile manufacturers had operated such a scheme in the Lauder Institute, Dunfermline, and in 1914 the Albion Motor Company had asked Renfrew School Board to organise day classes for engineering apprentices. The taking over of the works by the War Office at the outbreak of hostilities killed that scheme. In 1918 six engineering concerns operated day release classes in their own works. A pioneer scheme begun by Edinburgh printers in 1919 was still in operation in 1951.[32] But the scheme as a whole never came into more than permissive effect. Several authorities on both sides of the border made efforts to comply, but twenty years later only one scheme, in Rugby, had survived.

The Act of 1936, which set a date for raising the leaving age, lent urgency to the problem of what to do with the year from 14 to 15. In 1937 the Advisory Council suggested the establishment of "pre-apprenticeship" classes to fill the gap. For various reasons, mainly non-educational, local authorities were slow to adopt the suggestion, but in 1938 about 12,000 young men and women were studying "preliminary" courses which were not dissimilar.[33]

THE POSITION IN 1945

The outbreak of the Second World War found further education in process of expansion and prevented that expansion from happening. The arrangements for higher technological education were as good as any in Britain and better than most; it was at the technical level that much remained to be done. There was general agreement that the apprenticeship system was haphazard and collaboration virtually non-existent between industry and the schools (or for that matter the universities.) "Pre-apprenticeship" and "day release" schemes had never really got off the ground. It was no mean achievement that Britain was able to fight a highly mechanised war at all; as it was her tanks never competed on equal terms with Germany's, though her aircraft fortunately did. In the battle for world markets after 1945 Britain – and therefore Scotland – had to transform her technical education or fall hopelessly behind.

REFERENCES

1. *S.E.D.R. 1939*, 91
2. DOBIE, *S.L.C.*, 28, 126-7
3. *Report of the Scottish Education Reform Committee 1917*, qu. C. A. B. CAMPBELL, *The Scottish School Curriculum 1885-1923*, Glasgow University Ed.B. Thesis, n.d., 44
4. *C.C.M. 1887* Scougal, 199; *1892-3*, 87; *1893-4* Kerr, 289
5. KERR, *Scottish Education*, 330
6. *S.E.D.R. 1946*, 12
7. WOOD, *T.E.S.*, 2 September 1966
8. MORGAN, *Scottish University Studies*, 213
9. *Report of the Royal Commission on Technical Education, 1884*
10. *Technical Instruction Amendment (Scotland) Act 1892*
11. *S.E.D.R. 1952*, 8
12. *C.C.M. 1888-9*, 265; *1890-91*, Kerr, 247
13. *S.E.D.R. 1952*, 8-9
14. *S.E.D.R. 1952*, 9, 91; *1955*, 105; *1961*, 121
15. OSBORNE, *Scottish and English Schools*, 185
16. SMITH, SIR SWIRE, qu. CLARKE, *T.E.S.*, 30 March 1962
17. *Royal Technical College Calendar 1914-15*
18. *S.E.D.R. 1957*, 100
19. *T.S.A. City of Aberdeen*, 402-3

20. *S.E.D.R. 1952*, 19-20; LAUDER, *Glasgow Athenaeum*, 112, 125, 134, 140-41
21. KERR, *Annotated Code of 1905*, article 21 (*c*) (2) footnote
22. Edinburgh Education Committee *Education Week 1936*, 121
23. TOCHER, "Agricultural Education and Research in Scotland", *A.U.R.* xxiv, 70, November 1936
24. Edinburgh Education Committee, *Education Week 1936*, 47
25. *Education (Scotland) Act 1908*, section 10
26. *C.C.M. 1910-11*, H/5
27. *S.E.D.R. 1939*, 99
28. *S.E.D.R. 1939*, 101
29. FAIRLEY, *Compulsory Education*, 116; MORRISON, *Compulsory Education*, 66; COWIE, *Arbroath*, 173
30. *S.E.D.R. 1952*, 12
31. *Education (Scotland) Act 1918*, section 15
32. *T.S.A. Fife*, 342; "Fifty Years in Further Education", *S.E.J.* 31 May 1963; *Edinburgh Education Report, 1949-51*
33. *S.E.D.R. 1939*, 43

CHAPTER 10

The Universities

THE foundations of the modern Scottish universities were laid by the 1858 Act, but their modern shape was determined in the eighties and nineties of last century. The Act of 1889 and its executive commissioners gave a pattern to curriculum and administration which was to endure with few alterations until long after the Second World War, but for a decade before the Act change had been in the air, especially in student life. The days of master and pupil were over; the talk was increasingly of the "rights of the student", especially when the end of the first World War brought up "the most rumbustious generation in the University's history".[1] The aftermath of 1945 was to see the process of democratisation carried much further.

The 1870s therefore were the last days of the *ancien regime*. The universities were still being administered by the Act of 1858. Students lived in a different world from their successors of the twentieth century:[2]

There is nothing anywhere quite like a Scottish university class as it was then (before 1892). It was a heterogeneous but united body from first to last. One entered and, allowing for wear and tear, one left College with the same body of students . . . The fact that one was a candidate for honours did not separate him from the class. The work for honours was something additional, done entirely by private reading . . . The effect for the student was an enormous volume of eager and generous emulation. The mathematical student contended for a good place in the Latin and Greek class; the classical student for a good place in mathematics and physics; both for distinction in philosophy and literature . . . Our intercourse had not the charm and grace, the freedom of mind and wide range of cultural interests, the critical spirit that one found in intellectual circles in Oxford. But no one who remembers it in tranquillity but must feel he owes a deep debt to the spirit of arduous and generous emulation which breathed from these lads carving out their own careers on the rudely cut and hacked benches of King's College.

The seventies and eighties of the nineteenth century saw the last florescence of several Scottish university traditions. One was the poor student, dependent on his own resources and tenacity, drawing heavily on his physical capital merely to endure while he completed his course. In Aberdeen until 1904, when a deposit of a pound was exacted for borrowing books from the university library, many students were too poor to join. There was also a great drain on physical strength: Professor Bain of Aberdeen predicted that of his three most distinguished pupils – Robertson Smith, Hunter and Minto – not one would reach the age of fifty and he was right.

Further tradtiions were the adherence to religious observance and to formal methods of class teaching:

> The chapter from the Bible reverently read, we commence the morning's work and pursue it for a solid hour. A "man" is called up and scrambles through a few lines of the passage prescribed. The *Orestes*, Arrian's *Anabasis*, fragments of Theognis and Solon, and of course the *Iliad*, were some of the works we read. As the translation proceeds, Geddes corrects and helps, kindly and sympathetically, and often reproduces the text in his own, his very own English, which he mouths in his efforts to fit it to the original.

Professor Fuller of the Mathematics Department rattled through his prayer at top speed, concluding "Amen yesterday gentlemen I was discussing the area of the parabola". Professor Trail of Botany locked latecomers out till after roll-call.[3] Too commonly, in Aberdeen at least, learning was regarded as completely the business of the student: "Let us deliver our teaching to them, and if they don't work, reject them at the examination; we are Professors, not schoolmasters".[4]

There was an air of *gravitas*, of earnest endeavour and seemliness about much of the work. Professor Robert Macpherson of Aberdeen, "in private life the most genial of men . . . was always grave and serious in the Chair, as was becoming, and never uttered a sentence that could provoke a smile". When the legendarily learned William Robertson Smith was a student in the same university in the seventies, we are assured that some of his best efforts in class were greeted by rounds of applause from his fellows. Failures in arts, of which there were not many, were known as "wasters"; in medicine, less earnest perhaps, they earned the name of "chronics".[5] There was no organised sport; only a few hardy spirits in Aberdeen played Rugby on the links, keeping their poles and touch flags in the backyard of a sympathetic householder nearby.[6] The conviviality of the fifties, which had involved much hard drinking, had so far dwindled that there was now a University Temperance Society. The professors were regarded with something like awe: the first class supper in Aberdeen with a professor in the chair did not occur until 1874 and most of the student speakers were struck dumb by his presence.[7]

Yet for all this concentration the standard of work was not universally high. There were still too many cases in which the "abundant leisure of a professor in a Scottish university quenched instead of stimulating his

K

literary ambition".[8] Professor Martin of Aberdeen, by no means an exception, was a byword for vanity and portentousness. He knew three books by heart and these were his canon, yet he "honestly believed his lecture the greatest thing in the eloquence of the world". Even where the professor was a man of weight and ability, the content of his syllabus might be less than imposing: Frederick Fuller's second-year class in mathematics dealt with Euclid, algebra and trigonometry, his third with conic sections, analytical geometry of two dimensions, differential calculus and the elements of integral.[9] Many subjects later to be regarded as of the first importance had still no chair. English, for example, was dealt with in a short course of "rhetoric" by the Professor of Logic, and in Aberdeen at least under Dr Bain it consisted mainly of grammar and composition.[10] Graduation was still uncommon, the 1876 Commission estimating that in Glasgow only one arts student in six or seven ever proceeded to take a degree.[11]

SOURCES OF THE 1889 ACT

It was obvious that the 1858 Act had not gone far enough in fitting the universities into the modern world. There was, for example, an unresolved problem in the structure of the arts curriculum. It was part of Scotland's presbyterian tradition that the central and commanding subject in all courses, scientific as well as literary, was philosophy. The Scottish ordinary degree aimed at producing liberally educated men, who might later specialise in one or other intellectual discipline, building their expertise on a broad foundation. Attempts begun in the 1820s to change to the English system of earlier specialisation and greater utility were defeated more than once. A determined effort by Principal Shairp to influence the 1858 Commissioners against the philosophical bias – indeed, to reduce philosophy for non-philosophers to formal logic – was not successful. The Commission gave more approval to the views of Professor Lorimer, who advocated postponing specialisation until after the general degree.

The reformers however continued their agitation. They quoted Dr Johnson in alleging that the ordinary course "gave every man a bite and no man a bellyful". They were able to point to the moderate performance of Scottish candidates in the examinations for the Indian Civil Service; the papers seemed to favour classical and mathematical scholars rather than philosophers. The alterations of 1872 in the school system suggested that a process had begun of assimilating the Scottish to the English pattern and the Anglicisers took encouragement from this. In 1876 a Commission under the chairmanship of Lord Inglis considered the universities yet again, and its report, published two years later, was solidly in support of the English type of specialisation.[12] It was another eleven years before legislative action could be engineered

however. Then the 1889 Act and its executive Commission under Lord
Kinnear set the pattern of Scottish university education for the twentieth
century.

CURRICULAR DEVELOPMENTS

Perhaps the most important steps the Commissioners took were in alter-
ing the arts curriculum. The specialists won. A wider range of honours
groups, alternative to the ordinary course, was introduced: Ordinance
11 of 1892 added Semitic Languages, Indian Languages, Modern
Languages, English and history to the already existing groups of Classics, Natural Science, Mathematics and Mental Philosophy, and the
statistics of the next forty years in Edinburgh show a trend away from
some of the older schools:

Period	Total honours degrees	Classics	Philosophy	N.Ph. Maths.	English	History	Modern* Langs.
1895-1915	926	320	81	179	155	61	168
(%)		34·6	8·7	19·3	16·7	6·6	18·1
1922-1931	973	114	32	213	207	140	204
(%)		11·7	3·3	21·9	21·3	14·4	21·0

In the first of these two periods twenty-four students took double and
one triple honours; in the second there were five double honours
graduates. There was also a change in the allocation to categories. Third
class honours were gained by twelve per cent in both periods, but the
percentage of Firsts dropped from forty-two to thirty-one, a process
which was to continue.[13]
    The two main features of the old ordinary degree course were swept
away. The fixed curriculum was abolished, and it became possible, as
one critic pointed out,[14] for two men to take the same degree without
attending a single class in common. By the same token, the philosophical
prescriptions vanished, a fact which was still being deplored in an
influential book almost seventy years later. The old ordinary course, it
was felt, had made students think; they had been required to grapple,
however unwillingly, with general ideas. The new freedom left them
without central guidance, dependent on the regurgitation of facts and
second-hand opinions, and often compelled by competing subject
prescriptions to spend their whole university time cramming.[15] The
raising of standards by the introduction of "double" or "advanced"
courses was not regarded as sufficient compensation. In the event
Regulations in the nineteen-twenties accepted these criticisms: various
general programmes were established, with items of choice in each,
and it became compulsory for all arts candidates to study a science, a

* including French-Latin.

modern language and either moral philosophy or logic. In the view of
the critics however it was too late: the damage had been done.

The long dominance of the arts faculty in Scotland was also assailed,
though not yet destroyed. Science had been by tradition part of other
programmes. The first modern chemistry teaching in Glasgow and
Edinburgh, for example, had been in the mid-eighteenth century under
the cloak of medicine; in Marischal it began in 1783 as an arts class, in
King's similarly in 1754. For over a century however chemistry in
Aberdeen remained in the hands of amateurs: Professor Patrick Forbes,
at King's in the early nineteenth century, lectured on Latin as well as
chemistry and was also one of the ministers of St Machar's Cathedral.
The attitude of Professor French of Marischal was interesting: he first
carefully described the existing corpus of chemical knowledge, then
cannily remarked:

> There's a man of the name of Davy who is now telling us that this is
> all wrong. He's a troublesome man, Mr Davy, but we'll bide a wee
> till we see.[16]

It was not until the 1870s that the earliest bachelor of science degrees
were awarded in Glasgow and Edinburgh, while Aberdeen's first came
in 1890. An Ordinance of 1892 constituted faculties of science in all
the Scottish universities. But the students could only be led to the water;
it is notable that in the nineteen-sixties, when expansion was at its
height, there were still empty places in science.

The applied sciences began to claim a place at the end of the nineteenth century. Edinburgh in 1885 was the first university in the United
Kingdom to develop a School of Agriculture and a regular course in
forestry appeared there in 1890. Agricultural classes in Glasgow were
held at the Royal Technical College. In Aberdeen there had been a
lecture course in the same subject since 1840; now in 1895 a School of
Agriculture, with four lecturers, was set up and a B.Sc. degree introduced, and 17 years later a chair was established. Engineering, already
well grounded in Glasgow, reached the dignity of a chair in Aberdeen
in 1923. Two years later a partnership was begun in Glasgow with the
Royal Technical College whereby civil engineering was taught at the
university, mechanical and electrical in the college, and in 1926 the
B.Sc. in engineering made its appearance.[17]

Law remained a minor attraction, judging by the number of candidates. The 1889 Commissioners, following the practice in Edinburgh
and Glasgow, instituted a lower degree, known as the Bachelor of Law
(B.L.), which unlike the LL.B. set up in 1858 could be taken without
holding a prior arts degree. Expansion however was slow. In 1906 it was
claimed that the teaching staff and equipment in Aberdeen were less
than when the Faculty of Law had been founded centuries before, and
as late as 1933 St Andrews still had no Faculty, only a Board of
Studies.[18]

An Ordinance of 1893 established a faculty of music in Edinburgh, where under the will of General John Reid there had been a professor since 1839. It was hardly to be expected that such a study would command multitudes of students, and the example was not followed elsewhere, though Glasgow set up a chair in 1930 and degrees of B.Mus. and D.Mus. in 1931.[19] Medicine on the other hand grew solidly in importance; the course was extended everywhere in 1911 from four to five years.[20] A Bachelor of Commerce degree – the only one in the period – appeared in Edinburgh in 1919.[21] Divinity began the long, sad process of wasting away in numbers, though not perhaps in scholarship.

If we compare all degrees awarded at Glasgow in various sessions, we see the changing trend in choice[22]:

Faculty	1913-1914		1923-1924		1933-1934	
	Number	Percentage	Number	Percentage	Number	Percentage
Arts	282	49·8	352	32·2	586	54·7
Divinity	14	2·5	10	1·0	24	2·2
Law	19	3·4	32	2·9	69	6·4
Medicine	139	24·6	423	38·6	187	17·4
Science	112	19·8	278	25·4	135	12·6
Engineering	—	—	—	—	71	6·6
Total	566		1095		1072	

The figures for 1933-4 were affected by the economic depression which offered comparatively few opportunities in industry and most security for the well-qualified teacher, once he had gained a post.

It was in the last quarter of the nineteenth century that departments of education and psychology appeared at all four universities. Chairs in the Theory, History and Practice of Education were founded in 1876 at Edinburgh and St Andrews, preceded as British teaching chairs only by that in the College of Preceptors. Their foundation was made possible by money left by Dr Andrew Bell in 1831 for general educational purposes. £18,000 of this was applied in 1872 to establish the two chairs.[23] The Bell benefaction was made on condition that the professors appointed adverted from time to time in their lectures to his "Madras system"; in time this provision became less honoured. Professor S. S. Laurie, the first incumbent of the Edinburgh chair, and "the most outstanding educationist in Scotland in the second half of the nineteenth century",[24] stated his conception of his duties in more general terms[25]:

> to give the students of the subject an ideal and also a method; but above all to inspire them with a sense of the infinite importance and delicacy of their task. He has to show them that they are not mere exactors of lessons, but trainers of the human spirit; and also *how*, animated by this large conception, they may, in teaching subjects, educate minds. He will expose the popular fallacy that the schoolmaster's work is a drudgery, and convince his students that it is a privilege.

At their inception the Bell chairs were much handicapped by inadequate endowment as well as by the "inferior status" of their subject. The older disciplines, already besieged by the claims of upstart subjects like history and English, were not disposed to grant equality to a study like education which had little separate tradition and few discernible frontiers. Lectureships in the subject were created at Aberdeen in 1893 and Glasgow in the following year, but there was no third Scottish chair for another half century. Lectureships in psychology, a suspect "science", were instituted in Glasgow in the nineties and Edinburgh in 1906. Aberdeen and Edinburgh went on to acquire professors, but there was no chair in Glasgow until after the Second World War.

Edinburgh took the lead in offering students educational qualifications. As early as 1885 a "Schoolmaster's Diploma", suitable for teachers in primary or secondary schools, was offered. It could be taken after a year of study and an examination in the "theory, art and history of education" with special reference to Locke, Milton and Comenius. The University Local Committees built on this foundation, but in 1905 the training of graduates as teachers was transferred to the new Provincial Committees. It was felt in Edinburgh however that there remained a place for a Diploma of Education, certifying theoretical studies on a higher plane than any undertaken in the training centres. One was inaugurated in session 1913-14, and in 1918 a second year was added to the course, with a degree of Bachelor of Education as the goal. Glasgow had instituted the same degree in 1917, and other universities followed.[26] A comparatively small number of students presented themselves for the degree between the two world wars, sixty-eight for example in Edinburgh between 1918 and 1931. Full-time study could cover the prescription in two sessions, but most students preferred to spend a longer period concurrently with training or teaching. The effort was probably worth making: many higher educational posts as lecturer, inspector or administrator came to demand such a qualification.

UNIVERSITY ADMINISTRATION

The Act of 1889 consolidated the administrative structure of the universities. There were still three main officials. The Chancellor was elected by and President of the General Council. He nominated an assessor to the Court, and when present conferred degrees at the appropriate ceremonies. The Lord Rector was elected triennially by the student body and acted as Chairman of the University Court when (seldom) he wished to exercise his right. His election was taken throughout the period mainly as an excuse for student rowdiness and a chance to honour a great man, generally a politician. In the nineteen-thirties however there was another movement towards the appointment of "working Rectors" like Compton Mackenzie and Cunninghame

Graham in Glasgow.[27] The Principal was Chairman of the Senatus and, as Vice-Chancellor, performed the capping ceremony on most occasions in place of the Chancellor. All but one of the Principals were appointed by the Crown, on the nomination of the Secretary of State for Scotland. By no means a free agent, the Principal's authority was well described by Professor Mackie as like that of the Doge of Venice: he was chairman of most of the important committees.[28] The extent of his power might be seen in the small but very influential Committee of Principals and Vice-Chancellors of British Universities, convened as a congress in 1910 by the Principal of London and achieving official recognition in 1931.[29]

One important part of the administrative system not set up by the 1889 Commissioners was the Secretariat. Each university arrived at its own answer to this problem by its own route, but the answers were similar, and the Secretary or Registrar, although he had no statutory rights, had very real influence, particularly when he came to serve both the Senatus and the Court.

The Court consisted of 14 members, elected from the Senatus and General Council, with one or two members *ex officio*. The highest authority in the University, it controlled general administration and, as a corporate body, governed property, revenues, ordinances and appointments to the staff. One suggestion, the establishment of a General University Court for all the Scottish colleges, was allowed to lapse: like Gladstone's optional clause for a University of Scotland in the 1885 Act, it met little acceptance.[30]

The *Senatus Academicus*, constituted of the Principal, professors and some lecturers, lost its executive functions to the Court in 1889, but maintained control of educational policy and discipline: its business included the content of courses, degree standards and requirements and the general policy of the University. The General Council, to which all graduates belonged on payment of a small fee, was entirely advisory, but had the right to appoint four assessors on the Court. The Scottish Universities Committee of the Privy Council, consisting of the Lord President of the Council, the Lord Justice General, the Lord Justice Clerk, the Lord Advocate and the University Chancellors and Rectors, was the ultimate court of appeal and adviser to the Queen.

UNIVERSITY FINANCE

In many ways the thorniest problem for the twentieth century was finance. To keep in step with the rapidly changing needs of the world required much more money than could be raised by the old methods of fees, bursaries and bequests – State money, in fact, was necessary, and whosoever accepts State money incurs with it responsibilities to the

State. The terms of the problem were set out in this period; the danger
was not to become oppressive until the next.

Regular government grants in aid of the universities began with the
settlement of an annual sum of £42,000 under the Act of 1889. This was
however a "poor bargain"[31] and it was soon increased. When a large
sum became available in 1892 to provide free education in England and
Wales, Scotland received an "equivalent" of £265,000 a year; since
Scottish elementary schools were already free, the money was used for
higher education, and £30,000 of it went annually to the universities.
The Act of 1908[32] substantially added to this provision: the Secretary
for Scotland was empowered to make payments to the universities out
of the new Education (Scotland) Fund on the application of the Courts
and the advice of any special committee he might set up; these payments
were to be in addition to the older Equivalent Grant. Finally in 1919 a
permanent University Grants Committee was established for the United
Kingdom as a committee of the Treasury. It had a stipendiary Chairman
– the first was Sir William McCormick – and it had strong advisory
powers, including wide extension of grants, essential in days of expansion: direct Treasury grants to the Scottish Universities through the
U.G.C. rose from £1·5 millions in 1920 to £23 millions in 1950.[33] The
Committee was greeted with suspicion, partly because, as a United
Kingdom body, it tied the Scottish colleges uncomfortably closely to
what they regarded as foreign bodies, but chiefly as an ominous hint of
state control. The safeguard was that all eight members of the original
committee were or had been academics themselves; in time the membership increased to fourteen, but the vast majority were University men.[34]

Meanwhile the traditional sources of funds continued. Endowments
and fees are difficult to disentangle, since about half of the former were
intended to defray the latter. The revenue to be gained from fees was
made much less complicated and more readily available after 1889, when
the Executive Commissioners put an end to the practice of making class
fees a perquisite of the professor and introduced a general Fee Fund.
Before that the first day of term had been a memorable occasion: some
popular professors were believed to walk home with £300, not all in
notes, bulging in their pockets.[35] It was of course another assault on
professorial independence, and contributed in its way to the comparative
aggrandisement of the Principal.

A large proportion of students received bursaries to assist them with
fees and living expenses. The principle, as we have seen, was well
established in Scotland, though in this period the total endowments
devoted to scholarships and bursaries expanded greatly. Edinburgh for
instance, which had comparatively few before 1860, was presented with
£142,000 for this purpose in the next two decades.[36] Of Aberdeen's 889
students in 1890, 291 held bursaries worth £5,290; in arts there were
227 recipients out of 401. Ten years later the total was 350, valued at
£8,000, and it was written that

the bursary system is better developed here than at any other Scottish
university . . . Education may be regarded as the most distinctive of
the industries of Aberdeen.[37]

In 1908 however the number had contracted to 285, and the other
universities were overhauling Aberdeen: Glasgow possessed 454,
Edinburgh 326 and St Andrews 147. Moreover St Andrews could boast
sixteen higher scholarships and Edinburgh a hundred and eleven, with
nineteen open research endowments. All universities offered a number
of monetary prizes.[38]

One feature of the late nineteenth and early twentieth centuries was
the growth of open competition outside Aberdeen, where it had been
firmly rooted for centuries: the first mention of a "bursary" there was
in 1549, and the competition had been fixed on the last Monday of
October since 1659 at least.[39] The rules varied, often with premiums
for the Classics, but the principle of an annual competition was firm.
Of the awards listed for 1908, 82·7 per cent were for open competition –
95·1 per cent in Edinburgh and 89·6 per cent in Glasgow, but only
70·2 per cent in Aberdeen and 59·6 per cent in St Andrews.[40] Moreover
the Aberdeen tradition of regarding the competition as a league table
for local schools – "44th! Most disgraceful!"[41] – increased and spread.
In the 1870s and 1880s the nature of the Aberdeen competition may be
gathered from the fact that of a total of 1,200 marks, 400 were allotted
to the Version (English into Latin), 150 to Latin-English translation,
175 to Greek, 175 to English, 200 to Euclid and 100 to Arithmetic. The
marking of the Version was often absurd: no word was admitted unless
warranted by Cicero, Caesar or Livy (Tacitus and Sallust were "doubtful"), while by contrast a common question in the English paper was
"Correct, if need be, the following sentences".[42] The presentation
bursary of course never completely disappeared: in the 1930s residential
and nominal qualifications were still more important than intellectual
for some awards. By that time moreover local authorities were providing
assistance for deserving children of their citizens.

But the most important financial accession of the early twentieth
century was the Carnegie Trust Fund. Andrew Carnegie, son of a
Dunfermline weaver, had emigrated to the United States in 1848 at the
age of thirteen. When he retired from business in 1901 he had amassed
an immense fortune in steel. His methods were not always kindly, but
the last eighteen years of his life were spent dispensing charity on the
grandest scale: he gave away 288 million dollars in the United States,
twelve million pounds in Britain, as "the greatest educational benefactor
of all time".[43] In 1898 he bought Skibo Castle in Sutherland and lived
there quietly after his retirement. His attention was drawn to the needs
of the universities by an article in the "Nineteenth Century" written by
Thomas Shaw, K.C., which, as a contribution to "The Educational
Peace of Scotland", suggested doing away with university fees. Four

years later Carnegie made available ten million dollars in bonds of the United States Steel Corporation for the aid of the Scottish universities. This meant in British currency a lump sum of two million pounds, producing an annual income of just over a hundred thousand pounds.

The Trust Deed consisted of three clauses. Clause C had least influence on the universities, since it dealt with extra-mural activities and evening classes. Clause A was devoted to building and research. Four main lines were laid down – a scheme of research fellowships and grants, capital building projects, the endowment of chairs and lectureships where required, and the development of libraries. Grants were made quinquennially: the first series amounted to almost forty thousand pounds, of which £11,500 was allocated to Edinburgh, £11,000 to Glasgow, and £8,500 to each of the others. In the first fifty years of its existence the Trust assisted the publication of three hundred books and over five thousand papers; it gave considerable aid, for instance, to the Scottish Research Council. By 1950 research fellowships were absorbing thirty thousand pounds a year. Several new buildings were also made possible – the Chemistry Institute in Glasgow, St Salvator's Hall at St Andrews, the Zoology Department and Bush House, Edinburgh, new King's College and the Foresterhill Medical School, Aberdeen, and the Dundee Physics Laboratory.

Clause B helped to pay fees for students. Any man or woman whom the universities would accept was entitled to apply for such assistance; after 1927 about £50,000 a year was being expended on some 60,000 students. At Glasgow for instance, when the fees in arts were fifteen guineas a year, the Trust provided nine pounds. About 1930 seventy per cent of Scottish students were receiving aid.[44] On one point Carnegie would have been disappointed. "The main consideration", he wrote,[45]

should be to help others by helping them to help themselves, to provide a part of the means by which those who desire to improve may do so; and to give those who desire to rise the aid by which they may rise; to assist, but rarely or ever do all. Neither the individual nor the race is improved by almsgiving.

He believed that the native independence of spirit of the Scot would take more kindly to his offer if he left it open to the student to repay as much of the grant as he could in his own time. By 1950, 60,000 had been helped, but only 1,777 had made some repayment, and the total returned was £77,348.

Carnegie's gift suffered virulent attack in its early days. Sir William Sinclair, professor of midwifery in Manchester, accused him in 1907 of softening the fibre of Scottish students. Principal Donaldson of St Andrews thought there were enough bursary funds to pay the fees of all genuinely deserving cases. Professor Harrower of Aberdeen attacked the Trust in 1913 for stressing the need to graduate and therefore directing students into soft options, for killing several useful classes in medicine and arts, for encouraging dissipation in "a class of men in whose case poverty was an all-powerful safeguard", for discouraging by its entry requirements many good self-taught men, for paying the fees of thousands who could quite well pay their own, and for making possible an enormous increase in amusements in the Scottish universities.[46]

Yet the extent of the benefaction made by Carnegie, measured purely in monetary terms, was immense. A fair estimate of the expenditure from the Fund over the years from 1901 to 1950 was almost £5,500,000, divided as follows:

Head of expenditure	Total (£)
Fees, grants, awards	2,400,000
Buildings and equipment	1,200,000
Research fellowships	606,000
Chairs and lectureships	553,000
Libraries	277,000
Halls of residence	245,000
Federated superannuation	51,000

The Trust brought a university education within the grasp of many young people who before the days of education authority assistance would have been deprived of the opportunity or killed themselves getting it; indeed it may be said to have postponed for many years the open argument over state control. The extension of learning by assistance to research was also praiseworthy: many investigations could never have been undertaken or books published without the generous support of the Fund. Principal Adam Smith of Aberdeen went so far as to remark that during the First World War, when the fee income was substantially reduced, Carnegie may have made it possible for the Universities to remain open.[47]

ENTRANCE EXAMINATIONS

The principle that entrance to any university should depend on an examination, thus ensuring a reasonable general standard of preparation, was settled in 1892 by the Commissioners. Various individual departments and faculties had previously imposed tests, but the unevenness of secondary schooling and a desire not to exclude any needy young man had militated against a general rule: the Commission of 1876, for example, saw the necessity but would not recommend unequivocally. A pioneer like Professor Chrystal of Edinburgh might suggest a National Examination Board, on which the Scottish Education Department, the schools and the universities should co-operate, but in this he was eighty years ahead of his time. With the institution of the Leaving Certificate in 1888 however there was no point in further delay, and an Ordinance of 1892 established University Preliminary Examinations.

Even then success in the examination was not made a condition of entrance: to encourage students from country areas and less favoured schools, junior non-qualifying classes in Latin, Greek and mathematics were retained.[48] But for all degree courses the preliminary examination demanded certain entrance requirements – in arts passes in English, Latin or Greek, mathematics and another language or dynamics; in science the same with the substitution of French or German for Latin or Greek; in medicine English, Latin, elementary mathematics, with Greek or French or German. Meanwhile from 1888 passes in the new Leaving Certificate had been accepted by the universities as denoting that students were capable of entering the ordinary classes.[49]

The universities were conferring on the standard of preliminary examinations as early as 1894 and a Joint Board of Examiners was constituted. It was another quarter of a century however before a Universities Entrance Board was set up. This was in 1918; its headquarters were in St Andrews and it had the right from time to time to indicate which subjects would qualify for entrance, though each Senate reserved the right under an Ordinance of 1918 to apply additional tests for admission to any faculty or class.[50] General Regulations for admission came into effect in 1927: they were based on an attestation of fitness for university studies, certifying the achievement of a certain group of passes in the preliminary examinations or the Leaving Certificate tests. That these were of comparable difficulty was ensured by using the same papers for both in the Spring diet.

The general standard of the entrance examinations was felt at first to be too high. In 1908 Dr Kerr pointed out that it was certainly more severe than the corresponding tests for Oxford and Cambridge,[51] though this cannot be regarded as evidence of high quality. If it was too stringent, the test was unnecessarily severe for the work to be done in an ordinary class, at which level Scottish university work was certainly, and continued to be, less advanced than that in England. The effect of the examination, to raise the average age of entrants, left it at seventeen or eighteen, still a year younger than south of the border.

STUDENT LIFE

Even if the 1889 Commissioners had never existed, student life would have changed radically during this period; in the eighties it had already begun to do so. With men instead of boys as students, "corporate life" was becoming a reality, and the eighties seem to have produced in every university a crop of outstanding young men. Professor Minto of Aberdeen called the class of 1880-4 "the most extraordinary and able that has ever passed through the University".[52] "Unions" appeared at which these men could meet and organise their own affairs; Glasgow's dates from 1885. Clubs multiplied. A few of them, generally Literary or

Debating, had existed, some briefly, during the past hundred years. Edinburgh had had its Dialectic, founded in 1787, its Diagnostic (1816), its Philomathic (1858). St Andrews' were the Literary and the Classical Society. Glasgow had seen the Triampherian, Anticappadocian and Eleutherian Clubs, the Dialectic being first mentioned in 1776. The Disputing Society met in Marischal in 1795, considering such grave matters as "whether ambition has done more good or evil?" and "whether has Satire or Panegyric the greater tendency to excite men to the Practice of Virtue?"[53] After 1880 there was mushroom growth: in 1932 Edinburgh had sixty-one.[54] Sport became organised. The Glasgow University Athletic Club was founded in 1881, with rugby and athletics as its active sections and held its first Sports Day in 1882. Aberdeen's Athletic Association followed eight years later.[55] Playing fields were laid out, and the authorities admitted a certain responsibility with Student Welfare Funds and Directors of Physical Education. There were student songs, most of them set down in Dr Millar Patrick's *Scottish Student Song Book* in 1891, and a number of hallowed student traditions. Some of these were genuinely old, for instance the exclusive right of Aberdeen magistrands to carry walking-sticks, but a good many, like "Daft Friday" in Glasgow, were the fruit of such inventive minds as James Bridie's.[56] A lively innovation after the First World War was the annual Charities Rag, begun in Aberdeen and spreading to Glasgow in 1921, to Edinburgh in 1932. At its Glasgow peak in the late twenties Charities Day was producing £15,000 a year, and that at a time when social conditions were so bad that a quarter of it had to be given to the Lord Provost's Unemployment Fund. In all the universities the most famous parts of the campaign, which came to occupy a week every year, were the Student Show, sometimes an opportunity for future talents of stage, screen and broadcasting, and the annual "stunts", of which perhaps the most famous was Miss Anne d'Apenny's Atlantic swim, which brought 40,000 people to the Broomielaw in 1926 to greet her.[57] It has been suggested that the great achievement of Charities Day was to kill the traditional hostility of Town and Gown.[58]

Magazines, always a popular student activity,* now achieved something like permanence, and the era of fugitive and sometimes scurrilous publications came to an end. St Andrews had had its *Argus* in the eighteen-twenties, its *Literary Magazine* in the thirties and its *Comet* from 1865 to 1866; *College Echoes* arose out of the S.R.C. News Sheet in 1889.[60] The *Glasgow University Magazine* (GUM) made its appearance in 1882 and seven years later achieved continuous life; it followed the *Universalist* of 1813, the *Student* of 1817, the *Philosophical Tatler* of 1826, the *Academic* and the *Collegian* of 1827, the *Scalpel* of 1836, which was put down by the Faculty, the *College Squib* of 1846 and the somewhat heavy *College Album* which lasted from 1828 to 1874.[61]

* At least with the writers. GUM was "always admired by the authors and condemned by the rest of the university".[59]

Among the early contributors to "GUM" were James Bone, John Buchan, Gilbert Murray and J. J. Bell, but its form and tone for many years were fixed in Edwardian times by O. H. Mavor ("James Bridie") and Walter Elliot. The *Edinburgh University Magazine* (from 1887 *Student*) was founded in 1871, following another production of the same name which had a brief existence in 1831, the *Edinburgh University Journal* and *Critical Review* of 1823 and the *Lapsus Linguae* of 1824.[62] *Alma Mater*, the Aberdeen student magazine, began an uninterrupted existence in 1887; its predecessors included the *King's College Miscellany* (1846), and the *Academic* of 1876-7, "often written inside the moral philosophy class while the boy waited outside for copy".[63] Each established journal had from time to time to fight off rivals, like the Edinburgh *Gambolier* which managed to exist throughout session 1908-9, its contents fairly typical of such journals – an article in verse on "The Happy Student", a diary of various societies (the Fabian attracted Bernard Shaw to the Synod Hall in November) theatre and sporting notes, much straight verse (Verlaine translations, for example) complaints about the Union food, some resolute naughtiness about Union dances and debates and a great deal of plain talking on other students.[64]

Students' Representative Councils began to appear spontaneously in the eighties – Edinburgh and Aberdeen in 1884, St Andrews the following year, Glasgow in 1886. The model was the *Studenten Anschluss* in Strasburg, visited in 1883 by Robert Bell, one of Edinburgh's first presidents, though there had been a "Student Society" in the capital since 1876.[65] The 1889 Act gave the S.R.C. official status, and the Councils in turn did much to alter the nature of the universities by fostering the concept of a student body instead of a group of struggling individuals.

THE ADMISSION OF WOMEN

Perhaps the most far-reaching of all the reforms of the 1889 Commissioners was in opening the universities to women. They found them attending classes in arts* and even medicine – Sophia Jex-Blake and her companions in Edinburgh – but not permitted to graduate. Edinburgh in 1872 had instituted a Certificate in Arts, marking a pass in three subjects. St Andrews, due largely to the efforts of Professor Knight, "the man who, I think, did most to advance the higher education of women in Scotland",[67] offered from 1876 the diploma of "Lady Literate in Arts" (L.L.A.) which, though hardly a degree, placed a worthy goal before women students. Although latterly it required passes in seven subjects, it had quite a vogue, and more than 4,000 women took it before its abolition in 1920.[68] A similar though less advanced goal

---

* In Aberdeen the daughter of Professor Patrick Forbes appears to have attended her father's chemistry class in the 1820s.[66]

appeared in the local and higher local examinations run by all the universities from the late sixties of the nineteenth century.

The history of higher education for women in Glasgow may serve as the national type. Mrs Campbell of Tullichewan, at a dinner party in 1868, prevailed upon Professor John Nichol to offer a course of "lectures for ladies" in English literature. The series, held in the Corporation Galleries, attracted capacity audiences, and in the next few years several professors and Principal Caird himself lent assistance. In 1877 the organisation flowered into the "Association for the Higher Education of Women in Glasgow and the West of Scotland"; professors, by permission of the Senatus, delivered lectures to members in their own classrooms. Six years later Mrs John Elder presented North Park House and its grounds to the Association and in 1884 it was opened as "Queen Margaret College". There many separate lectureships appeared: during its life there were classes in botany, chemistry, anatomy, materia medica, bacteriology, surgery and the practice of medicine, diseases of the eye, English, logic, moral and natural philosophy.[69] In 1892 the Commissioners opened full membership of the Scottish universities to women and the owners of Queen Margaret College offered the building to the Court of Glasgow, which accepted the gift. A large number of classes in arts and medicine continued to be held there and the term "Queen Margaret" came to be attached to every woman student of the university.

A series of milestones was then duly passed. Eleven women enrolled in the Aberdeen English class in 1894; the oldest, aged twenty-eight, was known to the student body as "Granny". In his first year as professor of English at Aberdeen, Herbert Grierson's first prizeman was "the most gifted and interesting student it has been my lot to encounter",[70] Miss Rachel Annand from the Free Church Normal College. The first women graduates in Aberdeen were capped in 1898 and the following year saw the first woman to gain first class honours. The first female lecturer was Miss Johanna Forbes, appointed in 1903 to the Humanity department.* There was a Women's Union in Edinburgh from 1905.[71]

But it would be wrong to claim that women were received at once on equal terms with men. One lecturer at Gilmorehill in the eighties apologised to his ordinary class of men for the feebleness of one of his lectures by saying that it had been "prepared for the weaker intellects of Queen Margaret College". Women were unable to exercise their university votes until the Franchise Acts of 1918 and 1928. Some remarkable arrangements were proposed for segregation, for instance a wooden partition in the Humanity classroom at Glasgow which would have permitted only the professor to see both sexes at once, and separate tuition in the embarrassing subject of anatomy; indeed, although women could graduate in medicine in Edinburgh after 1892, they were

* It was another sixty years before the first woman professor appeared.

not admitted to the medical school until 1916. As late as 1911 some gentlemen were seriously advocating a separate university for women. The novelty of their appearance was slow to wear off: "to us", wrote one Edinburgh graduate, remembering classes in 1900, "the mind of the front benches was a sealed book".[72] And although there were 631 women in attendance at Glasgow in session 1907-8, the historian of the university in 1909 felt constrained to make the arch observation that[73]

> of the women who have graduated in medicine not a few have ob-
> tained public appointments, and the number of women graduates
> who have entered into marriage has been remarkable.

Posts, inside the universities and out, were still hard to win[74];

> They approve the women in theory, but in practice always find the
> man the more distinguished candidate.

For better or worse however the women had arrived, Queen Margaret College in Glasgow had 1,700 students in 1929-30, but the accommodation provided there was cramped, and too far from the main university buildings. In 1935 all women students were absorbed into the classrooms at Gilmorehill, and the College building was sold to the British Broadcasting Corporation.[75] By the end of the thirties a quarter of Scottish undergraduates were women.

UNIVERSITY STAFF

One comparatively minor provision of the 1889 Commissioners, a sensible recognition of changing circumstances, was in time to change the pattern of university staffing. In 1892 the status of "lecturer", as recommended by the 1876 Commission, was recognised, and the rapid expansion thereafter of all university departments meant posts for many such subordinates, whose appointments, unlike those of professors, were not necessarily permanent. A new hierarchy appeared, descending from the professor through readers, senior lecturers and lecturers to assistant lecturers and assistants. By 1950 well over 1,500 men and women were employed in subordinate posts. Their security and status were guaranteed by the Universities (Scotland) Act of 1922, which admitted them to the General Council, allotted them a quarter of the seats on the Senatus, and made them eligible for nomination through the latter to the University Court. In addition a Federated Superannuation Scheme for professors and lecturers was introduced: they contributed five per cent of their salary, the university ten per cent, and since this applied to all universities in the United Kingdom, it helped to improve the mobility of staff. Finally, powers were given to each Court to fix the retiring age for each member of its staff on a scale between seventy and seventy-five for Principals and between sixty-five and seventy for others.[76]

Conditions of service were on the whole good. Principals and professors lost their life tenures in 1922, but might still remain in post to an age far beyond the permitted limit in most walks of life. The session became longer, it is true: an Ordinance of 1908 set the minimum at three terms totalling at least twenty-five weeks. Arts and Divinity adopted this; Medicine and Science tended towards longer sessions of about thirty weeks. Law had a thirty-week session, but many of its classes extended only to one or two terms. The fact that almost half the year was left without class meetings was justified by the universities' function in research. Ordinance 61 of the 1889 Commissioners instituted the very useful category of Research Fellow. Research degrees of Ph.D. were established in 1919 in three of the universities, and two years later in Aberdeen.[77] Private benefactors provided foundations to enable learned lectures to be delivered; perhaps the most famous was that under the will of Adam Gifford, Senator of the College of Justice, who left £100,000 in 1887 for short courses on Natural Theology in the four universities. Gifford Lectures like those of Macneile Dixon on the "Human Situation" have since taken a high place in scholarship. There was a steady improvement in the ratio of staff to students. Edinburgh in 1884, for example, had thirty-nine professors, three lecturers and twenty-six assistants, a ratio of one teacher to every fifty students; in 1933 there were fifty-nine professors, nine readers, one hundred and forty-eight lecturers and ninety assistants, and the ratio was one to fourteen.[78]

The effect over the period was greatly to improve the range, if not always the quality of individual research. On the other hand, although there was an "efficiency bar" on the salary scale for lecturers there was no insistence on attaining some teaching standard, either by training or certification. The consequence, despite the existence of several brilliant lecturers in each university, was to inflict on too many students talented men incapable of communicating their ideas in comprehensible language. Changes in methods were reluctant: in the Edwardian era the teacher still did most of the talking, while the students scribbled industriously and in the examinations reproduced exactly. In most classrooms indeed the benches were adapted only to sitting forward and writing; leaning back in comfort was impossible. The student "sold his birthright for a mess of knowledge".[79] One of the main aims of an Ordinance of 1908, which reduced the minimum number of lectures from a hundred to seventy-five, was to make room for new methods, especially tutorials. In popular subjects like English and French however first year classes might number several hundreds, and even in the nineteen-thirties it was uncommon for arts students to have any tutorial work before their junior honours year. One thing which also remained unaltered from earlier days was the reverence for prizes and prize-winners: the Logic classroom at Edinburgh bore on its walls the names of all First Prize-men after 1836, the year in which Sir William Hamilton came to the chair.[80]

L

There was a notable change in this period in the sources from which teaching staff was recruited. Increasingly – in the arts faculties by the 1930s almost exclusively – posts were available only to Oxbridge men, often but by no means exclusively Scots. Professors of Classics in St Andrews before 1858 for example were all Scots-educated; of the first nine thereafter seven had been to Oxford, six had been Fellows, six had been at Balliol and five were Snell Exhibitioners.[81] A pattern was established – First Class Honours in a Scottish University, First or very good Second B.A. at Oxford or Cambridge, then return to Scotland and begin the long climb up the college ladder. In general, however, rewards were not such as to attract the most brilliant minds of their generation to pass their whole careers in Scottish academic life. Aberdeen notably was famous for its glittering birds of passage – Sir George Thomson in natural philosophy, Sir Frederick Soddy in chemistry, Ritchie, Hogben and Hardy in natural history, Grierson in English, Learmonth in surgery, Baillie in moral philosophy. With the rapid multiplication of new universities in England in the second half of the twentieth century the probability was that lecturers would be attracted south even earlier in their career.[82]

EXTRA-MURAL CLASSES

From time to time the universities made efforts to extend their work outside their own walls. In the sixties and seventies of the nineteenth century, when secondary education in Scotland was seriously in need of a final aim to help focus effort, they provided certificates awarded on the results of Local Examinations. With the appearance of the Leaving Certificate this work was done, and the Local Certificates were discontinued, but they had been of great value in the higher education of women. In the following century the universities transferred their efforts to organising evening classes on a fairly high level for laymen, mainly in such studies as history, literature and philosophy. These "university extension" classes received a form of permanent administration in 1919 with the establishment of extra-mural adult education departments, dealt with in the preceding chapter.[83]

DEVELOPMENTS IN THE INDIVIDUAL UNIVERSITIES

One notable trend after 1889 was the wasting away of individuality in the universities, virtually inevitable with greater dependence on public money and rapidly accelerating after 1945. Occasional outbursts of protest against "anglicisation" – against halls of residence for instance in the eighties and nineties – were stimulated by a reaction against this process. There were few changes however in the national structure. In

1895 one of Her Majesty's Inspectors alluded to the possibility of a new college at Inverness, but this appears to have been no more than a pious personal wish.[84] In fact only one new college was founded in the period, at Dundee. This was first proposed in 1874, and lecturers from St Andrews delivered regular courses in the city, even before there was a Tay Bridge, though the professor of chemistry told the Commissioners of 1876 that the exertion had half killed him. In 1880 Miss Baxter of Balgavies made a gift of £120,000, and three years later the college was opened with chairs in classics, English and eight scientific subjects.[85] Fourteen years afterwards the foundation was admitted to full membership of the university of St Andrews and new faculties followed. In 1898 a conjoint medical school was opened in Dundee, thus allowing St Andrews to grant medical degrees like the other Scottish universities; lack of hospital facilities had prevented this. In 1899 the first lectures in law to be given in St Andrews for three hundred years took place in the Dundee college, a manifest source of new strength.

Meanwhile the parent university was passing through difficult times. In 1876 there were only 130 matriculated students, while Aberdeen had 677, Glasgow 1,773 and Edinburgh 2,351. Relations between the Senate and students were not harmonious: the "Kate Kennedy" procession, begun as an undergraduate rag in the eighteen-forties, was becoming increasingly rowdy and in 1881 it was suppressed. More than one student was sent down at this time for insubordination.[86] In the circumstances it was to be expected that several men in authority should feel the oldest Scottish university had passed its period of usefulness. The first Universities Bill, introduced in 1883 as a consequence of the Inglis Report, included a clause proposing the abolition of the St Andrews colleges. There was great opposition however, and the report for 1883 of the General Assembly's Education Committee stated that the forthcoming abandonment of the clause was "generally understood".[87]

The straitened condition of the university continued nevertheless until the end of the century and there were further proposals in the nineties to close the colleges and divert their endowments. In the end, with difficulty, the danger was circumvented. Part of its legacy however was an increasing conviction in Dundee that the college there was oversupervised. There was a strong separatist movement which soon began to demand university status, and relations with the mother university became increasingly strained. When Henry Jones became professor of moral philosophy in the eighties, he expected an inimical reception from the students at St Andrews because the pattern of voting at his election suggested that he was a "Dundee candidate", and throughout his time there he found meetings of the Senate made distasteful by the perennial feud.

St Andrews remained a university with a strong personality and a collegiate tradition quite different from any other in Scotland. Virtually all the students lived in hostels or lodgings, and the advantages of corporate residence and the pursuit of studies with few distractions were clear. St Andrews, particularly in winter, was first and foremost a university town. It had its giants, of whom one of the most distinguished was D'Arcy Wentworth Thompson (1860-1948), son of a professor in Queen's College, Galway, who had been classical master at the Edinburgh Academy. Thompson was a professor of natural history for no less than sixty-four years, thirty-three at Dundee then thirty-one at United College, and he was also something of an encyclopedist, with a remarkable depth of classical knowledge.[88]

Among the other universities Edinburgh could show a fine record of progressive work. It took the lead in instituting Local Examinations and encouraging the higher education of women. In the last quarter of the nineteenth century it expanded rapidly to be the largest Scottish institution, with 2,351 students in 1876 and 3,341 in 1882. Later Glasgow was to rival her in population, but Edinburgh remained best provided generally with chairs and lectureships. Several of the incumbents had international reputations – Grierson and Saintsbury in English, Alexander Gray, political economist and poet, Macmurray the philosopher, James Drever in psychology and Godfrey Thomson in Education.

Numbers in Aberdeen increased from 656 in 1872 to 909 in 1888 and 1,258 in 1938. The most striking increase in the early part of the period was in medicine – from 256 in 1872 to 450 in 1888. On the whole, however, Aberdeen remained the "Teacher's University", famous, as John Stuart Blackie said, for her beef, granite and Latin.[89]

Glasgow showed most rapid expansion. It was as though the site of the Old College in the eastern slums had confined its energies. Within a few years of the transfer to Gilmorehill new buildings were springing up. In 1874 the Western Infirmary was opened, designed from the outset as a teaching hospital. The facilities of the Royal however were too good to waste and a new college of medical studies was opened there in 1876, to flourish for over seventy years. The first new buildings inside the university grounds were erected just after the beginning of the new century. The Botany buildings, opened in 1901, were followed next year by the James Watt Engineering Laboratories (extended in 1920) and in 1907 by new departments of Materia Medica and Natural Philosophy. A large Zoology building appeared in 1923 and a circular Reading Room in 1939. Meanwhile in 1935 the Observatory had come from Horselethill to the neighbourhood of the university.

The medical school, less celebrated than Edinburgh's but still high in prestige, shared in the general Scottish fall in numbers in the first decade of the twentieth century. Two independent Glasgow colleges moreover offered a qualification to practise medicine. One was the famous Anderson's College; in 1886, when the main part of the institution was incorporated in the new Technical College, the medical faculty moved to accommodation in Dumbarton Road and provided courses

there for the Licence of the Royal College of Physicians. Its most
famous student was David Livingstone. The other college, providing
similar courses, was founded in 1876 by the managers of the Royal
Infirmary; in 1889 it took the title of St Mungo's College and ten years
later it was incorporated. For some time there was a Faculty of Law
there also, but almost all its work was medical. Glasgow also had a
Dental Hospital and School and a Veterinary College, founded in
1862.[90]

The University's great men included Richard Jebb and Gilbert
Murray in Greek, Bradley, Raleigh and Macneile Dixon in English,
Edward Caird, later Master of Balliol, in philosophy, William Macewen,
Robert Muir and the Glaisters ("old John" and "young John") in
medicine. Among her students in the nineties were John Buchan,
Robert Horne and A. D. Lindsay; in the nineteen-hundreds, besides
Elliott and Mavor, there were Thomas Johnston, James Maxton and
John Boyd Orr.[91] Lord Kelvin held the chair of natural philosophy
until 1899.

But there was a growing approximation, at least in Glasgow and
Edinburgh, to the conditions later described so vividly in "Redbrick
University". In Glasgow, particularly, students attended the university
as they would a day school. Classes, even in the higher ordinary or
advanced stage of some subjects, might number hundreds. For many
the University Union was a restaurant and a dance hall rather than a
club. Although at the honours level in the thirties professors sought to
develop a tradition of individual work, there was a growing feeling of
mass production. The effect might be seen in the adolescent conduct
at rectorial addresses and elections, when ebullience sometimes sur-
passed the boundaries of good manners and even commonsense. It
might also be traced in the disadvantage under which a Scottish youth
laboured beside his English cousin where social graces were handy;
the most brilliant student might show himself tongue-tied in ordinary
intellectual conversation, and he was often a bad arguer, mistaking
loudness for conviction and boredom for defeat. The Officer Selection
Boards of the Second World War showed many Scots in a light which
did them less than justice.

THE POSITION IN 1939

The Scottish universities on the eve of the Second World War were on
the brink of transition. Rapidly as their numbers had expanded however
there were only hints of the vast changes to come. Arts was still the
largest faculty. The applied sciences were barely noticed in popular
esteem – or for that matter by many professors – as university subjects
at all; there was a place for them, of course, but it was in the central
institutions. The formal lecture system was still deeply entrenched.

The Bursary Competition exercised a powerful – some thought baleful – influence on all secondary schools with any pretension to scholarship, and the bursaries themselves were important, often essential, to those who won them. State interference was still a cloud little bigger than a man's hand.

One feature of the period is worth remarking – the steady growth of a university mystique. In 1899 it was still possible for the biographer of Professor Minto to write[92]:

> The natural tendency of graduates from the Scottish university system is to swear at, not by their *Alma Mater*.

Already however the rosy glow of sentiment was suffusing college memories, so that Andrew Lang could assert

> St Andrews by the Northern sea
> A haunted town it is to me,

and the "Crown of King's" had a life-long attraction for its graduates. Principal Sir William Geddes remarked to a friend[93]:

> I sometimes believe it will be found in my heart, as Calais was in Mary's. I can remember like yesterday the feelings with which I first beheld it as a boy. Well I hope it is the last object I shall see.

And such devotion was not restricted to professors, nor to King's. Marischal too was well remembered[94];

> Marischal College, the College of Dugald Dalgetty, a house rude and plain of feature, but ever memorable and dear, a thing to lift his imagination to the frosty stars.

Even drab, grimy Glasgow, of whom an Aberdonian could write in 1917 that he had never heard any graduate express any attachment to the old buildings or "the present pile", had its devotees[95];

> I must henceforth tread Life's highways;
>   Never more may I invade
> Those enchanted lanes and byways
>   Sacred to the genus "blade";
> For alas! that primrose way is
>   Closed against us once for all
> When we cross the crimson dais
>   Of the Graduation Hall.

This sentimental attachment, in a century increasingly unsentimental, to institutions whose rooms might be dark and uncomfortable, their lecturers dull and prosy, their "corporate life" unknown to thousands of daily commuters, is a strange but rather charming phenomenon.

REFERENCES

1. OAKLEY in *Five Hundred Year Book*, 116
2. GRIERSON, *The Problem of National Education*, 319-22, qu. G. E. DAVIE, *The Democratic Intellect: Scotland and Her Universities in the Nineteenth Century* (Edinburgh University Press 1961), 101
3. SHEWAN, ALEXANDER, *Meminisse Juvat, being the Autobiography of a Class at King's College in the Sixties* (Aberdeen University Press 1905), 14, on Principal Geddes; LEASK, *A.U.R.*, xxxviii, 123; MCGREGOR SKENE, *ibid.*, 464
4. *Aurora Borealis Academica*, 231
5. *Aurora Borealis Academica*, 159, 190; BULLOCH, "King's College in the Early Eighties", *A.U.R.* xxv, 73, Nov. 1937, 39
6. MATHESON, "University Sport in Earlier Days", *A.U.R.* xxiv, 72, July 1937, 248
7. MACLEAN, *Northern University*, xxviii; LEASK, *Interamna Borealis*, 46-7
8. *Aurora Borealis Academica*, 165
9. *Aurora Borealis Academica*, 37, 98-9
10. GRIERSON, "Development of English Teaching in Aberdeen", *A.U.R.* i, 1, Oct. 1913
11. MACKIE, *Glasgow*, 287
12. DAVIE, *Democratic Intellect*, 6, 80-86
13. TURNER, *Edinburgh*, 196-8
14. *Classical Association of Scotland, 1908-9*, 62
15. DAVIE, *Democratic Intellect*, 6-7; WILLOCKS in *Five Hundred Year Book*, 87
16. BARRER, "Chemistry in Aberdeen", *A.U.R.* xxxv, 108, Spring 1953, 43; FINDLAY, *Chemistry in Aberdeen*, 5, 14, 43, 44, 48
17. TURNER, *Edinburgh*, 263; HENDRICK, "Rise and Progress of Agricultural Study in the University", *A.U.R.* ii, 5, Feb. 1915, 119; HENDRICK, "Early History of Agricultural Education in Aberdeen", *A.U.R.* xxv, 73, Nov. 1937; BLACKADDER, "Engineering in the University", *A.U.R.* xvii, 49, Nov. 1929
18. *Quatercentenary Book*, 302; MORGAN, *Scottish University Studies*, 110
19. MORGAN, *Scottish University Studies*, 130-32; MACKIE, *Glasgow*, 297
20. MACKIE, *Glasgow*, 299
21. TURNER, *Edinburgh*, 208
22. *T.S.A. City of Glasgow*, 904, my percentages
23. MORGAN, *Makers*, 159-69
24. MORGAN, *Makers*, 193
25. LAURIE, Inaugural Lecture
26. KNOX, *250 Years*, 196; MACKIE, *Glasgow*, 297

27. MACKENZIE in *Five Hundred Year Book*, 36-7
28. MACKIE, *Glasgow*, 291
29. HETHERINGTON, "The British University System 1914-54", *A.U.R.* xxxvi, 112, Spring 1955, 8-9
30. KNOX, *250 Years*, 163
31. PEDDIE, J. R., *The Carnegie Trust for the Universities of Scotland: the First Fifty Years, 1901-51* (Edinburgh 1951), 16
32. *Education (Scotland) Act 1908*, section 16
33. MACKINTOSH, *Education in Scotland*, 184
34. HETHERINGTON, "British University System", 6
35. TURNER, *Edinburgh*, 44
36. GRANT, *Edinburgh*, ii, 145
37. WATT, *Aberdeen and Banff*, 386; *Aurora Borealis Academica*, 221
38. KERR, *Scottish Education*, 378-88
39. LEASK, notes to Maclean, *Northern University*, 344
40. KERR, *Scottish Education*, 378-88, my percentages
41. MACLEAN, *Fordyce Academy*, 118-19
42. SHEWAN, *Gymnasium*, 110-127
43. MORGAN, *Makers*, 147
44. MORGAN, *Rise and Progress*, 155
45. Article in *Northern Review*, qu. MORGAN, *Makers*, 153
46. ROBB, *Carnegie Trust*, 144-66
47. SMITH, "Universities of Aberdeen", *A.U.R.* xxii, 65, March 1935, 108
48. MORGAN, *Rise and Progress*, 150
49. STRONG, *Secondary Education*, 234; *C.C.M. 1888-9*, xxviii
50. *C.C.M. 1894-5*, 201; MORGAN, *Rise and Progress*, 150-152
51. KERR, *Scottish Education*, 271
52. LEASK, *Interamna Borealis*, 79
53. FERGUSSON, R. MENZIES, *My College Days, the Autobiography of an Old Student* (Gardner 1887), 61-63; WILLOCKS in *Five Hundred Year Book* 83; YOUNG, "The University's Disputing Society of 1795-6", *A.U.R.* iv, 10, Nov. 1916, 48
54. TURNER, *Edinburgh*, 352
55. CUNNINGHAM in *Five Hundred Year Book*, 159; STRATHDEE, "Playing Fields of King's", *A.U.R.* xl, 4, Autumn 1964
56. BRIDIE in *Five Hundred Year Book*, 17; *Aurora Borealis Academica*, 104
57. OAKLEY, in *Five Hundred Year Book*, 116-122
58. OAKLEY, *College Courant*, xvii, 30, 33
59. MAVOR, O. H., qu. *College Courant*, xvi, 31, 39
60. CANT, *St Andrews*, 128
61. MURRAY, *Old College*, 523-544
62. GRANT, *Edinburgh*, ii, 490
63. LEASK, "University Magazines", *A.U.R.* ii, 4, Nov. 1914, 13

64. *The Gambolier, a Light Journal*, Edinburgh 1908-9
65. TURNER, *Edinburgh*, 338; *The Old Quadrangle: Edinburgh University MCM-MCMV by Four Graduates*, Hay, Edinburgh, 1907, 112
66. SHEPHERD, "Women in the University", *A.U.R.* xxix, 87, Summer 1942, 180
67. *Laurel Bank School*, 3; HORN, *Edinburgh*, 191
68. CANT, *St Andrews*, 120; KNOX, *250 Years*, 160-61
69. KERR, *Scottish Education*, 361; CAMPBELL in *Book of the Jubilee*, 129-134
70. GRIERSON, "Development of English Teaching", 50
71. SHEPHERD, "Women in University", 171-7; TURNER, *Edinburgh*, 351
72. MACMILLAN in *Five Hundred Year Book*, 55; KNOX, *250 Years*, 160-161; *Old Quadrangle*, 19; LUMSDEN in *Votiva Tabella*, 235; MCMILLAN in *Book of the Jubilee*, 141
73. COUTTS, *Glasgow*, 459
74. SHEPHERD, "Women in University", 178
75. *Five Centuries*, 80-81
76. MORGAN, *Rise and Progress*, 153-4
77. MORGAN, *Scottish University Studies*, 192-200
78. TURNER, *Edinburgh*, xiv
79. *Old Quadrangle*, 21, 40, 114
80. TURNER, *Edinburgh*, 202; *Old Quadrangle*, 40
81. WRIGHT in *Veterum Laudes*, 50
82. MACKINTOSH, *Scottish Education*, 185
83. MORGAN, *Rise and Progress*, 161
84. *C.C.M. 1894-5*, Stewart, 412
85. MACKAY and PURDIE in *Votiva Tabella*, 189-192
86. CANT, *St Andrews*, 117
87. *General Assembly E.C.R. 1883*
88. BURT in *Veterum Laudes*, 116-17; JONES, *Old Memories*, ch. 7
89. *Aurora Borealis Academica*, 120, 217
90. MCNEE in *Fortuna Domus*, 192; *Five Centuries*, 31 ff; MUIR, *John Anderson*, 84; AIRD, *Old Glasgow*, 188
91. OAKLEY, *College Courant*, xv, 29, 33-7
92. *Aurora Borealis Academica*, 69-70
93. *Alma Mater*, Feb. 1900, 148
94. SYMON in *A.U.R.*, xxxviii, 4, 307
95. BROWNING, "Emeritus", *University Verses* (Hodge, n.d.), 41

PART II

The Contemporary Situation

CHAPTER II

Features of the Period

SCHOOL POPULATION

IN a speech delivered in 1901 at the Ninth Jubilee celebrations of the University of Glasgow Lord Rosebery remarked with foreboding[1]:

> I wish I could foretell as happy circumstances when celebrating the Tenth Jubilee as you now enjoy. Before that you will have passed through conditions which will have shaken the world.

The prophecy was not perhaps inspired: even in 1901 there was a strong likelihood of armed clash in Europe. But there is no doubt how amply events justified his prediction. The world of the fifties and sixties bore little more resemblance to that of 1901 than it did to Renaissance Europe, a fact for which there were three main causes, the Russian Revolution, the harnessing of nuclear power and the establishment in Europe and North America of universal education. As Mark Twain put it, "soap and education are not as sudden as a massacre, but they are just as deadly in the long run".[2]

More people were being educated at a time in Scotland in the two decades after the Second World War than at any other period in her history, and the number rose every year. Families were larger than they had been since Victorian days. The death-rate had been spectacularly reduced. The immediate post-war "bulge" in the birth-rate subsided in the early fifties but only a few years later it rose again, to remain permanently high. Compulsory school life became longer: the Act of 1945 reiterated the provisions of 1918, but went further. The leaving age was to rise to fifteen as soon as possible, and thereafter, when the Secretary of State deemed it advisable, to sixteen. The first part of the measure came into force on 1 March 1947. Within a year there were 40,000 extra pupils in the schools and various newspapers were conducting a campaign – still alive ten years later – for a return to fourteen or the raising of the age of entrance to six. Far from bowing before the storm however successive governments of both major parties fixed 1970 as the date for enforcing the second part of the plan and it was only in face of economic necessity that the Socialist administration announced, "with the greatest reluctance", a postponement till 1972.

The early sixties also produced what came to be known in educational cant as the "Trend". For one reason or another pupils stayed longer at school. On practical grounds there was the appearance of a national certificate examination in the fourth instead of the fifth year, the growing demand of employers for paper qualifications, the fact that apprenticeships began at sixteen, but at a deeper level there was the growing conviction that higher education should no longer be reserved for the few. In 1954 6·7 per cent of Scottish children attended school until they were seventeen, twelve per cent in 1962, and the number rose even more steeply thereafter. The number of young people in attendance over that age more than doubled, from 7,218 to 15,152, between 1956 and 1966.[3]

The effect was a total school population in 1966 of almost 903,000 in public and grant-aided institutions and another 21,000 in the independents. The figure in 1947 had been just over 760,000, and with the exception of a small decline (3,000) in 1963, it had never ceased to rise since then. About 60,000 of the 1966 children were volunteers – that is, they had passed the leaving age and were in the fourth, fifth and sixth years of their secondary course.[4]

NURSERY SCHOOLS AND YOUTH SERVICE

The education of children for ten years of their lives was not however the whole story. The 1945 Act, as we have seen, laid a duty on education authorities to establish nursery schools wherever there was enough parental demand. In the event this clause had to be held in abeyance until there were places for all children of school age, and in the sixties the proposed raising of the upper limit to 16 postponed further action on nursery classes to the dim future. Some authorities did convert private houses or make temporary arrangements, and Aberdeen city showed some foresight in constructing infant schools designed ultimately to include nursery classes. After 1951 however there was no nursery extension. There were 81 public schools in that year with 4,822 pupils, but thirteen years later the numbers were 86 and 4,542. Forty-one of the schools in 1964 were in Glasgow.[5] In addition a few children, less than a thousand in the country, were to be found in private "preparatory schools".

Education after 1945 also occupied itself with children at the other end of the compulsory period. Before the Second World War there had been few attempts to inaugurate youth clubs; it was felt that this was best left to voluntary organisations like the Scouts, Guides and the peculiarly Scottish "Boys' Brigade", which had its origins in the west of Scotland in the 1880s. Aberdeen experimented in 1924 with a "Youth Recreation Club" in connexion with a continuation class, and its success led to an expansion of the scheme. By 1939 there were nine clubs in existence,[6] and when two years later the Scottish Education Department issued a circular on the subject, it recommended three of them as models. In 1942 Circular 244 established a Scottish "Youth Service", to be run by each local authority in its own area, with the advice of a Youth Council; ten years later the service had 13,400 voluntary centres and clubs, with about 400,000 members.[7] A report entitled "The Needs of Youth in these Times" was issued in 1945 by the Scottish Youth Advisory Committee, and gave a comprehensive estimate of the problems to be tackled. In general it suggested that the duty of the authorities should be to provide facilities where the voluntary organisations had failed to do so adequately: first however they should give liberal assistance to these groups. The Committee gave many detailed suggestions for the conduct of youth centres, and the types of activity to be encouraged.[8] The Acts of 1945 and 1946 confirmed many of them, particularly the advisability of assisting voluntary bodies: indeed any organisation providing facilities for social and physical training was entitled to apply for a grant from the Education (Scotland) Fund.

Local authorities on the whole fulfilled their duties carefully. Most appointed youth organisers for full- or part-time work: East Lothian for instance had four, and was particularly proud of its undenominational centre in Tranent and the eleven children's clubs in its primary schools in 1948.[9] There were national sports competitions – a football cup was one – and many authorities ran youth festivals of drama and music. Glasgow provided a building, the "Palace of Art" left by the Empire Exhibition of 1938, as a show-case for its youth service; every year there were displays of work, sports demonstrations and choral and dramatic competitions. The story of the youth service was not one of unblemished success: juvenile delinquency continued to be a growing problem, and many youth leaders were discouraged by the stupidity and amorality of their charges. But, especially in urban areas, youth clubs brought opportunities for cultural hobbies and organised sport within the grasp of many children otherwise deprived of them.

The beginning of the sixties saw a movement to renovate and extend the service. There was evidence that while most children belonged at some time to a club – one investigation in the west of Scotland in 1961 put the figure as high as seventeen out of every twenty – many allowed their membership quickly to lapse and comparatively few were vividly enthusiastic. They joined because their friends did, through curiosity, by parental pressure or to learn some specific activity like swimming or dancing. They left whenever they began to feel the activity was "kid stuff", when their friends left, when they found stronger interests, or because of domineering, inefficient or unsympathetic leaders: "Brown Owl was rotten."[10]

By far the most important document produced in this field at the time was the Albemarle Report on the service in England and Wales, presented in 1960 by a special committee appointed by the Minister of Education, and widely discussed on both sides of the border. The most important recommendations envisaged a ten-year development programme for the youth service, a national campaign for more voluntary workers and the continuation of the voluntary services, extensive and intensive training of leaders, doubled in number, financial help on a wider scale to voluntary bodies and research into the whole system.[11] In Scotland conferences were held under the auspices of the Department and Moray House College of Education, and a Standing Consultative Council, under the chairmanship of Lord Kilbrandon, made a determined effort to foster efficiency by training competent leaders. Regional Committees were established in the mid-sixties, their work a locally determined blend of advice, provision and supervision, and a board was set up to conduct tests for national leadership certificates.

Nevertheless achievement, by no means inconsiderable, fell short of planning and even, to many people's disgust, of English performance, partly from lack of funds in a time when there were higher priorities, partly because much of the work in camps and excursions which had formerly been the prerogative of youth clubs was now being done by the schools, but also from the fact that this was by tradition an amateur field. To give it over entirely to the professionals was unthinkable, indeed, with few trained, impossible, but in the meantime the voluntary organisations were prickly in their dealings with authority, training courses did the best they could with leaders whose principal qualification was enthusiasm, and the youth of the country did not convey the impression that they were clamouring for the service. In the circumstances it was surprising and indeed encouraging to see how much was achieved.

HIGHER EDUCATION AND FINANCE

There was also, especially in the sixties, a dynamic expansion of higher education. The number of students in full-time courses at Scottish universities, central institutions and colleges of education grew from 20,000 in 1954-5 to 31,000 in 1962-3,[12] largely as part of the same process which made pupils stay at school after the leaving age as a privilege to be enjoyed.

The natural result of the whole process was that more money was spent annually on education than ever before. In a time of economic inflation of course prices steadily rose. Exercise books, which had cost 9s a gross in 1939, were 66s 5d in 1951; science notebooks rose from 7s 6d to 49s 10d a dozen over the same period, and pen points from 6½d to 4s 6d a box.[13] Paper, printing and labour costs throttled initiative in the publishing of textbooks until the market overseas opened it again in the late fifties. For a time the particular needs of Scottish schools were notably unmet, because there were not enough buyers for books of history, literature and language with a distinctively Scottish aspect. The proposal of the Saltire Society in a pamphlet of 1953 was that publishers, directors and teachers' organisations should confer to pro-

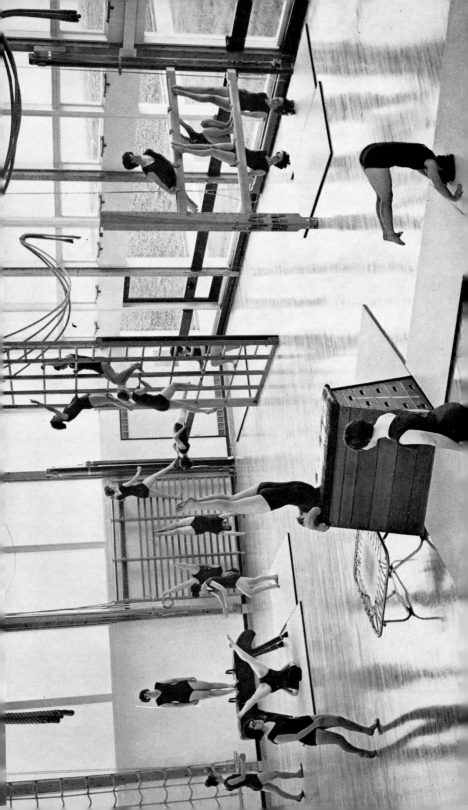

duce commissioned books for a guaranteed market; after the mid-fifties however a few Scottish books, especially in history, began once more to appear.[14]

Despite a cascade of figures in official reports total expenditure on Scottish education in any given year is impossible to compute with accuracy. Public revenue expenditure alone in 1965-6 was over £150 millions and this did not include the work of independent schools and voluntary organisations nor the proportion of university funds made available by the Grants Commission. On the public figures the cost per head of the Scottish population had increased fourfold since 1950. There was a forty per cent rise in real cost between 1957 and 1963. What was more important however was whether education had its fair share of public money and here evidence could only be comparative. One set of figures was encouraging: in 1945 education received 2·3 per cent of the British national product, in 1963 4·7 per cent, and the rise was continuing.[15] But in the latter year the percentage in the United States was five, in Russia seven, and in 1959 the Soviet budget had allocated almost exactly the same sum to education as to defence.[16] The United Kingdom (and therefore by the Goschen formula Scotland) was taking education very seriously in the sixties, but there was still some way to go.

THE STATE AND THE POLITICAL PARTIES

Socially and politically education had at last reached the front rank, when political parties found it worth while to feature it in their election programmes. All three, Conservative, Labour and Liberal, promised extensive building, more teachers and smaller classes, especially in the primary schools. From the mid-fifties however the main issue was educational "privilege" and the right of every child to an educational career as long as possible. Both Conservative and Labour in 1951 were vaguely pledging "better selection", the Conservatives for age, ability and aptitude, the Socialists more specifically for grammar school places[17]. By 1955 the battlefield had been chosen – comprehensive secondary schools. In all its manifestoes during a long period out of office Labour made a feature of this policy, claiming that[18]

> the ideal of a comprehensive educational system is part of the Scottish tradition.

Selection at "11-plus" (in Scotland 12) was to end, fee-paying in state schools was to be abolished and independent schools might either come within the system or forfeit government assistance.[19] When they did at last come to power the Socialists made it clear that these were no empty promises: local authorities might propose any scheme they wished but unless it was "genuinely comprehensive" the Secretary of State sent it back for reconsideration. The Conservatives over the same period

Modern gymnastics at Dunfermline College of Physical Education

opposed the principle, which in their opinion submerged the gifted minority:

> We know it is not the 11-plus that causes inequality, it is an inadequate educational system.[20]

But they promised better methods and if necessary longer periods of selection, and the Liberals, driving up the middle of the road, proposed "continuous selection from 11 to 13" and "various forms of non-selective secondary education", with a special enquiry into the independent schools.[21] Respect for the right of a parent to choose freely what education he would give his child and how much he would pay left the Liberals in a difficult position.

All parties also guaranteed a massive expansion in higher education, especially technology, though the public would have to be educated into accepting the latter.[22] The Conservative government moreover accepted at once the recommendation of the Newsom Committee in 1963 that the leaving age should be raised to sixteen, fixing 1970 as the crucial year, and Labour immediately stigmatised this as a blatant attempt to steal Socialist thunder. Despite grave warnings from many responsible bodies neither party would retreat from the decision until the economic crisis of 1968 brought a two-year deferment.

All such policy was clearly designed to satisfy a strongly-felt public need. Education was generally recognised to be valuable and every citizen wanted as much of it as possible for himself and his family. Junior secondary schools were "grand places no doubt – grand places for other people's children".[23] It was a Conservative minister, Mr Eccles who pointed out in 1960 that the demand for wider educational opportunities now came from the nation as a whole, not from a handful of middle-class enthusiasts,[24] and although this applied more south of the border it was by no means invalid in Scotland. Egalitarianism and a demand for democratic responsibility were to be seen everywhere in the sixties, in the provision of courses suitable for all pupils and not merely the academics, in the demand by teachers for some say in regulating their own professional affairs and by lecturers for places on the University courts, and significantly by the granting of such demands. The General Teaching Council, the Universities Act of 1966 and the Primary Memorandum of 1965 with its tacit departure from the autocracy of the 1962 Code, were all aspects of the same process. Most striking of all in Scotland was the change in attitude to intelligence and "native capacity". In 1921 a member of the Scottish Education Department was able to write[25]:

> However hard the saying may seem, there is no denying the fact that in every country only a relatively small percentage of the population will be endowed by nature with the mental equipment which they must possess if they are to profit by Secondary School or University study.

Only forty years later there was fairly general, though by no means unanimous approval of the dictum of the Crowther Report:

> It may well be that there is a pool of ability which sets an upper limit on what can be done by education at any given time. But if so it is sufficiently clear that the limit has not been reached . . . What is extracted from the pool of ability depends much less on the content of the pool than on the effectiveness of the pump.

In short, stop trying to change the pupils; change the universities and the secondary schools. The extremist's point of view was put in 1963 by a speaker at the E.I.S. Congress[26]:

> I feel convinced that an ordinary degree at any of our British universities is within the compass of anyone who is not a congenital moron – provided he or she is interested and puts in a certain amount of work.

Comprehensive education, as the leader-writer of the *Scottish Educational Journal* remarked, was "primarily a social experiment. The educational dividends are to some extent a bonus".[27]

It was strange therefore that the increasing stress on democracy and individual liberty should be accompanied by a progressive decline in the powers of voluntary educational agencies – strange but not surprising, with governments becoming increasingly sure of their own wisdom. There was no marked change in the position of the Church schools which, apart from religious matters, were indistinguishable from the ordinary seminaries. In 1958 one Scottish child in five was attending a church school, all but 0·3 per cent Catholic.[28] In the sixties however the independent schools found themselves in an odd position, their existence threatened on philosophical grounds at a time when their application lists were the longest in their history. In 1966 they housed 2·3 per cent of Scottish pupils.[29] Their supporters justified them by reference to the conditions they enjoyed, with a comparatively stable staff and a small teacher-pupil ratio. They had excellent opportunities for experiment, though not all were seized. Their advocates also insisted on the right of a parent, so long as he paid his share of the public bill, to send his child where he wished, and drew attention to the Register of Independent Schools, set up in September 1957, which opened their work to inspection. In effect however, though many parents sent their children to independent schools for such positive reasons, there were many more whose motives were essentially negative: their sons and daughters were going not so much to the independents as away from the state schools, which lacked the cachet of the more select seminaries, and where the pupils might be from mixed social groups. A large factor in the popularity of private schools was snobbery. The introduction of an exclusively comprehensive system in the public area altered the situation. To the snobs were now added a very large company of parents who sincerely feared, like the Conservative policy statements, that in the struggle to deal suitably with all children in one school the brilliant ones would be neglected. On the other hand it was difficult to see any place in a truly comprehensive system for an institution whose *raison d'etre* was selection.

EDUCATIONAL PRAGMATISM

Another marked feature of Scottish education after 1945, perhaps because so many of the people had to be directly satisfied, was its practical slant. The curriculum, especially at the secondary stage, was increasingly designed on utilitarian lines. There was a reaction against vague theories of formal discipline which found reasons for studying certain subjects in training for the mind. "Relevance" became the watchword. The classics, once entrenched at the heart of the grammar school curriculum, found themselves in the sixties fighting their final rearguard actions, with Greek reduced to a few schools and only 645 out of 74,187 candidates at the 1966 examinations for the Scottish Certificate of Education.[30] Latin was still widely taught, but there were many critics who regarded its place as secured mainly by the vested interests of existing teachers, some of whom took the opportunity to acquire additional qualifications in a more "relevant" language like Russian. There was support for the view that the full Classical course should be retained only for a small band of future classical scholars, who would maintain the link with ancient civilisations, while for the rest of the pupils there might be a new subject, taught in English, known as Classical Studies. One by one the universities dropped Latin as an admission requirement except for "relevant" courses.

By contrast the "practical" subjects came into prominence. Group subjects ceased to exist in the Scottish Certificate of Education and by 1965 it was possible, though unlikely, to acquire higher grade passes in no less than five different technical subjects. The Bachelor of Education degree introduced in 1965 by Aberdeen College of Education and University included one category of practical-aesthetic subjects (art and craft, music, drama, physical education) a pass in at least one of which was compulsory. The "Brunton Report" (*From School to Further Education*, 1963) had a strongly vocational bias. The central institutions and technical colleges, though they tried under various schemes to foster "liberal studies", found students' eyes firmly fixed on practical matters. Borrowings by 4,161 day and evening students from one central institution library in 1958-59 were in the following numbers:[31]

Applied science	4,382
Pure science	2,368
Social studies	305
Philosophy, religion, fine arts, language and literature, history, travel and biography	186

and university figures for arts students showed the opposite imbalance.

There was evidence also of a growing pragmatic emphasis in the training of teachers, where formal philosophical instruction in the education course gave way in the fifties to investigations of the social background. In the circumstances the extension by the colleges of "cultural" courses for the higher education of their students, including such topics for primary candidates as modern languages and mathematics, might be regarded as swimming against the tide. Where it squeezed out direct "methods" training in one or two subjects it was heavily criticised by some headmasters, and its relevance was constantly questioned by the students themselves, whose image of valuable training consisted very largely of assistance with techniques and class management.[32]

In the classroom the sixties were the period of "hardware", of concrete practical teaching aids. For language teaching there were laboratories and reading cards, in arithmetic the Cuisenaire and Dienes rods. Mathematics and science in particular benefited by self-correcting programmes and teaching machines. In foreign languages like French where tape-recorders and film-strip projectors became essential, the aim was no longer to write perfect French but to understand and be understood in France. Radio and television programmes were well established in the smallest country schools, television becoming steadily more specific with the appearance in Glasgow of a city-wide closed-circuit system. The stress in many subjects was on personal experience by actual visits, as in geography, biology and modern studies, or by imaginative self-projection as in the "patch" method of history teaching. Experience, practical interest and relevance were the central features of the "new syllabuses" in science and mathematics. In the 1960s Dewey at last reached Scotland.

This pragmatic tendency was not unconnected with an increasing secularism in Scotland and her schools. Under the Education Act of 1946 no authority could discontinue religious teaching without a public mandate from its electors and no steps were taken in the next twenty years to seek a referendum. But when the Principal of St Andrews wrote in 1950 that[33]

the Collegiate Church . . . continues to be the recognised focal point of our university life,

he was either deluding himself or describing a tradition accepted without being generally approved. Until 1914, even after the state had assumed responsibility for providing schools, religion had been central, so that music for example ranked first in subsidiary subjects qualifying for the Dick Bequest because "it is a direct moral and religious agency" and the prize for the most deserving child in an Edwardian kinder-garten was to look after the altar.[34] After the Second World War however and a period of unease verging on hypocrisy, the drift away from church-going and "positive Christianity" accelerated. In 1956 barely a quarter of Glasgow's adult population belonged to the Church of Scotland and not much more than a quarter of these were regular attenders. Nine years later the Roman Catholic press was expressing worry about the number of its children – as many as 40 per cent – who left school and church at the same time. In 1967 the Professor of Systematic Theology at Aberdeen wrote:

The older Scottish universities were founded on theology. In the new without exception theology has no place.[35]

From the late forties there was also evidence that the drift was spread-ing through the schools. The usual criticism was that, although there was always time in primary and secondary timetables for the "Bible period", ranging from an hour to over two hours a week, too many teachers, particularly in the higher secondary classes, were neglecting their responsibilities. Many felt disqualified by doubt or disbelief to speak on religious topics. Others, too lazy to face the problem squarely, were prepared to read the Bible with their classes, but their obvious lack of interest did much more harm than good. Often the religious period was used as a convenient time for discharging the petty admini-strative duties like marking registers and collecting dinner money which encumbered a teacher's day. Occasionally a local minister was invited to take lessons or services. But religious instruction was widely regarded as a "frill", an irrelevancy in the serious business of preparing for examinations: "if the truth be told", wrote the Scottish correspon-dent of the Times Educational Supplement in 1964,

the school is devoted mainly to secular tasks, and seldom serves as an agency for the deepening of religious life or the spread of Christian belief.

An increasing proportion of university graduates did not attend the classes offered in the colleges of education, if necessary exercising their "conscience clause". Not surprisingly their pupils were "bored, sceptical or frankly hostile". The Christian ethic was in the minds of many teachers, parents and pupils a pious imagining, insufficiently practical to deal with the hard world of the mid-twentieth century. The excep-tions were the bigots, like the small group of parents in West Lothian who complained bitterly of a French student-teacher who played to Protestant children a popular gramophone record sung by a Roman Catholic nun.[36]

THE CLIMATE OF CHANGE

In the system of education however, especially in the sixties, the amazing, the far-fetched and the impossible came into serious contemplation; the utopian visions of four centuries were adopted as political programmes, even as practical policy. The effect was to erode traditional conservatism. Men in authority who had once regarded sweeping changes as unthinkable now undertook to tackle them, timidly at first, then boldly, and finally with a decisive attack which seemed very close to rashness. The climate in the sixties was one of constant change, theoretical and material; there was no longer a fixed pattern of class-rooms, of subjects, of methods. One "emergency" followed another:[37]

> The cry of Wolf has been raised far too often in the past fifteen years in the field of Scottish Education.

The impetus of change made it an exciting period to live and work in, but it also caused changes to multiply and acquire value in themselves. The most serious problem would arise when people ceased at last to travel hopefully and considered it was time to arrive. There was no substantial evidence in the late sixties that this time had yet come.

REFERENCES

1. GRAHAM, "The 20th Century Club", *College Courant*, xvi, Martinmas 1963, 38
2. TWAIN, *The Facts concerning the Recent Resignation*
3. CHAMBERS, *S.E.J.*, 4 March 1964; *S.E.D.R. 1966*, 7
4. *S.E.D.R. 1947*, 8 (with an allowance for independent schools); *1966*, 6
5. OSBORNE, *Scottish and English Schools*, 84; Secretary of State in answer to a parliamentary question, *S.E.J.* 22 May 1964
6. *T.S.A. City of Aberdeen*, 404-5
7. *S.E.D. Circular 244*, 3 Sep. 1942; *S.E.D.R. 1952*, 48
8. Scottish Youth Advisory Committee, *The Needs of Youth in These Times*, H.M.S.O. 1945, 92-5
9. *ibid*
10. SCOTLAND, JAMES, *Youth Service Membership and Attitudes* (1960, unpublished)
11. Albemarle Committee, *The Youth Service in England and Wales* (Cmnd. 929), H.M.S.O. 1960, especially 108-113
12. Robbins Committee, *Report on Higher Education*, H.M.S.O. 1963 (Cmnd. 2154), App. I, 163
13. *S.E.D.R. 1951*, 26
14. Saltire Society, *Scotland in the Schools, a Report on the Scottish Content of our Education*, Edinburgh 1953, 16

15. George Thomson, M.P., *S.E.J.* 10 May 1963; Sleeman, *S.E.J.* 25 March 1966

16. *T.E.S.*, 2 Jan. 1959

17. BUTLER, *T.E.S.* 19 Oct. 1951; HARDMAN, D. R., *ibid*

18. Labour Party, *Let Scotland Prosper*, 1958

19. Labour Party, *Learning to Live*, 1958; *Britain Belongs to You*, 1959; *The New Britain*, 1964

20. LLOYD, *T.E.S.*, 2 Oct 1959, quoting Sir Ronald Gould; *Election Manifesto 1964*, *T.E.S.* 18 Sep. 1964; BUTLER, *T.E.S.*, 19 Oct 1951

21. Liberal Party, *Opportunity in Education*, 1958; *Education*, 1962; *Election Manifesto*, 1964

22. Labour Party, *Let Scotland Prosper*, 1958; *Signpost for the Sixties*, 1961; *The New Britain*, 1964; Conservative Party, *Election Manifesto*, 1964

23. *T.E.S.*, 7 Jan. 1955

24. ECCLES, *T.E.S.*, 2 Dec 1960

25. *Circular 11, 1921*

26. MACDONALD, "Education in an Affluent Society", *S.E.J.* 3 Jan. 1964

27. *S.E.J.*, 18 July 1958

28. *Report of the Day School Committee to the Board of Education*, 3 March 1959, 2-3; figures from the Roman Catholic authorities

29. *S.E.D.R. 1966*, 6

30. *S.C.E.E.B. Report*, 1966

31. *S.E.J.*, 5 Feb. 1960

32. CLARK, *S.E.J.*, 24 Jan. 1964

33. IRVINE in *Veterum Laudes*, 3

34. DOUGLAS, "James Dick and the Dick Bequest", *A.U.R.* xiii, 38, March 1926, 108; HARDY, *Diary of a Free Kindergarten*, 111

35. HIGHET, *Glasgow Herald*, 9 Oct. 1957; *T.E.S.* 5 Nov. 1965, 19 May 1967

36. *T.E.S.* 18 Sep. 1964; RUTHVEN, *S.E.J.* 18 Nov. 1966; *T.E.S.* 5 Nov. 1965

37. Scottish Correspondent, *T.E.S.*, 2 Feb. 1962

| # The Sources of Power

CENTRAL DEVOLUTION

IN 1945 and indeed a dozen years later the Secretary of State, largely through the advice of the Scottish Education Department and responsible only to Parliament, was the central repository of almost all power in Scottish education. He did not provide schools, but his Inspectors oversaw their work and his suggestions had the backing of two thirds of the money on which they ran. He was responsible for the supply of teachers and for supervising their training; his was the right to grant a teacher his certificate and to take it away. He had the last word on salaries. The only national examination was organised and its certificate issued by his officers. How much of his power was exercised by the Secretary of State, how much by his Departmental civil servants depended on the interplay of personalities; no Secretary was a tyrant and none a cipher.

The late fifties saw the beginning of an overt process in which he devolved many of his duties to other authorities, effecting an appreciable redistribution of power, though always within the public sector: Scottish educational administration, as Osborne has pointed out, was and is essentially more "professional" than English.[1] Some of the earliest changes were in the field of teacher training, where the colleges were permitted to acquire increasing independence in their work. Although until the mid-fifties inspectors continued to be nominated for duties in training, they held the lightest of reins and were regarded as available for consultation rather than supervision; they had private instructions indeed to avoid treading on any toes. The colleges took full advantage in extending their areas of effective responsibility, and it was the financial constriction of the National Committee which they found irksome rather than any departmental officiousness. The Central Executive Committee not only approved the general college estimates but demanded particular oversight thereafter of such trivial purchases as a new wheelbarrow for a gardener.[2] The logical development of the liberating process came in the Teachers (Training Authorities) Regulations of 1958, which made the training centres Colleges of Education with independent governing bodies much more loosely under the supervision of the Scottish Council for the Training of Teachers. This

body, which was to exist only until 1967, had a progressive and successful record as the Secretary of State's principal source of advice on
training. It scrutinised college estimates and proposals for new courses
and transmitted them with obervations to the Department, a function
which it exercised in a consistently constructive spirit. It also advised
the Secretary of State on exceptional admission to teaching and here
its Committee worked with exemplary efficiency; on the few occasions
when its recommendations were not accepted it was because the
Secretary of State was more willing than the Council to lower the
barriers. By contrast the Council showed a desire to adjust general
standards of entry to the profession in a way that was more acceptable
to the Department than to the teachers' organisations.

The establishment of a General Teaching Council in 1966 took the
colleges a step further on the road to independent action. The Scottish
Council was abolished, and although the principle of "visitation" by
the new body was introduced it was clear from its first pronouncements
on the matter that the G.T.C. proposed to handle relations with the
colleges very delicately indeed. Meanwhile wherever the effective
power in training was to lie in future it would not be with the Department. Except of course in one important matter which might prevail
over all others, finance.

The appearance of the G.T.C. marked a crucial step in the process
of devolution, for the Secretary of State, by what he described as an
"act of faith",[3] gave away his power not only to control admission to
the profession, normal and exceptional, but also his right to expel or
discipline unsatisfactory teachers. The new body had a difficult birth,
but the complaints of the professional organisations were against the
extent of its powers, the manner in which it proposed to exercise them
and the balance of its membership, never against the powers themselves.
Another stormy issue in the sixties concerned the arrangements for fixing
teachers' salaries. A National Joint Council set up during the Second
World War to advise the Secretary of State moved from one crisis to
another. The system envisaged was one of triennial "awards", and the
word is important. Whatever the views of the N.J.C., the Secretary of
State "awarded" the new scales, and on several occasions he rejected
the Council's advice. The aim of the teachers' organisations in the
sixties was that he should commit himself in advance by having his
representatives attend as full negotiating members, with a final sub-
mission where necessary to arbitration. The battle, which appeared to
have been won by the organisations in 1967, flared up again when the
government proposed to appoint the arbiter not from the Scottish legal
system but from the Ministry of Labour. It is not without significance
that, so much devolution having been granted elsewhere, the Secretary
of State showed himself most conservative in the field of finance.

By this time the Department had also relaxed its direct influence on
the secondary curriculum. In the late fifties teachers were first employed

to mark the papers of the Leaving Certificate examination. In 1959 the Association of Directors of Education, in evidence given before the Advisory Council, proposed the setting up of an Examination Board,[4] and four years later such a body was established to administer the Scottish Certificate of Education. The inspectorate, which had run the examination with conspicuous success since its inception in 1888, withdrew from participation, the Department retaining only assessors. The extent of the Secretary of State's influence was immediately, though not openly, an issue. A suggestion by the Working Party on the Secondary Curriculum that there should be an advanced grade had been on the whole accepted by teachers, even welcomed, but specimen papers and a timetable had aroused strong opposition. The new board was now asked to "reconsider the matter" but given a clear indication that the Secretary of State had made up his mind, and that the form, not the existence of a sixth-year examination was for discussion. A board longer established might have taken a different line; as it was their Certificate of Sixth Year Studies attracted much criticism for decisions which were not really theirs. Nevertheless the Secretary of State had set up an influential body of which he was not in command, and he took a similar step in 1965 with the appointment of a Consultative Committee on the Curriculum, though here the Chairman was the Secretary of the Department.

LOCAL AUTHORITY

In local affairs changes were slower in coming. Controversy centred round three issues, of which one was the extent to which local authorities might take their own decisions. Here the limiting factor was finance: if education, like politics, is the art of the possible, more was possible for the central authority, which provided twice as much money. A certain freedom was allowed to local planners after 1958 when the Local Government (Scotland) Act instituted the "block grant" principle, whereby educational expenditure by local authorities, except on milk, meals and the removal of war works, was met, along with various other services, out of a general grant. This represented a Departmental policy to integrate education in "the main stream of local administration"; as long ago as 1918 block grant had been proposed, but withdrawn to meet the objections of the new authorities and the E.I.S.[5] There was a good deal of opposition in 1958 to the arrangement, largely from teachers who feared that in competition with other local services education would suffer, but the fear was hardly justified by events. What was most impressive was the trial of strength in the mid-sixties, when attempts by various local authorities to modify the government's "comprehensive" policy were almost entirely defeated.

A second problem in local administration was the obvious fact that the majority of committee members had no special knowledge of educational problems, and some might even be downright ignorant of their existence. The situation was not improved by the express exclusion of teachers from committee membership. Since the only contact of many councillors with the schools had been in their own childhood or in specially organised visits, their experience was about a generation out of date. Such a comment however applies to any branch of democratic government, central or local. It might be met partly by the wise use of co-opted members and largely by entrusting all administrative detail – and not a few general principles – to the judgment of permanent servants, chiefly the directors of education. Legally the powers of these officers were not large; in practice they might be sweeping. The director might be no more than an imposing chief clerk, or he might determine the education of many thousands of children and alter the educational tradition of a large area of Scotland.

Another solution to the problem of preserving local knowledge was the *ad hoc* principle, which had operated from 1918 to 1929, with specially elected education authorities. The Association of Directors of Education, in evidence in 1967 to the Royal Commission on Local Government, advocated that these should be reintroduced, and supporters pointed to the suggestion that they had been abolished "almost in a fit of absence of mind": the aim of the 1929 Act had been to reorganise local administration generally and education had fallen by the way although there was no evidence that the authorities had failed in their work. The Scottish Education Department on the other hand claimed that the financial complexity of a system of requisition on the rating authorities had been quite unjustified by any public interest shown in electing the *ad hoc* bodies.[6] The value of the principle had been estimated by Walter Elliot in 1928 when he was Parliamentary Under-Secretary for Scotland:[7]

An *ad hoc* body is undoubtedly useful at the inception of a service, since creative ideas, undivided attention, specialised knowledge and a strong driving force are then necessary to overcome inertia and launch the new scheme. When the public have become accustomed to the service and things are running smoothly as part of the established and accepted machinery the need for the special body diminishes and in time disappears.

In the view of the Department, expressed in 1967 like that of the Directors to the Royal Commission on Local Government, the service was running smoothly; the Secretary could see no reason for a return to the *ad hoc* principle.[8]

Nevertheless the third problem of local government kept the issue alive in the sixties. This was simply the size of the efficient unit: there were many in favour of dividing the country not into counties but regions. Both the Directors and the Department favoured amalgamation of the 35 existing authorities into 12 or 15. Of the two main difficulties attending this proposal one was geographical. "A region" had to have a centre and not all the suggested areas possessed an obvious one: Orkney and Shetland were diverse communities and neither looked naturally towards a centre in the other, still less on the Scottish mainland, while in the regions around Glasgow and Edinburgh the natural centres were in the cities. The Directors of Education did not mention the northern islands in their evidence and were rebuked for the omission, while the unit they proposed around Glasgow, with $2\frac{1}{2}$ million people, was too big for smooth working without loss of local interest and knowledge. The Departmental spokesman recognised this when he proposed to resuscitate school management committees, yet these had been failures in the decade after 1918, since they were unwilling to content themselves with menial tasks like checking attendance. That such local interest still existed was demonstrated nevertheless by several protests against the closing of rural schools; few were successful.

The principal requirement of regional, as of all governing committees, was to achieve a body containing perhaps six or eight thoroughly knowledgeable and interested members who would examine matters on the educational, not the party political plane, while the rest allowed them to get on with it. Human nature made such a situation difficult to realise.

ORIGINS OF CURRICULAR CHANGES

There is further evidence on this question of power in the origins of the very considerable curricular changes during the period. There was some progress in research: at least one county had its own research panel,[9] others constructed their own intelligence tests for use in transferring children to secondary courses, and many provided their own attainment tests until these became unfashionable. Increasing popularity of the Bachelor (later Master) of Education degree in the universities produced a steady flow of papers reporting experiments, mainly related to the psychology of learning. Various voluntary bodies like the Scottish Educational Film Association and Programmed Learning Groups set up their own research sections, and all over the country work was done, sometimes in very difficult circumstances, by enthusiastic teachers and headmasters. There were interesting projects in the University and College Departments of Education. The most energetic body was the Research Council, but it was not until the sixties that the Department took steps to encourage experimental work strongly there and elsewhere: in 1962, when £100 million was being spent on Scottish education, the official grant for research was only £5,000.[10] By 1966 the programme had greatly expanded. The Research Council was spending over £37,000 on 23 projects, two-thirds of which was

subscribed by the Department, and there were 15 other investigations
to which specific grants of over £27,000 were contributed.[11] Few changes
however could be attributed in this period to the findings of research.
Certainly the most important was the procedure between 1945 and
1965 for promotion to secondary education, which was founded specifically on work done in the thirties by Professor William McClelland.
Perhaps it is wrong to expect certainty from any research. The conclusion
generally drawn is that the evidence is partial and more research is
needed.[12]

Publications, with the exception of one group, had no great influence.
The journals of the teachers' organisations, especially that of the
Educational Institute, had some pretensions to professional status, but
in the main were regarded as mouthpieces for their parent bodies;
much of the *Scottish Educational Journal* and virtually the whole of
The Scottish Schoolmaster were devoted to teacher politics. The *Times
Educational Supplement* opened an office in Edinburgh in 1965 and
launched a Scottish edition. Although its leaders were admirably
impartial and occasionally outspoken, it contented itself on the whole
with reporting the educational scene, and this was also true of such
local products as *The Dominie* in Fife and *Education in the North*, the
annual publication of Aberdeen College of Education. The most
influential documents were undoubtedly the Reports of the Scottish
Advisory Council immediately after the War and those of various
Departmental Committees and Working Parties in the late fifties and
the sixties.

The Advisory Council issued reports on the training of teachers
(1946), technical education (1946) and a series surveying the problem
of children requiring special educational treatment (1950-52). Most
outstanding however were the volumes on primary (1946) and secondary
education (1947). The former was described by an English historian
as[13]

the most valuable official study yet made on the primary school, and
(it) contains much of interest for English as well as Scottish teachers.

In general there was nothing in the report that had not been said before.
Its strength lay in two directions – the freshness and clarity of style
which made reading it a pleasure, and the careful and sensible attention
to detail which gave meaning to many otherwise windy phrases. The
Council agreed for example with the Saltire Society in discerning
certain characteristics typically Scottish and worthy of perpetuation;
among these it numbered a sturdy spirit of independence, an insistence
on democratic self-government and the capacity to be "good Euro-
peans". It then suggested various methods by which these traditions
and characteristics might be impressed on children in the primary
school – by the teaching of the rich Scottish language, by lessons on
Scottish poets before Burns, by singing folk tunes and learning folk

dances, by attention in some degree to Gaelic life and legend, by field study in geography and by treating Scottish history as more than a useful source of anecdote. The chapter showed the constructive and practical nature of the Report at its best.

It remained a volume of suggestions, but the Secretary of State was legally obliged to consider its points and give his proposals for action. Circular 122, issued in December 1947, was his first attempt to do so. All the main suggestions were accepted in principle and some in practice: the whole system of transfer from primary to secondary education for instance was reorganised, and the principle of transfer by age rather than attainment was accepted.[14] In several respects however there were practical difficulties and a more cautious approach. A class maximum of 30 was desirable, but the supply of teachers and the available accommodation put the paper figure at 45 and the actual numbers even higher. The suggestion that Scottish traditions should be fostered was heartily endorsed, but the Secretary was not prepared to recommend a weekly period or a closer study of Gaelic life and traditions. Significantly, although the fundamentals – physical education, handwork and speech training – were accepted as stated, the place given by the inspectors in their own Memorandum to the three Rs showed them still paramount.[15]

The Advisory Council's Report on Secondary Education appeared in 1947 and was received with equal acclaim, but Circular 206, which gave the specific views of the Secretary of State, did not appear until March 1951. The Council's principles governing the aims of secondary education were accepted, but there were many practical departures from the detailed suggestions. The unfortunately named "senior" and "junior" secondary schools continued in existence, at least in some areas, for another decade; some attempt was made to encourage reduction of size, but the difficulties of accommodation defeated the effort. The attempt to promote subject co-operation by combining history and geography as social studies was rejected. The Council's proposal that there should be fourth and sixth year certificates was rejected for the time being, though it was to reappear in 1959. The group certificate, however, had already, in 1950, been abolished.[16]

To sum up, the Secretary of State might in theory reject all the recommendations of the Council. In practice he met their suggestions where he could, but in the fifties, where administrative difficulty reared its Hydra head, the Department was reluctant to take adventurous action. And where the Department took no action, action was seldom taken.

Another group of influential publications was produced in the late fifties and the sixties by "Working Parties" set up by the Department. These took the place of the more ambitious and much more cumbersome Royal Commissions of Victorian times, the last of which, on Physical Training, reported in 1903. The Advisory Council was a step towards this more specific arrangement, and there were also in the early fifties Departmental Committees, formed entirely from the Inspectorate, on Primary and on Junior Secondary Education. The credit of introducing the working party technique has been given to Sir William Arbuckle, who was Permanent Secretary of the Department from 1957 to 1963, and who had himself been a teacher.[17] Their main feature was their composition, including teachers, local administrators and lecturers as well as inspectors, and the extent of their influence may be seen by considering four reports. One on the Curriculum of the Senior Secondary School, published in February 1959, set the pattern for a reorganisation of Scottish secondary education through its certificates, proposing a new examination structure which would confer a "Scottish Certificate of Education" with an "ordinary" grade equivalent to that of the General Certificate of Education (and therefore appreciably less exacting than the existing Lower Grade) and a "higher grade" continuing. The ordinary grade examination would be taken in the fourth secondary year, the higher in the fifth or later. There would be no compulsory subjects and the subjects themselves would be radically altered. The Working Party also recommended the introduction of a third, or "advanced" grade, to be taken after a sixth secondary year.[18]

The Secretary of State accepted the recommendations with few modifications. The most significant reservation was that a District Inspector should "retain authority to require a course which he found unsatisfactory to be altered"; presumably he did not place implicit trust in the judgement of individual headmasters, but he claimed that such a proviso "would not seriously interfere with the freedom of head teachers and education authorities".[19]

Another working party, under the chairmanship of Lord Wheatley, examined the recruitment, supply, training and government of the teaching profession in Scotland. Its Report, delivered in June 1963, was hailed as a "Teachers' Charter" since it recommended the setting up of a Teaching Council, and proposed a remarkable degree of self-government for the profession. The Secretary of State accepted all its main suggestions, embodying them in the Teaching Council (Scotland) Act of 1965, and gave wide powers to the new Council, including advice on "such other matters relating to the education, training and fitness to teach of teachers as they think fit".[20] He retained in his own hands the ultimate control of entry to the profession, but this had been recommended by the Wheatley Committee. The fact that he refused to finance the new Council, expecting its support to come from teachers themselves, demonstrated his desire that it should enjoy full independence.

The "Brunton Committee" on the transition from school to further education was named after its chairman, Her Majesty's Senior Chief Inspector; its Report, issued like Wheatley's in June 1963, recommended

Bernard Street Supplementary School, late nineteenth century

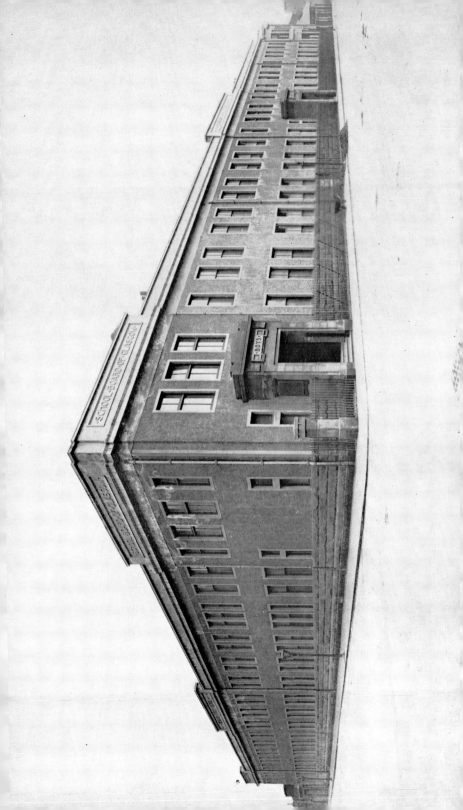

"vocationally-biased" courses beginning in the third secondary year with a broad approach to particular industries, special short courses for school leavers, a great extension in vocational guidance and in "day release", and much closer relationships between teachers and industry; it also came out strongly against an external examination like the English C.S.E. Again the Secretary of State accepted all its major proposals: in collaboration with the Confederation of British Industry for example the Scottish Education Department instituted an Industry Scheme for Teachers by which many were seconded to firms for periods of three weeks. Courses of the "Brunton" type were encouraged, and some authorities made rapid progress; the disappointing development elsewhere was not the fault of the Department.[21]

Potentially one of the most influential documents of the period was the Memorandum on Primary Education issued in 1965 by a Committee composed like the others of teachers, inspectors, lecturers and administrators, though its impact was much less resounding at first than that of, say, the Wheatley Report. It was generally held to do no more than crystallise the lessons of the best work being done in adventurous schools, but its aim was to make such work the normal pattern in Scottish primary classrooms, and this demanded a major effort in rethinking by serving teachers. Moreover its message was one of freedom for the child, something which could not be precisely enjoined in regulations, and its effect was therefore bound to be vague. Within a year however the demand for explanatory courses in such subjects as primary school mathematics was outrunning the resources of the colleges of education and local authorities. At least one college "methods" department could have employed its staff continuously throughout the year on such courses.

Be it noted, these were all "official" documents, sponsored by the Department and published by Her Majesty's Stationery Office. It was the Department which had constituted the working parties and accepted their recommendations. This was to be expected in an educational tradition as authoritarian as Scotland's, and there is no evidence that the majority of teachers had been eagerly awaiting the opportunity to experiment in curriculum and methods; there were indeed not a few examples of resistance in the schools to change.[22] The colleges of education from the fifties onward had a good record of experiment and encouragement for new methods, especially in primary education, but they had to contend constantly with an element of suspicion. In general most credit for change must go to the inspectorate; as its historian writes,[23]

> Since the inception of the service in 1839-40 the Inspectors have been the principal promoters of educational advance in Scotland.

The chairmen of three of the four working parties considered were inspectors. But more important still was their influence in working out the new ideas in school: inspectors were largely responsible for the success of the new syllabuses, especially in physics, of new subjects like modern studies and of new methods, as in language teaching. The changes noted in the pattern of power in the sixties radically altered the function of the inspectorate. The Examination Board took over the running of the only national certificates. The General Teaching Council became responsible for the system of probation and for discipline within the profession. Education Committees appointed more and more "organisers" and "advisers" whose work was very similar to that of the English "local inspectors", and the creation of regional authorities would greatly extend the province of such officers. The aim of the inspectorate in the sixties was increasingly to "provide leadership through co-operation";[24] the word "inspector" was becoming a misnomer. There remained however one important function. They were still responsible for ensuring that public money was well spent, and while they were doing this they were still "inspectors".

The two decades after 1945 then saw a notable willingness by the central authority, on paper at any rate, to delegate some of its duties. But there were critics who questioned whether in the second half of the twentieth century any such delegation could be real. They pointed to the wide and powerful influence which the Department could still wield through its assessors and even more by its control of the public purse. Plans for expansion before 1970 for instance were seriously hampered both in schools and colleges by financial restriction; even comparatively minor local proposals waited a long time for approval. Few questioned the need for such economy, but while the Department was no doubt genuinely reluctant in its parsimony, the whole exercise was a lesson in where the true power continued, and must continue, to lie.

REFERENCES

1. OSBORNE, *Scottish and English Schools*, 40
2. INGLIS, *T.E.S.S.*, 24 March 1967
3. ROSS, WILLIAM, at an E.I.S. dinner, January 1965
4. *S.E.J.*, 6 Nov. 1959
5. ROBERTS, *Dunbartonshire*, 177
6. *T.E.S.* 19 May 1967; ROBERTS, *Dunbartonshire*, 174; *S.E.J.* 12 May 1967
7. *S.E.J.* 23 Nov. 1928
8. *Glasgow Herald*, 10 May 1967
9. *T.S.A. East Lothian*, 155
10. NISBET, Gilchrist Lecture, Aberdeen, November 1962
11. *S.E.D.R. 1966*, 95-8
12. *I.T.A. Report 1967*

13. CURTIS, *Education in Great Britain*, 258
14. *S.E.D. Circulars 108* and *122*
15. S.E.D., *The Primary School in Scotland*, H.M.S.O. 1950
16. *S.E.D. Circular 157*
17. BONE, *Inspection*, 310
18. S.E.D., *Report of the Working Party on the Curriculum of the Senior Secondary School*, H.M.S.O. 1959
19. *S.E.D.R. 1959*, 25
20. *Teaching Council (Scotland) Act 1965*, section 2(1)
21. *S.E.D.R. 1966*, 23-4
22. cf. SWANN, address to the E.I.S. Congress, 1963
23. BONE, *Inspection*, 346
24. BONE, *Inspection*, 318

CHAPTER 13

The Schools

PROVISION OF SCHOOL PLACES

THE most pressing problem immediately after the Second World War was shortage of space. The birth-rate rose sharply from 1946; the leaving age became fifteen a year later; the Code of 1950 materially reduced the permissible size of classes, though with forty-five in primary, forty in the first three secondary years and thirty thereafter these were still larger than in England. Each successive government in the fifties and sixties promised every effort to reduce them and each failed. Moreover, whether from conviction or convictions – almost certainly the former – compulsory attendance was now really working, and it was a remarkable event when the figure in any school fell below ninety per cent. The effect of all this in the late forties was to create a demand for thousands of extra classrooms. The H.O.R.S.A.* Scheme provided 1,350 of these, with over 40,000 places, but though fairly long-lived they were never intended to be more than temporary. Meanwhile the cost of erecting permanent buildings had soared: whereas the James Hamilton Junior Secondary School, built in Kilmarnock in 1936, cost £46,000, a similar institution at Shortless in the same town was estimated in 1947 to require £200,000.[1] Since houses were also short and demanded first priority, new schools were inevitably delayed. The larger town created new suburbs housing many thousands, but did not provide schools there, and makeshift arrangements whereby countless busloads of pupils were transported from the outskirts to older schools in less thickly populated districts produced the phenomenon of "bus children", a nondescript race owing allegiance neither to their school nor their home locality.

Many authorities faced the expense courageously and launched ambitious building programmes: in the last half of 1953 Glasgow was opening a new school every month and Edinburgh was busy on fourteen. Cranhill Comprehensive, opened at the end of 1960, was the 75th new school in Glasgow since the war, and at the same period the city was building eight primary, six secondary and five special schools, three further education colleges and a community centre.[2] The new institutions incorporated many improvements – gymnasia, assembly halls with

* Hutting Operation for the Raising of the School Age.

theatre stages, classrooms with an entire southern wall of vitaglass, furniture of the appropriate size for each class, space for the latest visual and aural aids. Between 1957 and 1962 thirteen new Scottish schools were opened with swimming pools, thirteen building included them, and twenty-three more had them in their plans.[3] Not all the schools of course were perfectly planned: at least one "progressive" school could not install a cinema projector until arrangements could be made for darkening one of its many-windowed rooms, and another had its opening delayed for weeks by the flooding of its site. The general effect however was very encouraging.

Such buildings took time to plan and build. In the meantime authorities had to make such provision as they could to meet specific problems. In Dunbar new buildings approved in 1939 had not been begun a decade later, and there were so many pupils in the senior secondary school that the authority had to rent local church halls.[4] A similar situation might be found in most counties in the early fifties, when the term "annexe" became one of the commonest in scholastic usage. Many secondary headmasters moreover found themselves short of accommodation for specific departments and it was not uncommon for pupils studying commerce, science, homecraft or technical subjects to be sent for part of the day to a neighbouring school with the necessary equipment. This difficult and complicated situation affected the size of classes, the courses which could be offered, the framing of timetables and even methods of teaching. It was hardly practical for inspectors, directors of education or training tutors to advocate experiments when the teacher was bound in the straitjacket of physical surroundings. Nevertheless the herculean task of modernising Scottish school buildings was well advanced at the end of the fifties. Between 1946 and 1959 just under 400,000 new places were provided, and in the last year a further 50,000 were approved or in construction: that is, new places were or soon would be available for half the children in Scottish schools.[5] With the raising of the leaving age fixed for 1970 the late sixties saw a further building expansion, with half as much again spent on new school projects in 1967-8 (£26 millions) as in 1965-6 (£17 millions).[6]

NURSERY EDUCATION

Public nursery schools were normally open for seven hours a day; independent ones tended to restrict themselves to the mornings. Children were accepted by the former at the age of two and a half, by the latter a year later. Criteria of selection were seldom exclusively or even predominantly educational: in the public schools they were primarily social – unsatisfactory environment, personal defects, mothers at work; in the independents they were usually financial. Qualified teachers were generally employed in the public schools; under the 1956

Code at least one in each school had to be qualified and trained.[7] Two thirds of the staff of private schools on the other hand were not recognised as teachers. Accommodation generally was not good: a report in 1958 by a panel of the Research Council summed up the position:[8]

> Nursery school provision in Scotland is both inadequate and unbalanced. The demand far exceeds the supply, which at present provides nursery education for only one child in twenty. The child whose environment is bad or whose personal development is unsatisfactory has a chance – though, considering the long waiting lists, rather a slender one – of receiving public nursery education . . . The child of fairly well-off middle or upper-class parents, especially if his intelligence and personality are considerably above average, has a chance of nursery education in an independent school. The majority of children between these extremes would seem at present to be almost completely excluded from the possibility of nursery education.

The value of such schools could not be truly estimated until economic conditions made it possible for them to develop freely. Margaret Macmillan had no doubts:[9]

> The Nursery School, if it is a real place of nurture and not merely a place where babies are "minded" till they are five, will affect our whole educational system very powerfully and very rapidly. It will quickly raise the possible level of culture and attainment in all schools, beginning with the junior schools.

Certainly there was evidence in the Soviet Union, where something like five million children were attending nurseries and kindergartens in 1957, that the influence of these institutions could be strong. In Russia however compulsory education did not begin until seven, and "kindergarten" was not another name for nursery school. Meanwhile the principles underlying the organisation of nursery work were to be found in the Scottish infant classrooms, and the curriculum and methods there showed the clearest evidence of change towards a freer and less "intellectual" attitude, changes which were slow to penetrate into the higher classes.

PRIMARY CURRICULUM AND METHODS

The timetable in most primary schools altered only slowly before the sixties. The range of subjects taught was a little extended, but the "fundamentals" were left unshaken. The Advisory Council, in its Report on Primary Education issued in 1946, had made an effort to approach curriculum-building from a fresh angle: in place of the three Rs it nominated speech, handwork and physical education. Since

reading and writing in all their primary facets were included in speech
and handwork, this left only arithmetic's place in danger. The official
attitude on this topic however was less adventurous, as a memorandum
of 1950 by a panel of inspectors showed:[10]

> Although educational thought and criticism have been intensely
> active in the last fifty years, the main structure of the primary
> curriculum has remained unchanged; indeed, despite the importance
> now rightly attached to physical education, music, art and hand-
> work, the basic skills of reading, writing and arithmetic can never
> cease to be fundamental in the primary school.

At the age of six the child, it was here recommended, should spend
twelve hours out of the seventeen and a half in a school week on the
three Rs, at eight, thirteen and a quarter out of twenty-two and a half,
at eleven, twelve and three-quarters out of twenty-two and a half. Of
these times arithmetic was to occupy three, four and four hours.[11]
The practice in most schools at the beginning of the fifties was to spend
even more time than this on the rudiments, and especially on arithmetic:
many teachers were occupied with "sums" from 9.30 to 11 every
morning.

The Code of 1956 prescribed in sections 20 and 21 the subjects to
be taught in Scottish schools. In every year of his primary course the
child had to receive instruction in reading, writing, arithmetic, training
in speech, physical and moral education, music, art, handwork and
nature study. Moreover when he had matured sufficiently to profit he
was to be taught history, geography and composition, the girls needlework. In Gaelic-speaking areas there was to be reasonable provision
for learning the language. For the rest it was the duty of the primary
school staff to foster in the pupil such democratic and Christian virtues
as fair-mindedness, honesty, truthfulness, self-control, love of beauty,
industry, self-reliance, forethought, responsibility to the community,
goodwill towards other peoples, personal hygiene and cleanliness, good
speech and manners and consideration for man and beast. The list
read glibly but the principle was sound: it would have been even vaguer
and less valuable to promote the teaching of "democratic virtues"
without some attempt to specify what they were.

The methods used in teaching however were often criticised. Reading
aloud was still common and composition was most valued when it
was free of grammatical and spelling errors. Much of the arithmetic
period was taken up in working complicated, repetitive examples.
Teaching aids other than the blackboard were slow to appear and often
neglected when they did. History was still a chronological story, set
aside when the promotion examination loomed. Music meant class
singing. Art, craft and needlework were prescriptive rather than expres-
sive. Physical education depended on the age of the teacher and the
availability of visiting specialists.

In the fifties however there were increasing signs of change, fostered by inspectors and young teachers fresh from their training, and generally spreading upwards from the infant departments, traditionally the most progressive area. "Assignments" and "projects" became the rule in many schools, sometimes with considerable success: Carradale primary in Argyll for example studied herring fishing in 1948, forestry in 1949, dairy farming in 1950 and the highest classes kept individual notebooks.[12] Primary V in the Aberdeen Demonstration School in 1947-8 wrote and acted their own play and built a model of an Elizabethan theatre.[13] The children of Abingdon primary produced in 1961 a survey of their area. The "shop" or "post office" was a feature of most infant rooms. In the fifties the fashionable experiment was in group methods, attempting to harmonise the learning of the brilliant and the dull and to preserve the interest of all. Its introduction met some opposition however; experiments could not shake the firm belief of a Scottish teacher that there was an irreducible amount which he had to tell the children, which they could not discover for themselves, and that the most convenient way of doing this was by standing at a blackboard in front of the whole class.

In short teaching methods in the main remained formal. The 1950 Memorandum still found it necessary to point out that "slates and slate pencils should not be used" and that commands like "fold your arms" and "neck rest" could not be too strongly condemned.[14] It also saw a place still for corporal punishment, which remained firmly entrenched throughout the period. Sudden prohibition of the strap by Dunbartonshire in the early fifties brought chaos and had to be rescinded. A resolution by Dundee in 1958 to move towards abolition caused the Educational Institute to advise its members that if any such decision were taken, they should not carry it into effect.[15] The problem remained unsolved. By 1965 only seven authorities had made regulations governing the use of corporal punishment and the training colleges were under constant criticism for giving no guidance. Much of this was unjustified: there was discussion in several departments there. But what teachers wanted, as often in other fields, was not discussion but prescription, and this, in a field of delicate human relationships, was not available. An E.I.S. Memorandum on Discipline issued in October 1965 recognised the fact and suggested that this was fundamentally a matter for teachers themselves.[16] Nevertheless, after all the discussion and all the experiment, the atmosphere was often as described by J. C. Milne in Aberdeenshire:[17]

> As I gaed doon by kirk and toun
> I heard the larkies singin,
> And ilka burnie treetlin doon,
> And wid and welkin ringin.

> As I gaed doon by kirk and toun,
> Quo I, "A skweel, gweed feth!"
> And there I heard nae sang nor soun'
> But bairns quaet as death!

On the whole there might be a little more noise and less regimentation
in a classroom of 1962 than there had been in 1902, but a child from
the latter entering the former, at least above the infant stage, would
soon have been at home.

There were no melodramatic changes of heart like those claimed by
the countries of eastern Europe in their reports to UNESCO.[18] Nevertheless a period of increasing transformation can be noted. In 1962 the
Code was still prescribing subjects and demanding local schemes of
work, but the Memorandum issued three years later lent official backing
to a much less authoritarian view. The head teacher was seen less as
an autocrat and more as the democratic leader of a team, and so to
some extent was the class teacher. Group and individual attention were
taken for granted; in the interests of the latter "streaming" as in the
secondary school gave place to "setting". Experiments were encouraged,
not as a relief from necessary drudgery, but as part, even a major part,
of school work. A visit to a museum or a factory or a film might become
the centre of practical learning activity for days or weeks. These were
the concepts of the "new methods" – "practical" and "activity". Reading might be simplified and revolutionised by the International Teaching
Alphabet (though research in 1966 left this in doubt because of difficulties in transferring to traditional orthography).[19] Arithmetic benefited
from concrete material like the Cuisenaire and Dienes apparatus.
Spoken English filled a growing part of the day. Fuller understanding
by looking more deeply at a narrower area was fostered by the historical
"patch" and the geographical "sample". New subjects – new at least
in Scottish public schools – were introduced to primary pupils, who
found themselves speaking and listening to French, discovering scientific principles and learning through mathematics some of the pattern
of their environment. The direction and consolidation which the 1965
Memorandum gave to these experiments was a necessary process, for
the first instinct of many teachers, when they attempted the new subjects,
was to teach them with the same formalism they remembered from their
own secondary schooldays.

In the late sixties the Scottish primary school, with new subjects and
"no subjects", with team-teaching specialists and individual methods,
with new educational aids and techniques to be mastered almost daily,
was a confusing place for many teachers. The pattern emerging, far
away from the regular, strict, easily classified and communicated technique of tradition, not unnaturally roused frustration and resentment
in older teachers, partly because they found its concepts harder to
grasp, partly because their conscience bothered them: "Very well, it

may be much more pleasant, but when you add it all up, have they really *learnt* anything?" The usual reply condescended to their old-fashioned approach, but in fact the new methods were largely an act of faith.

SECONDARY CURRICULUM AND METHODS

The raising of the leaving age in 1947 may have inaugurated a new era of "secondary education for all" in England; north of the border it meant that most children would now complete a three-year course instead of leaving after two-thirds of it.[20] Circular 108 of that year made it clear that virtually all children should be transferred out of the primary schools between the ages of eleven and a half and twelve and a half and none after thirteen. Whether the course was truly secondary, even as intended "junior secondary", is open to doubt: at least in the early fifties there were many schools in which it was no more than a diluted version of the traditional programme. Nevertheless completing the course, even where it did not lead to a certificate, became more common. By the mid-sixties two out of three young people were finishing such courses, and the proportion dropping out of leaving certificate work on reaching the age for leaving fell from 38 per cent in 1956 to 17·4 per cent ten years later.[21]

This division of courses into "certificate" and "non-certificate" was intended as an administrative convenience, but it raised the question of the nature of secondary education. The chief aim, in the view of the Advisory Council in 1947, was to foster the full and harmonious development of the individual, though he must also realise that he was part of a greater whole. The function of the secondary school therefore was to provide a rich social environment where character and understanding grew from the interplay of personalities. On this basis the Council recommended a larger place for practical and aesthetic activity, constant co-operation between departments and the presentation of "subjects" less as disciplines than as fields of human endeavour. The English scheme of grammar, technical and modern schools, based on a division at the age of eleven, was held to be unsound. The ideal was a fairly small school, with a roll not far above six hundred, presenting a plentiful variety of courses and providing fully for transfer as mistakes were rectified and development occurred. The intention was to avoid a situation far too common still in which the non-academic child was regarded as essentially inferior to his more intellectually gifted brother. In the event there continued to be two courses, and the ideal in both was vocational. The Brunton Report of 1963 specifically said so about the "non-certificate" group, while the five-year courses, whatever their expressed aims, went on conforming to the requirements of the leaving certificate, the key to higher education and so to the professions.

The certificate itself had already moved away from being a university entrance test towards a guarantee of work completed, especially after 1924 when the minimum "group" of two higher and two lower passes was not enough to satisfy the Universities Entrance Board, but it is significant that the criticism of the secondary course by the universities as mere fact-gathering was based on the concept of what a university entrant ought to be.[22]

The certificate course, secure in a long tradition of successful preparation for higher studies, carried on for many years with pre-war content and teaching methods. Modern languages was a study of printed texts, with "unseens" (written translations into English) as a test of efficiency, "sentences" to demonstrate familiarity with idioms, and essays and "proses" (written translations out of English) to throw up the better scholars. Classics were in a similar mould, omitting the essay but laying greater emphasis on proses. The format of their higher papers in 1960 showed little change from those of 1920.[23] In 1959, although there had been a swing to the modern side, two-fifths of the pupils in the first year of Scottish secondary courses embarked on the study of Latin, and one-third of all fifth-year pupils included it in their course.[24] Many were following utilitarian motives: they had to study Latin because certain university courses demanded a leaving certificate pass on at least the lower grade. The Code recognised the problem in staffing, with large numbers of classics masters and slowly falling numbers of pupils, by permitting principal posts to be held in departments offering only thirty in place of the normal sixty hours a week.[25] Greek disappeared from many secondary schools, though traditionally minded institutions took some pride in maintaining its place. The plight of these subjects however in a utilitarian age may be measured from the number of their champions whose defence rested on the unsafe doctrine of transfer of training.

History in the secondary department still had its impact muffled by the practice of teaching towards certain questions "spotted" as likely to come up in the leaving certificate examination. It was still possible in the fifties to walk into a fourth or fifth year classroom and hear the teacher droning out notes at dictation speed on the fiscal policy of Walpole or the causes of the French Revolution. Questions on Scottish affairs were introduced in 1951, but they were neither numerous nor compulsory.

English literature was too often a process of memorising labels and regurgitating accepted theories; here also the "note" flourished. Plays especially those of Shakespeare, were taught as words on paper, not as dramatic pieces, and the impression contributed by one lecturer in 1964 to the *Scottish Educational Journal* was not a caricature:[26]

"How now, a rat? Dead for a ducat, dead!" . . . How much was a ducat? Peter? Margaret? . . . Well, look it up at the back of the book, that's what the notes are for . . . What? It doesn't tell you? Och well, it can't have been very much . . . Tell you what, look at the next sentence. Now here's something you can really do. Analyse it.

The three-year course had no tradition and no external certificate; the schools were free therefore to experiment, and the Department phrased its advice in very general terms. Its Memorandum on Junior Secondary Education, written by a panel of inspectors and published in 1955, described good work in a number of "progressive" schools, encouraged experiment (though on the whole it did not recommend a topical rather than a subject-centred approach) and took great pains to avoid even the suspicion of prescription. But many teachers were unable to make use of the liberty offered. Some took the certificate course in the subjects they knew and simplified it for meaner intellects; others, when the Department issued a circular setting out exemplary timetables, simply "operated courses 1, 4, 8 and 11". The absence of a terminal certificate was often more of a handicap than a liberation, and various authorities established their own: Edinburgh for example offered one from 1940 to 1958 based on internal estimates, then in the latter year introduced a City Certificate, set by a panel of teachers, on mathematics, technical subjects and the basic skills and marked in the candidates' own schools.[27]

The Report of the Working Party on the Senior Secondary Curriculum, issued in 1959, "shattered the complacency of the secondary schools".[28] It criticised the existing system on a number of grounds – its rigidity; the fact that too many pupils left school early; the lack of courses which contributed materially towards future vocations; and an excessive preoccupation, despite the abolition of the group certificate, with work in just that direction. The changes proposed were wide in their implications. There was to be a new examination structure, with ordinary grade in the fourth, higher in the fifth and advanced in the sixth year. New subjects like "modern studies" were proposed and older ones – science, commerce, technical and domestic subjects – would sub-divide. There should be no compulsory subjects: freedom of choice would be given to local authorities and headmasters. A decision on the grades to be attempted could be postponed until the end of the second year. Stronger links would be forged with further education by allowing students to be presented by colleges or education authorities.

Virtually all the Working Party's recommendations were implemented. The new Scottish Certificate of Education appeared in 1961. The higher grade examinations were deferred from March to May to bring them into line with the new ordinary grade papers. The number of separate subjects was substantially increased and this led to a much longer examination period. The conditions for presentation were extended as suggested, so that candidates could be put forward by colleges, local authorities and "any other body approved by the Secretary of State".[29] Examinations were not provided on the advanced level however until 1968.

The new certificate was an almost immediate success, and its influence was immense. The number of candidates rose sharply from 42,276 in 1962 to over 74,000 in 1966.[30] Since a third of the latter group were in four-year schools, further education colleges or were "external" candidates, there was ample evidence of a break-down in the old stratified structure of Scottish secondary education. The old Leaving Certificate had been within the reach of about fifteen per cent of pupils; the Scottish Certificate of Education was a reasonable goal for over thirty per cent, and a Working Party of the Educational Institute in 1967 suggested that the figure should be raised dramatically to seventy per cent. The boundaries between "academic" and "non-academic" courses were becoming blurred.

The balance of courses also changed. A paper in "modern studies", which concerned themselves with the history, geography, politics and economics of the twentieth century, was introduced at ordinary level in 1962, and succeeded so well that within half a dozen years there was also a higher grade and a working party was considering the place of the subject in non-certificate courses. By contrast joint subjects of the past split into their component parts: on the higher grade alone in 1965 it was possible to gain passes in four separate sciences and six technical subjects, and domestic and commercial groups were also sub-dividing.[31] Since there were no compulsions and the old concept of a group certificate had been abandoned as early as 1950, schools had great freedom in planning their pupils' courses. The normal requirement of a language and a scientific subject for admission to a university placed an effective limit on such freedom, but even here the refusal of the newer universities to adhere to the Scottish Universities Entrance Board altered the picture away from prescription.

The Scottish Certificate of Education Examination Board, which in 1963 took over the award of the certificate, showed itself no less willing than the Department to experiment with papers. The mid-sixties saw the destruction of the old rigid curriculum and methods in mathematics and the sciences. Research originating in the United States and applied to the British system with the help of the Nuffield Foundation resulted in "alternative syllabuses" in physics, chemistry, biology and mathematics, introduced at first side by side with traditional work but gradually replacing it. The emphasis in science was on methods of discovery by the pupil rather than dictation by the master; examinations placed the candidate in an experimental situation and asked "What would happen if . . .?" Moreover the study of energy, radio-activity and organic chemistry, over half a century after the pioneers, at last reached the Scottish classroom. The "new mathematics" dispensed with Euclidean geometry and introduced a more dynamic approach, with work on sets, inequations and bases other than ten.[32] The Examination Board fostered the development by setting papers on the new syllabuses.

In languages the move was towards oral work, in the belief that for all but a few future specialists the value of any French or German they learnt would lie in their ability to make themselves understood among Frenchmen, Germans or Swiss. "Language laboratories" gave the opportunity for learning spoken as well as written idiom. But here as elsewhere old methods died hard, and the stern hunt for grammatical accuracy continued in a number of schools, thanks to specialists whose training in accuracy perpetuated itself in their own teaching. An examination at ordinary grade in spoken French however assisted the process of change, and experiments began in 1967 in a similar course in spoken English. A working party on the teaching of classics undertook the formidable assault on the old regime there. Its report in 1967 recommended reduced time spent on language study, grammar and syntax, the use of a wider range of material, including such medieval sources as George Buchanan and the *Carmina Burana*, greater practice in oral work and the allocation of as much as forty per cent of marks to the study of classical history and civilisation. "Classical studies" were already established in some colleges of education, and experiments with new techniques included the teaching of Virgil in Aberdeen, the fortress of classical study, by means of programmed learning.[33]

The Government's declared intention of raising the leaving age again in 1970 increased interest in the secondary curriculum. A Consultative Committee was established in October 1965, with the Secretary of the Department as chairman, to keep the general situation in review and make arrangements for dealing with particular problems as they arose. It set up committees for example to review the teaching of English, to discuss the implications of the change to decimal currency, due in 1971, and to consider the balance of examined and unexamined subjects. In 1967 there were parties working on mathematics, physics, chemistry, modern studies and coordinated courses for girls. The difficulties of the large non-certificate group were dealt with in a Departmental Memorandum published in November 1966, which suggested courses to meet the raising of the leaving age. Like the 1955 Memorandum it was the work of the inspectorate and no less determined than its predecessor to avoid laying down any laws. It suggested however that subjects should be abandoned and courses constructed round three basic (and obvious) elements – social and moral education, preparation for leisure and vocation-based activities. Experiment was encouraged, in certain schools by direct invitation.[34] The document, even more permissive than that of 1955, was not acclaimed. Many teachers simply did not believe that the age could be raised without precipitating a crisis; the only memorandum they would have applauded would have been one issuing

precise and numerous orders. Vague encouragement and broad general-
isations, none of them new, commanded no respect. Meanwhile in a
few areas experiments were conducted, including some on ideas begun
south of the border – the "inter-disciplinary enquiries" for instance
commenced in London and Manchester, and the "Teachers' Centres"
advocated by the English Schools Council.

The changing balance of secondary courses was shown in the comparative popularity of various subjects. English, mathematics and
French remained well entrenched. The classics faded. The practical
subjects advanced their position: between 1962 and 1966 presentations
in technical, domestic and commercial subjects on the ordinary grade
doubled in number. It was in the mid-sixties also that the proposals of
the Brunton Committee increased the weight given in non-certificate
courses to "vocation-based" programmes, in which teachers of practical
subjects had a major part to play.

One effect of this altered balance was to shake the long-accepted
Scottish tradition that an academic teacher was much more valuable
than a non-academic, a graduate than a non-graduate, an honours man
than anyone else. At the material level the resultant commotion was
felt in grim battles over training, status and salary, with the establishment of pressure groups among, for example, honours graduates,
non-graduate women and art specialists, and many attempts to grapple
with the particularly intractable problem of training technical teachers.
About a quarter of all teachers certificated between 1945 and 1966, and
40 per cent of all secondary specialists professed practical and aesthetic
subjects and some of the worst shortages were in these categories.
Such a large minority felt its importance ought to be acknowledged.
On the other hand it remained more than doubtful whether the new
value placed by the educators on practical subjects was shared by the
general population. Given a choice for their children of two languages
or a technical (or domestic) course, few parents would have chosen the
latter. While the government set aside finance for ambitious scientific
and technological expansion, students preferred to overcrowd the arts
faculties. As for the "practical" pupils, the three-fifths who did not
aspire to a Scottish Certificate of Education, what most of them wanted
was not a vocation-based course but a vocation. They would have liked
to learn on the job, and their elders on the whole agreed with them:[35]

> There is a general feeling that with the new leaving age of fifteen,
> a boy destined for farming loses more in physical vigour than he
> gains in mental alertness in the extra year.

TEACHING AIDS

Quite as striking as the curricular changes were the multiplication
and diversification of teaching aids. More and more learning took

place outside the classroom, with pupils collecting information, conducting surveys, sketching, photographing and even tape-recording.
The British India Steam Navigation Company devoted two ex-
troopships entirely to educational cruises, the first of which in April
1961 transported 750 pupils, with classes meeting on board, to Corunna,
Gibraltar and Lisbon.[36] Later excursions went regularly to Leningrad
or the Eastern Mediterranean. There were physical education centres
at Glenmore Lodge and Inverclyde. Many authorities and some schools
ran their own residential colleges and "adventure centres", while
every Easter and summer vacation found hundreds of organised
parties travelling to London, Stratford and all the countries in Western
Europe.

Inside the classroom mechanical aids were rapidly developed. In
1949 fifty-seven per cent of Scottish schools had radio sets, in 1966
over ninety-four per cent, and almost all listened regularly. The Schools
Broadcasting Council for Scotland arranged a comprehensive service
of programmes, some like "Music and Movement" and "Exploring
Scotland" popular for years throughout the country, others designed
to meet minority needs in, for example, sixth form work. Between
1950 and 1959 the Joint Production Committee of the Scottish Educational Film Association and the Scottish Film Council produced a
hundred and seven films, film-strips and sets of slides, and in 1966
alone five new films were completed, with eleven in production. The
Central Film Library in Glasgow held a stock of over 4,000 titles.
Films were the commonest aid in use in the sixties, with filmstrips
and slides close behind.[37] The subjects best served were science and
geography.

In 1953 the first experiments in schools television were made in
southern England. At the end of September 1957 the B.B.C. televised
a series of short programmes to junior secondary schools in Scotland.
Sixty-six, including forty-two specially outfitted by education authorities, took part in this pilot experiment, and in one sponsored by the
Independent Television Authority. Following a report of the Schools
Broadcasting Council in 1959 the B.B.C. doubled its schools television
service in September 1960. By that time schools were acquiring sets
at a rate of about forty a year.[38] The sixties brought local television:
the independent Grampian station in the north, advised by an educational committee of teachers, directors, college lecturers and inspectors,
transmitted series like "Let's Make It" and "Let's Explore" to primary
schools in the region from Dundee to Wick, while Glasgow Education
Authority in 1965 set up its own educational television station, co-
ordinating its efforts with closed-circuit installations in the Universities,
Jordanhill College and the College of Drama. Edinburgh proposed to
follow suit. Queen Anne school in Dunfermline made successful use of
closed circuit television, but it was still generally too expensive for
schools.

One new device followed another. Oral methods made use of the tape-recorder, and it was a development of this, the "language laboratory", which after 1962 helped to revolutionise the teaching of modern languages. Adding machines found a place in primary arithmetic. There was an effort to popularise "teaching machines", pioneered in America and introduced by various commercial firms. They promoted "programmed learning", by which pupils worked at their own pace through prepared assignment books which could be completed only if the correct answers were found at each stage. There was some useful experiment, notably in Aberdeen, but the process was slow to catch on, the machines especially being regarded with cautious scepticism. In the mid-sixties generally, although more teachers were using aids than ever before, there was much distrust of "gimmicks", especially mechanical ones, as evidence an article in *Punch* on BOOK (Built-In Orderly Organised Knowledge):[39]

> Anyone can use BOOK, even children, and it fits comfortably into the hands. It can be conveniently used sitting in an armchair by the fire. Once purchased BOOK requires no further upkeep cost; no batteries or wires are needed, since the motive power, thanks to an ingenious device patented by the makers, is supplied by the brain of the user. Altogether BOOK seems to have great advantages with no drawbacks. We predict a big future for it.

The success of teaching aids in fact, as critics tirelessly pointed out, lay in the use teachers made of them. At their best they opened doors out of the classroom into countries far away, in the world, in space or beyond the microscope. When "followed up" they might spark off such interesting work as did the radio programmes which in 1958 produced an anthology of local poetry in Peebles, a model house in a Dundee special school ("Exploring Scotland"), a discussion of moral standards by approved school children in Aberdeen, a tape recording of Glasgow infants dramatising a story from "Let's Join In."[40] They might on the other hand be no more than twenty minutes' isolated respite from the hard grind of "proper study".

THE ORGANISATION OF SECONDARY EDUCATION

It is hardly surprising that as ideas altered on the nature and content of secondary education arrangements for organising it had also to change. It was in this post-war era, as we have seen, that what was done for non-academic children was at last accepted as "secondary" education. There were two main (and inter-related) administrative problems – how to place individual children in each category, and whether to educate them, once placed, in separate schools. Even twenty years after 1945, when the answer to both appeared to have

o

been, if not found, at least discerned, the image in most people's minds was still of two categories.

Circular 108 of 1947 settled the question of selection until the sixties. Each authority was required to submit a promotion scheme for approval, but the lines were laid down on which it should be constructed. The last scheme was approved early in the fifties; with small modifications they showed the same features, largely based on McClelland's work. Transfer was controlled by a promotion board, comprising usually committee representatives and teachers. A child no longer had to qualify for secondary work. Since the psychological disturbance caused by retaining him in a primary school was thought to outweigh the dangers of advancing him without full preparation, he was promoted not later than his thirteenth birthday, even when he had not completed his course. On the other hand, also for psychological reasons, very few children under eleven, even the most brilliant, were transferred: in Glasgow in 1952-3 for example only four out of twenty thousand. The average age of promotion was just over twelve. Until 1959 most counties imposed some kind of attainment test, intended as much to standardise teachers' estimates as to discover whether children had reached a necessary standard of achievement.

The child's intelligence was also tested. On the basis of all three measures – intelligence, attainment and teacher's estimate of capacity – his course in secondary school was decided. To avoid charges of dictation, every county made provision for consulting the wishes of parents, though in the last resort it was the welfare of the child which counted, and the decision of the Secretary of State was final. But for the average parent the attainment examination still appeared as the "qualifying", a brief but imposing barrier which had to be scaled in such a way that a poor scholar might qualify for a good school by a special effort and a clever boy condemn himself by laziness or misfortune on a certain day. It was difficult to see how this impression could be removed without the co-operation of those who held it; it died very hard. A decision to abolish the test was open to criticism that it was due as much to social expediency as educational advisability, but there was a growing conviction that too much of a child's future hung on his performance in the tests. An investigation conducted in Aberdeen in 1957 on the later university records of a hundred local children showed that correlations with performance in the promotion tests were all positive but comparatively low – with the first and second intelligence tests ·26 and ·22, with the standardised tests in arithmetic and English ·20 and ·15, with teachers' estimates ·07.[41] On the other hand a survey in West Lothian in 1956 which studied the leaving certificate passes of sixty-four boys and girls promoted six years before found that only two had an intelligence quotient under a hundred and seven and all those who were most successful showed a hundred and twenty or more.[42]

A special committee of the Advisory Council studied the question in 1961. They found that the transfer examinations had certainly narrowed the curriculum in many primary schools to English, arithmetic and little else, but accepted the need for some assessment of abilities at entry to secondary work. Their suggestion was that the promotion boards should divide candidates into three categories only, prospective "highers", probable "lowers" and others, with not more than twenty per cent in the first and at least fifteen in the second category. The tendency, they felt, had been to admit too many to higher courses – only a fifth in Aberdeen but approximately a half in some counties, notably Glasgow, and over a third in the country as a whole, of whom two-thirds were never presented. They sought justice for the extreme groups, the gifted, whom they found increasingly neglected, and the "modified", a term they wished to see discarded.[43]

The committee made one proposal which was very much in tune with the political thinking of the time: they recommended experiment with various patterns of comprehensive education. Throughout the fifties it had become increasingly clear that the junior secondary school would have to go. The "clean cut" policy after 1945 left too many poorly grounded pupils in courses run on the assumption that they were well prepared. Finding no interest and constant frustration, they became aggressive, and in some of the poorer quarters of the cities there were educational ghettoes where the best a teacher could do was to maintain a semblance of order. The fine work accomplished in other such schools went for nothing; in the minds of most Scottish parents the junior secondary was a school for failures, denied the double language course which was the key to higher education and condemned, literally, to hew wood if not to draw water.

The figures of "wastage" – pupils who left without completing their courses – fed this dissatisfaction. In thirty-two Glasgow schools in 1950 the first year roll amounted to 11,500, the third year to 5,200, the fifth to 1,500, the sixth to 480.[44] In the Scottish junior secondaries in 1952 only 20,000 out of 50,000 leavers had completed a full three year course. The trouble moreover ran through the whole system. In the same year 23,000 left senior secondary schools: forty-six per cent of these went as soon as they reached leaving age and seventy-four per cent did not complete the five-year course.[45]

Several local authorities sought a solution in forbidding the term "junior secondary". With the appearance in 1962 of the ordinary grade in the Scottish Certificate of Education moreover the trend was towards a type of school offering a four-year course. "Wastage" had by this time started to decrease: the number of pupils aged seventeen and over rose by a third between 1954 and 1963.[46] Thereafter political and social pressures refused to wait for educational experiment. The democratic solution was to place all children in a neighbourhood school, with equal care for each, whatever his particular abilities. This was the "comprehensive system", championed in all its manifestoes by the

Labour party, and introduced in principle as soon as the government gained a safe majority. The Conservative opposition was not happy:

> The Labour Government's attempts to spread comprehensive education throughout the country are a regrettable and in places a damaging irrelevance.

But even the Tories accepted that such a system might be suitable in certain areas.[47]

The debate on comprehensive education had been stormy in England in the early fifties, with Socialist councils at war with a Conservative government. Scotland then had pointed smugly to its ancient system of "omnibus" and "multilateral" schools, especially in country districts. Ten years later however it became clear that these were not an adequate answer: middle-aged people in Inverurie, for example, still remembered whether they had been taught at the Academy or "on the other side", though all had been nominally Academy pupils.[48] Government policy in the sixties was a deliberate assault on the traditional primacy given in Scotland to academic studies. It was significant in the new Training Regulations of 1965 for instance that there was no differentiation within the teacher's secondary certificate, as there had been before.

Circular 600, issued in October 1965, was an authoritarian statement by the Department that the Scottish educational system would henceforth be comprehensive, an ambitious decision since in that year 376 out of 668 Scottish secondary schools were still selective and 158 "mixed".[49] Local authorities were invited to submit schemes for bringing the decision into effect, and it soon became obvious that compromises were unlikely to be approved. Several authorities proposed a "two-tier" arrangement of junior and senior high schools, the former offering first to fourth year courses, with transfers for some at the end of the second year, the latter four-year courses beginning in Year III. Fife indeed had been operating such a system since 1962. The Secretary of State was prepared to admit these only in areas where geographical considerations were paramount; industrial counties, Renfrew for example, which put forward a two-tier scheme were advised to think again. In Aberdeen, when the Director of Education proposed this pattern, the strongly Socialist Education Committee refused to accept it. The Socialist answer was the "all-through" school: the Aberdeen scheme finally approved envisaged ten secondaries, all offering six years of comprehensive education, with the consequent destruction of the city's ancient Grammar School and its High School for Girls. The same issue in 1967 almost cost the Labour party its majority in Glasgow for the first time in decades.

The totally comprehensive school was a decision of the heart: there was no adequate evidence that pupils would do better in such a system. The problem for its opponents was to safeguard the brilliant youngster when his teachers were busy with diverse classes, some requiring techniques yet to be evolved. One solution, the Sixth Year College beginning at Class V, was impossible so long as the higher grade examinations continued to be held in the fifth year. Another was propounded by Edinburgh in 1966, the three-tier arrangement of primary (5-10), middle (11-14) and upper (14-18) schools. Since there would be no segregation at any stage, the system was fundamentally comprehensive, but it also offered some prospect of an economical deployment of teachers. It was experimental, being restricted at first to certain parts of the city, and so satisfied many observers who were shocked by what they considered the Government's headlong rush into complete comprehension.[50]*

In many minds the decision sounded the knell of independent and fee-paying schools. In 1964 55,000 pupils, 6·5 per cent of the whole school population, were being educated in these institutions, almost evenly divided in three categories. Certain local authorities, notably Glasgow and Edinburgh, ran schools in which nominal fees were charged; they were entitled to do so under the 1962 Education Act so long as they first ensured that free places were available for all who wanted them. The Department also gave direct grants to meet over half of the running costs of twenty-nine schools in various parts of the country, including the Hutchesons' Grammar Schools in Glasgow, Robert Gordon's College in Aberdeen, Dundee High School and the Merchant Company foundations in Edinburgh; the bill in the early sixties rose from a million to over a million and a quarter.[51] The third category comprised the completely independent schools like Fettes and Glenalmond, Gordonstoun, St Leonards and the Academies of Glasgow and Edinburgh. Under the 1945 Act these had to find a place on a Register (established in the fifties) and were subject to inspection if they wished to remain there. Several were "Scottish Public Schools" and although they had a fine tradition, it was probably true to say, as the writer of an article on a direct-grant school did, that whereas his was regarded with local affection, they were on the whole tolerated.[52]

The case for the continued existence of fee-paying schools rested on three foundations. First, they found it possible to provide better conditions for learning, partly by attracting more and better qualified staff, and partly, since they had powers of selection and rejection, by housing no unwilling pupils, and dealing only with co-operative parents. Second, they were able, by giving due warning in their prospectuses, to initiate educational experiments impossible within the state system. Such a school was Gordonstoun, conducted according to the doctrines of Dr Kurt Hahn, which gained considerable prestige in the sixties by being chosen for the education of the Prince of Wales. Another was Kilquhanity in Galloway, run as a "freedom school" in the pattern of A. S. Neill's Summerhill. There about 40 pupils selected their own courses, built their own common-room and theatre, ran their own farm

* It was in fact ultimately rejected.

and administered their own affairs through a School Council, on which teachers and pupils had one vote each and the chairman was a pupil. Discipline was introduced by the fact that, having chosen a course, they were expected to go on with it. "It's a funny place", said the post-office clerk giving directions to find it, "not at all like a school."[53] Its freedom might be gauged by comparing its career with the difficulties encountered by the headmaster of Braehead in Fife, who attempted a not dissimilar experiment inside the state system.

The third claim put forward for the fee-paying schools was that a parent, as long as he paid his share of the public bill and chose a properly inspected method, should be allowed to educate his children as he wished. But the very existence of independent schools destroyed the monolithic perfection of the comprehensive principle. It was claimed that in Aberdeen for example Gordon's, St Margaret's and Albyn would simply cream off all the brightest pupils, including many who had previously attended the Grammar and High Schools. Circular 600 recognised the danger in a phrase with ominous undertones:[54]

> Those authorities in whose areas there are grant-aided schools will no doubt wish also to consult the governing bodies of these schools as to the part they can play in a comprehensive system.

The most widely rumoured solution was that local fee-paying schools would disappear, those with direct grant be confronted with the alternative of coming within the system or standing on their own feet: Morrisons' Academies for Boys and Girls became in effect senior high schools in Perthshire's two-tier organisation.[55] In the late sixties however the future remained obscure.

SOCIAL ASSISTANCE

One process which accelerated rather than slackened during the period was the provision of social assistance, which became increasingly available not only to necessitous but to all children. The 1945 Act laid down for example that authorities, as part of their schemes, must provide facilities for recreation and for social and physical training. They might establish camps, holiday classes, play centres, playing fields, gymnasia, swimming baths, organise games and expeditions, and contribute some or all of the expense. They might even provide special clothing for physical training.[56] Authorities interpreted these instructions in their own way. Most urban committees for instance made provision for visits to nearby swimming baths; schools with their own pools were uncommon. Robert Gordon's was the only one in Aberdeen for long after 1945, and in Glasgow before the opening of the new comprehensives in the sixties, baths were restricted to certain schools built in the early part of the century.

All pupils under eighteen in schools and colleges of further education were entitled to free milk daily, and almost nine-tenths drank it, or at least accepted it: "free milk", according to the Third Statistical Account of Aberdeen, "now ranks with marbles as an item of barter." Four out of ten also took mid-day meals, one fifth of these without payment.[57] They were encouraged to be thrifty: in 1965-6 for example the Aberdeen Savings Bank carried out nearly 700,000 transactions in 291 schools.[58] Every effort was made to fit leavers into the right jobs. The Act of 1946 permitted authorities to maintain agencies for collecting and distributing relevant information, and two years later the Employment and Training Act left them to decide whether they would do so themselves or leave the business to the Ministry of Labour. Although most took the easier course, 60,000 leavers a year were being interviewed by 1960,[59] most schools had careers masters and there were periodic conventions and parents' nights besides "School to University" conferences. The demand increased greatly in the sixties, in one field with the proposals of the Brunton Report, and in another with the spread of higher education among many pupils whose parents knew nothing of the opportunities it created.[60] The task of guidance was beset with difficulties: information was of little value without investigation of abilities and interests and the essential immobility of children complicated matters further. This was a field where in the late sixties much had still to be done.

One form of social assistance increasingly offered in the sixties was "sex education." The topic was tinged with embarrassment; the generally accepted view was that it should have been left to parents, but if it was, it would seldom be properly done. Evidence was difficult to find, but in one survey in a Fife secondary school only 6 pupils out of 582 claimed to have had any instruction and then merely answers to childish questions. The stork, the little black bag and "tell you later" were, it appeared, quite common.[61] Various experimental schemes were established, for instance in Fife and Aberdeenshire, and there were radio and television programmes, films and film-strips, but all encountered basic problems in moving from instruction to education, from physical to temperamental and emotional factors. Nevertheless, difficult or not, the problem had to be tackled; the increase in premarital pregnancies and the spread of venereal disease showed that.

Where pupils were found to be in any way underprivileged, assistance became more generous. The rapid rehousing of urban population after the second world war led as we have seen to a wave of educational transport, with almost 17,000 Glasgow children for example conveyed daily in 1955 from eleven housing schemes in ordinary and special buses.[62] There were more hostel and lodging places for country children. But the effect on the pupils and the rural areas they left was generally deplored. The daily round trip for Braemar children to Banchory Academy was eighty miles, and Lismore and Appin pupils might be away from home from six in the morning to seven at night. Such long journeys undoubtedly contributed to early leaving: at Lismore in 1955 out of four hundred and nine children at school only four were in senior secondary courses. Yet bad accommodation and higher priorities were sounding the knell of rural schools, which were closing in many parts of the country. Where they remained, they usually filled the role of social as well as educational centres: at Little Glenshee in Perthshire for example there was handicraft on Monday evenings, carpet bowls on Tuesdays and Thursdays, a drama rehearsal on Wednesdays, a dance, whist drive or concert on Fridays and a church service on the fourth Sunday of each month.[63]

Bursaries were widely provided for higher and specialised education, partly by the local authorities and partly by the Department's Awards Branch, which took over the administration of allowances for courses in universities and colleges. The total cost of courses in 1964-5 for bursars and allowance holders was nearly £12 millions, of which the Department contributed 8, the authorities 1·4 and parents and holders the rest.[64] Every Scottish student in higher education was entitled to a basic grant (£50 in the mid-sixties); what else he got depended on his family's means.

Most public money per head was spent on severely under-privileged children. Over ten thousand in 1965 were in the care of local authorities at an average cost weekly of £5 10s each.[65] Throughout the period there was a move away from the "children's home" towards placing with foster-parents. They were much less costly, but that was not the reason for the trend, which was based on the emotional value of the family environment. About four thousand children a year, even in the affluent society of the sixties, also received free clothing.

Eleven thousand in 1965 required special educational treatment and another fifteen hundred were in schools approved for delinquents and unfortunates.[66] There were twenty-six institutions of this kind, two provided by the Glasgow authority, the remainder by voluntary managers, usually with a religious connexion, all largely financed by public funds. They were seldom used until other methods of dealing with difficult children had failed, especially probation. As might be expected, none were co-educational. The average length of stay was less than two years but the influence of the schools was not easy to determine. On the whole employers co-operated well in accepting ex-pupils; in 1959 two thirds of the girls and half the boys who had left three years before were in regular jobs. Moreover ninety-one per cent of the girls and sixty-four per cent of the boys had not reappeared in court[67]. This was hardly a perfect measure of success, but there were no others. Whatever was achieved, at a cost of £800 for each pupil in 1965, sprang from the tenacity and unsentimental devotion of the teachers.

The number of children in special schools and classes remained fairly constant throughout the period: in 1947 it was 10,829, 10,266 in 1956, 10,943 in 1965.[68] Upwards of three-quarters were described as mentally, about a tenth as physically, handicapped; and there were no more than a few hundred in any other category. This field was the subject of two separate series of investigations. Between 1949 and 1951 the Advisory Council produced several reports on all types of defective children; the Secretary of State in Circular 300 of 1955 accepted many of their recommendations. Notably he agreed that handicapped pupils were best served when educated along with their more fortunate fellows. Regulations issued in 1954 defined the categories of "special educational treatment" and the arrangements necessary in each. One difficult problem however remained only partially solved – how to ascertain with some confidence when a pupil came into any category. Several working parties reported on this in the sixties, dealing with the mentally handicapped, the maladjusted, those with hearing defects and the blind.

In 1966 provision was being made in eighty-eight special schools, fourteen of which were residential, fifty-nine special classes in the ordinary schools, fifty-eight "junior occupational centres" for children who could be trained but not educated, and child guidance arrangements under twenty-seven local authorities.[69] The largest group, over eighty per cent, suffered from mental handicap so grave that they were unable to profit from ordinary education. There was a gratifying decline in the number diagnosed as "physically handicapped" – from 3,948 in 1948 to 1,819 in 1965[70] – but some of this may have been due to altered standards of test. The poorest provision, with only 212 places in the country, was for maladjusted children, perhaps because their situation was least well understood. Emotionally disturbed children, especially if they were of above average intelligence, presented a very thorny problem indeed. There was an interesting attempt to find a solution at Lendrick Muir boarding school.[71] Teachers of handicapped children underwent an extra year of training at Jordanhill College of Education or in special courses for certain categories at Dublin, Manchester and Birmingham.

In the late twentieth century every western country, whatever the colour of its government, had to be a "welfare state", and the schools of Britain were the organised centres for dispensing much of this welfare. Here more than anywhere, more than at any previous time, the educational development of Scotland mirrored the general trends in her history. Social assistance spread everywhere: the decision for comprehensive education was one facet. It was still however far from perfect. Its methods were typically those of democracy, that "broad-based, stupid, blind adventure, groping towards an unknown goal" which assigns rights to the individual without guarantee that the result will be a workable community. But to continue with such methods was an article of democratic faith. One common criticism was that children, having too much done for them, were rapidly weakening in moral fibre. As in so many debates, there was little firm evidence, and it is difficult to see how there could be. Certainly more children were going on to higher education than ever before. They were taller and heavier and healthier. And probably – though here we enter again the realm of speculation – most of them were happier.

REFERENCES

1. *T.S.A. Ayrshire*, 215
2. *S.E.J.* 27 Jan. 1961
3. MACLAY, Secretary of State, answering a Commons question, S.E.J., 6 April 1962
4. *T.S.A. East Lothian*, 395
5. *S.E.D.R. 1959*, 128
6. *S.E.D.R. 1966*, 61-2
7. *Schools (Scotland) Code 1956*, section 5
8. NISBET, STANLEY, *Nursery School Provision in Scotland* (S.C.R.E. 1958), 20-21
9. MACMILLAN, MARGARET, *The Nursery School*, Dent 1930, 95
10. *Primary School in Scotland*, 7
11. *Primary School in Scotland*, 10-12
12. *S.E.D.R. 1950*, 15
13. *Demonstration School Logbook*, H.M.I. Report, ii, 220
14. *Primary School in Scotland*, 53, 100
15. *S.E.J.*, 24 Jan. 1958
16. *E.I.S. Memorandum on Discipline*, October 1965, *S.E.J.* 15 Oct. 1965
17. MILNE, *Poems*, 71
18. *U.N.E.S.C.O. Yearbook of Education 1949*, Czechoslovakia
19. *Report of London University Institute of Education Reading Research Unit*, 1967
20. OSBORNE, *Scottish and English Schools*, 26
21. *S.E.D.R. 1966*, 7
22. ROBERTSON, Presidential Address to the Education Section of the British Association, Sep. 1959; OSBORNE, *Scottish and English Schools*, 125-6
23. TRAIN, *S.E.J.* 9 Dec. 1966
24. *S.E.D.R. 1959*, 30-31
25. *Schools (Scotland) Code 1950*, section 7(4); *1956*, section 6(8)
26. SCOTLAND, *S.E.J.* 28 Aug. 1964
27. *S.E.J.* 7-14 Feb. 1958
28. BONE, *Inspection*, 313
29. *S.E.D. Circular 452*, 20 Feb. 1961
30. *S.E.D.R. 1962*, 27; *S.C.E.E.B. Report 1966*
31. *S.E.D.R. 1965*, 108

32. *S.E.J.* 5 March 1965, 26 March 1965, 25 March 1966
33. BROWN, qu. TRAIN *S.E.J.* 9 Dec. 1966; *S.E.D., Report of a Working Party on the Curricula in Latin and Greek* (H.M.S.O. 1967)
34. *S.E.D.R. 1966,* 26-7
35. *T.S.A. County of Aberdeen,* 216
36. *S.E.J.* 14 April 1961
37. *S.E.D.R. 1959,* 28; *1966,* 13-14; BARCLAY, *S.E.J.* 17 Feb. 1967
38. *S.E.D.R. 1957, 1958, 1959*
39. HEATHORN, *Punch,* 1962
40. SCOTLAND, *S.E.J.,* 18 July 1958
41. NISBET, *S.E.J.,* 3 May 1957
42. *S.E.J.,* 27 Dec. 1957
43. *S.E.J.,* 15 Dec. 1961
44. *S.E.D.R. 1950,* 19
45. *S.E.D.R. 1952,* 25
46. *S.E.D.R. 1959,* 11
47. Conservative and Unionist Parties, *Putting Britain Right Ahead,* 1965
48. DIXON, *Education in the North,* Spring 1965, 20
49. *S.E.D.R. 1965,* 33
50. *S.E.J.,* 25 Nov. 1966
51. *S.E.D.R. 1965,* 89
52. "Morrison's Future", *T.E.S.,* 30 Sep. 1966
53. *T.E.S.,* 23 Sep. 1966
54. *Circular 600,* section 19
55. "Morrisons' Future", *T.E.S.,* 30 Sep. 1966
56. *Education (Scotland) Act 1945,* section 3
57. *S.E.D.R. 1966,* 16-17
58. Aberdeen Savings Bank, *Report on School Banks and National Savings Associations,* 1965-6
59. *Education (Scotland) Act 1946,* section 135; *S.E.D.R. 1960,* 89
60. DEWAR, *T.E.S.,* 3 March 1967
61. *S.E.J.,* 21 Nov. 1958
62. *T.S.A. Glasgow,* 521
63. *T.S.A. Aberdeenshire,* 443; *Argyll,* 163; YOUNG, *S.E.J.,* 24 Sep 1965
64. *S.E.D.R. 1965,* 128-9
65. *S.E.D.R. 1965,* 130, 132
66. *S.E.D.R. 1965,* 100
67. *S.E.D.R. 1959,* 91
68. *S.E.D.R. 1947,* 55; *1956,* 116; *1965,* 100
69. *S.E.D.R. 1966,* 30-31
70. *S.E.D.R. 1966,* 33
71. NICHOLSON, *S.E.J.,* 12 Feb. 1965

CHAPTER 14

The Teachers

SUPPLY OF TEACHERS

"I CANNOT remember a time when I wanted to do anything else." When over five hundred students in Scottish colleges of education were asked in 1965 to account for their presence there, almost a quarter answered thus. The picture of teaching as a vocation remained clear, though it was a double-edged weapon, since it also discouraged some possible entrants who felt that teachers were born, not made. The most attractive feature of the work, both to students in training and to children in secondary schools, was the opportunity to spend their days with young people. Material advantages ranked far below spiritual: money was not a commanding magnet, though for teachers in service it was a perennial topic of complaint. Young Scots became teachers because they were fond of children, because the work seemed interesting and varied and valuable, and occasionally because of "short hours and long holidays". A good many also drifted in.[1]

Whatever their reasons, there were not enough teachers. Every year after 1945 there were more in the schools: the total rose in twenty years from 29,000 to 42,317. But the number of children grew also, and the teacher-pupil ratio improved only slowly – 25·9 in 1946, 23·6 in 1964. Moreover the national average was forced down by the small rural schools: in Sutherland and Shetland the ratio was not much over fifteen, whereas only Aberdeen of the cities was really well staffed, with average primary classes of only twenty-two. In the industrial south-west such classes were twice as large, and the absence of a teacher might throw eighty children together in one room, to be policed rather than taught.[2] "Reserve" teachers had become a lost luxury; principal assistants and infants mistresses usually took classes for at least part of the day; and headmasters, even in large schools, were no strangers to the classroom. Outsize classes remained such a problem that all political parties considered it necessary to promise reduction in their manifestoes.

The problem was self-perpetuating. Worn down by the struggle many teachers gave up early, especially women, whose average age of retirement in 1966 was sixty-three.[3] The situation was worst in the central lowlands. Glasgow, which employed a fifth of the country's teachers, had five hundred oversize classes in 1961 and several hundred children on part-time education. Two years earlier the Deputy Director of Fife had written of a "creeping paralysis" afflicting schools in his county:[4]

> There is scarcely a subject for which an adequate supply of teachers is available, and many are the improvisations which must be made.

There was a seller's market for jobs. At the end of their training year students were able to choose posts according to amenities like new buildings, convenience of travel and prospects of promotion. In the mid-sixties only the city of Aberdeen could still afford to offer appointments without specifying particular posts.[5] The counties with many large schools suffered: there was one headmaster to every ten teachers in Scotland, but only one to twenty in Glasgow.[6] A Departmental Committee on the Supply of Teachers which found a total shortage in 1962 of 3,673 expected the figure to rise to 5,000 by 1966 and 7,000 by 1970, and the raising of the leaving age then would demand 5,000 more.[7]

Certain categories were chronically starved. Shortages in music, physical education and homecraft might be regarded without too much alarm in a tradition which considered these to be "frills", but even the most diehard reactionary could not fail to be dismayed by shortages in mathematics and science. The Departmental Committee sounded a tocsin when it pointed out that two thirds of the specialist mathematicians in 1960 were over fifty years old. Technical teachers and "subspecialists" without honours degrees were widely used to plug the gap, and the deficiency was expected to be over fifty per cent by 1975.[8]

A succession of working parties studied the general and the various specific problems. The Departmental Committee, composed of two officers of the S.E.D., two directors of education, the Executive Officer of the National Committee for the Training of Teachers and the General Secretary of the Educational Institute, was formed in 1950, and remained in being, with periodic changes in membership, for a dozen years. It reported four times and its statements, never less than grave, made the fourth report as gloomy a document as had appeared in Scottish education during the twentieth century. The Committee considered from the outset that without the use of recruitment schemes the normal output of colleges could never be reckoned to do more than offset wastage. The last report looked forward to a slight easing of the situation when the post-war bulge produced more teachers in the late sixties, but it went on to point out that the birthrate, after declining in the early fifties, had risen again and showed no sign of falling. From 1975 the deficiency in mathematics and science would be so severe as to threaten a complete breakdown of advanced instruction.[9] Moreover the shortage might be part of a general want of well-educated men and women in the community, and this might present an insuperable obstacle to improvement.

Another Committee, set up by the Secretary of State in 1953 under the chairmanship of Sir Edward Appleton to report on the supply of teachers in mathematics and science, reported in 1955. At the end of 1953 ten secondary schools in Glasgow could boast only one honours graduate apiece in mathematics, and the deadening effect of the situation was being felt in the poor standard of pupils going on to higher institutions. The Appleton Report pointed out that the demand in this field had grown out of proportion to the general increase in the number of pupils: between 1939 and 1954 the latter had risen by only $7\frac{1}{2}$ per cent, but the total number of certificated teachers over the same period had increased by 18 per cent. The Committee expected the shortage to grow, and proposed some interesting devices – full pay and pension for retired teachers who returned to service, special maintenance grants during training, higher salaries for holders of degrees in mathematics and deferment of national service. The Educational Institute opposed preferential treatment of any category and the national service proposal altogether, and in the event such concessions as were made were weakened by extension to all graduates.

In 1959 a Special Committee of the Advisory Council reported on measures to improve the general supply of secondary teachers. Its recommendations trod similar paths: full salary and pension for a teacher retired and re-employed, increased bursaries to attract pupils to staying on at school, higher salaries generally, better deployment of teachers, more responsibility for them in the administration of education, a wider pensions scheme and changes in training to admit graduates with third-class honours to special certificates and primary teachers to take backward classes in the secondary department. The last measure was adopted.

A working party set up in 1957 by the Department and the local authorities attempted to adjust the distribution of teachers in the country. Its report recommended voluntary self-denial by the better staffed counties on the lines of the English quota system, but whereas the latter was accepted by all authorities the city of Dundee immediately stated non-compliance in Scotland. Nevertheless there was some success: between 1960 and 1964 the worst areas raised their teaching force by four hundred and nineteen, the best by only four. A Departmental working party in 1966 under the chairmanship of Dame Jean Roberts recommended that the system should continue and proposed certain further steps whose advantages should not be available to non-compliers. In general these boiled down to additional salary and travel allowance for teachers in "designated schools" with a three-year history of understaffing.[10] The report had a lukewarm reception and the Secretary of State took some time to consider his comments.

Any differential financial inducement was bound to arouse opposition. Before 1939 there had been a "Glasgow allowance" of £50 a year, which had been one of the main targets of egalitarians fighting for standard scales. When the National Joint Council in 1963 gave way to pressure and proposed its reintroduction there was a fury of protest, especially from industrial counties like Lanark, Renfrew and Dunbarton, whose teachers were no better off than Glasgow's. The proposals were then amended to offer a bonus to teachers in certain specified districts in all these counties, but opposition by local authorities everywhere killed that too. A proposal by the E.I.S. that salaries instead of grants should be paid during training was rejected by the Department because of the repercussions it would have outside teaching. The suggestion made by virtually every Committee that retired teachers who returned on full salary should be allowed to keep their pensions was also refused, though a certain allowance was granted. In the event the best most authorities could do was to offer teachers some priority in housing, and the Roberts Committee, while rejecting a National Fund for this purpose, agreed with the general principle.[11]

The Secretary of State and his advisers showed ingenuity in the measures they adopted to cope with the chronic deficiency. The attractions of teaching were depicted in magazines and the daily press, in pamphlets and posters issued to schools and universities, and by visits of suitable serving teachers. Prospective entrants received preferential treatment in the community from 1956, when students with first and second class honours in mathematics or science were granted indefinite deferment of national service if they embraced the profession: in the next three years this concession was extended to all teachers and 564 students were deferred in the period before national service was discontinued.[12] Entrance requirements were reduced in some categories, notably candidates for the primary diploma, who from 1953 might be admitted with "near-misses" in their leaving certificates, and also "mature persons" over twenty-four. The training course was compressed in the Emergency Training Scheme of 1945 to 1959, which also reduced entrance demands: it produced 4,550 teachers for primary and secondary posts.[13] The course for honours graduates was reduced between 1958 and 1961 from three to two terms. Candidates with lower qualifications were admitted to superior posts: in 1960 a third-class honours degree qualified its holder to hold a special certificate, and from 1959 men and women with a general certificate might, after additional training, take classes of backward children in secondary schools. They received an extra annual payment of £75. Other financial inducements were also introduced like special assistantships in secondary departments offering £40 a year. The Special Recruitment Scheme, operating from 1951, provided fairly generous allowances for entrants from other fields of employment. Begun as a temporary measure it continued unexpectedly to attract a steady stream of entrants; by the mid-sixties the number of its beneficiaries was four times what it had been at the start, and in Jordanhill they constituted a steady 16 per cent of the student population.[14]

The most promising manœuvre was to persuade those who left the profession to think again. Retired teachers were invited to return and by 1954 almost five hundred had accepted. Although the age of compulsory retirement, at least in unpromoted posts, was raised thereafter to seventy about two hundred over-age teachers remained in service each year.[15] The other valuable group was composed of married women, who were increasingly urged to combine teaching with running a home and raising a family; several good reasons and many rationalisations were given in support of the practice. Colleges ran special "refreshment" courses. It was all very reasonable and all very healthy for the profession, and it all rang a little oddly only twenty years after marriage carried automatic resignation; many women served under both dispensations. It was also very successful; indeed it was the married women who kept the schools open in the sixties, when the number of single women in service fell almost every year. A quarter of the women who completed training between 1961 and 1965 were no longer teaching in the latter year, but 18·1 per cent, although they had married, still were.[16]

One useful contribution could be made by relieving teachers of administrative and social tasks, leaving more time presumably for "real teaching". Medical and clerical staff multiplied and there was a movement to introduce teaching auxiliaries who would undertake routine tasks in the classroom. Where all this meant the removal of duties like collecting dinner money, filling forms and supervising play at the interval it was more than welcome, but it could not be expected to make much difference in the manning of the schools. A teacher thus released could be expected to find plenty to do with the classes he already had, and in any case many apparently irrelevant chores were part of the complex social process known as teaching.

The readiest solution for harassed directors of education, faced with over-crowded classrooms and staffing vacancies, was to employ uncertificated teachers, men and women whose qualifications fell narrowly or widely short of the standards normally demanded. The teachers' organisations, which had fought a long battle against the use of such assistance and come in the thirties within sight of total victory, remained inflexibly determined never to capitulate. Nevertheless the numbers rose yearly – 1,626 in 1958, 2,198 in 1961, 2,958 in 1966.[17] In 1964 uncertificated teachers formed over six per cent of all teachers employed in Scotland. As always the position was worst in industrial counties like Lanark, where the percentage was 11·2, and would have been in Glasgow, had the authority not preferred to leave places unfilled. On the other hand rural counties like Kirkcudbright and Selkirk had almost none, and the city of Aberdeen was fortunate with only 1·3 per cent.[18] Many of those employed could claim some element of suitability for their particular task; there were untrained graduates for example and music specialists who were technically but not educationally acceptable.

There was also however a sizeable group – almost a thousand – who fell far short of any desirable standard, men and women who had failed early in a university course and some who had been unsuccessful in teacher training. One mordant critic suggested that the quickest way to get a teaching job in the south-west was to fail at Jordanhill. Such "teachers" were on one day's notice and the problem was made extraordinarily slippery by constant changes in personnel. The General Teaching Council made an effort in 1967 to grapple with it through a scheme of "conditional registration" for better cases and a time limit within which they must qualify; those seriously below standard were to be dismissed. The proposals gained some support from the Secretary of State but not from many teachers and local authorities (though for different reasons) and the issue became one of prestige and even survival for the Council itself.

One less radical concession was fought through in the sixties. Although the Educational Institute clung grimly to its ideal of a graduate profession the vision faded in the post-war years. The proportion of graduates in 1939 was forty-one per cent, and it rose after 1945 to almost forty-five, but thereafter, despite every effort, no substantial rise could be achieved. In 1960 it was 45·3, in 1966 44·7, and many of the serious shortages of the sixties were in categories usually open only to graduates. Two schemes were presented which struck at the heart of the principle involved. In February 1965 the Principals of the Colleges of Education proposed the institution of a four-year college associateship, with the same entry requirements as for the primary diploma, leading to a primary or a secondary or even a double certificate (for the "middle school"). The idea was approved by the Scottish Council for the Training of Teachers and by some teachers' organisations, but vigorously opposed by the E.I.S.; it could not command the support even of all college governing bodies. Meanwhile a proposal put forward by the Department in June 1960 for the admission of non-graduate men to the college diploma course on the same terms as women was equally strenuously resisted; nevertheless in 1966 it was recommended afresh by the General Teaching Council and enacted by the Secretary of State. It was still unwelcome to the Educational Institute, which pointed out with some reason that it would provide teachers for a sector where shortages were less acute, but it was finally accepted without strikes. The associateship idea was allowed to lapse.

No-one suggested that these many devices and concessions would solve the central problem. The core of difficulty lay in the likelihood that teaching was already deriving its fair share of benefit from higher education, for, as the Secretary of State pointed out in 1965, nearly half of the working populations of the country who had had such education were in the service of schools, colleges and universities.[19] A survey conducted by the Appointments Committee of Glasgow University showed that half the men and two thirds of the women graduating

P

in arts there between 1958 and 1962 entered a teaching career; so did half the ordinary and a quarter of the honours science graduates.[20] It was unrealistic to expect more.

Nevertheless the effort to attract had to be made, though many critics, notably in the E.I.S., suggested that the Secretary of State could expect no success unless he increased the incentives, with salaries paid during training and higher salaries in service.* On the other hand, if the statements of young people themselves were to be believed, poor payment was not the main obstacle before their eyes; in any case promotion was rapid in areas of shortage, and an honours graduate in mathematics in the sixties might be fairly confident, even where his ability was moderate, of finding a post worth £2,000 a year before he was thirty-five. Much more discouraging to young minds was the threat of frustration and strain, fear of disciplinary incompetence and the picture of teaching as a dull, unadventurous pursuit.[21] Its most valued feature, security, was not one to appeal to young people, save in periods of national economic restraint.

TRAINING OF TEACHERS

One handicap, especially in the mind of graduates, was the long period of preparation, which might keep men and women with all the vigorous urges of youth *in statu pupillari* until they were twenty-two years old or more. It was not strange therefore that the training colleges were under constant criticism from their students, particularly those who came from the freer atmosphere of the universities. What most of them sought was a few tips of the trade; anything else was regarded as unnecessary padding at the expense of people who could have been earning a salary, and in any case as largely irrelevant. When five hundred students in 1965 were asked to identify the subjects of most value in their course, nine out of ten said practice in teaching and only 6 per cent educational philosophy. Child psychology and "subject methods" came about midway between these.[22] More distressing was the attitude of too many serving teachers, as summed up by one College Principal[23]

> Teachers give us an incredible amount of help with students, but in their public utterances and conversations with students they do anything but create a decent public image of the work of the Colleges.

Their views were often based on memories of their own experiences decades before, possibly transformed by the alchemy of time; whatever the reason, the damage was done.

If their work was poor – which in fact and in sum it was not – the colleges had increasingly themselves to blame, for their history during the period was one of growing independence. A story is told of the

* See for example the E.I.S. Report on Teacher Shortage, November 1963.

Director of the Aberdeen Centre that when the new Training Regulations appeared in 1905 he studied them closely for 24 hours consecutively before pronouncing them "a masterly document".[24] He was clearly seeing them for the first time, a state of affairs very different from that in the nineteen-sixties when the Colleges of Education Regulations (before issue) were the subject of prolonged and meticulous discussions between the Department and the Committee of Principals. It was perhaps unfortunate that the most comprehensive review of the training system in the first decade after the Hitler War came too early to have its best effect; it was the Report issued by the Scottish Advisory Council, and it appeared in 1946, when the problem of providing hosts of teachers as soon as possible made the time unpropitious for radical changes. It proposed the establishment of university Institutes of Education, as in England, with two or three constituent colleges as well as a research centre in each province. The demand of the Educational Institute for a professional degree was firmly refused however: the Council held that its status would suffer in comparison with existing arts and science degrees.[25]

A number of other suggestions it made – on secondment to college staffs for example and the provision of a religious diploma – were enacted: many others, on financial or dogmatic grounds, were not. The system of administration, with the Central Executive Committee in power and professional members there often outvoted even on professional matters, was left untouched. In the late nineteen-fifties however the Secretary of State undertook a comprehensive review of the training system, conducted in two stages. The Teachers (Training Authorities) Regulations of 1958 were the culmination of the first stage: they set up a new system of management and administration, differing radically from the older structure. The most important step taken was to grant much greater autonomy to the colleges. Provincial Committees were replaced by governing bodies, self-governing corporations. The National Committee, with its Central Executive, ceased to exist, and there appeared the Scottish Council for the Training of Teachers, whose membership of twenty-five was recruited largely from the college governing bodies. Its functions were mainly advisory and co-ordinating, but it also formulated rules and principles for exceptional admission to training or award of certificates; its recommendations to the Secretary of State were usually, though not invariably upheld. The supervision exercised by the Central Executive Committee was gone: governing bodies for example now appointed their own Principals, and an occasion under the old system when one provincial committee sent a short list of three candidates to the Central Executive and was presented with a quite different nomination for the post could no longer occur.

The new financial arrangement also clearly showed the altered balance of power. Each governing body prepared its own estimates, which were passed on to the Secretary of State, with comments, by the Scottish Council; the latter had no powers to alter them. The Secretary of State on the other hand could, as was fitting in a guardian of public expenditure. If he chose to ignore the advice of any governing body, the latter had of course the right to resign.

Academic staffs of the colleges were granted a stronger voice in running them. Principals had wide powers in the admission and expulsion of students; academic matters became their province, with advice from Boards of Studies formed from the teaching staff. For all lecturing posts the duty of recommending appointments was laid on committees consisting entirely or mainly of lecturers; the only exception to this rule was in the appointment of a Principal. Eight years later a further step was taken in the process of granting responsibility to the staff when half a dozen of them were allotted places as full governors.

A change in the function of the training institutions was reflected in their altered name: the resolutely vocational "Training Centres" became "Colleges of Education". In addition to their work of producing qualified teachers and keeping them up to date, the new colleges were to play a larger part in the higher education of their students, in organising conferences and developing research, chiefly related to class-room conditions, and in training other groups in the community. Jordanhill and Moray House undertook a great deal of work in training youth leaders, Moray House in child care and social service, Moray House and Dundee in conducting courses for Commonwealth students.

A further interesting feature of the 1958 system was the greater reliance it placed on teachers. By a rather cumbersome process teachers and headmasters in schools and further education centres elected members to each governing body, with a representation larger than that of any other group. A strong teacher element was also ensured on the Scottish Council: at one time sixteen of the twenty-five members were certificated teachers and the number never fell below twelve.*

The teachers themselves remained unsatisfied. There were strong complaints that the number of their representatives was not greater, and when staff governors were admitted in 1966 the Educational Institute requested, without success, a proportionate increase. A move in 1959 by the Secretary of State to review the process of training further by examining entrance standards, form and content of courses and certification began with the issue of a memorandum to all interested bodies, but it raised a storm of disapproval. Points at issue included arrangements for training graduates: there was a powerful body of opinion, among teachers and others, that the proper place for this was in the universities, which were universally respected, though not, it must be admitted, for any efficiency they had ever shown in training teachers. They themselves, faced with herculean tasks among their

* "Certificated teachers" included directors of education, university lecturers and others who had at one time taught in schools.

own students, were by no means eager in most cases to accept the commission; Stirling was an exception. Much more vehement protest however was roused by the Department's suggestion that the three-year diploma course might be extended to admit men. In the event the review was suspended for several years while the Wheatley Committee undertook a wider examination of the whole standing and government of the profession.

Their most determined critics admitted that the Scottish Council and the governing bodies made a promising start. In other circumstances they would have been entitled to a longer proving period, but unrest in the early sixties was the chronic condition of the teaching profession. Responsible men and women were anxious to claim a larger measure of control over entry and discipline, and the new Committee, set up in 1961, was bound to spend much of its time considering possible changes in the training system. The final effect of its report was the establishment of a General Teaching Council, with rights of "visitation" in colleges comparable with those of the General Medical Council in the universities; there was also further growth in the independence of the colleges themselves. The key of course was still finance, and the Secretary of State, whose funds became the only source for the colleges, held that more firmly than ever. Nevertheless, even without an independent Grants Committee for Scotland as proposed by the Robbins Committee, the colleges were freer than they had ever been.

The use they made of their new powers was shown in the transformation of courses. Formal philosophy almost disappeared from the education syllabus, to be replaced by sociology. Changes in academic content occurred especially in the course for the primary diploma, with the appearance of elective "special" or "main" studies, in which such subjects as English, mathematics, classical and modern studies were read at some depth, and similarly exacting "practical" or "aesthetic" groups in music, art and crafts, drama and physical education. Much more training was done outside the colleges. Students of one college in the sixties could be found in the same session on geographical field studies in Yorkshire, Lanarkshire and Ross and Cromarty, on biological investigation in Angus and religious discussions at Pitlochry, sketching at Mallaig and Wick, digging on archaeological sites at Pennan and Lundin Links, acting and producing in London and Mull, making music and studying local history as well as drama at Stratford, climbing in Glenmore and sailing at Stonehaven. There was also a good deal of research in the colleges, especially of a practical kind, in various reading systems and mathematical schemes, closed circuit television and programmed learning, linguistics and curricular reform.

The growing number of students in higher education had a powerful impact in the sixties on the colleges of education, particularly since many of those concerned, while unable to achieve a university entrance certificate, found the lower academic requirements of the college diploma course within their grasp. The abolition of a prescribed number of "sittings" and substitution of the ordinary for the lower grade contributed to the expansion. Thus the population of the colleges grew from 3,496 in 1954 to 5,233 in 1960 and 8,719 in 1965; just before the war it had been 2,946. The most spectacular growth was in the primary diploma course, whose entrants increased in the same eleven years from 732 to 2,450.[26] Such was the pressure that three new colleges specialising in the diploma course were founded between 1964 and 1966 and a fourth was proposed for Roman Catholic students in Glasgow, while all the older institutions built large extensions.

The increasing number of candidates and the wider range of their educational background were probably partly responsible for a rising rate of failure. It was an old criticism that few entrants ever failed to complete their course, and this had certainly been true in the past: out of 120 graduates entering training annually at Aberdeen between 1919 and 1939 an average of only 0·3 did not complete their course, and only 0·9 more had theirs extended. From 1950 onward however the number refused certificates on grounds of inefficiency rose steadily in all the main centres; in Aberdeen for example between 1964 and 1967 the rate of "wastage" – students who began attendance but failed to complete at the appropriate time – was a little over ten per cent; in the diploma course it was fifteen per cent.[27] The trend was evidence in part of more stringent demands by the colleges, especially in classroom performance.

The late sixties brought two interesting experiments in training. One was the institution, long urged by the Educational Institute, of a teaching degree. The door was opened by the Robbins Committee, which proposed in 1963 that colleges should co-operate with nearby universities in offering instruction for a degree of "Bachelor of Education",* extending over four sessions with concurrent academic and professional study. The lead was taken by the college and university in Aberdeen, where the first ninety-four students enrolled in 1965. Glasgow and Edinburgh followed a year later and Dundee, where there was a new university, in 1967. Only the last of these schemes however conformed to the Robbins pattern, with the first two years common to degree and diploma courses and the last two devoted to graduating work. It met some criticism from the Educational Institute. In the other three cities admission was granted only to holders of an Attestation of Fitness and the pattern of the course was very similar to that of an ordinary degree, with professional subjects – education, psychology and (in Moray House) sociology – compulsory. Certain practical subjects not traditionally regarded as university studies, art and physical education for example, were available at Jordanhill and Aberdeen; at the latter a pass in one was compulsory. The degree was

* Existing "second" degrees of that name were to be retitled where necessary. Most became master's degrees.

conferred by the university, but taught mainly or almost entirely by the college.

Another more radical experiment received the qualified approval of the General Teaching Council in 1967. This was the concurrent course for a degree and teaching qualification offered by the new University of Stirling. By working in semesters and using some holiday periods, the university authorities were able to offer an honours course extending over four and a half instead of five years and an ordinary shortened from four years to three and a half. Many organisations welcomed the prospect of a break with the existing pattern, but there was speculation over possible repercussions, both in the colleges and the other universities, and the G.T.C. made it clear that no proposals should be made by other bodies until the progress of the Stirling experiment could be assessed. Both this and the B.Ed. courses required a very early decision by students to commit themselves to teaching; it remained to be seen whether many were willing.

IN-SERVICE COURSES

In one direction the work of the colleges expanded rapidly in the late sixties. It was inevitable in an era of sweeping change that teachers should find their qualifications and experience going quickly out of date. The need had never been more pressing for "in-service" or "refresher" courses. The colleges were not alone in offering these. Most local authorities held conferences and short courses, and some went much further: Fife for example opened a Teachers' Centre in 1964 in a converted school, Abbotshall, where teachers, auxiliaries and technicians could receive instruction on new developments and carry out their own experiments. Edinburgh converted Roseburn primary school in 1965 for a similar purpose.[28] University departments offered lecture series on recent discoveries and new programmes of study. But the Secretary of State made it plain that the colleges held the major responsibility in organising, mounting and often staffing in-service courses.

Up to 1966 their performance, though creditable, was less than spectacular. In that financial year, when revenue expenditure on the training of students before service was over two and a quarter millions, in-service work cost less than £50,000.[29] The main reason was the attitude of teachers. A quarter of the Scottish teaching force took refresher training of some kind in 1964-5, but for many this meant a day or two listening to lectures, watching a demonstration or hearing other people in discussion.[30] The summer school pattern common in Canada and the United States and the ambitious programmes in Russia had no counterpart in Scotland. There were signs in the late sixties however that the problem was being tackled very seriously indeed. Several colleges appointed Directors of In-Service Training and planned teachers' centres; experimental exchanges were arranged which allowed teachers to attend a three-weeks course while final year students took their places in school; the Department proposed a national supervisory committee. Most important, the Secretary of State gave approval in principle of the secondment of teachers during the school year and made the process financially possible.

SALARIES AND STATUS

Throughout the period Scottish teachers were chronically dissatisfied with their salaries. From time to time, especially in certain categories, these were claimed to be close to the poverty level, but on the whole they were criticised as evidence of the low standing of teachers compared with other groups in the community. A series of articles in the *Scotsman* in 1965, calculating the average salary a reasonably conscientious professional man should earn at his peak, between the ages of forty-five and sixty-four, showed that honours graduate teachers could expect to be better paid than bankers and insurance agents, but much worse than doctors, dentists, actuaries, architects, engineers, solicitors, surveyors and public relations officers – in short, members of virtually every other profession. The position was not so bad as in Canada, where salesmen averaged thirty per cent more than teachers, insurance and real estate agents twice as much, engineers and architects three times. Nevertheless in 1961 the holder of a primary diploma was paid less than a police constable.[31]

On the other hand teachers derived some benefit from the growing prosperity of the country. The starting point of most salary scales in 1966 was two and a half times higher than in 1945 and the maximum for an honours graduate woman was three and a half times the 1945 figure. The rise in terms of purchasing power was about twenty to thirty per cent, less striking but not inconsiderable.[32] The pattern of increase however had been distorted by the introduction of equal pay, which was conceded in 1955 after the same decision in the non-industrial civil service. Vehement claims by many male teachers, especially in the Scottish Schoolmasters' Association, that the change ought to be accompanied by a system of dependents' allowances were rejected, and after a seven-year period of working towards it, equal pay became a fact in 1962.[33] Two out of every three Scottish teachers in the sixties were women, and it was argued that the effect was to make a smaller bite of the cherry available to men, with inevitable handicap in competing with professions still predominantly male.

These were basic rates: headmasters in the largest secondary schools were at least as well off as the average general practitioner. But these men and women were intended to be the pick of the profession; the comparison should have been not with G.Ps but with consultants. In any case promotion, especially in the areas administered by large authorities, was notoriously slow and often dominated by the principle of seniority, so that it was freely suggested in at least one county that "the way to get on is to get older." Although several attempts were made to improve the situation by sub-dividing departments and appointing more principal teachers, and also by creating a hierarchy of intermediate posts like special assistantships, there remained too many people chasing too few desirable jobs.

The profession also paid the price of security in a period of inflation. In 1961, when the salaries of unpromoted teachers ranged from £470 to £1,400 a year, the average pension of all those, including headmasters, who had retired before 1948 was only £253.[34] Most of these pensions moreover died with their owners until 1965, when a scheme allowed teachers in service to contribute part of their salary to make some provision for widows and dependents.[35]

Teachers in short regarded themselves as chronically ill-paid, and many blamed the system for negotiating scales. During the Second World War a National Joint Council had been established, on which sat twelve representatives of the employing authorities and twelve of the teachers, with a neutral chairman. The duty of this body was to advise the Secretary of State on suitable rates of pay, but he was under no compulsion to accept its advice. Authorities had to pay their teachers on the scale he approved.[36] New "awards" – the term is significant – were made at intervals of about three years, and each proposed revision became an occasion for acrimonious outbursts in the public press and elsewhere. The teachers' endless grievance was that, even when the Council agreed unanimously on a new set of scales, the Secretary of State sometimes rejected it: in 1961 he turned down such a settlement out of hand and two years later he even refused to accept an arbiter's award. National economic problems might be put forward as reasons, but such behaviour made any pretence of free negotiation inappropriate. When the Secretary indicated in the mid-sixties that he might be prepared to reduce his absolute power there were lengthy manœuvres over the reconstitution of the Council and in particular over the issue of the publication of proceedings. The Department's representatives moreover were likely to become full members of the Council, and in the event of disagreement the case would go to an arbiter, but this became in turn a cause of dissension: the Secretary's proposal was that the arbiter should be appointed by the Ministry of Labour, while the teachers saw little real concession in an arrangement by which one government bound itself to accept the decisions of another.

Nevertheless if the acquisition of places holding some power was to be taken as evidence, teachers' status did improve in the late fifties and sixties. As governors of colleges of education and members of the Scottish Council they made good use of their influence. Certificated teachers formed more than half of the General Teaching Council established in 1965, though not a large enough fraction to satisfy the teachers' organisations. The Education (Scotland) Act of 1963 permitted local authorities to co-opt teachers to their education committees; by the end of 1964, 24 of the 35 had decided to do so.[37] But although the minister of Old Deer in Aberdeenshire might write after the Second World War that[38]

the dominie is still one of the chief figures of the rural scene, and is expected to be a leader in the community,

it is doubtful whether many teachers would have agreed with him. There was an argument from 1947 to 1950 for instance between the Department and the education committee of Lanarkshire over the powers of the local promotion board. The S.E.D. thought teachers should be in the majority, the authority that, if they were, all their decisions should come up for ratification. A dozen years later, despite an act of parliament, pressure from the Department and the recommendation of a national working party, eight education committees refused to co-opt teachers.[39] Many schoolmasters had been the best pupils in their classes and were irked to find duller spirits who had qualified in medicine or dentistry accorded a social position they were denied. This lack of status was not of course confined to Scotland: the story went that when Churchill wanted to punish Butler for having differed with him in the thirties he offered him the Board of Education.[40]

But the consequence of all this discontent was injurious to the profession: too much public washing of dirty linen, too many wild threats regarded by the man in the street as undignified. A member of parliament in 1963 wrote,[41]

Teachers as a group often give an impression of self-pity, of a stifling staffroom atmosphere in which petty discontents and complicated differences of academic status easily get out of perspective.

Years of devoted but unspectacular service were easily forgotten. A great many onlookers were exasperated; a great many more were frankly bored.

REFERENCES

1. SCOTLAND, JAMES, *Attitudes to Teachers and Teaching in Scotland* unpublished, 1965; ASHLEY, COHEN and SLATTER, *T.E.S.*, 12 May 1967
2. *S.E.D.R. 1947*, 8; *1966*, 65; *1965*, 17; *S.E.J.* 15 July 1966
3. *S.E.D.R. 1966*, 80

4. GRASSIE, *S.E.J.* 22 May 1959
5. *T.E.S.* 18 Nov. 1966
6. LEES, *S.E.J.*, 1 May 1959
7. *S.E.J.*, 26 Jan. 1962
8. S.E.D., *Committee on the Supply of Teachers in Scotland, Second Report*, 20-21; *Fourth Report*, 23, 40
9. *ibid*
10. S.E.D., Roberts Committee, *Measures to Secure a More Equitable Distribution of Teachers in Scotland*, H.M.S.O., 1966 8-9, 20-23
11. *Roberts Report*, 14
12. *S.E.D.R. 1960*, 76
13. *S.E.D.R. 1959*, 73
14. NOBLE, Secretary of State, answering a parliamentary question, 1964; qu. *T.E.S.*, 3 July 1964; *S.E.J.* 24 Feb. 1965
15. e.g. *S.E.D.R. 1965*, 56
16. *ibid*
17. *S.E.D.R. 1966*, 65
18. Secretary of State answering a parliamentary question, qu. *T.E.S.*, 13 March 1964
19. ROSS at an E.I.S. dinner, January 1965
20. University of Glasgow Appointments Committee, *Sub-Committee on Recruitment for School Teaching*, 5
21. *ibid.*, 6-12; SCOTLAND, *Attitudes to Teaching*, 1965
22. SCOTLAND, *Attitudes to Teaching*, 1965
23. WOOD, speaking to the E.I.S. Executive, qu. *S.E.J.*, 2 March 1962
24. MACKENZIE, "My Last Schoolmaster", *A.U.R.*, iii, 8, Feb. 1916
25. Advisory Council on Education in Scotland, *The Training of Teachers*, H.M.S.O. 1945, (Cmnd. 6723).
26. *S.E.D.R. 1965*, 123
27. Registers of Aberdeen Training College; Aberdeen College of Education, *Triennial Report 1964-1967*, 7
28. *T.E.S.* 10 Dec. 1965; *Edinburgh Education Report 1965*, 13
29. Scottish Council for the Training of Teachers, *Estimates of Colleges of Education*, Oct. 1965
30. *T.E.S.*, 10 Dec. 1965
31. GRAHAM, *Scotsman*, 15 Feb. 1965; *S.E.J.*, 12 Feb. 1965; *S.E.J.*, 17 March 1961
32. *Teachers Salaries (Scotland) Regulations 1945, 1966*; *S.E.J.* 23 July 1965
33. *S.E.D.R. 1955*, 68
34. *Teachers Salaries (Scotland) Regulations 1959*; Secretary of State answering a parliamentary question, qu. *S.E.J.*, 2 June 1961
35. *S.E.J.*, 5 Feb. 1965
36. *Education (Scotland) Act 1945*, section 50
37. *Education (Scotland) Act 1963*, section 4; OSBORNE, *Scottish and English Schools*, 42

38. *T.S.A. Aberdeenshire*, 376
39. *Education in Lanarkshire 1949-51*, 29; S.E.D. (Donnelly Committee) *Appointment of Teachers to Education Committees* (H.M.S.O. 1962)
40. THOMSON, *S.E.J.*, 10 May 1963
41. *ibid*

CHAPTER 15 | # Further Education

ORGANISATION OF FURTHER EDUCATION

FOR many years after 1945 further education remained the least interesting and the worst developed part of the Scottish system. The situation was a strange one, for each government was in no doubt that expansion in British industry and trade depended on improved technical performance, and there were several efforts by the state in the fifties and sixties to bring about improvement. Teachers in further education for instance, on the ground that their hours of work were more demanding, were paid on higher salary scales than those in day schools. There were important pronouncements in blue books and white papers every two or three years. Yet it was not until the late sixties that there was some satisfactory progress in, for example, day release.

The Advisory Council produced a report on Technical Education in 1946 and one on Further Education in 1953.[1] Regional Advisory Councils on Technical Education were established in 1949, and a staff inspector appointed by the Department. One chapter of the S.E.D.'s annual report in 1952, giving a survey of technical provision, was reprinted as a separate paper.[2] Circular 296 of 1954 stated the aim of the Secretary of State that local technical colleges should be available within reasonable travelling distance of any student's home. Two white papers, one on Technical Education issued in 1956 and a second, "Technical Education in Scotland: The Pattern for the Future", presented in 1961, marked the full acceptance by the central authority of the need to co-ordinate and foster technical education. The 1956 document envisaged a building programme of ten million pounds starting in 1961, three-fifths to be spent on local authority colleges; by the latter date seventeen millions were being spent under the programme.[3] An organised pattern of courses was drawn up by the 1961 paper. For technologists at the highest level there would be four years of study, either full-time or sandwiched between periods of work in industry, leading to university degrees, college associateships and Higher National Diplomas; entry requirements would be little lower than for admission to a university. For technicians there were Ordinary and

Higher National Certificate courses. For craftsmen and operatives there would be one-year pre-vocational studies and part-time programmes extending up to five sessions.[4] For executive officers there was instituted in 1961 a Diploma in Management Studies. To secure the strongest link between industry and education the Secretary of State appointed in 1959 the Scottish Technical Consultative Council, with representatives of employers, employees and colleges. Two years later a special committee of this body, established to consider ways of developing day release, recommended a scheme of compulsory registration as a necessary step towards enforcing attendance.[5]

Colleges of further education run by the local authorities were largely a post-war development. Over fifty were in existence by 1959, benefiting as we have seen from the special financial provision in the 1956 white paper. There was some success in promoting education in engineering, building, mining and the steel industry, but expansion was retarded by opposition to day release. The sixties brought an important change in the situation: the central institutions, which had increasingly concentrated on higher level work – two became universities – turned over their candidates for ordinary and some higher national certificates to the local colleges. Glasgow and Edinburgh built several new ones, of which Napier, opened in the capital in 1964 with over 6,500 students in its first year, may serve as example. Rural authorities also took a hand: Thurso Technical College, opened in 1959 by Caithness Education Committee, met the odd situation created by depositing an ultra-modern atomic power station at Dounreay. It was extended twice, and by 1966 had about seven hundred students, forty of them in full-time pre-vocational courses, the rest mainly seeking ordinary national and City and Guilds certificates.[6] In certain areas, notably Glasgow and Lanarkshire, colleges appeared at two levels, senior and junior, the former taking over some functions of the central institutions. Meanwhile continuation classes went on meeting in the evenings at various day schools, a valuable arrangement in country areas, though in the cities one of its stronger attractions was the economic use it made of educational plant.

A continuing weakness of the further education colleges was the number of untrained staff. Higher salaries were paid to those who did train and a Central Register was established in 1962 to promote this development, but it was not until 1964 that the Robertson Committee was set up to consider supply and training. Its report in 1966, accepted quickly by the Secretary of State,[7] proposed centralised training in Jordanhill College of Education, with candidates released on full pay by their own colleges to take the course; employers might be required to release them within three years after their appointment.[8] The new system of teachers' certificates introduced in 1965 established a separate qualification in Further Education.

VOCATIONAL EDUCATION

The development of vocational further education depended on good relations with the schools and also with industry. Each had its problems. Ties with the schools were much strengthened by the report of the Brunton Committee in 1963, "From School to Further Education".* This laid down the rule that the vocational impulse should be the core of the school curriculum for most pupils, and urged local authorities to promote co-operation between schools, colleges and industrial firms. There were so many educational crises in the sixties that the report made less than the impact it deserved on its appearance, but several counties produced ambitious schemes and virtually all carried out experiments. Ten secondary schools in Edinburgh for example had members of the city's Chamber of Commerce attached to them.[9] The link would have to be strong by 1972, when the raising of the leaving age would abolish the awkward gap before the age for commencing apprenticeship.

This gap from 15 to 16 was filled by some authorities with "pre-vocational courses, either in schools or colleges. In 1952 there were pre-nursing colleges in Glasgow and Aberdeen, agricultural schools in Dumfries, Stornoway and elsewhere, and a course lasting a year at Leith Nautical School for deck officer cadets in the Merchant Navy; there was also provision in mining and commerce.[10] The courses were of course voluntary, and they prepared boys and girls for a group of allied trades rather than for individual jobs.

A more interesting programme however was that already begun between the wars, which called on industrial firms to release their young employees for one day in each week. The English Education Act of 1944 contained provision for the establishment of "county colleges" on these lines, and the Scottish Act of the following year accepted the idea north of the border. On a date to be fixed "Junior Colleges" would be opened for young people between the ages of fifteen and eighteen not already in full-time attendance at any educational institution. These students, by an attendance order, would be compelled to attend the college for one day a week for forty-four weeks, or for a continuous period of eight weeks, in each session. They would receive a course of physical, practical and vocational training intended to develop their aptitudes and make them better citizens. Parents or employers who connived at the evasion of such duties would be liable to legal punishment.[11] In prospect of such a scheme operating, the Advisory Council issued suggestions for the curriculum, remembering that many of the students would be of low mental ability, with non-academic interests and often a positive abhorrence of study. The report suggested dividing the timetable into five sections – physical training for one period a week, a course on human relations including English, history, geography, civics, local

* See Chapter 13, "The Schools".

and central government, economics, commerce and the use of books (two periods a week), mathematics and science, mainly for boys and purely to arouse or maintain interest, workshop and vocational subjects, which would in the third year command as many as four out of eight periods each week, and music or art, with more time allotted here for girls. The main problems indicated by the Report would be the provision of hostels and concentrated courses in sparsely populated areas and the finding of expert staff to teach these subjects well.[12]

The Act of 1945 however raised many problems more urgent than day release, and two decades later there was no prospect of the sections concerning junior colleges being fully implemented. The fixing of a date in September 1948 for beginning "preparation for compulsory further education" had been proved a pious hope.[13] The general prospect of a national system faded even further into the future with the Government's decision, announced in March 1960, to give priority to raising the school leaving age to sixteen.

A number of local authorities, however, made moves of their own to implement the Act. In Glasgow day release classes were run in the Stow Colleges of Building, Engineering, Hairdressing and Printing, and in Langside College, which was a unique experiment. In 1948 it had four hundred students, including Post Office messengers, junior clerks, lads from rolling mills, sales assistants, young civil servants and factory girls. The education provided was interesting in being entirely non-vocational in the narrow sense – English, social studies and such options as craft or metal work and gardening. These youths were released one day a week by their firms, who entered into an agreement with the Glasgow authority and sent representatives to a board of management. There was a similar Day Nautical School in Aberdeen, but its popularity waned after 1945.[14] The weakness of the system, of course, lay in its being voluntary: an apprentice who chose to absent himself could be punished only by his firm, which might or might not regard the offence with gravity. Smaller firms, of which there are many in, for example, the building trade, often saw little point in paying a boy's salary to allow him to attend even a vocational course, of whose value they had only suspicion. Moreover the main problem had barely been scratched: in 1948 Ayrshire authority bought Glaisnock House at Cumnock as a junior college, but pointed out that to operate the full scheme within the county would require nine such institutions.[15] In 1959, when over 160,000 Scottish youngsters were eligible for day release, only 17,000 were actually attending.[16] The proportion, eleven per cent, was half that for England and Wales.

The Industrial Training Act of 1964 sought to establish a scheme to foster day release. A Clerical Training Committee instituted its first scheme for young office workers at Anniesland College in Glasgow in 1967; the Iron and Steel and the Engineering Boards produced programmes in Ayrshire, Falkirk and Dundee; there was a Water Supply scheme in Kilwinning and one for construction workers in Edinburgh.[17] But the structure of Scottish industry made group training difficult. Some of the larger firms were well ahead with the work: Colville's provided their own training centre at Mossend, instructing their apprentices in blocks of four weeks out of every twelve, with enthusiastic trainers and excellent visual aids.[18] The smaller firms dragged behind, but many were scarcely to be blamed. In the whole Highland area for instance there were only thirty-three firms employing more than a hundred workers and a group training scheme for the smaller units was impossible. Certain industries moreover were reluctant to co-operate: textile companies in Lanarkshire showed little alacrity in the early fifties.[19]

CULTURAL EDUCATION

Adult education, with the emphasis on cultural rather than vocational aims, enjoyed a brief spell of expansion after the war. There was marked interest for a time in such "disciplinary" studies as economics, psychology and international relations, and a number of local authorities were emboldened to offer courses in these, formerly the province of the university extra-mural departments. The hundred and seven centres of the Workers' Educational Association in 1944 became two hundred and seven in 1948 and the number of students increased over the same period from ten to fifteen thousand.[20] In 1952 in Scotland 223,000 people enrolled in part-time continuation classes, more than half for the study of such general subjects as English, foreign languages, handicrafts, music and drama, first aid and – most popular – physical training and country dancing. There were 28,000 enrolments in needle-craft and 6,000 in cookery courses.[21] The classes met usually on one evening each week for a total of twenty or twenty-four weeks in the session; each student paid a small enrolment fee of a few shillings, and was responsible for the cost of the material he used. Women especially filled classes in country dancing, leather work, china-painting, home dressmaking and "useful hobbies". After the early fifties however interest in the more formal subjects faded. At one extra-mural centre three psychology classes failed in one session. The general impression was that while there would always be a fair demand for classes in the "artistic" subjects and those, like languages, with some semblance of practical utility, there was little request for intellectual disciplines.

One institution however did manage to maintain its existence. Newbattle College reopened in 1950 as a residential seminary; its principal was an eminent Scottish poet and man of letters, Edwin Muir. Since it offered full-time courses including English literature, philosophy, political theory, psychology, history and economics, few men and women possessed money, qualifications and especially leisure

to attend. Nevertheless, aided by scholarships, it had twenty-two
students in its second session, drawn from various occupations and
ranging in age from eighteen to fifty. Short courses were also held
during vacations. During the fifties an average of over thirty students
took the residential course each year, while about five hundred attended
for short periods. There appeared to be a need for such a college in
Scotland, which could be satisfied by Newbattle.[22]

The shortcomings of adult education in the fifties were obvious.
Only a small proportion of the population showed interest enough to
enrol and fewer stayed the course. Accommodation was uncomfortable;
the lecturers were not always capable of gauging the intellectual level of
their students – teachers trained to deal with young children and
university professors accustomed to young men and women willing to
eavesdrop on their streams of consciousness were not the best-equipped
teachers for adults unused to the customs of higher study; libraries were
often inadequate. Courses could have been better advertised and equip-
ped. Community centres were badly needed to replace classrooms
intended for children of twelve. Even the most dauntless student and
the most devoted lecturer might be excused dismay at the prospect of
leaving his fireside on a wet, gusty January night to huddle into a
cramping, fixed desk under a dim electric light in an imperfectly heated,
institution-like classroom.

THE POSITION IN THE 1960S

The picture of further education between 1945 and 1960 was not a particularly cheerful one. In 1953-4 the percentage of boys and girls receiving
education between the ages of fifteen and twenty was unimposing:[23]

Age	School	University	Training College	C.I. and F.E. Centre Full-time	Part-time	Total
Boys						
20	—	5·5	0·1	1·1	18·7	25·4
19	—	4·3	0·1	1·0	26·2	31·6
18	1·2	2·9	0·1	0·8	35·6	40·6
17	8·1	1·3	—	1·3	39·9	50·6
16	13·0	—	—	3·1	30·8	46·9
15	23·2	—	—	2·5	12·6	38·3
Girls						
20	—	2·6	1·4	1·2	9·7	14·9
19	—	2·3	1·4	1·6	12·4	17·7
18	0·6	1·6	1·8	1·7	17·8	23·5
17	6·2	0·8	—	1·9	21·7	30·6
16	12·3	—	—	2·8	20·3	35·4
15	22·7	—	—	1·5	10·2	34·4

Moreover there was a very high rate of wastage among further education students. A report from Glasgow in 1955 painted a discouraging picture:[24]

> Hundreds enrolled in the first year of the classes: about ten per cent never attended a class; another ten per cent jogged along till Christmas and then vanished; eventually about forty per cent took the first-year examinations. About twenty-five per cent of the original enrolment began a second year and only about half of these persisted for the third and final year. The upshot was that, for the intermediate and final certificates of the City and Guilds of London Institute, about eight per cent entered and five per cent received some form of qualification . . . In the Higher National Certificate courses there was serious wastage in the junior and senior courses leading up to the group certificate. Only twenty-five per cent received this certificate – or less than ten per cent of those originally enrolling.

The effect of half a century of half-hearted technical education in Great Britain may be seen in comparative figures of the production of graduate engineers in 1954:

State	Number of new engineers per million of population
Great Britain	57
France	70
Switzerland	82
West Germany	86
Italy	39
U.S.A.	136
U.S.S.R.	280

To the British figures, of course, might be added 8,100 holders of Higher National Certificates – 164 per million – but engineers at this lower grade were also being produced in other countries, in Russia for example at the rate of 326 per million. In contrast, the output of pure science graduates in Western Europe as a whole in 1954 was 48 per million, in Russia 56, in Great Britain 105.[25] The achievements of Russian, American, German and Italian engineers in the post-war world guaranteed the standard of their courses of training. It remained to be seen whether by the end of the 1960s the British Government's programme of expansion would have overhauled the rest of the engineering world, and there remained the question whether the attempt by ruthless specialisation was being made in the right way.

REFERENCES

1. *Cmnd. 6786; Cmnd. 8454*
2. *Cmnd. 8813*; S.E.D., *Technical Education in Scotland* (H.M.S.O. 1953)

3. *Cmnd. 9703*, 32, 36; *S.E.D.R. 1961*, 58
4. *Cmnd. 1245*, Appendix
5. REID, *T.E.S.*, 24 Feb. 1967; S.E.D. (Technical Education Consultative Committee), *Report of the Day Release Committee* (H.M.S.O. 1962), 6-10
6. *S.E.J.*, 16 Oct. 1959
7. *Circular 619*
8. S.E.D., *Future Recruitment and Training of Teachers for Further Education in Scotland* (H.M.S.O. 1965), 28-9
9. *S.E.D.R. 1965*, 9
10. *S.E.D.R. 1952*, 13-14
11. *Education (Scotland) Act 1945*, sections 29-31
12. Advisory Council on Education in Scotland, *Compulsory Day and Continuation Classes* (H.M.S.O. 1943)
13. *S.E.D.R. 1948*, 20
14. *S.E.D.R. 1947*, 18; *T.S.A. City of Aberdeen*, 415
15. *T.S.A. Ayrshire*, 213, 218
16. Secretary of State, qu. *T.E.S.*, 10 June 1960
17. REID, *T.E.S.*, 17 March 1967
18. MACKENZIE, *T.E.S.*, 11 Nov. 1966
19. *Education in Lanarkshire 1949-51*, 102
20. *S.E.D.R. 1946, 1947, 1949*, *passim*
21. *S.E.D.R. 1952*, 95-96
22. *S.E.D.R. 1952*, 45
23. *Cmnd. 9703*, 31
24. *Report of a Sub-Committee of Glasgow Productivity Committee*
25. *Cmnd. 9703*, 38-40

CHAPTER 16

The Universities

There were changes in university life after 1945 which did not commend themselves to many observers. "To be occupied in and about a university", one Principal wrote, "is more of a business and less of a personal adventure".[1] The students, he lamented, were becoming too solemn: "we are getting into the era of less fun and more fuss". Sad though it might be, the change was inevitable: in the 1950s and 1960s the Scottish universities were very big business indeed. An enterprise costing many millions of pounds a year was presumably no place for fun.

The demand for places, especially after 1960, grew quickly. The Robbins Committee pointed out that while four per cent of young people had been at school after their seventeenth birthday in 1938, the figure had grown in 1962 to fifteen per cent, and over half of these were seeking places in higher education. Up to 1975 the demand was likely to expand even more rapidly.[2] Moreover students entering for the first time did not make up the total picture: post-graduate work required a massive expansion and there should be a place for part-time and correspondence courses. A survey conducted in 1960 by the Educational Institute of Scotland found 752 teachers who expressed themselves willing to study for degrees in these ways if the opportunity were offered.[3]

The attempt to meet even the orthodox demand involved the Scottish universities in a programme of expansion and diversification so immense as to alter their whole pattern. Between 1945 and 1952 their student population rose by eighteen per cent and the growth accelerated in the sixties; by 1966 Edinburgh had almost 10,000, Glasgow just under 8,000, St Andrews, Aberdeen and Strathclyde over 4,000, Heriot-Watt 1,200. The grand total was 32,000. Glasgow was 60 per cent larger than in 1939.[4] The rise was less steep than in England, which had ground to make up; whereas before the war, allowing for the difference in population, there had been two Scottish students to one English, the ratio in 1957 was three to two. Nevertheless the explosion had its effect. Professor Drever, Principal Designate of Dundee, believed that Edinburgh changed its character perceptibly somewhere between the five and six thousand marks.[5]

There were also changes in the meaning of the title "university". On the one hand the older institutions absorbed outside colleges and widened the province of their work. In 1947, after the report of the Goodenough Committee on Medical Education, the Anderson and St Mungo Colleges and the Dental Hospital became part of Glasgow, and a bachelor's degree in dental surgery replaced the licentiate. Two years later the Glasgow Veterinary College became the University Veterinary School and a B.V.S. was instituted.[6] In the mid-sixties several universities recognised the work of colleges of education by awarding degrees after courses taught there. On the other hand at least two of the newer foundations, Strathclyde and Heriot-Watt, made no attempt to adhere to the principle of *universities*; their work was predominantly in science, technology and commerce.

Remarkable as such expansion was, it did not satisfy everyone. The universities themselves claimed that in the years before Robbins further growth had been prevented by lack of funds, and there were complaints that qualified candidates were being refused admission, particularly in Edinburgh, which turned away 255 arts entrants in 1961 and accepted only 157 medical applicants out of over 1000. Some of course found places elsewhere, but in 1962 in Scotland 304 were excluded altogether.[7] There was also an attack on "wastage", with the claim that failure rates were too high. In the period from 1955 to 1958 one Scottish student in seven failed to complete his course; in 1955 one Glasgow arts student in ten passed in nothing at all at the end of his first year. Ten years later Professor Drever was quoting the failure rate in Aberdeen as 10 per cent, in St Andrews and Edinburgh 18, in Glasgow 19, at a time when it was 7·5 in Oxford and only 4·8 in Cambridge.[8] The demands of university courses were apparently too high for those students who held minimum passes in their certificates of fitness.

One striking result of the need for growth was the foundation of new universities, the first in Scotland for almost four hundred years. There were observers at the beginning of the sixties who did not regard the expansion of existing institutions as enough and contemplated with dismay the prospect of mammoth colleges on the American scale. But an even stronger attraction in their minds was the fact that new foundations need not conform to established patterns. Thus a National Committee which campaigned for a new university in 1964 advocated experiments in curricular structure and teaching techniques.[9] It became evident quite early that the government was in an adventurous mood. In 1962 the Conservatives took the crucial step. Two years previously an article in the *Scotsman* had suggested that as a "bold third alternative" to expansion of the old and foundation of the new, the Royal College of Science and Technology might be raised to university status; the suggestion was now accepted and the first students for the degree of B.A.* were admitted in October 1963. Six months later the Scottish

* The first B.A. students in a Scottish university for over a century.

College of Commerce, which had co-operated with the "Tech" since 1947 in a course of management studies, merged with the new foundation, and in May 1964 Strathclyde University received its charter.[10]

The Robbins Report, published in 1963 and accepted by the government the very next day, "with the despatch appropriate to an election year",[11] recommended the erection of one entirely new Scottish university and released a flood of speculation and manœuvre for its site. The Scottish National Party proposed a federal arrangement on the Welsh pattern with colleges at Inverness, Stirling and Dumfries and colleges of education attached. Various committees were set up to promote the claims of their own areas and to gather local support in ground and funds. The betting was heaviest on Inverness and Falkirk, but the final choice of the Executive Commission was Stirling. Meanwhile two other "conversion" universities appeared, Heriot-Watt in Edinburgh, announced in January 1964 with plans to expand its population from 830 to 3000 by 1975, and Dundee by separation from its parent institution, St Andrews. The promotion of Heriot-Watt may have had some influence in the choice of Stirling rather than Falkirk. The independence of Dundee, sited in a large and growing industrial city, brought a warning from the Principal of St Andrews that, having thus lost her medical and technological schools his university was in danger of declining into a "little arts college".[12]

The one completely new foundation, Stirling, gave early promise of taking its experimental function seriously. In 1966 it launched an appeal for £2 millions and received all but £300,000 in a few months. It planned a limited intake from 1967 to 1970, then an expansion to 3,000 in 1973, and a final population of perhaps twice that number. The most striking of its early proposals was the abandonment of the traditional Scottish terms and the substitution of American-type semesters, one running from September to December, the other from February to June, with two of the weeks between devoted to compulsory study. The first degree, like Strathclyde's, was to be a bachelor of arts and there were to be major courses extending to three semesters, subsidiary two and minor one. All students would take eight courses in Part I, which would cover three semesters; Part II thereafter would occupy three semesters for ordinary degree candidates, five for those seeking honours. There would be experiments in examination methods, but the traditional comprehensive test was to be retained at the end of each course.[13] Most publicity was given to the concurrent course proposed for candidates for teaching, which added only one semester instead of the full year required by the traditional pattern. Its implications made several observers uneasy, but it received the guarded approval of the General Teaching Council. The first students enrolled at Stirling in September 1967.

INTERNAL CHANGES

Apart from, but not unconnected with their immense expansion, the Scottish universities underwent many internal changes during this period. The abolition of the group demand in the Scottish Leaving Certificate after 1950 made the Entrance Board reconsider its requirements and further changes were necessary twelve years later, when the conversion of the S.L.C. into the Scottish Certificate of Education and the postponement of the examination dates from March to May led to difficulties in programming. Qualifications were re-expressed largely in terms of higher passes. But in the sixties the future of the Board itself was in doubt, and of the concept of attesting general fitness for university work. Edinburgh gave notice that it would withdraw from the Board and the new universities did not join. In 1967 Strathclyde dropped the traditional demand that every candidate should hold passes both in a language and in the mathematical-scientific group.[14] With competition for admission in some universities and certain faculties imposing their own requirements, the certificate of fitness steadily lost its significance; in 1968 it was abolished.

There were changes in the balance of numbers entering the various faculties, as the following table of matriculated students in Glasgow* shows:[15]

	Average (percentages)		
Faculty	1934-9	1952-7	1965-6
Arts and Social Study	42·8	27·8	32·6
Science	12·6	21·8	27·6
Engineering	7·2	14·9	10·3
Medicine	22·5	18·4	14·6
Dentistry	—	3·2	2·8
Veterinary	—	3·5	2·9
Law	10·5	8·9	7·9
Divinity	4·4	1·5	1·3

Sir Hector Hetherington, writing in 1954, discerned a shift of number "and even quality" out of arts,[16] but Scotland was still providing more than her fair share of places in that faculty and its proportion of the total rose again in the sixties. There was a steady growth in science, but not to the extent which the government wished to encourage. The actual numbers in divinity, law and medicine remained fairly steady, in the last because extra places were not created, in the first for lack of candidates. The Scottish universities were still essentially vocational institutions, but the vocations were changing. In a sample group of a hundred Glasgow men graduating in 1868 forty-six became ministers, twenty-eight doctors, ten lawyers and seven teachers. Comparable

* Including the Royal College of Science and Technology in some courses; the latter did not become independent until 1966-67.

figures for ministers in 1922 were thirteen, in 1952 only five; for doctors thirty-eight and sixteen; for lawyers six and three. The number of teachers on the other hand rose to twenty-one and thirty-one.[17]

For an increasing number graduation was not the end of their university career: one Principal regarded the expansion of graduate studies as "the most academically significant opportunity created by the Robbins Report",[18] both in work for doctorates and for comparatively new qualifications like master of science and bachelor of philosophy or literature. Many of these students stayed to teach in the universities, which, in arts at least, ate up their own most brilliant children.

The vocational emphasis led in the sixties to a further drift into specialisation and away from the traditionally philosophical and general pattern of Scottish higher education. The ordinary degree was accepted as second-best, a useful safety-net for those who could not aspire to the honours schools. There were changes in its form: compulsory philosophy remained, but the demand for at least one language and one science was remitted in Glasgow and Edinburgh to a choice between the two. Glasgow introduced third year studies in 1964, a move towards the English pattern in the pass degree. But although the general intention was to grant as much liberty to students as possible, there was a distinct danger that the ordinary degree would degenerate into a "rag-bag", and critics inside the universities were much concerned on this point.[19]

STUDENTS

Except for St Andrews, the vast majority of students at Scottish universities were native Scots. Immediately after the war the number entering Aberdeen from beyond the "Aberdeen region" (Shetland to Montrose) increased threefold. But in 1949 over four fifths of the students still came from the home area. In 1963 almost three-quarters of Glasgow students had their homes within thirty miles of their university and less than ten per cent hailed from beyond Scotland. Proximity remained the most significant factor in choice, though the advice of relatives was also important. In consequence nearly half Scotland's students lived at home,* the percentage varying from 69·1 in Glasgow to only 4·5 in St Andrews. The latter was the university for halls of residence; at Aberdeen, Dundee and Edinburgh well over half lived in lodgings.[20]

Rapid expansion meant a substantial increase in the number of first-generation students. Whereas one sixth of the Scottish university population in 1864 were the sons of manual workers, the proportion from 1955 to 1961 had risen to a quarter. (The percentage throughout Britain was slightly higher, and in Wales it was forty.[21] Critics of the

* The figure for the United Kingdom was 19·3 per cent.

"new breed" were not wanting: as one novelist made an old school-master reflect,[22]

> When they were poor they were always reasonably dressed, but now that they are supported by the state, they look like mechanics or police court cases or even Americans.

They were charged with being obsessed with material things: their vacations for instance, intended for rest and study, they spent in jobs. At Aberdeen in 1956-57 three out of every four worked during their summer break, more than half for nine weeks or longer out of the fifteen available.[23] They became tram and bus conductors, income tax clerks, waitresses and shop assistants and hotel maids, ward orderlies and general labourers, fun-fair attendants and holiday camp "redcoats". This was a distinctive development of the decades after 1945; before the war, when financial assistance was much less generous, summer work was by no means so common. In the sixties many industrial concerns and hotels depended on students for the major part of their labour force.

The other ground on which students were criticised was rowdiness and want of discipline. Periodically letters to the press condemned them for "frittering away" public money by indulging more in hooliganism than study. Their consumption of alcohol, generally beer, was a favourite target. The truth was that disciplinary systems evolved in and often little changed from earlier centuries were inadequate for dealing with young men and women in an aggressively democratic community. A *cause célèbre* in Glasgow in 1965, when several students were sent down in what many onlookers regarded as a very high-handed fashion, led the Senate to establish a new Code. Its cases of "serious misconduct" are significant: offences in connexion with examinations, falsification or serious misuse of university documents, false pretences and personation, theft and gross negligence with funds or property, and riotous and disorderly conduct.[24] The last was demonstrated mostly at rectorial elections, especially in Glasgow.

Not all comment however was censorious. Principal Drever of Dundee believed in 1966 that the general quality was higher than in the thirties.[25] When students failed many blamed the methods by which they were taught. First-year classes holding hundreds of listeners, with too few lecturers to permit useful subdivision, left many freshmen languishing as displaced persons. Standards of teaching, as distinct from lecturing and research, were often low. Many failures were among students who should not have gained admission; their high skill in memorising and reproducing second-hand information did not equip them for genuine university work. Nevertheless the universities themselves were not happy with their methods. The Hale Committee considered the matter from 1961 to 1964; among the evidence it received from the Scottish Union of Students were the opinions that it was still possible to pass by regurgitating notes, that research and publication carried far too much weight and that all new lecturers would benefit from a month's course in teaching methods. The Committee's report called for more work in tutorial groups and a reduction in their size, with better academic guidance, especially in the course for the ordinary degree.[26]

UNIVERSITY STAFF

Expansion of staff more than kept pace with that of student numbers. In 1966 there was one lecturer to every ten students. This was a good ratio: although the English figure, thanks to Oxford and Cambridge, was one to eight, in the United States it was one to fifteen and on the Continent as low in places one to thirty or forty.[27] But the increase was not proportionate at all levels. Whereas the number of professors in the four older universities grew from 127 in 1913-14 to 271 in 1952-3, the number of junior staff over the same period multiplied many times. In 1963-4 the same four employed a staff of 2,243, of whom only 246 were professors.[28] The effect was often to limit lecturers and assistants to unproductive, pedestrian labour with large ordinary classes, and the energy and ambition which in the past had been concentrated on work for promotion sometimes expended itself on university politics. The problem was tackled in the sixties with the creation of more promoted posts, especially "personal", second and even third chairs. Their existence could be justified on other grounds. University staff played a growing part in the work of the community as a whole: in session 1962-3 for instance professors on the Senate of Glasgow spent an average of forty-one days attending committees on extra-university matters, junior members an average of twelve.[29]

UNIVERSITY FINANCE AND GOVERNMENT

The cost of the universities soared after the Second World War. Between 1944 and 1954 the call on public money increased tenfold and the rise in the sixties was even more rapid. Direct Treasury grants through the University Grants Committee, £23 millions in 1950, had reached £60 millions by 1961.[30] In the mid-fifties half the students in Scottish higher education were receiving local authority bursaries; in 1962, following the report of the Anderson Committee, the Department took over full responsibility for such awards, and soon every student, no matter what his family circumstances were, was entitled to a grant of at least £50. Such lavish expenditure could have only one consequence: between the thirties and the fifties direct aid by the state more than doubled, and those in command of university affairs became steadily

more apprehensive of a threat to their liberty. Until 1963 responsibility
for their work lay with the Chancellor of the Exchequer, who operated
through the U.G.C., offering subventions for the discharge of duties in
the national interest. In that year however the responsibility in England
and Wales was transferred to the Ministry of Education and Science,
with two Ministers of State, one for schools, the other for universities.
In Scotland the threat was less immediately oppressive: while the Secretary of State supervised the schools, the universities remained under
the Grants Committee. But most vice-chancellors were alarmed. Sir
Charles Wilson of Glasgow saw evidence that the Minister tended to
lay down his policy and consult the universities only when he encountered difficulties. Sir Charles pointed out that once the public audit
engulfed the universities, independence would be hard to maintain.
Yet academic freedom, the right to make their own appointments and
organise their own courses without prescription, interference, or even
delicate suggestion, was

> a necessary condition of the highest efficiency and the proper
> progress of academic institutions, and . . . encroachments on their
> liberty in the interests of greater efficiency would in fact diminish
> their efficiency and stultify their development.[31]

The Robbins Committee recognised this when it recommended not
only the continuance of the Grants Committee but its extension to
other forms of higher education. Four years after the report however
fears of public interference had been by no means laid at rest.

Meanwhile the stress of the fifties and sixties had strained much of
the 1889 Act beyond the point of tolerance; university government had
become impossibly cumbersome. On the one hand non-professorial
staff sought responsibility in running their own institutions; Robbins
recommended this, and St Andrews allocated seats on its Court as
early as 1953. On the other hand Senates were already much too large,
with as many as 125 members in the biggest universities in 1965. The
Principal, who was *de facto* chairman of both Senatus and Court, was
asked to bear too heavy a load. But perhaps the most irritating
provision of the 1889 Act was that which compelled any change proposed by one university to be submitted for acceptance by the other
three.[32]

The removal of Queen's College Dundee from the University of
St Andrews made statutory changes necessary. The Universities
(Scotland) Act of 1966 removed some at least of the flaws and annoyances.
Readers and lecturers were allotted a quarter of the Senate places,
although this enlarged that body even further, and made government by
committee essential, with the Principal unrelieved of his manifold duties.[33]
The way was cleared for the foundation of a university of Dundee.[34]
Perhaps most welcome, the procedure for change was appreciably
smoothed. A new expeditious arrangement was introduced for passing

a "resolution" which would handle most affairs – the institution of new degrees for example, and the composition of faculties and boards of studies. Certain matters, such as the powers and functions of courts and senates, were still subject to ordinances, but these no longer had to be submitted to the other universities, and there were special arrangements to deal with matters of urgency.[35]

The opinion of the Robbins Committee in 1963 was optimistic:

> We suspect that a full comparative investigation would reveal that on its chosen ground the British university system is among the most efficient and economical in the world.

Since full investigation was not proposed it was impossible to test such a statement. Those who dealt with the Scottish universities in the sixties found them sometimes touchy, jealous of their powers and privileges, suspicious of sweeping change yet co-operative in what they considered prudent amendment, resolved to defend "standards" – the most repeated criticism of the Robbins recommendations was that they would reduce the quality of higher education – and, since they were governed by men of the highest intelligence and most profound ingenuity, remarkably skilful in defending their point of view, whether it was right or not. They were also not infrequently charged with autocracy. The intricate problem of harmonising their academic freedom with national demands was certainly in the sixties nowhere near a solution.

REFERENCES

1. HETHERINGTON, "The British University System 1914-54", *A.U.R.*, xxxvi, 112, Spring 1955
2. *Robbins Report*, 11, 16
3. *S.E.J.*, 24 Feb. 1961
4. *S.E.J.*, 7 Oct. 1966; University of Glasgow, *General Council Report, April 1967*, 23
5. REECE, "The Scottish Ordinary Degree", *A.U.R.*, xxxix, 127, Spring 1962; WATSON, *University Notebook*, qu. *T.E.S.* 11 Nov. 1966
6. MCNEE in *Fortuna Domus*, 192-3; *Five Centuries* 78-9
7. *University of Glasgow Survey, 1962-3*, 3; University of Edinburgh, *General Council Report, 1962*; University of St Andrews investigation, qu. *S.E.J.*, 5 July 1963
8. OSBORNE, *Scottish and English Schools*, 231; Dean of the Faculty of Arts, Glasgow, *S.E.J.* 25 Nov. 1955; DREVER, "Address to Dundee Business Club", *T.E.S.*, 16 Dec. 1966
9. CHAMBERS, *S.E.J.*, 28 Feb. 1964
10. *S.E.J.*, 5 March 1965
11. *Glasgow Survey 1962-3*, 3

12. *S.E.J.*, 18 Oct. 1963; *Scotsman*, 31 Jan. 1964; WATSON, *University Notebook*, qu. *T.E.S.*, 11 Nov. 1966
13. *S.E.J.* 18 Nov. 1966; *T.E.S.* 21 Oct. 1966
14. *S.E.J.*, 17 Feb. 1967
15. Glasgow University, *General Council Report, April 1967*, 23
16. HETHERINGTON, *A.U.R.* Spring 1955, 4
17. CAIRNCROSS, *Glasgow Herald*, 24 Nov. 1952
18. WILSON, "Address to the E.I.S. Congress", *S.E.J.* 3 Jan. 1964
19. REECE, "The Scottish Ordinary Degree", *A.U.R.*, xxxix, 127, Spring 1962, 211-15
20. O'DELL and WALTON, "Student Population of Aberdeen University", *A.U.R.* xxxiii, 101, Autumn 1949, 126; *Glasgow Survey 1962-63*, 11, 12
21. OSBORNE, *Scottish and English Schools*, 209
22. LINKLATER, *Roll of Honour*, 52-3
23. FISK, *T.E.S.*, 11 April 1958
24. Glasgow University, *General Council Report, April 1967*, 32
25. DREVER, *T.E.S.*, 16 Dec. 1966
26. *T.E.S.* 25 Aug. 1961; University Grants Committee, *Report of the Hale Committee on University Teaching Methods* (H.M.S.O. 1964)
27. DREVER, *T.E.S.*, 16 Dec. 1966
28. HETHERINGTON, *A.U.R.* xxxvi, 112, Spring 1955, 3; CROSLAND, answering a parliamentary question, *T.E.S.*, 5 March 1965
29. *Glasgow Survey 1962-3*, 7
30. MACKINTOSH, *Education in Scotland*, 184
31. WILSON, "Address to the E.I.S. Congress", *S.E.J.*, 3 Jan. 1964
32. ROSS, *T.E.S.*, 5 Nov. 1965
33. *Universities (Scotland) Act 1966*, section 7 (1)
34. *ibid*, section 13, schedule VI
35. *ibid*, sections 4-6, schedule II

PART III

The Scottish Tradition

CHAPTER 17

The Scottish Tradition in Education

SCOTTISH EDUCATIONAL PRIDE

> In proportion to their small numbers they are the most distinguished
> little people since the days of the ancient Athenians, and the most
> educated of the modern races.

AN Englishman[1] wrote that of the Scots in 1889. It is doubtful whether,
writing in the nineteen-sixties, he would have been of the same opinion,
though many of his countrymen continued to hold the traditional
belief. Throughout history indeed there have been many people to
agree with him, a high proportion of them Scots. National modesty is
not the most conspicuous Scottish characteristic, and her teachers and
educationists have been of much the same mind as her poets, engineers
and soldiers. The historian of Glasgow in 1817 remarked that

> the attention which has been paid to the education of the lower
> orders of the Scottish nation has been proverbial over Europe for
> several centuries past.

"Come away, sir", said Dr Adam of the Royal High School to a
visiting English inspector in the eighteen-sixties, "come away, sir,
you will see more done here in an hour than in any other school in
Europe". The visitor described the school as "one of the most celebrated
educational establishments in Europe", but he found arithmetic and
mathematics unsatisfactory and the general impression disappointing:
"It was not", he wrote, "one of the best schools I saw".[2] For a country
so proud of its educational heritage moreover, it is strange that "Scottish
traditions" – in history, music, literature and art – have had such a
grim struggle to find a place in the curriculum.

The truth of the matter is, of course, that much of Scotland's pride
in her educational tradition is unreasoning and unreasonable. Yet the
educated Scotsman is a citizen of no mean city; there is much in the
history of his schools and universities of which he can be justly, if
not exuberantly, proud. There are also certain recurring features of
which no country ought to boast. A short examination of the main
factors which have influenced Scotland fairly steadily throughout her
history may throw some light on the way her educational system has
developed.

R

PIETISM

The strongest of these influences, certainly until late in the nineteenth century, has been the pietism of her people. For the devout Scot education was always seen as a weapon – a weapon to fight ignorance and establish the truth, but also a weapon to combat error, to keep the flock in the paths of righteousness by closing all other paths. There are therefore two opposing elements in the influence of religion on Scottish education – construction, but also constriction.

The constructive work is obvious: it is perfectly fair to generalise that almost every forward step in Scottish education before 1833 or even 1872 was taken either by a Church, established or not, or by private citizens and associations for religious ends. In the era of the Celtic and Roman Churches, it was Columba who brought schools to the country. It was the abbeys and the cathedrals which developed them, calling on teachers from far beyond the Cheviots, like John of Ferrara at Kinloss, and educating a number of scholars of international repute, like Duns Scotus. The universities were founded by, and depended for their support, on interested bishops – Elphinstone in Aberdeen, Wardlaw in St Andrews, Turnbull in Glasgow – and such colleges were set up "to the end that there the Catholic faith may be spread".[3] G. G. Coulton[4] thinks that the importance of the educational work of the Roman Church in Scotland has been exaggerated, but there is evidence of much solid achievement.

With the Reformation the centre of education moved from the abbey to the parish, but it remained the business of the Church. The New Faith, which stressed the importance of the personal approach to God and individual reading of the Scriptures, was bound to show even greater educational zeal than the Old: within a dozen years after 1560 the Assembly had granted commissions for planting schools all over Scotland, "to diffuse Presbyterian virtue". From the outset the plan was for a national system, something which had never been expressly proposed under the Roman Church. Despite frequent Assembly petitions for the use of the funds of the Old Kirk, the money never became available on a national scale, but the scheme set out in the First Book of Discipline became a tradition and a blueprint in itself for the system of parish schools which was developed over three hundred years.

But Protestantism was essentially a movement of revolt, an attack on Rome, and much of the educational work of Knox and his colleagues was intended to be destructive. The system of licensing, begun in 1567, forbade the employment of any teachers in schools or universities "but sic as shall be tryed by the superintendents or visitors of the kirk",[5] and this clerical control continued until 1861. Teachers were tested before they were admitted to posts, and dismissals on grounds of religious deficiency occurred throughout the seventeenth and eighteenth centuries. The animus of the Reformers against the Old Faith was also manifested in an attempt – by the Assembly Act of 1578 – to force parents to call back all children being educated in Papist countries like France.

An "anti" bias was not of course peculiar to the New Faith: long before the Reformation the Church had been advised of the advantage of being "wisely unlearned". From 1560 onward, however, it took a more prominent place in education, so that many admirable enterprises were blemished by positively vindictive religious prohibitions. The Society in Scotland for Propagating Christian Knowledge brought education during the eighteenth century to three hundred thousand children who might very well have received none, but it would employ no teacher unless he promised to "deny, disown and abhor the tenets and doctrines of the Papal Romish Church", and by setting its face against the Gaelic language and attempting to root it out, the Society warped the development of education and culture in the Highlands. When the Free Church broke away in 1843 from the Establishment, the latter, requiring all its teachers to subscribe to its Confession of Faith, drove many of them out of their posts; in effect, the division was to produce an artificial situation with not much more than sixty per cent of the pupils in either the Church of Scotland or the Free Church schools adherent to the appropriate sect. As late as 1853 anti-Roman feeling was still so virulent that one of Her Majesty's inspectors was prompted to write of the difficulties in producing school buildings in Glasgow that[6]

it seems to be considered praiseworthy either to offer sites for such institutions at thrice their real value, or to refuse them altogether.

It would be rash to suggest that since 1918 prejudice has decreased, but it is a fact that the freedom given to Roman Catholic schools at the present day has avoided a number of problems which have vexed other countries.

POVERTY

Second only to religion as an influence on Scottish education has been the poverty which for much of her history has plagued her people. According to the somewhat alarmist Fletcher of Saltoun, writing about 1700, one in five of the population was a beggar and the figure had seldom fallen in the past below one in ten. The failure of the Darien scheme wiped out almost a quarter of the national wealth. Even the lords and the lairds could hardly afford to attend the Scottish Parliament: after its sittings many of them spent a period in the Canongate gaol for debt. The commercial and industrial prosperity which came to the central region after 1707 produced some alteration, but also created the new poor of the eighteenth and nineteenth centuries. The educational endowments of all the burgh schools and universities in Scotland in 1864 did not equal in combination the endowment of Eton.[7] Moreover, as with so many unpleasant necessities, people learned to live with poverty by converting it into a virtue. Even among those, especially in the early nineteenth century, who could have afforded moderate expenditure, frugality became the acceptable pattern of behaviour; it was related to the strong vein of puritanism in the Scottish character.

The effect of such poverty on education was seen in two distinct ways. Education became desirable as an economic as well as a religious weapon: for many young Scotsmen it offered a prospect of release from the narrowest of worlds. Thus it was that the parish school system was built and maintained by one public decree after another over three centuries, and the land rental of Scotland paid far more proportionately for education than that of England. Thus it was also that so many poor boys contrived to secure at least part of a university education. On the other hand it was enough that education was provided at all; there was never enough money for refinement and experiment. Large classes and long vacations made university study cheap, but less fruitful than it might have been for all but the most brilliant. The inadequacy of teachers' salaries – "the maximum of mouth honour and the minimum of oatmeal"[8] – was and remains a chronic complaint. And in more recent times, among "working people", a strong tradition of leaving at the earliest possible date led to the strange situation whereby Scotland, offering many more grammar school places than England at the age of twelve, had in fact a smaller proportion of pupils continuing their studies beyond fifteen.

RELATIONS WITH ENGLAND

Such a comparison with the situation in England draws attention to a third powerful influence on Scottish education – indeed on the whole course of Scottish history – the constant presence of a giant on her southern border. In the thirteenth century it was still possible for Scottish youths to study in England – at Balliol College, for example – but the outbreak of almost three centuries of war between the two countries put an end to that. Scottish students still travelled abroad, but to the universities of the Continent – Padua, Bologna, Louvain, Geneva, but most commonly in France. There was a Scots College in the University of Paris from 1326 until the Revolution.

By the time of the Treaty of Paris in 1560, when a slow improvement began in Anglo-Scottish relations, the two educational traditions were firmly disparate in aim and concept: while English schools were allowed to develop from private beneficence to meet individual needs, Scotland sought to create a national system, partly as a religious weapon. Her universities displayed a European rather than an English pattern. For over two centuries after the Union of the Crowns, for over a century after the Union of the Parliaments, Scots continued to learn in their own way; during the eighteenth century indeed, education tended to be an economic as well as a religious weapon, presented against the wealthy southern merchants.

This independent development was made possible mainly because England steadfastly refused to take education seriously. Once she did, the way was always clear for English influence to permeate Scottish schools and universities. The first Privy Council grant to education was made in 1833; a year later a similar grant was made to Scotland, and this sketched a pattern of legislation whereby every English measure was followed within a year or two by a Scottish. 1870 and 1872; 1902 and 1908; parallel acts in 1918; 1944 and 1945. Such a pattern would have been comparatively simple to operate if the English system had been in advance of the Scottish, but throughout the nineteenth and part of the twentieth centuries, the opposite was generally the case. The consequence was a struggle by the Scots to avoid accepting acts meant to deal with problems which in Scotland had already been solved. The 1870 Act was an attempt to battle through to general literacy in England, to establish a national system of schools; Scotland by that time was ninety per cent literate, and she already had a national system. The right of every child to a secondary education, hailed south of the border with acclaim in the 1944 Act, was nothing new in Scotland, where for many elementary education had been a stage and not a type for forty years. The complication of the situation was much increased by the location for many years of the Scotch Education Department in London.

For about a century therefore educational relations between the two countries have presented something of the aspect of a running battle. Payment by results, successful south of the border, was imposed on Scotland after an enquiry into English conditions, and caused damage to the teaching in many Scottish schools before it was abolished. At the university level the fight to retain the old Scottish philosophical tradition and the general or "ordinary" degree occupied the pundits between 1858 and 1889 and has not yet been decided. By the middle of the twentieth century there were many indignant letters in the public press and speeches on educational platforms, protesting that the Scottish system was being dragged at the tail of the English. "Comprehensive" schools in Glasgow followed a pattern made popular in London, but they had much in common with the omnibus secondaries of Scottish rural areas. This was perhaps no more than a prestige argument; more dangerous was the partial assimilation of the Scottish public examination system to that of England. The Ordinary Grade test was accepted for sixteen-year-olds in 1962, but the Higher Grade for seventeen-year-olds was not abandoned. Within a few years the need for an Advanced Grade for eighteen-year-olds was accepted, but the Higher Grade

remained in existence, and it was hard to resist the impression that it
did so for largely sentimental reasons. It is more than doubtful whether
any responsible educationist, constructing from zero a national certificate system, would have put forward a scheme for searching examinations on three different levels in three successive school years. Attempts
to prevent the same pupil sitting all three tests were not likely to
command much success.

THE INFLUENCE OF THE GREAT EDUCATORS

At first by reaction therefore, and later by imitation, the Scottish
system has been powerfully influenced by the English. From time to
time a debt can also be discerned to other countries. We have noted a
French influence in the universities. The system of teacher training, in
its early days at least, owed something to experiments in Prussia. But,
despite inspectorial visits, particularly about 1900, to various nations
in two continents, Scotland shows little evidence of borrowing on a
grand scale. There has never been anything, for example, like the
wholesale reorganisation of education on the Russian pattern seen in her
satellites after 1945. More influential in Scotland has been the work of
the "great educators", her own and those of other countries. We have
already remarked the enduring effect of the proposals in the First Book
of Discipline; it should be added that many of these are essentially
Platonic. Andrew Melville, a Platonist like the six Johns, gave the
universities their form for centuries. Two examples are sufficient of the
Platonic influence – the stress on the academic and the persistent
undervaluing of techniques; the long rearguard action in the universities
to retain philosophical studies in a central position.

Of later educators the most influential have been Froebel and Herbart.
The latitudinarian views of Rousseau and Pestalozzi were not welcome
in many Scottish schools, where stern discipline was considered to
build character. But the Froebelian version of these views, coming in
the second and third quarters of the nineteenth century, created an
impressive impact in the fast-developing infant schools, and spread
through them to the other primary classes. The primary curriculum
set out in detail in *The Education of Man* might have been seen at
work in thousands of Scottish schools at any time in the next hundred
years. After the First World War the principles evolved by Maria
Montessori had some success in the nursery and infant classes, but in
the nineteen-sixties the Froebelian system still held the fort against all
novelties. The same resistance to change is seen in the comparative lack
of penetration shown by Dewey's doctrines before the nineteen-sixties:
project and problem teaching and activity methods were much lectured
on in Scottish universities and colleges, much discussed in professional
assemblies, but little practised in schools throughout the author's long

life. In a country with a strong tradition of Platonic idealism, Dewey's pragmatist attitude could hardly expect to be welcome, nor could a doctrine which stressed the need for the learner to do the work appeal in a system where the dominie was king.

It was a different matter with Herbart. He, like Froebel, was an idealist, and, unlike the latter, he had a strong vein of authoritarianism. His psychological doctrine of apperception was generally accepted as the basis of learning theory in the training of teachers, and his famous "steps", worked out from the same theory, had a firm, dictatable precision which endeared them to a harassed pedagogue with a large class of apprentice pedagogues.

DEVOTION TO EDUCATION

Conditioned by these influences, what are the main features of "the Scottish tradition in education"? We may consider several, real or merely supposed. In the first place, there is the claim, often repeated, that, whatever her shortcomings, Scotland has always remained firmly, even superstitiously devoted to the concept of education. The first education act in European history was passed in Scotland in 1496, though there is no evidence that it achieved its intent. The systematic planting of schools in every parish, and, when these proved inadequate, in slums and glens throughout the country testifies that men in authority continued for centuries the struggle to provide places. Private benefaction regarded education as its natural outlet: famous work was done by the Society in Scotland for Propagating Christian Knowledge, by the Gaelic Societies, by the Education Committees of the Church of Scotland and the Free Church, by the Merchant Company of Edinburgh, by the Dick Bequest, and by scores of individual donors. The first real Mechanics' Institute in the United Kingdom was formed in Edinburgh, and there was a celebrated course of evening classes for working men in Glasgow before the end of the eighteenth century. From an early date access to the universities was easier than in almost any other country: in the mid nineteenth century the ratio of university students to the population was twice that in Germany, six times that in England, and a century later, for all the rapid expansion south of the border, the rate in the north-east of Scotland was still twice as high as the English. Horace Mann, the American who in 1843 visited schools in Scotland, England, Ireland, France, Holland, Belgium and all the main German states, placed Scotland third after Prussia and Saxony in the attention paid to education, its system being the most thorough he found. He described a country[9]

so long and so justly celebrated among the countries of Europe for the superior education of its people.

Not only was there willingness to provide places; there was eagerness to take them up. The "lad o' pairts" whose parents made grinding sacrifices to give him his chance, and who would trudge miles daily through all weathers to attend school or university has always been a focus of popular sentiment and pride:[10]

> Gae owre the braid Atlantic main,
> Haud roon the warld and hame again,
> Ye'll find, whare'er the sons of men
>   Mak habitation
> Some wha in this bit toun I name
>   Gat education.

This was true from the poor boys fostered in its abbey schools by the Roman church, through Thomas Ruddiman and Colin Maclaurin, to the groups of distinguished men produced by small country districts in the early nineteenth century, the heyday of the parish schools. It was at this time too that there were reports of grown men returning to school in quest of the education they had missed when younger: in winter it was common for farm labourers in Aberdeenshire to "tak a raith at the coontin", and Lady Abercrombie's assistant gardener spent a guinea tip on a quarter of Greek.

Nevertheless the longer one studies the history of Scotland, the more familiar one becomes with the details, the more one tends to question whether much of this vaunted devotion was entirely superstitious and unconsidered. As early as the sixteenth century the master of Linlithgow complained bitterly that "so little respect has ever been had to the grammar schools" and throughout the existence of the parish system its records are full of remarks on the paltry remuneration of dominies, who were accorded generosity only in "mouth-honour". There is also some evidence that the twentieth century has seen the devotion in decline: the proportion of children staying at school after the statutory leaving age rose in Scotland after 1945, but it rose much more sharply in England and Wales.

Whether real or imagined, this educational preoccupation has had plain effects in Scottish history. It has meant, for one thing, constant attempts to establish a system: a nation so convinced of the value of education could not be content, like the English, to rely on individual effort. It has spurred many poor families to considerable sacrifices, and their sons to stern self-denial, so that they might take advantage of the cheap university education available. But not all its effects have been admirable. Cheapness of university training was secured only at the cost of crowded classes and long vacations, with mass lectures and parroting examinations. And this over-pressure on pupils came from every direction – from their parents, from their masters, from themselves. Scottish school discipline has been traditionally harsh, and it dies hard, so that in the mid-twentieth century the "tawse" remains an unenviable article of wonder in foreign eyes. Worst of all, "a university education became something like a test of character, and systematic overwork, bad housing, poor diet and lack of exercise took their toll in chronic under-health and nervous strain". The Aberdeen University Magazine contained some verses which commemorated a case only too sadly typical:[11]

Shon Campbell went to College
    Because he wanted to,
He left the croft in Gairloch
    To dive in Bain and Drew;
Shon Campbell died at College
    When the sky of spring was blue.

Shon Campbell went to College,
    The pulpit was his aim;
By day and night he ground, for he
    Was Hielan, dour and game;
The session was a hard one,
    Shon flickered like a flame.

Shon Campbell went to College,
    And gave the ghost up there,
Attempting six men's cramming
    On a mean and scanty fare;
Three days the Tertians mourned him –
    'Twas all that they could spare.

MILITANT DEMOCRACY

A second tradition of Scottish education is its militant democracy, hardly surprising in a strongly presbyterian land. The main reason for the existence of Calvinism in the sixteenth century was its insistence on every man's right to meet his personal God without any priest to take him by the hand. Every man had the right to read the Bible for himself, but first every man must learn to read. As a poor country, moreover, Scotland was forced in times of trouble to mobilise as a nation. Not for her the easy life protected by mercenaries; every man had to take up his arms. This is what makes the Declaration of Arbroath such inspiring reading, and it accounts in large part for the success of a small country in war against the Plantagenets, and in religion against the Church of Rome. Thus we read in the First Book of Discipline of the necessity of a school in every parish, "for the schools are the seed of the kirk and the common wealth". Thus too we read on many occasions of a mixture of social classes at the desks: "I used to sit between a youth of a ducal family and the son of a poor cobbler".[12]

In these circumstances it is odd, though not perhaps incomprehensible, that schooling was not free until the 1890s; indeed in 1864 the Secretary of the Committee of Council pointed out that fees were higher in Scottish elementary schools than in English. In a poor country, where schoolmasters also had to live, this is logical. As with the claim of educational devotion, however, closer scrutiny makes the assertion of democratic equality less unchallengeable. Children of noble families rarely attended the parish or even the burgh schools. It was different with the sons of lairds, but many of these were as impoverished as their tenants. The stated aim of the John Neilson Institution in Paisley that social classes were mixed, "thus using the higher as a lever power to elevate the lower in the scale of society", suggested a disparity which would not be warmly acceptable to the "higher" classes. From the nineteenth century at least it became the practice of the landed gentry to send their sons to boarding schools, often outside Scotland, and by the twentieth this had spread to the merchant and higher professional groups. In the 1950s and 1960s the matter had become a battleground of political principle, with long waiting-lists for all the fee-paying schools, while town councils dominated by doctrinaire Socialists sought to reduce the operation of the selective principle at too early an age. Scotland still provided places in a full secondary course much more lavishly than England – some critics said too lavishly – but dissatisfaction with the nature of these places drove many parents to seek schools outside the public system.

ACADEMIC BIAS

One striking feature of the Scottish institutions whose operation was and is essentially undemocratic is its academic bias. There has always been deference to the aristocracy of intellect, and by the mid twentieth century pupils in junior secondary schools – about two-thirds of their age-group – were in many ways treated, if not regarded, as second-class educational citizens. Such stress on verbalism, on the magical powers of words, was perhaps inevitable in an educational system which owed so much of its inspiration to the Platonism of sixteenth-century divines: in the schools the classics, especially Latin, ruled, while the universities centred their curricula on various branches of philosophy. Whatever its origins, the bias was perpetuated by men who had been brought up in the faith and returned to pass it on; and its effects were seldom beneficial to the community. Games and hobbies played a much smaller part in the life of a school than they did south of the border; even in the twentieth century, though they secured a place, there was a widespread impression among teachers and parents that they were brief intermissions in the serious business of education. Verbalism led also to an over-valuing of the examinable; there was too much attention to inspection, by the minister, the presbytery, or later Her Majesty's Inspector, and from the nineteenth century, too much teaching towards certificates.

Inevitably, where one group of school subjects achieved such importance, others found themselves undervalued. Voltaire's remark that "we have never claimed to enlighten shoemakers and servant girls, they are the portion of the apostles" might have been spoken by many authorities and many schoolmasters in Scotland. Like games and physical education, classes in the arts and music have been almost universally regarded as recreative rather than self-expressive, while those in technical and domestic subjects have been generally reserved for the academic "failures". Specialist teachers have shared the contempt suffered by their specialties. The consequence has been prolonged distortion of the school curriculum.

The same disdain for the practical has been seen in higher and further education. "Here's to pure science, and may it never be any damned use to anyone" holds the kernel of an important article of faith, but it leads also to the attitude which considers all technical and vocational colleges as much less than intellectually respectable and in their work far below the university angels. This idea is not of course confined to Scotland. The products of teacher training colleges in England have had a low status in the community, and there remains in the 1960s a common notion that it is more suitable for a grammar school teacher to go straight into the classroom from his university, preferably Oxbridge, and certainly without risking the contagion of the training course. This is one facet of the strange English myth of the gifted amateur and the distrusted professional; it is odd however that a similar idea should have spread to Scotland, where the status of the colleges of education, although – perhaps because – university graduates must attend them for training, is no higher than that of the better training colleges in the south. It is hardly worth pointing out that the colleges of education do not and cannot attempt to compete with the universities in the intellectual standard of the work they do, or that the universities cannot and do not compete with the colleges of education in many more practical activities; there is a non-academic tinge about much of the work in training and technical colleges, and this *ipso facto* makes them "inferior".

But perhaps the gravest and most distressing feature of the academic bias in Scottish education is the influence it has had in drawing the schools in on themselves, and out of the general life of the community. As far as the majority of Scottish schools and schoolmasters before the 1960s were concerned, John Dewey might never have lived: Scottish children had one language, one set of values, one code of conduct for the school, others for what they regarded as "the real world". There is little evidence, moreover, that this situation was of late growth. Criticising secondary education in Scotland in 1868, two French visitors commented tartly: "Ce n'est pas les Georgiques à la main qu'on laboure la terre". In short, Scottish schooling has been and remains something artificial and apart, a kind of compulsory acrostic which, for many children, has not even the saving grace of passing the time agreeably. And this is not only true of less gifted children intellectually: the brighter ones may enjoy "performing intellectual minuets", but they are often hard put to it to discern any relevance to daily life. Furthermore at the university and college level there is the same complaint.

In some cases of course the fault lies with the student; because he fails to appreciate relevance, it does not follow that it does not exist. But with too many junior secondary courses planned and run by men of scholarly habit and experience, there is enough substance in such complaints to demand a careful scrutiny of the system. It is not necessary to go to American extremes in vocational curricula, but there is a good deal to be learnt from American, Russian and French experiments where the schools play a real, constructive part in the work of the community, and where the links between school and apprenticeship are much stronger. The comment that "I left school, and then my education began" is glib, but it ought to be also patently ridiculous, and at the moment it is not.

CONSERVATISM

One consequence of the academic bias in Scottish education has been so marked that it has become virtually a tradition in itself. This is the strict conservatism to which the system has always adhered. This habit of mind has no doubt been partly due to national poverty and the necessity of frugality; even Scotsmen who wanted to experiment could seldom afford to do so. It may also have been a typical manifestation of a national "canniness", a reluctance to attempt change. It might also be attributed to a national passion for careful logic. Englishmen have been content to admit exceptions to their rules, and exceptions to their exceptions: English law, English education and the British constitution are witnesses to this. Americans have been even more empirical in their approach: their insistence on flexibility has on occasion gone so far as to implant a positive distrust of any rules. But the Scottish philosopher has generally been attracted by the generalisation, with exceptions, if possible, eliminated in advance by arriving at the most valid rule, and Scottish educators have generally been philosophers. To such men, change and experiment were and are projects not to be lightly undertaken; conservatism is in their bones. And it is interesting to observe the same principle at work whatever the politics of the people in power: in the mid-twentieth century, when Socialist education authorities carried out prolonged assaults on fee-paying schools and similar "strongholds of privilege", there was a definite impression that one of the causes was intellectual neatness and the removal of exceptions.

The advantage of educational conservatism has been the way standards have been jealously preserved – an advantage so long as the standards remained satisfactory. The stipulation in the twentieth century that all male teachers of general and special subjects must be graduates of a university is an example of such conservation of standards, and the uproar caused by proposals to abandon it is significant. The history of the Scottish ordinary degree is another illustration. The schools have been on the whole fortunately free of the more hysterical kind of experiment. But conservatism has also had its less attractive results. The curriculum in the universities was still largely medieval in the eighteenth century. The "academies" founded in that century to meet the demands of the Industrial Revolution gravitated quite soon to the older, academic type, and became virtually grammar schools, with a fashionable new name. Methods of teaching congealed in a formal pattern, with a great deal of rote learning, memorising and chanting; many lessons from the thirteenth century onward were called "lectures", (readings) and the system of reading round the class and expounding continued to the present day, with stress on note-taking and regurgitation. New subjects found it almost impossible to squeeze into the syllabus, and in 1961 there were in the examinations for the Scottish Leaving Certificate 111 candidates in Russian and 244 in Spanish, but 419 in Ancient Greek.[13] "Scottish traditions", in a country insistently proud of its "heritage", have found no important place in the schools. The opportunity to experiment offered by the Scottish Education Department in 1940 when it abolished the national certificate at the end of a junior secondary course was accepted only occasionally by teachers or authorities. Formalism reached its peak in the tyranny of examinations, which, at least in the last two years of primary and senior secondary schooling, completely dictated the timetable. In a world demanding more and more paper qualifications, it is difficult to see alternatives, but the dominies and their employers might have struggled a little harder. This tradition made all the more amazing the atmosphere of change in the sixties which varied in some eyes from the stimulating and the adventurous to the plainly reckless.

AUTHORITARIANISM AND TEACHER STATUS

It has been suggested that this conservative, strongly academic system, with its emphasis on the passing on of acquired wisdom and its roots deep in philosophical idealism, was bound to be perpetuated by teachers because it gave teachers the central place. Certainly such authoritarianism required a tradition of firm discipline to keep it in the saddle. The fool's cap, the fox's skin, the bone necklace, the tessera, the jar of salts or wormwood, the cane and the tawse all had their part in the educational drama, and although they were no doubt given too much of the limelight because of their dramatic impact, they seem to have occupied a more prominent role than in many other educational systems. Certainly in the twentieth century visiting pedagogues do not find this facet of Scottish education admirable.

The point is not perhaps unconnected with another which must be discussed – the status of the Scottish dominie. There is a sentimental tradition of the wise, couthy, scholarly country schoolmaster, intellectual guide, consultant philosopher and humane friend to his pupils, labouring with no thought of recognition to discover lads of parts and set their feet on the road to national eminence. There were teachers like that – there are in every generation – but the picture is removed from the general reality. Particularly in the north-east, the standard of scholarship in parish schoolmasters was high: one Banffshire parish had thirty-eight masters between 1631 and 1841, and at least twenty-four of these were university graduates, while in another between 1612 and 1804 the corresponding figures were thirty and twenty-five.[14] But, as we have seen on many occasions, the dominie, however he stood in public respect, was never highly rewarded in material ways. From the first act settling emoluments in the seventeenth century to the present day salary scales for teachers seem always to have been unsuccessfully chasing the cost of living. The best that can be said for the twentieth century is that in this period the gap was not so wide. Even the fixed scales, moreover, were often unpaid by the heritors and tenants whose duty it was to find the money, or else paid in kind, a device more economically ingenious than dietetically satisfying. There were no schemes for pensions in retirement, and such provision as existed for widows had to be made by the dominies' own efforts. Even genuine respect, unconnected with salaries, seems often to have been absent. As Professor Blackie pointed out to two French visitors in 1868, teachers were not highly regarded, and "even a professor of the university in Scotland is hardly regarded as a gentleman".[15] Even in the twentieth century teaching was a profession only in its own eyes and those of the non-professional man.

Probably the most damning evidence that the job has not been highly regarded is the number of men and women on the one hand who came to teaching after failing elsewhere – as ministers, lawyers, merchants, cobblers, soldiers or simply ladies of leisure – and on the other the fact that the dominie's desk was widely held to be a convenient step to the pulpit. In the same two Banffshire parishes mentioned above thirty of the sixty-eight masters mentioned between 1612 and 1841 went on to become ministers, and several put in "substitute masters" for part of their service while they attended divinity classes in Aberdeen.[16] The twentieth century version of the same trend, in a period when the ministry has been less highly respected, is the attitude among university students that they will consider careers in industry, the civil service and scientific research, with the comforting reflection that there is always teaching "to fall back on".

With such a history, it is not perhaps surprising that the Scots dominie has had to fight to impress his authority on his pupils. The tradition of stern discipline becomes more readily comprehensible.

EDUCATION AND RELIGION

The high percentage of teachers who went on to become ministers is only one manifestation of a tendency which remained strongly fixed in Scottish affairs until the end of the nineteenth century, and whose influence lingers still – the tendency to make education the handmaid of religion. As we have seen, the strain of puritanism in the Scottish character was a powerful influence in educational affairs – so powerful that in the mind of anyone who gave thought to the matter at all schooling was Church business. Under the Roman Kirk what teaching there was was left to abbeys, cathedrals and chantry chapels; the man most responsible for the maintenance of the average parish school was the local minister; bishops founded the universities; committees of the Church of Scotland and the Free Church controlled the first training colleges. The advantages of this state of affairs were considerable when there were no alternative candidates as promoters of education, but when these appeared two grave disadvantages began to show their effect. The first was an undue stress on certain facets of the pupil's personality: spiritual and moral education have great importance, but they should not be so central in the scheme that all other aspects, the intellectual, the physical, the aesthetic can only be introduced, if at all, for the contribution they make to spiritual and moral development. The second effect was to import into the Scottish educational system an incorrigibly amateur element, which ensured that the man in charge of maintaining and inspecting the school system were seldom if ever experts in education. The first reports of Her Majesty's Inspectors in the nineteenth century wage incessant warfare against the annual presbytery examinations, which they describe as "a pleasing practice, but a mere farce as examinations: schools that we should consider 'good' are in the language of the presbytery 'very excellent' or 'excellent'; and those that we should consider 'very bad' are in their accounts "indifferent".[17] In short, with the best intentions in the world, religion would not allow education to stand on its own feet. This was at least partly to blame for a situation which caused Joseph Chamberlain to remark in 1870:[18]

> The object of the Liberal party in England, throughout the continent of Europe and in America has been to wrest the education of the

young out of the hands of the priests, to whatever denomination they might belong.

It may also explain why the transition from church to state control in 1872 was comparatively easy, though the co-operation and goodwill of the church authorities at the time should be warmly acknowledged.

ECONOMY

Steadfast devotion to the concept of education, democracy in the classroom, an academic bias, conservatism in curriculum and teaching methods, the central position of the teacher, a constant close relationship between education and religion – these have all been present in the Scottish educational tradition. One more must be mentioned – the unvarying practice of economy, arising out of the comparative poverty of the country. The need for thrift, for paring expenditure to eliminate luxuries, has contributed not inconsiderably to the shape of Scottish education. In the first place it helps to account for the recurrent stress placed by the authorities, once convinced of the importance of schooling, on evolving an educational system; for them *laissez-faire* was too extravagant. "No father", wrote the six Johns, "of what estate or condition that ever he be, can use his children at his own fantisie, especially in their youth-head, but all must be compelled to bring up their children in learning and virtue".[19] The surest and most economical way of imposing compulsion was the establishment of a national system, and the parish organisation was the Church's attempt to carry out the state's duty.

This continued adherence to a system accounts in its turn for certain features of Scottish education. It explains the general vague distrust of private schools. The public school idea, with its attendant cluster of preparatories, has put down only shallow roots in Scotland. The "experimental" school, exemplified south of the border in Summerhill and various types of approved institution, has seldom flourished. Even the "hospitals", founded from the seventeenth to the nineteenth centuries by private benefaction, came within the systematising influence in the 1880s when the Educational Endowments Commission opened the way for most of them to convert themselves into fee-paying secondaries. The twentieth century saw many drawn within the state system, and by the 1960s comparatively few were flourishing outside those of the Merchant Company of Edinburgh.

There is also an explanation here of the importance, stronger in Scotland than England, of the central authorities. The continuing influence of the First Book of Discipline has often been mentioned. The licensing of teachers by the Church, the inspection of parish and other schools by local ministers and elders, the fact that such training as there was for teachers could be had only in colleges provided by the Churches – these factors, in the days of ecclesiastical control, ensured a certain uniformity throughout the country of curriculum and methods. When the state acknowledged some educational responsibility, more-over, the early Permanent Secretaries of the Scotch Education Depart-ment, Craik and Struthers, had a powerful and creative hand in deter-mining the pattern of Scottish education for the next century, probably more effective and with much less adverse comment than that of Morant in England.

The necessity for economy not only encouraged the establishment and maintenance of a national system; it also determined certain elements in that system. For one thing, it is difficult to assign any more philoso-phical reason for the Scottish tradition of coeducation. It is tempting to extend the Platonism of the Book of Discipline to include equal opportunity for girls, but they are not specifically mentioned in the scheme, and one might have expected an idea so revolutionary in the sixteenth century to be expressly stated. Nevertheless mixed classes of boys and girls became the rule in most Scottish schools at all levels, as it remained the exception in English secondary departments. Claims that the presence of the girls had a soothing and refining influence on their ruder classmates were too flimsily based to carry conviction. It is more likely that girls were in the schools simply because the places were there. Their presence in secondary classes arose indirectly from the same economy, for it was the Scottish tradition – one still ungrasped in the nineteenth century across the border – to conduct primary and secondary work in the same burgh or parish school.

Here we touch one of the most striking differences between the two national systems. Until well into the twentieth century the English had no straight ladder of education. For the schoolboy there were two kinds, and they were alternative. One was elementary: it aimed at making him literate but very little more, and it ended when he was fourteen and went out to work. The other was secondary; the way was prepared for it in preparatory schools, and its products went, as no elementary pupils could, to a university. Barely a fifth of the population were in the secondary branch, and there was hardly any transfer between the two. The Scottish tradition was sharply different. Until almost the end of the nineteenth century there were really only two stages – not kinds – of education. One was the school, the other the university. The school enrolled all the children in its neighbourhood at the age of five or six. To many it taught the rudiments and little more, but wherever a child combined ability, diligence and parental support, the school would continue to inculcate the somewhat narrow, academic but indubitably higher stages of education. Inevitably, since the curriculum was more demanding, better educated teachers were required; inevitably also, since the higher instruction was available, a greater proportion of pupils took advantage of it. The second stage was

S

the university, and because its students came from a more broadly based system of schools, the university undertook in its first and even second year studies at a comparatively elementary level. In short, except in the larger burghs, the secondary school hardly existed in Scotland before 1872; the work of its lower forms was done by the so-called 'elementary' school, that of its higher forms by the universities.

Undoubtedly this made for cheapness. It is difficult to imagine how a national system could have been more economically constructed. The arrangement left its mark, however, for better or worse, on Scottish education. The kind of study in depth which has been customary in the best English grammar and "public" schools – scores, if not hundreds of them – has appeared seldom north of the border. Even in the best Scottish senior secondaries the comparatively low standard of university entrance examinations has made it hardly worth while to dig deeply. There has been frequent criticism of the huge, superficial first-year classes in the universities, and the strong suggestion that professors have had to waste too much time expatiating on the rudiments of their subjects. The introduction in 1968 of an Advanced Grade in the Scottish Certificate of Education could be the most momentous single step in changing the pattern of national education.

CONCLUSION – THE SCOTTISH TRADITION

These are the components of the Scottish tradition in education. None has worked entirely for the good of the people; each in its way is open to severe criticism; yet the general impression is of a heritage worth remembering and building upon. Its formalism is to be deplored. The excessive reverence it pays to the academically gifted pupil has made Scottish technical and technological education notably backward; colleges of further education in the 1960s were freely described as the "Cinderellas of the system". Yet, as the Americans ruefully discovered in 1957, there is a place for formality, and academic studies are important. The dominie, denied material rewards for centuries, found his compensation in asserting a kind of dictatorship in the classroom. This led to grave disciplinary problems and an unwillingness to experiment where dignity had to be sacrificed. But it also safeguarded in many cases the operation of the profound educational principle that, in the last analysis, it is the personal relationship that counts – the relationship not only of one learner with another, but also of master and disciple. The vaunted Scottish devotion to education may often have been superstitious, illogical – often, but not always. For centuries education was respectable, but it was more than that. There were in each generation men who cared sufficiently about it to spend their money and their energy and their time freely on its development – men like Andrew Melville and Bishop Kennedy, Robert Owen and David Stow, Robert Gordon and Allan Glen and Andrew Carnegie, the founders of the Gaelic Societies, the Education Societies, the Infant School Societies, the S.S.P.C.K., the Free Church Committee. The sentimental image of Scottish educational democracy, personified in the lad of parts who was to become a colonial governor or a university principal or a law lord, may be idealised through an intellectual soft-focus lens. But there were many lads of parts, and they did attain eminence, and its was easier for a Scottish boy to reach a university than for his brothers in most countries of the western world.

The Scottish educational tradition then may be found in a few positive dicta:

that education is, and always has been, of paramount importance in any community;

that every child should have the right to all the education of which he is capable;

that such education should be provided as economically and systematically as possible;

that the training of the intellect should take priority over all other facets of the pupil's personality;

that experiment is to be attempted only with the greatest of caution; and

that the most important person in the school, no matter what theorists say, is not the pupil but the (inadequately rewarded) teacher.

In every generation it is easier to discern the shortcomings of a tradition than its virtues. It is rigidly idealistic, certainly inflexible, but it holds to a number of valid truths. At its best the Scottish tradition in education has served the people of Scotland well.

REFERENCES

1. HAMERTON, *French and English*, 437
2. FEARON, *Burgh Schools*, 115; CLELAND, *Annals of Glasgow*, 250
3. Papal Bull founding Glasgow University, qu. MARWICK, *Glasgow*, 31-35
4. COULTON, *Scottish Abbeys and Social Life*, 175-186
5. *Act of the Scottish Parliament, 1567*
6. *C.C.M. 1852-1853*, Marshall, 1062
7. MORGAN, *Rise and Progress*, 97
8. WILSON, *Tales and Travels*, 256
9. MANN, *Report for 1843*, 238, 258, 362
10. SAUNDERS, *Scottish Democracy*, 308
11. MACKENZIE, *A.U.R.*, xxxviii, 4, Sep. 1960, 309

12. MORGAN, *Rise and Progress*, 78
13. *S.E.D.R. 1961*, 23
14. BARCLAY, *Banffshire*, 227-229, 257-258
15. DEMOGEOT and MONTUCCI, 452
16. BARCLAY, *Banffshire*, 227-229, 257-258
17. SELLAR and MAXWELL, qu. SIMPSON, *Aberdeenshire*, 60
18. qu. DAWSON, *The Crisis in Western Education*, 103
19. *First Book of Discipline*, ed. Dickinson, 295

Glossary

Academies	schools founded in the late eighteenth and early nineteenth centuries to teach a more "modern" secondary curriculum.
ad hoc authorities	education authorities operating in Scotland from 1918 to 1929; members were elected expressly for educational duties.
advanced department	section of the elementary school in the late nineteenth century working for the Merit Certificate.
advanced divisions	post-primary courses in elementary institutions from 1923 to 1936.
adventure schools	private schools run for profit, usually by individuals.
ad vitam aut culpam	form of tenure of teaching post – for life or until found guilty of a major delinquency.
Argyll Commission	commission under the chairmanship of the Duke of Argyll which investigated the condition of Scottish education, 1864-67.
ars grammatica	Latin in medieval schools and universities.
assembly schools	schools founded, mainly in Highland parishes, by the Education Committee of the General Assembly of the Church of Scotland; nineteenth century.
Bajan	*Becjaune*; first year student in Aberdeen university.
bedellus	head janitor of University of Glasgow.
burgh schools	schools run by the town council, usually with a secondary curriculum.
Bursary Comp.	competitive examination for university scholarships; especially celebrated in Aberdeen and Glasgow.
Candlemas Day	2 February, when pupils brought gratuitous offerings to the teacher and might get a half-holiday.
Canonist	Professor of Canon Law in Aberdeen.

s*

central institutions	centres of higher technical instruction recognised after 1901 by the Scotch Education Department.
central schools	urban schools in which supplementary courses were centralised in the early twentieth century.
Chancellor	*a.* cathedral dignitary with the right to license all teachers in the diocese; medieval; *b.* titular head of a Scottish university.
Civilist	Professor of Civil Law in Aberdeen.
clandestine censor	pupil set to spy and report on his fellows.
cloistral school	school attached to a medieval monastery or abbey.
coal-money	subscription paid by children to their master in lieu of fuel.
collegiate school	medieval school attached to a collegiate church, generally where a patron made a special bequest to ensure the saying of prayers for his soul.
collegium	place of lodging for medieval university students.
commissioners of supply	body charged with deciding where schools were to be planted in seventeenth century and thereafter.
conscience clause	clause permitting parent to withdraw a pupil on the grounds of conscience from religious instruction; 1872 Act.
Culdees	kind of clergy under the Celtic Church.
Dame school	school run by a woman, generally elderly, at her own risk.
Dean of Faculty	university officer elected by the Faculty, who supervised admission to courses of study.
demonstration school	school attached to a training seminary.
dictates	university lectures in the seventeenth century.
discharge	forbid.
disputations or disputes	formal debates in Latin.
Disruption	the breaking away of many ministers and members of the Church of Scotland in 1843 to found the Free Church.
doctor	assistant master in a grammar school.
dominie	schoolmaster, from Latin *dominus*.
donatt	Donatus' Latin grammar book, and then any such book.

Elder	lay member of the governing body of a presbyterian church.
endowed school	school provided by a private benefactor.
extension courses	university extra-mural courses for adult students.
Faculty	a. group of university departments, as faculty of arts, faculty of law, etc.; b. professional body, e.g. Faculty of Procurators (lawyers), Faculty of Surgeons.
Fastern's E'en	Shrove Tuesday, when there was cock fighting in school in the seventeenth and eighteenth centuries.
ferleyn	Celtic Church dignitary.
First Book of Discipline	plan for organisation of the new Protestant Church in Scotland, 1560.
Gallery	tiered seats in classrooms for pupils and students observing.
General Council	body consisting of all graduates of a university.
gilds	medieval craft brotherhoods
grammar school	school teaching Latin and one or two other secondary subjects.
Half-timers	pupils who spent half their time in school, half at work; nineteenth century.
heritors	local landowners.
higher class schools	schools beyond the elementary level.
higher class public schools	schools of this type run under the 1872 Act by the school boards.
higher grade schools	schools providing secondary courses set up in 1899 under the school boards.
highers	Leaving Certificate examinations introduced by the Scotch Education Department in 1888.
Highland Clearances	movement by landowners to drive people off the land in order to create deer parks and sheep-runs.
horn book	piece of wood covered with horn; letters, numbers, etc., set out on it for learning.
hospitals	charitable trust funds in aid of unfortunates.
hospital schools	schools provided by these trusts.
Improving Movement	movement in the eighteenth century to develop better agricultural methods.
industrial schools	in the seventeenth and eighteenth centuries schools giving vocational instruction; later schools for vagrant youths.

Inglis Commission	Universities Commission of 1876.
Junior instruction centres	centres offering classes for unemployed juveniles during the 1930s.
Kinnear Commission	Universities Executive Commission of 1889.
kirk session	council of minister and elders running the affairs of a parish church.
Labour certificate	certificate issued by the Scotch Education Department from 1878 to 1901 to children between 10 and 13 years of age who passed certain examinations; it allowed them to leave school.
lad o' pairts	gifted boy from a poor family.
laird	local squire.
lecture school	school to teach the elements of reading.
local examinations	examinations conducted by universities for grammar school pupils, especially girls, in the late nineteenth century.
Madras System	Dr Andrew Bell's system of teaching with monitors; nineteenth century.
maill	allowance as rent – e.g. chamber maill.
maxies, minies and medies	grades of error in Latin prose.
Mechanics' Institutes	associations of working men for purposes of self-education and improvement in the nineteenth century.
Mediciner	Professor of Medicine in Aberdeen.
Merit Certificate	certificate issued by the Scotch Education Department from 1891 to pupils aged 13 and over who passed certain examinations in elementary subjects.
merk	old Scots coin; in the eighteenth century 100 merks were worth £5.11.1 sterling.
mission schools	schools set up in the nineteenth century in the poorest areas of cities.
model school	school attached to a training seminary.
Moncrieff Act	Act of 1861 introducing tests for schoolmasters.
monitorial systems	methods of class organisation whereby some pupils contributed to the education of the rest; there were two main systems, sponsored by Bell and Lancaster.
mortification	bequest payable on death of donor.
Munro Act	Education (Scotland) Act of 1918.

Nation	group of students, usually determined geographically, for university rectorial elections.
night school	evening continuation classes.
Normal Schools and Normal Colleges	teacher training institutions.
Nova Erectio et Fundatio	new foundation of Glasgow University under Andrew Melville in 1577; similar arrangement two years later in St Andrews.
Oblations	offerings by pupils to their master at Candlemas.
Old Faith	Roman Catholicism.
Oure Tounis Colledge	name given to the college founded in Edinburgh in 1583, later Edinburgh University.
Paedagogium	building in which study occurred in a medieval university.
pandy	stroke on the palm of the hand as corporal punishment.
parchment	full teaching certificate.
parish schools	schools founded in ecclesiastical areas under the Acts of 1696 to 1803.
Parker Committee	Committee on Training Colleges and Secondary Schools, reporting in 1888.
parliamentary schools	additional schools set up in the parishes under the Act of 1838.
pars	prescribed task in Latin grammar.
payment by results	system whereby government grant was earned partly by performance of individual pupils.
perquisites	sources of a schoolmaster's income other than salary or fees.
piece	children's packet of food taken to school to eat at the interval.
pound Scots	old Scots unit of currency; in the eighteenth century twelve pounds Scots equalled one pound sterling.
precentor	a. master of music in a cathedral or abbey; b. choir leader in a presbyterian church.
presbytery	local court of the Church of Scotland, above the kirk session and below the synod.
primar	a. first book of the elements of reading; b. noble university student at St Andrews in the seventeenth century.
Provincial Committees	teacher training bodies between 1905 and 1958.

Quadrivium	second part of the traditional medieval arts curriculum – music, arithmetic, geometry, astronomy.
qualifying examination	test to determine whether a pupil was fit to proceed beyond primary education, instituted in 1903.
Ragged schools	schools catering for very poor children.
Reader	*a.* assistant minister, sometimes also used as a teacher, in parish church; *b.* university lecturer, next in seniority to professor.
rector	*a.* medieval university officer, who supervised its working; elected by students in Glasgow and Aberdeen; elections continue today (as Lord Rector); *b.* headmaster of a secondary school.
rector scolarum	medieval church dignitary, in charge of the schools in an episcopal see.
regent	university lecturer in charge of a year-group of medieval students.
Revised Code	the Schools Code which introduced payment by results.
Sacrist	head janitor of Aberdeen University.
school offices	lavatories.
school of industry	school giving vocational instruction.
scoloc	Celtic churchman, perhaps a teacher.
Scots Colleges	institutions of higher education for Scottish students on the Continent from the sixteenth century onward; Roman Catholic foundations much used to train priests for the Counter-Reformation.
secondar	student (local gentry) at St Andrews university in seventeenth century.
Second Book of Discipline	second document establishing organisation of the new Scottish Protestant Church in the sixteenth century; virtually no reference to education.
Senatus	body of university professors and later some lecturers, responsible for curriculum and discipline.
sessional schools	schools founded by minister and session of a parish, usually urban.
shed	covered shelter for pupils in school playground.

side schools	additional schools founded by the heritors in very large parishes after 1803.
sir	bachelor of arts not yet at full graduation; medieval term.
six Johns	authors of the First Book of Discipline – Knox, Winram, Spottiswoode, Row, Willock, Douglas.
skallie	slate pencil.
slate and slate pencil	writing materials carried by pupils till the early twentieth century.
sma' yill	small ale.
song school (*sang scule*)	school teaching music and Latin for service.
specific subjects	certain subjects which pupils might study beyond the rudimentary level from 1891 to 1898; one was included in the Merit Certificate.
spinning school	school to teach girls textile processes and the elements, largely in Highland areas.
S.S.P.C.K.	Society in Scotland for Propagating Christian Knowledge.
Statistical Accounts	nation-wide descriptions of counties and parishes in Scotland; the First was issued in the 1790s, the Second in the 1830s, the Third after 1945.
stent or stint	tax on heritors for settling school.
studium generale	origin of a university – place where scholars congregated.
subscription schools	schools provided by parental contributions.
superintendents	Presbyterian supervisors; successors to bishops.
supplementary courses	post-primary courses in primary schools between 1903 and 1923; later advanced divisions.
synod	largest regional area of the Church of Scotland.
Tawse	stiff leather strap used as instrument of punishment.
ternars	students from common families in St Andrews university in the seventeenth century.
Three Estates	Lords, Commons and Clergy; the Scottish Parliament.
trivium	first part of the medieval secondary curriculum – Latin grammar, logic, rhetoric.
University Court	Governing body of Scottish university after 1858, dealing with finance and administration.

upland parishes   rural parishes.

Vacance   holiday.
version   translation from English into Latin, the most
                         important part of the university bursary com-
                         petition.

Whisky money   money originally earmarked as compensation
                         for publicans in the 1890s; in Scotland made
                         available for educational purposes.

INDEX

Aberdeen Church of Scotland Training College, 88, 99, 114
  College of Education (Training Centre), 107, 111, 116, 124, 180, 190, 227, 230
  College of Physical Education, 114
  Demonstration School, 16, 48, 50, 75, 79, 90, 200
  Free Church Training College, 103, 107, 114
  Grammar School, 62, 66, 124, 212
  High School for Girls, 212
  University of, 107, 108, 109, 114, 135, 145, 146, 148, 150, 152, 153, 154, 157, 158, 159, 161, 162, 163, 164, 180, 182, 230, 245, 246, 249, 250, 258, 265, 270
activity methods, 201, 262
Adam, Dr Alexander, 257
Adams, Sir John, 106, 107
adult education, 133-5, 162, 241-2
advanced department, 57, 64
advanced divisions, 57-8, 59, 74
adventure schools, 4, 18, 35, 46
advisers and organisers, 194
Advisory Council on Education, 28, 29-30, 55, 80, 129, 141, 187, 190, 191-2, 198, 202, 210, 217, 222, 227, 237, 239
aesthetic education, 267
age, school, 6, 17, 18-19, 57, 80, 173, 178, 196, 239, 264
agriculture, colleges of, 139-40
aids, teaching, 54-6, 181, 207-9
Airdrie Academy, 70
Albemarle Report, 175
Albert Road School, Glasgow, 69
Albyn School, Aberdeen, 214
Allan Glen's School, Glasgow, 37, 38, 64, 66, 72, 136, 138, 275
Anderson College, 38, 138, 164, 246
Anderson Report (1962), 251
Andrew, Mr (H.M.I.), 57
Annand, Rachel, 159
Anniesland College, 240
Appleton Committee, 222
approved schools, 216

Arbuckle, Sir William, 29, 192
Argyll Commission, 3, 34, 42
Arnold, Matthew, 103, 135
'article 39'. 113
Ashridge College, 135
assembly schools, 43
'assignments', 200
associateships, College of Education, 225
Athenaeum, Glasgow, 139
Atholl Crescent College of Domestic Science, Edinburgh, 139
Atkinson Institution, Glasgow, 38, 138
attendance, school, 16-19, 22, 189, 196
Ayr Academy, 62

Bain, Professor, 145, 146
Balfour Commission, 38, 39-40, 64, 72, 138
Balliol College, 162, 260
Bathgate Academy, 38
Bell, Dr Andrew, 103, 149-50
Bell, J. J., 158
Bellahouston Academy, 15, 69, 72
Blackie, Professor J. S., 164, 270
Blind School, Royal, Edinburgh, 94
'block grant', 187
Board of Education, English, 29-30, 72, 136
Board of Education, Scottish, 22, 23, 24
boards, school, 6, 13-19, 22, 27, 28, 36, 37, 39, 43, 46, 48, 50-51, 54, 62, 64, 65, 66, 72, 80, 87, 109, 110, 111, 115, 125, 140
Bologna, University of, 260
Bone, James, 158
Bonnybridge case, 44
Boys' Brigade, 174
Bradley, Professor A. C., 165
Braehead School, Fife, 214
'Bridie, James', 157, 158, 165
British Broadcasting Corporation, 160, 208
broadcasting, schools, 55-6, 208